P9-AQA-386

The Decline of American Communism

A VOLUME IN THE SERIES

COMMUNISM IN AMERICAN LIFE
Clinton Rossiter, General Editor

David A. Shannon

THE DECLINE

A History of the Communist Party

OF AMERICAN

of the United States since 1945

COMMUNISM

THE CHATHAM BOOKSELLER
CHATHAM, NEW JERSEY

77128

© *1959 by David A. Shannon*

*All rights reserved. No part of this book may be
reproduced in any form or by any mechanical means,
including mimeograph and tape recorder, without
permission in writing from the publisher.*

Library of Congress Catalog Card Number: 78-151615
Printed in the United States of America

Reissued 1971, by the Chatham Bookseller
By arrangement with Harcourt Brace Jovanovich

To

J. R. S. and E. J. S.

This book is one of a series of studies of Communist influence in American life. The entire survey has been made possible through the foresight and generous support of the Fund for the Republic. All of us who have taken part in it are grateful for this exceptional opportunity to study the most confused and controversial problem of the age and to publish the results exactly as we find them.

CLINTON ROSSITER

PREFACE

For more than a decade, the American people have been concerned about the presence of an active, organized, and dedicated Communist party in their midst at a time when relations between the United States and the Soviet Union have been strained and mutually suspicious. This concern has given rise to a flood of oratory and print on the nature and purposes of Communism, some of which has been intelligent, dispassionate, and informed, and some, perhaps most, inadequately researched, hysterical, and dangerously wide of the target. Yet this book is the first devoted exclusively to a history of the Communist Party of the United States itself during the years it has caused the greatest anxiety, the years since World War II.

The American Communist Party's recurrent political and ideological shifts result in explosions that bring to light many hidden facts. This book is a history of the party from the 1945 upheaval, which ejected Earl Browder from leadership, through the biggest explosion in the party's career, detonated by Khrushchev's speech on Stalin's crimes and the Russian intervention in Hungary, an explosion that rocked the party from early 1956 to early 1958. This book is not a guide to the detection of Communists, but a history of the party itself in the postwar years. The story of the American Communists since 1945 is, in a sense, a complete story, for it has a beginning, a middle, and an end.

In the writing of any book one becomes indebted to others, but I am embarrassed as I contemplate the number of people who have helped me to write this one. To all of them I express my gratitude.

My thanks to my colleagues and the administrators of Teachers College, Columbia University, for affording me a leave from teaching to do research for this book and to the Fund for the Republic for the financial assistance that made the leave feasible. My thanks also to the Graduate School of the University of Wisconsin for a summer-session salary grant that enabled me to spend full time for a summer finishing the book.

My colleagues in the study of Communism in American Life, which has been sponsored by the Fund for the Republic, were stimulating, helpful in criticism, and generous of time. I owe special thanks to Clinton Rossiter, director of the project, but all of the following aided me: Theodore Draper, William Goldsmith, Daniel Bell, Daniel Aaron, Ralph Roy, Nathan Glazer, Moshe Decter, Earl Latham, Robert Iversen, John Roche, and Joel Seidman. George Rawick and Mrs. Nancy Goldsmith assisted me for a time in research.

Many people who were either participants in this book in some way or another or who helped me in some manner with their special knowledge corresponded with me, allowed me to interview them, or both. They were of inestimable help. They were: C. B. Baldwin, Jack Barbash, Bruce Bliven, Merle Brodsky, Earl Browder, Joseph Clark, Joseph Freeman, John Gates, Max Gordon, Nissen Gross, Mrs. Gilbert Harrison, Dorothy Healy, Philip Jaffe, Mrs. Ida Landau, Val Lorwin, Curtis MacDougall, Joseph Starobin, Michael Straight, Irwin Suall, Norman Thomas, Rexford Tugwell, Henry Wallace, and David Williams. I also had some interviews with Communist rank-and-file members who prefer to remain anonymous.

Finally, I owe thanks to my wife, Jane Short Shannon, who helped in many ways, above all by reading the manuscript in all its stages with a kindly and encouraging attitude and yet with a coldly critical eye.

DAVID A. SHANNON

Madison, Wisconsin
March, 1959

CONTENTS

Preface ix

Part One
THE AMERICAN COMMUNIST PARTY: POSTWAR READJUSTMENT

I   *New Leader and New Line* 3

     PATRIOTS ALL: THE WARTIME LINE 4
     EARL BROWDER VERSUS WILLIAM Z. FOSTER 9
     RIGHT AND LEFT DEVIATIONISTS 15
     FOREIGN-POLICY LINE 23

II   *The Party Line for America* 34

     ANOTHER GREAT DEPRESSION? 39
     THE LINE FOR LABOR 44
     THE PARTY AND RELIGION 52
     "ART IS A WEAPON" 54
     THE PARTY AND THE NEGRO 58

III   *Party Organization, Party Strength, and Party Life* 68

     BROADENING THE PARTY'S INFLUENCE 82
     INDICATIONS OF PARTY STRENGTH 91
     THE COMMUNISTS AT THE POLLS 97
     THE PARTY AND THE TRADE UNIONS 101
     "THE LIFE OF THE PARTY" 106

77128

Part Two
THE UNPOPULAR FRONT

IV   *Creating Gideon's Army—The Progressive Party* 113

NON-COMMUNISTS AND ANTI-COMMUNISM 122
NEW YORK AND CALIFORNIA: A DOUBLE GAME 131
THE RUSSIANS, THE COMINFORM, AND AMERICAN
     POLITICS 134
PERSUADING HENRY WALLACE 140

V   *Professional Soldiers in a Campaign That Failed* 152

THE PROGRESSIVE PARTY CONVENTION 164
THE CAMPAIGN FAILS 176

Part Three
YEARS OF SUSPICION

VI   *The Party and Anti-Communism* 185

EXPECTATIONS OF FASCISM AND WAR 191
THE SMITH ACT CASES 195
"PEACE" AND WAR 203
THE LAST DAYS OF THE PROGRESSIVE PARTY 210
THE C.I.O. EXPULSIONS 214
THE ROSENBERG CASE 218

VII   *The Party's Internal Security* 227

THE "LOYALTY" PROGRAM 228
THE CAMPAIGN AGAINST HERESY 239

Part Four
THE AGE OF KHRUSHCHEV

VIII   *Slow Thaw in the Cold War* 251

THE END OF THE AMERICAN LABOR PARTY 256
TRADE-UNION "UNITY" AGAIN 259
ANOTHER CHANGE IN THE NEGRO LINE 262
"THE AMERICAN WAY" 265

IX   *Tarnished Heroes: Stalin and Foster* 272

THE TAX AFFAIR 278
JOHN GATES CRITICIZES 281
SOVIET ANTI-SEMITISM 284
SHIFTING PARTY WINDS 286
THE RUSSIANS AGAIN 292
FOSTER COUNTERATTACKS 302

X   *Hungary and Further Disillusion* 309

BOLTING THE PARTY 317
THE 1957 CONVENTION 321
FOSTER GAINS THE UPPER HAND 332
THE BICKERING FLICKERS ON 338
THE END OF AN ERA 344

Conclusion: An Impotent Party 354

SUICIDE AND INFANTICIDE 364

Bibliographical Essay 375
Notes 379
Index 413

PART ONE

THE AMERICAN COMMUNIST PARTY: POSTWAR READJUSTMENT

We are the most consistent opponents of imperialism and the staunchest champions of American-Soviet friendship. Consequently, we cannot accept the viewpoint of those who find both the U.S. and the U.S.S.R. responsible for the increased war danger. We maintain, as a matter of fact and record, that the Wall Street interventionists and bipartisan warmongers alone are to blame for the real and growing danger of a new world war.

—EUGENE DENNIS *to the fourteenth national convention of the Communist Party, August 1948.*

ONE: NEW LEADER AND NEW LINE

When the war in Europe ended with Germany's surrender in May 1945, the American Communist Party was at its peak, with between 75,000 and 85,000 members. In 1944, the Communists had recruited more than 4,000 new members a week. It had money of its own as well. Far from being the recipient of "Moscow gold," it was able to send funds to Communist parties abroad. It enjoyed a measure of prestige in at least some sections of society and of indifference in others. A public-opinion poll taken soon after the war revealed greater toleration toward Communists than there had ever been earlier, a reflection, to at least some extent, undoubtedly, of the regard with which Americans generally held the military exploits of their Soviet allies. The party had widespread influence beyond its own boundaries. Between one-fifth and one-fourth of all the members of the Congress of Industrial Organizations (C.I.O.) belonged to unions led by Communists or men close to the party. The party could count upon one-third of the votes of the C.I.O. executive board. The Communists had some strength at the polls. In November 1945, they elected two members of New York's city council on their own ticket, and two other city councilmen, elected on the American Labor Party ballot, worked hand in glove with the Communists.

Today, the Communists look back upon their power in 1945

wistfully. Their party has become a shambles. The membership has left in droves. There is one acknowledged party member for each twenty-five of 1945. The party has fewer dues-paying members than it had when it split off from the Socialist Party of Eugene V. Debs in 1919. Today, the party is almost bankrupt. It has been forced to stop publication of its daily newspaper, to close its schools, and to trim its staff to the quick. The Communists have lost almost all their influence in the trade unions. The C.I.O. has expelled the Communist-controlled unions and then raided their membership until almost no one is left. No longer do Communists make a good showing at the polls. In the fall of 1957, a Communist candidate for the New York City council received only 1 per cent of the district's vote. Instead of prestige or even toleration, Communists today receive social ostracism. It goes almost without saying in today's politics that the Communists are universally despised.

In 1945 the outlook for the American Communists had never been brighter; by 1959 it had never been darker.

What had happened in that decade and a half? Why did the Communists decline to political insignificance? The answer involves some factors beyond the party's control, and some factors within its control, decisions of the party leadership that proved disastrous from the party's own point of view. The *coup de grâce* came, ironically, not from America, but from Moscow.

This book is a description of the Communist Party's decline after 1945.

PATRIOTS ALL: THE WARTIME LINE

During the last months of the war, when victory seemed within the Allies' grasp, the foreign policy of the Soviet Union toward its Western comrades in arms gradually changed from uneasy alliance to hostility. The change was apparent at the Yalta conference in February 1945. Inevitably, the changed direction of

Moscow's policies would have a jolting impact on the American Communist Party.

But American party leaders detected no departure in Russian policy until they discovered in May that an important French Communist official, Jacques Duclos, had published the previous month in one of his party's magazines, *Cahiers du Communisme,* a biting criticism of the American party's wartime line. Duclos was especially critical of the 1944 decision of the top American leader, Earl Browder, to dissolve the Communist Party and re-make it into the Communist Political Association, the C.P.A. This criticism from abroad awakened the American Communists to a realization that the postwar world they had anticipated was not the one foreseen in Moscow. No criticism such as that Duclos had written, they thought, could have been made without the approval of the Soviet Union. Duclos was too important a leader in too important a Communist Party to have made such criticisms of a sister party without being sure of his position in Moscow.

The Communists' wartime line was a curiosity in the history of American Communism. After the Nazi invasion of Russia, their emphasis was upon national unity to win the war against fascism, now a "peoples war" instead of an imperialist adventure. They submerged their traditional criticisms of American capitalism until they were, on many issues, to the right of many non-Communist liberals. A minor detail at the 1944 convention, which founded the C.P.A., indicated a great deal about their mood and tactics. Browder sprinkled professional singers through the audience so that the assembly could sing what Browder still calls "the best rendition of 'The Star Spangled Banner' ever performed by a large amateur group." [1] It was in this nationalistic all-out-for-unity mood that Browder, in a Bridgeport, Connecticut, speech, offered to "clasp the hand" of the junior J. P. Morgan in the unlikely event that that gentleman, dead for nine months, proved himself to be a progressive capitalist member of what the Communists called "the democratic anti-fascist coalition." [2] Not only in such peripheral matters, but on issues of significance to Communists—

race relations, organized labor, and political action—the wartime Communist line revealed itself.

Traditionally, the Communists have been, in their own way, vigorous champions of the rights of minorities, although Communist policy toward minority racial groups has vacillated more than is generally known. During the war, however, the Communists soft-pedaled this issue. California Communists endorsed the federal government's removal of the West Coast Japanese to what were euphemistically called "relocation centers" in the country's interior. American Communists did not help Negro leaders in their efforts to pressure the administration to end color segregation in the armed forces, and they criticized Negro militants. Indeed, in early 1941, before the German invasion of Russia, when the American Communists' slogan was "The Yanks Are Not Coming," the Communists had opposed A. Philip Randolph and his "March on Washington" movement, which wrung from Franklin D. Roosevelt the executive order establishing the Fair Employment Practices Commission.[3] During the war, the Communists took the position that unity for the war effort demanded that racial discrimination be at least temporarily tolerated if not condoned.

The Communists adopted a similar attitude toward trade-union militancy. American workers during the war encountered only opposition from the Communists when they considered strikes or slowdowns against grievances. *Political Affairs,* the official magazine on Communist theory (called the *Communist* until the party dissolved and set up the C.P.A.), proclaimed that to strike or even to permit a strike "would be a crime against the war effort. . . . Co-operation on the basis of the nation's war-time program alone has provided the solution of the workers' problems." Communists in the United Auto Workers tried unsuccessfully to persuade the membership to accept piecework and incentive pay to increase production. On one occasion in San Francisco, when longshoremen protested to their union that employers required them to load more cargo into the freight slings than they considered safe, Harry Bridges ordered the men to put even more in the slings.[4]

In 1944, the Communists vigorously supported Roosevelt's re-election, and, after the election, Browder expressed his gratification and warned against independent political action: "We must discourage every project of organization of new parties . . . the lesson of this election campaign points toward reducing the number of parties and not increasing them." Browder was not disappointed, as were some New Dealers, at the refusal of the Democratic convention to renominate Henry A. Wallace for vice-president. "I think . . . it is probably fortunate for the country and for Wallace that he was not nominated in this past election." In early 1945, when Edward Stettinius, a former president of United States Steel, replaced Cordell Hull as Secretary of State, many liberals were alarmed. But not the Communists. The New York newspaper *PM* expressed its displeasure with the appointment and was rebuked by the Communists for being "irresponsible." Browder urged "unconditional support" of Roosevelt's national war-service proposal, which would have made liable for military or industrial service all able-bodied men and women; many liberals opposed it.[5]

The C.P.A.'s postwar strategy called for a continuation of the wartime line. Browder, in *Political Affairs,* predicted Russian-American harmony after the war, despite the obviously deteriorating relations in the last months of the European war, which he described as *"a conflict of mood and opinion but not a conflict of interest."* As Browder saw it, there were but two alternatives to continued Russian-American harmony: war, which would be "military and political insanity"; or armed peace, "another name for diplomatic and economic war without drawing the military conclusions." The West would reject both alternatives because they would "cancel all prospects for a rapid extension of the world markets so vital for America's postwar economy." [6]

If Browder's crystal ball was cloudy, his followers did not perceive it. They filled out the details of the Communist line for the postwar period to conform to Browder's general position. Post-war universal military training, "the most effective and democratic method by which the United States can build and maintain a military establishment geared to the needs of the post-war world," was a plank in the Communist platform for the world of peace. It was a pity indeed that the American people had not heeded George Washington's advice and established universal military service in 1790. Labor was urged to extend its no-strike pledge. Postwar strikes, Communists believed, would only endanger the goal of full employment. Furthermore, strikes would prevent the maintenance of high wartime take-home pay. The Communists were to maintain the C.P.A. and not reconstitute the old party, wrote the Communist organization secretary, John Williamson. The C.P.A. was the "most indispensable weapon" in maintaining "national unity in the post-war period, including the long-time collaboration of Communists in the democratic coalition." [7]

The Communists' rationale for this whole soft line was that there were profound changes developing in American capitalism. The war against fascism, as the Communists saw it, was making the American business community, or at least a large part of it, democratic and responsive to the needs of the whole nation. Here and there, reactionary capitalists remained, but they were on the defensive, even in retreat: the "decisive sections of the American capitalist class have abandoned the old policy of hard-boiled reaction and imperialism, and are seriously trying to adjust themselves to the democratic currents and needs of the nation at war." With such a development, obviously the Communist position toward the capitalists would have to change. "The problem," wrote Browder, "is no longer how to combat the whole bourgeoisie but how to strengthen the progressive against the reactionary sector. . . ." [8]

EARL BROWDER VERSUS WILLIAM Z. FOSTER

But, said Jacques Duclos, this wartime line of Browder's was "revisionist" nonsense, and the American Communists saw his "letter" as an international signal to scuttle the Browder position and adopt a harder line, although Browder wrote an introduction to the *Daily Worker* translation of the Duclos letter in which he tried to minimize the differences between his position and that of Duclos. For weeks, the American Communists were in turmoil. The national board met in almost continuous session in the last half of May 1945. The pages of the *Daily Worker* carried discussion from any Communist who wanted to write, quite in contrast to periods of normal party stability, when the membership was quiet on all important matters and nothing suggested anything but perfect party unanimity. When equilibrium again came to the American Communists, confirmed by their special emergency convention of July 26-28, there was a new reconstituted party organization, a new leadership, a partial outline of a new line, and, most important, a new leftist mood.

The two antagonists in this ideological duel were Earl Browder and William Z. Foster. Foster was the most important Communist leader to oppose Browder in the national board meetings following the *Daily Worker*'s translation of the Duclos letter. He had been in and around leftist politics for almost a half-century. Born in March 1881, in Taunton, Massachusetts, the son of an Irish immigrant father and a mother of English-Scottish background, Foster grew up in the Philadelphia slums, quit school at the age of ten, and worked at a variety of jobs all over the country, as a dock worker, a seaman, a streetcar conductor, a lumberjack, and a farm hand. In 1901, he joined the Socialist Party of Eugene Debs, which expelled him in 1909. He then went into the Industrial Workers of the World, where he tried unsuccessfully to persuade the Wobblies to join the American Federation of Labor and "bore from within." In 1912, Foster formed his own organization, the Syndicalist League of North America; it lasted two years. Another short-lived organization followed. During the war, he rose within the American Federation of Labor in Chicago as an organizer in the meat-packing industry. In 1919, he came to national prominence as the A.F. of L. leader of the violent but unsuccessful steel strike. The next year, he founded still another of his own organizations, the Trade Union Educational League (T.U.E.L.), spurned at first by the American Communists but accepted by the Russians' Red International of Labor Unions, or "Profintern," at its first congress in Moscow in July 1921. No Communist when he went to Moscow in 1921, Foster returned to the United States to join the American party and, at the Profintern's direction, to be the head of the American Communists' labor branch. T.U.E.L., the American section of the Profintern, had its headquarters in Chicago; the central political office of the Communist Party was in New York. Thus Foster moved into the American Communist organization as a top leader. In 1928 and 1932, he was the Communists' candidate for the Presidency.

But in the 1930's, Earl Russell Browder had passed Foster and become the number one man in the Communist Party. Browder was a complex and contradictory person. Born in Wichita, Kansas, on May 20, 1891, the son of a teacher and the grandson of a Methodist circuit-riding minister, he never fully lost—apparently did not want to lose—his Kansas ways. He made many trips to Moscow, he served the Comintern as one of its agents in China, he married a Russian, and he was proud of his friendship with certain leaders of the international movement, particularly Georgi Dmitrov. Yet he continued to speak in the flat accents of a Kansan (he pronounced the word "cadre" to rhyme with ladder), and he dressed like a small-town Midwestern businessman of a generation ago (even with long underwear tucked neatly inside his socks). Although in his political career he was ever sensitive to the wishes of the Soviet Union, he remained something of an American nationalist. He is likely today to tell strangers a few minutes after meeting them how proud he is of the way Americans have treated his three sons, who are disinterested in politics.

Foster had chafed under Browder's party leadership during World War II. His heart had not been in the party's wartime line. He opposed the idea of Communist co-operation with "sections of the bourgeoisie." In January 1944, Foster had declared his dissent in a letter to the Communist national committee. But neither this letter nor any other indication of Foster's disapproval reached print until after the Duclos letter. Browder, of course, opposed publication of Foster's views, and Foster was not sufficiently sure of himself to fight the Browder machine. He did not come out into the open until the Duclos letter made him confident of Russian support. During the war, he had published articles that agreed with the Browder line, even after the early 1944 letter of dissent to the party's national committee. Indeed, as late as June 1945, two months after the Duclos affair, *Political Affairs* carried a Foster article that included these words: "By far not all American capitalists favor a policy of aggressive imperialist expansion. Large numbers of them followed the general Roosevelt line. These more far-sighted elements among the capitalists, the Kaisers, Krugs, Nelsons, etc., realizing that their class interests dovetail with the nation's interests and understanding that any attempt of the United States to go it alone in the world would result in sure disaster, are accepting the general policies laid down at Teheran and Yalta." Foster's acknowledgement of "more far-sighted elements among the capitalists" implied the same distinction among capitalists that Browder had made, and the distinction was the basic tenet from which the whole Browder soft line flowed. Further, Foster's statement that the "class interests" of the capitalists "dovetail" with the nation's interests was a good example of the kind of "revisionism" he was already pledged to stamp out.[9] His article was diametrically opposed to his position at the national board discussions in his efforts to depose Browder. This was not the first time, however, that the mechanics of Communist publication could not keep pace with Communist ideological change.

Foster had two important lieutenants in his struggle against Browder: Eugene Dennis and Robert Thompson. Dennis, born Francis X. Waldron, Jr., was also of Irish extraction. Reared in the Pacific Northwest, Dennis had got into the labor movement as a teamster and had joined the party in 1926 after a strike of agricultural workers in California. The party sent him to the Lenin School in Moscow, from which the Comintern sent him to China. Arriving back in the United States in the mid-1930's, Dennis became a member of the party's national committee and state secretary of the Wisconsin organization. His work there attracted Browder's attention, and he moved Dennis into the national office. Browder's protégé turned against his sponsor; in the process, Dennis made himself the party's number two man.[10]

Unlike most party leaders, Thompson had little political or trade-union experience. Barely thirty years old when he became Foster's lieutenant in charge of eliminating the influence of Browder and the Browderites, Thompson had spent much of his adult life as a soldier. He had been a member of the Abraham Lincoln Brigade and had fought and been wounded in the Spanish Civil War. As a staff sergeant infantry platoon leader in New Guinea in World War II, he had earned the Distinguished Service Cross. He received a medical discharge long before the end of the war. The ruthlessness and toughness of a good infantryman were the qualities Thompson brought to the battle against Browder. During the party upheaval, Thompson was heard to say to a friend who found it difficult to vilify Browderite friends that he did not find it difficult at all—"just like killing Japs." Thompson's reward for his services in routing the Browder heretics was one of the most important positions in the party, state secretary of New York, by far the biggest of the state organizations and, with its offices at the national headquarters on East Twelfth Street, the most influential.[11]

Neither Dennis nor Thompson could lay claim, as did Foster,

to Marxist purity and opposition to Browder's "revisionism." Dennis had written articles in the spring of 1945 in which he saw eye to eye with Browder about the postwar world, and Thompson felt obligated to take considerable space in one of his attacks on Browder to describe how he had been misguided. In language reminiscent of a repentent backslider from a total-abstinence pledge, he explained: "I conditioned myself to swallowing an opportunist gnat and as is inevitable in such cases wound up by swallowing elephants." [12]

On June 2, 1945, the national board of the C.P.A. adopted a draft resolution entitled "The Present Situation and the Next Tasks," which became the basis of the Communists' official discussion and which, slightly amended, became the main resolution passed by the special party convention, July 26-28. The draft resolution was a thorough repudiation of Browder and his wartime soft line, as well as an outline of the new line.[13] From the time the draft resolution passed the national board, Browder was in actuality no longer the top Communist leader. He remained a member of the C.P.A.'s thirteen-member national board and of the national committee (of which the national board was an executive committee), but he had been repudiated. The special national convention dissolved the C.P.A., re-established the Communist Party of the United States of America, the C.P.U.S.A., and refused to elect Browder to its national committee. After the convention, Browder was just another rank-and-filer, and a disgraced one at that. Several months later, in February 1946, the party expelled him altogether.

The fundamental difference between the old Browder line and the new Foster line was the denial of progressive tendencies in capitalism. The Communists now said American capitalism was inherently reactionary and imperialist; those who defended it or the policies of the government, in their eyes only the instrument of reactionary imperialists, were retrograde. If the defenders of American policies were honored leaders of the working class, their defense proved only that they were "misleaders" of labor.

From the premise of the inherently reactionary nature of capitalism and its agencies, it followed that Communists should do all in their power to fight capitalists rather than to collaborate with them in any kind of alliance.

The Communists did not discard the idea of alliance with non-Communists who were not staunch defenders of capitalism or of American policy—especially foreign policy. The "democratic antifascist coalition" should become even stronger. To the Communists, the unity of all noncapitalist working-class groups was paramount. Co-operation with non-Communist labor, farmer, and Negro groups remained one of the Communist goals.

The Communists had once referred to "the united front of struggle from below." In a similar mood, the Communists hoped to woo the masses away from their "misleaders." Whereas the party had once refrained from attack on many popular leaders, or had spoken kindly of them, they now would attack them if they supported governmental policies or were outspokenly anti-Communist. Thus, Walter Reuther now became an object of Communist scorn and vilification; Walter White, of the National Association for the Advancement of Colored People, who supported American foreign policy, now was labeled a hateful betrayer of his people. The Communists were not prepared to pull out of unions that had anti-Communist leaders; they would try to overthrow them instead. However, they did maintain "dual organizations" against the N.A.A.C.P. The new coalition was to be an alliance, but one with a difference. It never really developed.

For some time, there were ideological lags and even internal inconsistencies in the Communist position. The Communist draft resolution, for example, contained an endorsement of the Labor-Management Charter which United States Chamber of Commerce President Eric Johnston, C.I.O. President Philip Murray, and A.F. of L. President William Green had signed in early 1945, until a revision made after the resolution's passage by the C.P.A. national committee.[14] Endorsement of a document written in part by an officer of the National Chamber of Commerce was obviously at odds with the new line. The endorsement was withdrawn from the document's final draft, but a plea for an extension of federal aid to small business remained. James S. Allen, one of the party's theoretical writers who strongly favored a hard line, was justified somewhat in calling the draft resolution "full of inconsistencies, contradictions and confusion." [15]

The new line did jell before 1945 was over. Communists soon learned what ideas they could express and what ones they should banish.

RIGHT AND LEFT DEVIATIONISTS

Back in the 1930's, the Browder party's two ideological bogies were, on the right, Jay Lovestone, expelled from the party in 1929 for professing the heretical view that special American conditions and traditions required a unique Communist party, and, on the left, the Trotskyists. Now, after World War II, Browder himself became the bogy on the right of the line; an assorted collection of former Communist extremists, lumped under the label "left deviationists," became the bogy on the left.

When Browder was toppled from the leadership, he remained a party member in his party club or branch, the lowest party echelon, until his expulsion from the party. The decision to expel came from the top rather than from the rank and file. On January 27, a convention of the Manhattan party passed a resolution urging the national committee to expel him; the next day, the Bronx convention passed the same resolution. Only then did Browder's party club in Yonkers take any action against him, ousting him on February 12. Browder did not bother to appeal the decision. He did not even go to the club meeting to defend himself. On February 13, the national committee affirmed the Yonkers club's action, adding that the party "must root out all vestiges of revisionism and all rotten liberal attitudes toward Browder and the conciliators of Browderism." [16]

The new leadership kept a sharp suspicious eye on Browder, worried lest he split the movement or try to recover his former position. But Browder's first concern was to make a living from a mimeographed newsletter he called *Distributors Guide*. A group of businessmen whom Browder described as "periphery sympathizers" of the party promised him support, and his first issue appeared on January 5, 1946. The circulation was very small, and since it contained nothing but Browder's analyses of economic conditions and international events, neither of which was anything new to veteran readers of the Communist press, there was nothing in the venture to threaten the new leadership's security. The leadership was nevertheless alarmed. It threatened to expose the business supporters of *Distributors Guide* as Communist sympathizers if they did not withdraw their support—even Communists find occasional advantage in Red baiting—and the newsletter quickly collapsed.[17] Browder's next venture was a trip to Moscow, and the new leadership panicked.

He had decided to go to Moscow "just to see what was going on."[18] He denied then and has denied since that the purpose of his trip was to appeal his removal from party leadership.*

The State Department granted Browder a passport and the Soviet Government granted him a visa. He left New York by plane on April 26, 1946. The next day's *Daily Worker* carried

* The New York *Times* of September 15, 1946, quoted Browder as saying there was no "shadow Comintern" to which he could have appealed, and that Duclos in 1945 had never intended his article "as an intervention of international leadership." Browder's argument was that Duclos had "washed his hands of responsibility for the results, which is something no kind of international leadership could do." He also quoted Duclos, as reported in the London *Daily Mail*, as saying that American Communists were "an immature and uninfluential group." Foster cabled Duclos on September 16, saying that Browder had used Duclos' name to discredit the American party. Duclos replied that the London paper had distorted what he had said but did not reply to the main point of Browder's assertion (*Daily Worker*, September 21, 1946). This was a curious byplay; Browder, who obviously was removed from office by international intervention, denied the real intent was to remove him; and Foster, who could never admit that it was Communists from abroad who had elevated him to power, argued by implication that the orders had come from overseas.

the headline BROWDER LEAVES FOR STOCKHOLM TO EXTEND ANTI-
PARTY INTRIGUE. Dennis said the trip was "calculated . . . to
create confusion and uncertainty in the ranks of the Party." The
party secretariat hastened to issue an official statement calling
Browder "an unreconstructed revisionist . . . a social-imperial-
ist . . . an enemy of the working class . . . a renegade . . .
[and] an apologist for American imperialism." [19]

Browder arrived in Moscow on May 6, received a warm welcome from minor Russian officials, and moved into a three-room
hotel suite provided by the Russians. Then nothing happened.
He called upon several Soviet officials, all of whom were cordial
but careful to avoid discussion of anything important. Years later,
Browder reported the impression that there were "wheels within
wheels," all of which were in motion, and said he did not understand what was happening in the Russian leadership. On May 20,
a group of Browder's friends and acquaintances arranged a lavish
dinner at a Moscow restaurant to celebrate his fifty-fifth birthday.
The feast began in midafternoon. By about eight o'clock, Browder
felt his part in the celebration had gone too far, and to escape
further vodka toasts he slipped out and returned to his hotel.
There in his suite was a very impatient messenger from the office
of the foreign minister, Vyacheslav Molotov. Browder was to be
ready for an interview with Molotov by ten o'clock that night.
"Apparently the only person in Russia authorized to talk to a
foreigner was Molotov." Browder drank a quart of black coffee
and went for a long walk. When Molotov's limousine came for
him, he was ready for what he thought would be "a historic crisis in
my life."

In a conversation ten years later, Browder recalled that there
were three people in Molotov's office during the interview—Molotov, Browder, and an interpreter. Molotov, who had returned that
day from a foreign ministers' conference in Paris, asked Browder
to state his mission. Browder first asked if the Communist International, or Comintern, dissolved technically in 1943, were to be
re-established. Molotov said it would not be. (The next year, the

Soviets founded the Communist Information Bureau, or Cominform.) Browder then talked about what he thought could be done in the world if there were Russian-American co-operation; he maintained such co-operation was possible. He enumerated his many criticisms of Foster's leadership of the American party and described the kind of party and movement he thought there should be in the United States. According to Browder, Molotov listened intently but did not indicate by word or facial expression what he thought of Browder's position. After an hour, Molotov asked him to elucidate further on certain points, and Molotov's questions indicated that the foreign minister understood him perfectly. As midnight approached, Molotov said he was very tired and, without revealing his own views in any way, brought the interview to an end. Browder arose, and Molotov said casually that on his desk was a proposal that Browder be appointed the American representative of the Soviet book-publishing industry. Was Browder interested? Browder said he would accept the appointment, for it would prove to the world that he was a friend of the Soviet Union.

Browder's venture as representative of Soviet publishing proved as disastrous as the *Distributors Guide* venture. For several years, an American woman Communist had been in business as the Soviet representative for fiction and photographs, leaving only nonfiction for Browder to try to sell to American publishers. Browder invested and lost his savings. He sold only a few scientific works to American publishers. In 1949, he canceled the contract, sold the office furniture to pay the last month's rent, and went out of business. There was no market in the United States for Russian books, and, said Browder, "By that time I wasn't sure I was a friend of the Soviet Union anymore anyway." [20]

When the American press released the news of Browder's appointment, Foster announced the party would intensify the fight against Browderism. The party had already done a great deal to eliminate Browderism from its ranks. It had expelled Browder's brother and one of its wealthy angels, A. A. Heller, whose money had helped to establish International Publishers, which publishes

Communist books.[21] But now anti-Browderism became a frenzied ritual. Nearly every issue of *Political Affairs* denounced "Browder revisionism." [22] The editors of *Political Affairs* even managed to work a condemnation of Browder into an article about May Day celebrations.[23]

In July 1948, Browder humiliated himself by asking his enemies in the party to reinstate his membership. In a letter to Alexander Trachtenberg, of the cadre and review commission, the office charged with the party's "internal security," Browder said that Tito's recent defection from the Soviet orbit was a serious threat to Communism, and added, "In such a moment all other considerations must give way to the necessity of unity of the world movement and the protection of its achievements. . . . The enemy camp, making use of my expulsion from the Party, now tries to manipulate with my name to extend their disruptive efforts. This is a weapon to which they are not entitled; my only desire is to strengthen the camp of peace, democracy and socialism."

Robert Thompson assumed the task of handling the case. He got the floor at the national convention in August 1948, read the Browder letter, and to the delegates' applause called the communication "an attempt . . . thinly disguised by demagogic phrase-mongering about Tito" to further Browder's "anti-Party factional activities" and his "anti-Marxist bourgeois political line." The delegates unanimously rejected Browder's application for membership.[24]

No Communist dared say anything that could be construed as "rightist" Browderism. And this was important to Foster, for there were top Communist leaders who had once been close to Browder. Dennis, for example, had been Browder's right hand, a fact that Foster could never forget. Dennis lived that down only after years of party conformity. Foster elevated Dennis to the job of general secretary of the party in 1946 when the anti-Browder campaign was at its peak, gaining for himself the administrative assistance he needed because of his own age and poor health. Dennis was now beholden to him. Rooting out "revisionism" and "rotten liberal attitudes toward Browder" bolstered Foster's position in the party; it also seriously limited the party's flexibility. It had to be cautious about doing anything that could be interpreted as Browderite.

The Communist leaders inflated "leftist tendencies" into another bogy. Here and there within the party, small groups of "superleftists" now argued that Foster's leadership was as "revisionist" as Browder's. In the fall of 1946, the party initiated a wave of expulsions. Among the first "left deviationists" expelled were the writers Bruce Minton and his wife, Ruth McKenney, author of *My Sister Eileen*. In August 1945, the Mintons had written a letter to the editors of *New Masses* criticizing it for its "reformist editorial policy" and resigning as contributing editors. The following spring, after several exchanges of letters, *New Masses* had dropped the Mintons from its masthead. In September 1946, the state committee of Connecticut expelled them "for conducting a factional struggle against the line of the Party and its national leadership" and warned the membership to beware of those who "resort to ultra-revolutionary phrase-mongering and factionalism." [25] The Mintons then dropped out of the Communist movement altogether, but others who were expelled organized little splinter groups and published bitter criticisms of the party's leadership.

The primary Left-deviationist groups were these: the New Committee for Publications, which published *NCP Report* beginning in the fall of 1946, with Carolyn Burkhart as chairman and Lyle Dowling as editor; the PR Club CP (Expelled) of the Bronx, which published *Spark: A Marxist Monthly* beginning in April 1947, and which consisted largely of the family of a man named Earl Price; the Maritime Committee for a Communist Party, which operated on the New York waterfront with William F. Dunne, Sam Darcy, and Charles Keith as leaders; a small group in California under the leadership of Harrison George and Verne Smith; and a short-lived group in Queens, the Workers Freedom League, led by Bert Sutta, an expelled section organizer. None of these Left deviationists had ever been in the party's top leadership, but some of them had been in the party for years. In 1948, some of these groups succeeded in forming an alliance, and published *Turning Point,* which as late as 1956 was occasionally on sale at a few newsstands in mid-Manhattan.

The spectacle of the party lashing out at these Left deviationists with all the furious epithets at its command was both comic and tragic. It was comic because the groups were quite unimportant, a handful of fanatics armed with no more than revolutionary indignation and mimeograph machines. They polemicized against one another almost as vigorously as they did against the party leadership, each maintaining that it and only it had the true message. These little sects were no more than gnats to the party itself, but the party treated them as a major threat. Communist writers took pages and pages for diatribes against the "renegade cliques," the followers of "semi-Trotskyism and unprincipled Leftist adventurism," and "degenerate factionalists." The national board even hinted darkly that the Left groups were a plant of "reaction": "It would be odd if reaction did not seek to combine its attacks against our Party from without with attempts at organized disruption from within." [26]

The party went to great lengths to quell the Left deviationists. The strange story of Francis Franklin is revealing. Franklin was a Communist graduate student at the University of Virginia in the late 1930's. Browder met him at Charlottesville and thought he had promise, and Franklin soon came to New York City. He taught American history at the Jefferson School, the party's adult-education institution, but in 1947 was fired for "disruptive activities." Finally, his section expelled him after he had distributed an open letter to the party membership charging the leadership with Browderite tendencies. He began then still another leftist mimeographed periodical, *Towards Socialism,* with which he engaged in the esoteric polemics of the deviationist fringe. Then, quite without warning, his periodical announced in October 1949 that the whole venture was a mistake. The party was not what it should be, but the way "to Bolshevize" the party was to work within it rather than to criticize it from the outside. Another fringe periodical told its version of the story under the headline FRANCIS FRANKLIN TURNS RAT. "F. F. . . . is now ready for a deal. He has lists, he has correspondence with expelled and CP members. . . . He has put in his bid to become the National Committee's 'finger man.' " [27]

But the spectacle was also tragic in that the party cast out some old men who had sacrificed much for the Communist movement only to find themselves ostracized in their old age. Among these old men was Verne Smith, who had come into the party from the I.W.W. in the 1920's and had served for years on the *Daily Worker* and the *Daily People's World,* the party paper published in San Francisco. Another was Bill Dunne, who had been coeditor of the *Daily Worker* when it began publication in 1924. Another was Harrison George, who had joined the Socialists in 1910 and the I.W.W. in 1914 and become a charter member of the Communist Party in September 1919, joining from his cell in Leavenworth Penitentiary.[28] An interesting case was that of Max Bedacht, who began his Marxist associations in Europe in 1902 and continued them in the party of Debs after he came to the United States in 1908. In 1919, he was on the executive committee of the Communist Labor Party, one of the left groups that split from the Socialists. For years, Bedacht was president of the International Workers Order, one of the party's most important fronts. When Browder was removed, he aspired to a higher position in the leadership, but Foster kept Bedacht in the I.W.O. Bedacht was spoiling for a fight. He found it in 1946. He charged that the party's plan to establish an old people's home for each of the several nationality groups in the I.W.O. was "bourgeois nationalism." For two years, he harped on this theme, and in October 1948, the party expelled him. He moved to New Jersey and became a poultry farmer.[29] These old men were classic "true believers," dedicated revolutionaries. Now when their lives were almost over they found themselves rejected and despised by the party they had helped to build. The movement devoured its own.

The Communist leadership and the party line were secure from internal dissent. The party could quote Lenin against both the Left and the Right: from *"Left-Wing" Communism: An Infantile Disorder* against the left bogy and from *What Is To Be Done?* and several other works against the Browderite witches. The party used Lenin, who was nothing if not flexible, to help make the Communist line rigid. By 1948, the American Communists had set themselves such tight ideological boundaries that they had little room in which to turn around. When the crisis came in Moscow after the death of Stalin, the American Communists could break out of their ideological box only by tearing their party to pieces.

FOREIGN-POLICY LINE

The most important part of the entire Communist line was its position on foreign policy. Minor aspects of the line on domestic matters could change a little, but the line on foreign policy, with its defense of the Soviet Union and its attack on American policies, was a firm anchor. The positions of non-Communist labor and Negro leaders on foreign policy became the touchstone to determine whether the Communists would support or criticize them.

The rationale of the Communist line was that American capitalism and capitalists were inherently reactionary and imperialist. Their reasoning was straight from Lenin's "classic," *Imperialism,* which argued that imperialism was the last inevitable stage of capitalism. As domestic capitalist economies become incapable of absorbing their product, argued Lenin, capitalists seek markets and investment opportunities overseas. Overseas adventures bring the various national economies into conflict and result in war. Foster acknowledged the argument's source: ". . . the United States is an imperialistic country . . . the most aggressive empire in the world. This country displays all the features characteristic of imperialist capitalism as analyzed by the great Lenin." [30]

To the Communists, of course, it followed that such imperialism must be fought tooth and nail. To do otherwise, to their way of thinking, would be to compromise with evil.

Dozens of Communist editorials, articles, and speeches alleged that it was American policy to 1) protect and extend capital investments—"Anglo-American international cartel investments"; 2) reduce the Soviet Union to weakness and to isolate it from the rest of the world—"the policy of hostile encirclement"; 3) make the defeated Axis powers American satellites; 4) "resurrect a decadent feudal-reaction" everywhere and keep democracy to a minimum—"Washington likes what Franco is doing in Spain and wants all of Europe to follow the Franco model"; 5) establish American hegemony over the colonial areas breaking away from the British, Dutch, French, and Belgian empires; 6) strengthen its grip on Latin America; 7) operate the United Nations as its instrument for extending its strength and reducing the power of "the peaceloving peoples"; and 8) force Great Britain into a junior partnership with American imperialism.[31]

Another fundamental assumption of the Communist foreign-policy line was that the Soviet Union was not imperialist, that it was, on the contrary, anti-imperialist and the major defender of peace and democratic values on the world scene. The Communists inverted Lenin's dictum on imperialism, that imperialism is the last stage of capitalism, to argue that the Soviet Union, not being capitalist, could not possibly be imperialist. Foster put it this way: ". . . the charges of 'red imperialism' against the U.S.S.R. are ridiculous on their face. Imperialism . . . is the final stage of capitalism. . . . The U.S.S.R., on the other hand, is fundamentally non-imperialist. The Soviet Union has no capitalism and hence no capitalist monopolies to drive it into policies of oppression and exploitation of other peoples. In consequence, Soviet policy, dictated by the structure of the socialist regime itself, is inevitably one of peace and friendly collaboration with other nations." [32]

When critics of the Soviet Union pointed out that, despite what

"They want to reduce that country to their sway, to put it in its place, so to speak, as they are now proceeding to do with the lesser capitalist countries of the world." [39]

The Communists identified Winston Churchill's famous "Iron Curtain" speech at Fulton, Missouri, as a part of the conspiracy; it was a "chapter in a whole series of American imperialist provocations against the American people themselves and against the Soviet Union." [40] As for the Iron Curtain itself, the Russian policy of denying Western journalists free access in Eastern Europe sprang from a desire to maintain harmony between the Soviet Union and the Western powers. Imperialist Western reporters would only poison the well of Big Three unity. In the past, said Foster, the Soviets had extended to Western journalists "every facility to observe what is going on in the new land of Socialism only to have these correspondents once they have put foot outside of the USSR launch the most outrageous broadsides of attacks and slanders against the country whose guests they were." [41]

American concern with Russian espionage was altogether artificial, claimed the Communists. When the House Committee on Un-American Activities was trying to get Gerhart Eisler to testify early in 1947, Eugene Dennis claimed the committee was "Cooking up for the United States something akin to the 'Reichstag fire' conspiracy." "A crude plot to whip up hysteria against any reasonable calm discussion of atomic disarmament," said the editors of the *Daily Worker* as they coined a new slogan, "A spy scare a day keeps disarmament away." [42] When the Canadians revealed the existence in their country of a Russian wartime espionage ring, the *Daily Worker*'s foreign editor declared, "Some miserable stooge— no doubt planted in the Soviet Embassy . . . another brush in the current attempt to make all the English-speaking people believe that we cannot cooperate with the Russians." [43]

The year 1947 saw two new developments in American foreign policy, the Truman Doctrine and the Marshall Plan. Since late in the war, the anti-Communist government of Greece had been harassed by Communist guerrillas, and the British had given the

Greek Government financial and military support, probably preventing Greece from moving into the Soviet orbit. In February 1947, the British notified Washington that its internal economic problems and its troubles in the shaky empire made it imperative that they pull out of Greece. Fearing that without continued support for the Greek Government, the Communists would soon control Greece and possibly also Turkey, President Harry Truman went to Congress to ask for an appropriation of $400,000,000 to be used for economic and military support to the Greek and Turkish governments. In the course of his speech, Truman said it should be American policy "to support free peoples who are resisting attempted subjugation by armed minorities or by outside pressure." This became known as the Truman Doctrine.

A few months later, Secretary of State George C. Marshall described at the Harvard University commencement a program that came to be known as the Marshall Plan. He suggested that the United States offer economic aid to any European government, including the Soviet Union and those under its influence, in order that the European economy might revive and "permit the emergence of political and social conditions in which free institutions can exist." Europeans, rather than Americans, were to work out the details, and they should understand that Marshall Plan aid would be the last from the United States in the foreseeable future. The response from Western Europe was enthusiastic; the economies of those nations were in truly desperate condition. The Russians themselves raised only minor objections until the European foreign ministers' meeting in July. In April of the following year, the Marshall Plan became law.

Many Americans were worried about the Truman Doctrine and the Marshall Plan, new departures in American policy. A great many continued to believe, as had their fathers and grandfathers, that involvement with foreign countries should be no more than temporary, the sooner ended the better. Defenders of democracy were concerned about the Truman Doctrine's support of the conservative Greek regime although they wanted Greece to remain outside the Soviet sphere. Defenders of old-fashioned capitalism were disturbed by the prospect of some of their tax money going for Marshall Plan aid to the Labour government of Great Britain.

The Communists aimed considerably more fire against the Marshall Plan than the Truman Doctrine, although the Truman Doctrine was the more vulnerable to Communist criticism in a variety of ways. It was more openly anti-Soviet than the Marshall Plan, it bolstered an undemocratic regime in Greece, and since it did not involve the co-operation of the European powers as much as the Marshall Plan, it was easier to charge it with domination of foreign countries. But the Truman Doctrine became law quickly, before the Communists could organize a major campaign against it. Truman made the proposal on March 12 and signed the bill on May 22. The Marshall Plan, on the other hand, took ten months from announcement to enactment, giving time for Communists the world over to follow the Russian lead in denouncing it.

Yet the Truman Doctrine came in for its share of Communist attack. It was a doctrine of "unabashed imperialism [that] flows from the 'get tough' program of the biggest monopoly capitalists." Further, it was "an attempt to make a big new advance for American imperialism," an advance that would provide a base for the "possibility of eventual attack" on the Soviet Union.[44]

The American Communist attack on the Marshall Plan was massive. Communist periodicals made the plan the major object of attack for months, and so vigorous was the party's opposition that it made the Marshall Plan a major issue of conflict between the Communist unions and the national C.I.O. leadership and thereby hastened the day of Communist isolation from the labor movement.

Perhaps one reason for the unusual vehemence of Communists everywhere against the Marshall Plan, aside from the fact that the plan obviously would work to the long-term disadvantage of the Communist parties of Western Europe, was that with the plan the State Department had outsmarted the Soviets. Marshall's Harvard address left the door wide open to Soviet-bloc participation in the plan, and he underscored the point in a press conference a few days later. The strategy was that Moscow would refuse to participate but that it would be put in an embarrassing position by so doing. The strategy worked perfectly. Had the strategy backfired, had Moscow permitted Warsaw, Bucharest, Budapest, and the other Communist capitals to undertake Marshall Plan agreements, the State Department would have been in a precarious position. Many observers doubted that Congress would have voted the necessary funds. And it may be that the Soviet Union considered calling the State Department's bluff. At the beginning of the meetings of the European foreign ministers at Paris in July, Soviet Minister Molotov's objections to the plan were only minor, but a telegram from home reversed his mood to his usual truculence.

The Communist position on the Marshall Plan was that it was just another imperialist maneuver, "a cold-blooded scheme of American monopolists to establish their ruthless domination over harassed world humanity," as Foster put it,[45] but imperialism with a difference: the plan was a deliberate attempt to rebuild the German war potential and pave the way for a resurgence of Nazism. One of its purposes was "support of the German Nazi industrialists," and such an alliance would only lead to the rise of anti-Semitism in the United States and "an emerging native fascism." [46]

If the Marshall Plan was indeed a Wall Street gambit to extend control over the economies of Western Europe, as the Communists claimed, then the Communists were up against the obvious question of why the capitalists of Europe, in defiance of Lenin's theories, should want Marshall Plan aid. The Communists answered that the Western European capitalists, though still devilishly clever, were in retreat. "The 200 families of France and the monopolists of Britain today deliberately chose 'junior partnerships' with the American trusts in the hope that they will succeed in preserving capitalism and in assuring for themselves a sizeable share of the profits." [47]

Curiously, the Communists failed to criticize the Marshall Plan as being partially motivated, as it was, by the beneficial effect it would have on the American economy. Both American management and American labor foresaw the salutary effect that Marshall Plan orders, a kind of federal subsidy, would have on the economy, and they rushed to Washington to partake of the largesse. The shipping industry, for example, both labor and management, got a provision into the act requiring that at least half of all Marshall Plan goods had to be sent in American ships. Communists argued instead that the Marshall Plan would bring depression. "The Marshall Plan takes every possible step, in the name of recovery, to see to it that the European standard of living is drastically reduced. . . . Every major provision of E.R.P. blocks recovery." The resulting European depression would hasten an American depression, always "just around the corner," the Communists asserted. Using an argument reminiscent of Republican campaign literature in the 1920's, the party asked, "What will Phil Murray tell his steel workers when the steel corporations attempt to use the low-paid German workers as strikebreakers by transferring orders to their Ruhr plants?" [48] The Communists never made clear whether the Marshall Plan would hurt American workers with imported depression or imported manufactures, but, in any case, their opposition to the plan was clear.

In response to each development of foreign relations after the Marshall Plan, the Communists continued to reflect Russia's line of criticism. Early in 1949, the United States, Canada, and ten nations of Western Europe signed an agreement creating the North Atlantic Treaty Organization. The twelve nations agreed to coordinate their military organizations and to take common action in the event of an Eastern attack. To the Communists, who called the treaty the "North Atlantic War Pact," N.A.T.O. was another "advance in the domination of American ruling class circles. . . . Wall Street now has a new instrument to advance its insane program for world domination." Capitalism's governmental puppets had heightened the "danger of an atomic war instigated by Wall Street. . . ." [49] President Truman's Point Four program, announced in his inaugural address in January 1949, was a "scheme

. . . to spread the Marshall Plan over the colonial and semi-colonial world. The general economic aim of these proposals is to help bolster up the shaky American economic system . . . to secure financial domination over the colonial and semi-colonial areas, and to build up more military allies for the planned war against the U.S.S.R." [50]

The Communists were as critical of American foreign policy for Asia as they were of the policies for other parts of the world. The purposes of America's China policy, the Communists charged, were the same as its European policy: to encircle and isolate the Soviet Union, to support reactionary regimes, and to reduce the area to the status of "an American tool and appendage." Furthermore, it was American policy to be "soft" on the conquered Japanese just as it was "soft" on the Nazis, which not only revealed the true political sentiments of American imperialists, but afforded them allies against the Russians.[51] When one reads the Communist attacks on the China policy of President Truman and Secretaries of State Marshall and Dean Acheson before the Chinese Communist victory and the "Asia First" attacks on these officials after that victory, one wonders if the two groups were writing about the same people.

For all the Communists' articles hailing Chinese Communist military victories, their attacks on American Far Eastern policy, their abuse of the Chinese Nationalists, and their filiopietistic pieces about Mao Tse-tung, their inspiration and interest lay in Eastern Europe rather than in Asia. To all but a relatively few Americans, Chinese history and the Chinese civil war were a confusing jumble; not fully understanding, most Americans knew only they did not approve of the Chinese Communists. No more sophisticated on these matters than the rest of the population, the American Communists knew only that they and Mao Tse-tung were on the same side.

In the most serious and lasting split in the Communist world to date—the break between Yugoslavia and Russia in June 1948—the American Communists supported the Russians without hesitation. Although the American party was not a member of the Cominform—when the Cominform was established in the fall of 1947 the American party stayed out "because of the present political situation in the United States" [52]—it jumped on Tito as heavily as did any of the Cominform members. Until Tito's excommunication, the American Communists had praised him, and the party had officially backed Yugoslavia in the Trieste dispute with Italy; when Foster returned from a trip through Europe in early 1947, he made a glowing report on Tito and Yugoslavian socialism.[53] After the break, however, Foster and Dennis were quick to belabor Tito for having "deviated from Marxism-Leninism," and they managed to publish their statement in the first issue of the Cominform newspaper to appear after the schism.[54]

In 1945, the American Communists had perceived that the Russian view of the postwar world had changed drastically. Consequently, they abolished their soft wartime line, overthrew their leadership, and developed a new and harder line more in keeping with their understanding of Russian desires. The internal consistency of their new line did not always shine brightly, but they were consistent in their support of the Soviet Union. In guiding and adjusting themselves as world events developed, the American Communists never took their eyes away from the red star in the East.

TWO: THE PARTY LINE FOR AMERICA

I n July 1946, at a routine meeting, the Communist top leadership echelon—the national committee—heard Max Weiss deliver an abstract theoretical report called "The Struggle on the Ideological Front." Weiss had been a leader of the Young Communist League before the war; now he was moving up to the heavyweight class as a party theoretician. There was little that was original in his report, but Weiss ably put into a few pages the fundamental theoretical position of the new line. Through his report, as through the line in general, ran two main threads: the devil-conspiracy theory as an interpretation of the drift of events; and a swing to the left.

The "devils" behind American domestic policy were the same ones who made American foreign policy: Wall Street and its agents, commonly called "lackeys," "puppets," or "tools." As the monopolists were imperialist abroad, they were reactionary, even inclining toward "fascism," at home. And they were as cunning at home as they were abroad. According to Weiss, they were currently engaged in a propaganda campaign to inculcate "a pragmatic contempt for theory among the masses," and they had been quite successful in their sly campaign to popularize the term "management" and take the more personal word "boss" from circulation. "It is time we threw off the 'management' veil and helped the workers uncover the face of the enemy—the trusts, the 60 families!" [1]

The devil-conspiracy theory explained facts that conflicted with basic Communist theory. The Communists had always begun with the assumption—only occasionally explicit—that political virtue resided in the proletariat. But the proletariat did not always behave virtuously by Communist standards. There was, for example, its "pragmatic contempt for theory," or at least for Communist theory. How could this ideological deficiency of the inherently virtuous be explained? The explanation was to blame the bourgeoisie for corrupting the proletariat. Communists used the same method to explain racist attitudes among workers: the bourgeoisie had "infected" the workers with the "virus of white chauvinism."

The Communists clearly had shifted left. That is to say, they were less inclined than they had been to compromise or water down their Communist principles in order to achieve immediate goals short of the ultimate aim of a Soviet America. Yet they were acutely aware that to shift too far left or to appear to be too far left would endanger their position with the groups whose support they needed—the labor movement, non-Communist political liberals, and the Negro movement for equality. Yet they did isolate themselves—as they admitted after the damage was done. There seem to be three main factors in the party's becoming isolated. First, and most importantly, the Communists put their main effort into propaganda and agitation to persuade other Americans to their pro-Soviet views about United States foreign policy. To the Communists, foreign policy had nothing to do with their being in a leftist or rightist, "hard" or "soft" stage; the party always followed their Russian comrades in foreign policy. From 1941 to mid-1945, the United States and Russia were military allies. During these years, the consistent American Communist support of Russia's foreign policy did not harm the party's relationships with non-Communists because the primary aim of Russia's policies was also the main objective of American policies. Indeed, the American party's identification with the Soviet Union actually lent it prestige during the war years, when the might of the Red Army and the tough resistance of the Russian people against the Nazis earned the respect of most Americans. But after the war, American and Russian foreign policies were in conflict, to put it mildly, and the American Communists' support for Soviet foreign policy became a serious disadvantage in their efforts to influence non-Communists on any matter. Second, after the war, the Communists became increasingly negligent, even reckless, about maintaining their bridges to the non-Communist publics whose support, or at least whose neutrality, they vitally needed. Third, the drift of the general non-Communist population after the war was undeniably to the right, toward acceptance of the *status quo,* abandonment of the demand for social reform that characterized the 1930's, perhaps even return to the dominant social values of the years before the Great Depression. While non-Communists drifted right, the Communists shifted left.

One essential Communist tactic to minimize the danger of self-isolation while making a turn to the left was their attempt to build a "broad coalition of all democratic and antifascist peoples" against "the postwar program of Wall Street [which] is directed against the people of our country, no less than against the democratic forces the world over." [2] The tactic required that the Communists not appear to be too far left for popular acceptance; the party understood the problem, the necessity of waging "its fight in such a manner as to achieve the maximum unity—unity within the C.I.O., unity of C.I.O. with A.F. of L., the Railroad Brotherhoods, the miners, unity of labor with the farmers, the Negro people, the veterans." [3] But the party had other devices as well in its effort to make itself attractive to non-Communist "democratic and antifascist peoples."

One device was to intensify the courtship of some middle-class elements that the party had begun in the 1930's. Immediately after the war, the Communists made quite a play for support from middle-class professionals and intellectuals in their belief that "the Battle for the Middle Class is a central issue." The Left Wing president of the United Office and Professional Workers of America, Lewis Merrill, declared there was "no future for creative workers, whether they are in the sciences and professions or elsewhere, in a country completely dominated by the policies of monopoly industry and monopoly finance." The pitch for professionals reached a peak with the republication of an article by the British Communist and scientist J. B. S. Haldane. Haldane described the Soviet Union as a professional's paradise and promised professional people that if they were good at their jobs in a Communist society "you would have more power and more responsibility than you have now." [4]

Another device was to concentrate on issues that they actually scorned as bourgeois reforms. During the summer of 1946, the *Daily Worker* incessantly editorialized in favor of price controls because the cause was popular among non-Communists whose alliance Communists wanted. Party members participated in neighborhood tenants' councils, and they worked hard for rent controls and public housing. In a self-critical mood, the party confessed it had not done enough to "mobilize the American people in the fight for progressive taxation." [5]

Still another method was to exploit some of the style and flavor of the Browderite–Popular Front period of the party but in a different context, to use some of Browder's more successful techniques for different ends. In Browder's era there had been the slogan "Communism is twentieth-century Americanism." The slogan disappeared, but the sentiment did not. The Whitmanesque "We too sing America" theme became even stronger for a few years after the war. There was even an attempt to install pragmatic old Benjamin Franklin, the symbol of the self-made man and the author of Poor Richard's capitalistic homilies, into the pantheon of Communist heroes.[6] Ever prone to glorify the common people in its art—Communist artists had a special weakness for big-muscled, square-jawed men and big-hipped, peasant women as subjects—the movement now went all out for folk music. Back in 1929, during the textile strike at Gastonia, North

Carolina, the Communists had discovered folk music in the person of a little hillbilly striker named Ella May Wiggins, the mother of five children who was killed by a policeman. Browder was a man with small-town Kansas musical tastes and a former flute player in the town band who still gets the instrument out occasionally. He had always encouraged folk music, and after Gastonia the song took root in the movement.[7] But in the postwar era, folk music flourished in the party as it never had before. Guitars were everywhere, and the party member who did not appreciate Pete Seeger, a singing "peoples' artist," was an independent soul indeed.[8]

But for all their Popular Front tone, the Communists had no intention of watering down their Marxism–Leninism in the coalition they hoped to build, of compromising their goal of winning the American masses to "a Socialist outlook." On the contrary, their support of such reformist measures as progressive taxation, public housing, and price and rent control—New Dealish measures, in general—was a trap for non-Communist liberals and a device by which they hoped to further acceptance of Marxism–Leninism. Foster put it this way, using the example of labor: "Organized labor can and should support many of the economic reforms and make-work projects of the New Dealers or Keynesians. . . . Lenin long ago taught the workers to support reforms as by-products of the general class struggle. But, as Lenin also taught, the unions cannot, save at their own peril, accept the general conclusions of these reformers that their proposals will put the capitalist system upon a healthy and progressive basis." Dennis, in a 1946 report to the party's national committee, was a little more candid, saying that "we have correctly warned against and opposed raising the issue of Socialism in the U.S.A. as an immediate slogan of action. But . . . *what is on the order of the day* is the issue of educating and winning millions of American workers and anti-fascists *to a Socialist outlook* . . . the mass education of the American working masses toward the attainment of Socialist consciousness." Perhaps Gilbert

Green, one of the younger members of the national committee, expressed the idea most clearly and succinctly during the up-heaval after the Duclos letter. "Even when we support certain reform measures advanced or supported by liberal-bourgeois forces, we are duty bound to make perfectly clear to the workers and the people that these measures are inadequate . . . while propagating socialism as the ultimate answer." [9]

The Communists recognized that winning the American masses to "a Socialist outlook" would not be an easy task, but they thought a severe economic depression was imminent, and depression would facilitate their task and help them to victory. With depression would come a sharpening of the class struggle, and the workers would soon understand that the "superficial reforms of the New Dealers or Keynesians cannot solve basic problems which grow out of the decay of the capitalist system." The workers would then accept the leadership of the Communist party, "the vanguard party . . . integrally linked with the masses, not separated from them, helping them to move forward [to socialism] and leading them in their forward movement." [10]

The balance of this chapter discusses Communist attitudes and actions on five aspects of American society on which the party took a strong position in the years after the war: the health of the American economy, organized labor, religion, literature, and the Negro. Examination of the Communist position on these five subjects reveals the party's reliance upon the Soviet Union for guidance even on matters peculiarly American, shows the quality of thinking that characterized the party leadership, and indicates much about the party's internal power structure, its methods, and its style.

ANOTHER GREAT DEPRESSION?

During the war, Communists had been optimistic about the post-war economy even when most other people were apprehensive.

During the last days of the European war, Dennis had written optimistically of "the possibility of achieving an expanding post-war domestic economy and a growing world market . . . as well as a constantly rising standard of living. . . ." [11] But then Duclos tipped the party over into a somersault, and the same American economy suddenly was filled with indications of impending doom. The facts were the same but the shape of the lens through which Communists saw them had changed.

Classic Marxism maintains that cyclical convulsions are inevitable in a capitalist economy, and, in their reaction against Browderism, the Communists clutched at this tenet with tenacity. Communists were by no means alone in predicting an economic crisis. Theoretical economists, businessmen, and labor leaders of all shades of political opinion were anxious about a downswing in the business cycle with the end of the war, and they had some justification for their fears. After all, the American economy had emerged from depression only with the advent of war.

The Communists were far more reckless in their predictions of depression than the academic economists. As the postwar boom took shape, they vacillated between denying that prosperity really existed and insisting that the depression was just around the corner. Every tremor in the stock market they heralded as the advent of a crash. When the stock market quivered in early September 1946, the editors of the *Daily Worker* plastered their front page with big type: "Wall Street Hit by 1929 Jitters. Another drop in stock prices . . . which heralds the volcanic eruption to come . . . sharpest drop since 1940. But it is only the beginning. Even before the promised postwar paradise has had a chance to materialize, the inner rottenness of the present social system shows itself. The ghost of the coming crisis stalks the Stock Exchange." [12]

Communists argued that Keynesian measures might delay the depression but could not avert it, though they might minimize the effect of the depression when it came.[13] They ignored programs like the Full Employment Act of 1946, the G.I. Bill of Rights, and the "52-20 clubs," and insisted that business had rejected Keynesian measures because it actually wanted a depression. Foster said businessmen believed "an eventual economic crisis, after an orgy of profitmaking, would advance their overall reactionary plans. . . . They are convinced that with ten or fifteen millions of workers unemployed and half-starved they, patterning after Hitler, would be able to mobilize these hungry multitudes for struggles against democracy in this country and for imperialist aggression abroad." Of course, the capitalists were wrong in thinking that the hungry would turn to fascism. "In a great economic crisis, with the workers in their present militant mood all over the world, things would certainly turn out very differently than the reactionary capitalists now calculate. . . ." [14]

The postwar years moved on, and no depression came; but the Communists continued to predict economic ruin. "It may not take more than two or three years, if that long, before the bottom drops out of the domestic market," said a 1946 party pamphlet. Three years later, the depression was still on its way. The number of predicted unemployed varied from Foster's "ten to fifteen million" to "perhaps thirty million" and "tens of millins." [15] Not until the crisis in the party after the downgrading of Stalin in 1956 was there any hint in Communist literature that their economic "perspective" was faulty, and the article that appeared then was labeled "A Discussion Article" to indicate that the ideas expressed, while they might be considered seriously, were not official.[16]

Why the Communists persisted in their predictions of an imminent major depression is a complex question. No small part of the explanation is the fact that Russian economists insisted that the American economy simply could not behave the way it actually was.

Late in 1946, Eugene S. Varga, an outstanding Soviet economist, published a book entitled *Changes in the Economy of Capitalism as a Result of the Second World War*.[17] Varga was an eminent figure in Russian academic circles. Born in Hungary in 1879, he had become a professor of political economy in Budapest during World War I. In Hungary's Communist regime after the armistice, he was People's Commissar of Finance. When the Hungarian Communists fell from power, he went to Moscow, and in 1929 he became chairman of the Institute of World Economics and World Politics. Varga also enjoyed a considerable reputation abroad. Early in 1944, an American business newspaper published a translation and condensation of one of his articles on postwar currency stabilization.[18] American Communists knew his writings well. He had written regularly for *Inprecorr*, the Comintern journal, during the 1920's and 1930's. In early 1946, *New Masses* published a translation of one of his articles that had appeared in a Russian magazine.[19]

Varga's book was a dry piece of economic analysis—he said in his preface that the book "is not easy reading"; but it attracted world-wide attention. The main question discussed was how the capitalist economies would develop in the postwar era; the book was based on extensive data, much of it from published official material.[20]

Varga discussed the impact of the war upon the American economy and predicted the economic future of the United States. The war had impoverished the capitalist economies of Europe, but those of the United States and, to a lesser extent, Canada had been "really enriched." They had become technologically more efficient during the war. Labor conditions in America had been better in the war years than they had been in Europe, civilian consumption had been markedly better, and industrial production had approximately doubled while production in Europe, particularly in Germany, had declined. Because of these conditions, the United States would not suffer a crisis of underproduction after the war such as Europe would; on the contrary, there would be an economic upsurge for two or three years after the war. But all was not to be rosy for the United States, by any means. The postwar boom would be followed by a crisis somewhat longer than the depression of 1920-21, to be succeeded by an economic cycle less like the cycle of 1921-29 than that of the "special type of depression" which America had after 1929. In general, the postwar period would see a "deepening of the general crisis of capitalism," against which capitalist recovery methods would prove ineffective.

In January 1945, Varga's work had been discussed by prominent Soviet scholars at his institute. The assembled scholars had several carping criticisms to make, but Varga proceeded with his book. In May 1947, twenty leading Soviet scholars gathered again to criticize the finished product. Their meeting was quite an impressive show, and they were merciless in their criticism. In their eyes, Varga had not been sufficiently anticapitalist or anti-American. One of the critics revealed much when he charged that Varga should have given a "clearer" and "more optimistic" answer as to when exactly the "longed for . . . collapse of capitalism" would occur. The scholars were mild compared to the attacks that were to come in the Soviet press. The tenor of the attacks was revealed in *Bolshevik,* February 15, 1948: Soviet economists must be "free of bourgeois objectivism." The American press had noted Varga's writing before all the stir and had characterized it as vigorously anti-American, but it was not anti-American enough for Stalin's postwar society. Varga was "non-Marxist" and "reformist." [21]

Remarkably, Varga did not immediately capitulate before his critics. He defended his main points at the May 1947 meeting, conceding only that he may have made minor errors that did not affect his general conclusions. He stuck to this position for two years before the attacks and the humiliation became too much for him. He was removed as head of his institute. In the Soviet journal *Problems of Economics* in 1949, he recanted completely.[22]

The American Communists reprinted in *Political Affairs* a translation of one of the attacks upon Varga predicting that a severe American depression was imminent. They also printed a translation of one of Varga's *mea culpa* articles, a piece embarrassing even to read, so abjectly did the author strip himself of all dignity. He was as critical of himself for defending his book for two years as he was of the book itself.[23]

The year Varga recanted, American party intellectuals held a "Conference on 'Managed Economy,' the 'Cold War,' and the Developing Economic Crisis" at the party's Jefferson School. They demonstrated they were not Vargas. Party Chairman Foster could not attend the conference, but he sent the group a communication that was quite explicit about what the conference's conclusions should be. For two days, the intellectuals pondered —and came to the recommended conclusions: the new Great American Depression was still just around the corner.[24]

THE LINE FOR LABOR

Since the Communists saw a major depression about to strike America, bringing with it social conditions advantageous for their party, it was imperative to strengthen their position in preparation. And of all elements of the American public, none was so important to the Communists as organized labor, for without considerable direct strength and influence in the labor movement, a Communist party is nothing in an industrial nation. The core of Communist theory is the proletariat, and throughout the Western world the trade union is the institution that most directly and clearly represents industrial workers. Wherever in the Western world there are vigorous Communist parties, the parties have major strength in the trade unions. Western Communist parties that have failed conspicuously have done so primarily because they failed to develop a strong and lasting base in the trade-union movement.

Communists got a foothold in the C.I.O. soon after its foundation in the mid-1930's. C.I.O. President John L. Lewis needed experienced organizers, particularly for the industries with little tradition of unionism. Unorganized workers were ripe for recruitment. The Communist Party and other left political groups were more than willing to offer organizers, and Lewis and other C.I.O. leaders were willing to use the Communists' experience. The C.I.O. leaders did not anticipate that the Communists would use their position to further their own ends. Lewis thought he could use the Communists and not be used by them. He asked David Dubinsky, of the International Ladies Garment Workers Union, when Dubinsky protested the use of Communists, "Who gets the bird—the hunter or the dog?"

In industries where strong unions existed before the birth of the C.I.O., like coal mining, the Communists made little progress. Neither did they gain much in the industries in which Lewis or Sidney Hillman or other established union officers led the organization of workers, such as steel and textiles. But in others, where there was a legacy of union radicalism, like nonferrous mining and smelting or in those like electrical appliances, municipal transport, maritime, and, to a lesser degree, auto, where there was almost no unionism at all and where established C.I.O. leaders did not themselves organize, the Communists were able to establish almost immediate control. Ironically, the vacuum which the Communists filled existed at least partly because the A.F. of L., which was noisily anti-Communist, failed to organize the unskilled workers of basic industry.[25]

A survey of Communist strength in the C.I.O. will come in the next chapter. Suffice it for the moment to say that at the end of the war, from one-fifth to one-fourth of the C.I.O. membership was in unions controlled by Communists or pro-Communists, that several important state and city C.I.O. councils were under Communist influence, and that there were Communists or fellow travelers in significant posts on the national C.I.O. staff.

Almost immediately after the end of the war, there began a wave of strikes unlike any the United States had ever experienced. In 1946, labor set a record for man-hours lost by strikes. The basic reasons for the strikes were many: the release from the generally observed wartime no-strike pledge, which had built up irritation and discontent; a desire to affirm that a unionized

America was really here to stay, and to prevent an antiunion drive from management like that which followed World War I; a wish to maintain wartime take-home pay, swollen by overtime; and a will to raise real wages in the face of steadily mounting prices. The party did all it could to capitalize on the strike wave.

The party now had two designs for the labor movement: to exploit the labor-management crisis to bring about greater labor unity; and to extend the economic fight to politics generally. Repeatedly, the party urged that a national labor strategy committee be set up representing all the major branches of labor— the C.I.O. the A.F. of L., the railroad brotherhoods, and the independent unions. This committee, the party argued, should direct national wage policies and co-ordinate strike strategy. Such a committee, it fondly hoped, would prove to be the nucleus of a united labor movement and an instrument with which the party could extend its influence. A united labor movement would have an important job to do in the economic field, but the real struggle, the party argued, was in politics. Only through political action could come, for example, "the fight against monopoly prices, against monopoly dictation of prices." [26]

But things did not develop to the party's liking at all. Despite the heat of the struggle in the postwar strikes—the strike of the auto workers against General Motors lasted for 118 days—and despite the vacillating policies of the Truman administration toward the strikes, policies that the Communists hopefully thought would disrupt the C.I.O.'s marriage to the Democratic Party, the tide was against the Communists in the trade unions. In fact, the tide of popular opinion generally was turning against the Communists in 1946. Anti-Communism was growing rapidly, a product of the cold war. Early in the year, there was a crisis in the United Nations over the U.S.S.R. and Iran. In March, Winston Churchill delivered his "Iron Curtain" speech, and although the speech did not have as warm a reception as it would have had a year or two later, it was influential. In August, Communist Yugoslavia shot down two American planes, and passions began to grow hot. Throughout the year, apostate Communists told their stories to Congressional committees and to the press. A sharp fight raged between the Communists and the non-Communists over control of a new veterans' organization, the American Veterans Committee. And in November, the voters responded to the new conservative mood that had come over them and elected the first Republican Congress since 1928.

Communists found themselves fighting a losing defensive battle rather than an offensive in organized labor. At the March convention of the United Automobile Workers (C.I.O.), by a narrow vote the vigorously anti-Communist, social-democratic Walter Reuther wrested the presidency of the union from the Communist-supported incumbent, R. J. Thomas. The Reuther group had not won control of the union's executive committee, but the Communists' campaign against Reuther had ended in defeat. Throughout the C.I.O., pressure increased for a purge of Communists from union office.

By the time the C.I.O. met in its annual national convention in Atlantic City in November 1946, the battle between the Communists and the anti-Communists in the organization was too hot to be ignored. The party, of course, wanted no mention of the conflict. Recognizing that they did not have a chance of getting any pro-Communist resolutions from the convention, the best the Communists could hope for was that there would be no anti-Communist resolutions. But as it developed, anti-Communist resolutions were passed, and, ironically, the Communists at the convention voted for them. They even helped to write them.

At a convention of a national labor federation, as at a political convention, the real work is done off the convention floor in committee meetings. At the meetings of the executive board, composed of the presidents of the C.I.O.'s constituent unions, before the convention opened, it became evident that the Communists were going to have a difficult time. The executive board passed a set of amendments to its constitution designed to tighten the national organization's control over the state and local C.I.O.

councils, measures obviously aimed at restraining the activities of
the Communist-dominated councils, of which New York City's
and California's were the most important. Strategic retreat seemed
the best course for the Communists. They remembered the ad-
monition of the party's labor secretary, John Williamson: "We
must avoid tactics that separate the Left and progressive forces
and organizations from the mass of the labor movement." [27]

A factor in the distance of the Communist retreat was the
complex personality of the C.I.O.'s president, the widely respected
Philip Murray. Murray was no ordinary man, or one easy to understand. A Scottish immigrant and coal miner, he had risen in
the ranks of John L. Lewis's United Mine Workers. When the
C.I.O.'s Steel Workers Organizing Committee organized the steel
industry, the mild little man with the Scottish burr was in the
middle of the fight. He became president of the United Steelworkers of America, holding the respect of all factions. A de-
vout Roman Catholic and personally strongly anti-Communist,
Murray was also libertarian. He did not like the Communists in
the C.I.O., but he believed that so long as they were good unionists and adhered to C.I.O. principles they had a right to C.I.O.
membership and to their opinions. Furthermore, although he had
come to be what he was through struggle and had helped to lead
the C.I.O. to what it was through conflict, he was a man of peace.
He did not like feuds, especially feuds that might endanger the
position of the C.I.O. Murray arranged for a compromise between the Communists and the anti-Communists, which was not
as anti-Communist as some wished or as the Communists feared.

Without consulting anyone first, he brought up the matter at
a meeting of the executive board before the convention opened.
He explained that the C.I.O. had been attacked as Communist-
dominated and that in the recent elections candidates had tried
to win votes on the issue. He had stated categorically before that
the organization was not dominated by Communists, but now he
wanted action from the executive board and from the convention
that would refute the allegations. In typical fashion, he appointed

six members of the executive board, three "lefts" and three "rights," to study the matter and report their recommendations back to the full board. The three "rights" were Walter Reuther, Milton Murray, of the Newspaper Guild, and Emil Rieve, of the Textile Workers; the three "lefts" were Ben Gold, of the Furriers and an acknowledged party member, Michael ("Red Mike") Quill, of the Transport Workers Union, and Abram Flaxer, of the State, County and Municipal Workers. The special committee brought back a compromise, and their resolution received a unanimous vote from the presidents of all the constituent unions.

Before reading the resolution before the convention on November 18, Murray gave an obviously extemporaneous speech which briefly explained the resolution's background, its purpose, and his interpretation of it. The resolution, he told the delegates, "should not be construed to be a repressive measure, calculated to do certain things of a repressive nature, but it does provide definitely certain charts and certain courses, that when this subject matter is disposed of, should be and in fact must be adhered to within the councils of the National CIO and all of its affiliates." While at Atlantic City, many people had told him and written him "that this organization of ours should indulge itself in the extravagances of repressive legislation. As the President . . . I should like to be distinctly understood that I am definitely opposed to any form of repression in this movement of ours." But, on the other hand, "there should be strict adherence" to the resolution. He ended on a note that showed his personal view of the party: "It [the resolution] portrays rather vividly this Union's allegiance to one country, and that is the United States of America."

He then read the resolution, of which these are the significant parts:

In our efforts to win economic security and social justice and to unite our movement against the forces of reaction and the enemies of democracy, we reaffirm our faith that these goals can be achieved for the American people through the democratic process and without sacrificing any of our basic human freedoms. . . .

In pursuit of the principles set forth herein and adopted by the CIO Executive Board, we, the delegates . . . *resent and reject efforts of the Communist Party* or other political parties and their adherents *to interfere in the affairs of the CIO.* This convention serves notice that we will not tolerate such interference. [Italics added.]

President Murray put the resolution to a voice vote, and it was unanimously adopted. There was no debate.[28]

Reaction was mixed. *Time* published a photograph of an aging, brooding, and tired Murray walking Atlantic City's boardwalk. Murray, *Time* said, had compromised, but the Communists had suffered a setback. The New York *Times* saw the resolution as a Communist defeat, and published a cartoon of Murray sweeping Communists from the house of labor.[29] The *Jewish Daily Forward* of New York, which had been fighting Communists since the early 1920's, accused Murray of running away from a battle with the party. The Communist rank and file was bewildered. How could it be, they asked themselves, that the presidents of the "left-led" unions, as they were called in the Communist press, assented to a resolution that implied the party interfered in C.I.O. matters and that this interference was resented? The *Daily Worker* hastened to explain. The resolution was unfortunately necessary, the labor editor explained, to prevent "a knock-down and drag-out fight, sharpened division and possibly splits in the C.I.O, more factionalism, possible purges—just what the reactionaries have been looking for hopefully." The editors cheerfully headed their editorial "A Rebuff to Reaction." Ten days later, after seeing how most people had regarded the resolution as a rebuff to the Communists, the *Daily Worker* was not quite so cheerful. George Morris, the paper's labor columnist, wrote, "I don't know of a single Communist who does not feel that the C.I.O. yielded unjustly to reactionary hysteria. . . ." But then, in bold-face type, he said that "there can be no doubt of the correctness of the action of the Communists and all 'lefts' in the convention by their agreement to vote for the statement after they succeeded in eliminating all the major damage that the right wing sought to include in it. That is how a united front works." [30] But not all the damage had been eliminated, and certainly that was not the way the party wanted to see a united front work.

To explain the fact that the Communists in the labor movement were on the defensive, the party fell back upon its devil-conspiracy theory. Big business was corrupting the labor movement, and the devil's imps were the social democrats; big business used social democrats to do its dirty work in labor circles. "It is a noteworthy fact that Wall Street imperialism finds it useful and necessary to build up . . . Social Democratic labor leaders . . . for its own reactionary purposes. . . . Social-Democrats pose as progressives. . . . They are, in fact, masked reactionaries who perform their disruptive role in their own distinctive way." No term was too harsh for a social democrat. Foster called Norman Thomas a "drum major for imperialism," Victor Riesel's labor column a "pipeline" from Wall Street, and Riesel himself a "Pinkerton." [31] Riesel by 1946 was no longer a social democrat, but since he had once been managing editor of the *New Leader* when it was published by the Social Democratic Federation, he was fair game. But it was another former social democrat, Walter Reuther, who drew the lion's share of Communist abuse. To the Communists, Reuther's rise in the union was proof that "the bourgeoisie resorts to methods of hot-house cultivation and forced growth to produce the needed crop of Social-Democratic spokesmen who may assume leadership in its behalf within labor's ranks." [32]

Working with the social democrats, of course, were the party's special demons, the Trotskyites.[33] And in the years after the war, the Communists rediscovered a forgotten or neglected enemy, the Vatican.

THE PARTY AND RELIGION

It is clear that the party after the war hardened its opposition to religion. It became more opposed to organized religion than it had been, or at least it now expressed its opposition openly, and it also became more outspokenly opposed to religion itself as distinct from religious institutions.

Meanwhile, the American people in general were moving in the opposite direction. There had been a resurgence of religion in the United States since Pearl Harbor. Granted that some of the resurgence reflects appearance rather than reality, granted that there is a secular motivation for some people's religious activities, and granted that there is a considerable amount of religiosity in the United States with only a superficial religious significance, nevertheless, there seems to have been a growth of truly religious thought and feeling.

The Communists were most disturbed about Roman Catholicism. Historically anti-Marxist, Roman Catholics constitute a very large part of the American working class. To offend these workers' religious sensibilities while trying to attract them ideologically would seem to be poor tactics, but that is the course the Communist Party took. During the Browder period, the party had played down its antireligious views and had developed the "outstretched hand policy" toward Catholics. Now the party withdrew the outstretched hand. "We must avoid our error of the past in which we told ourselves that we were extending the 'outstretched hand,' when clerical reaction was offering us a mailed fist," wrote the editor of *Political Affairs*. "That illusion was part of the Browderite roseate prospect of the progressive postwar role of 'enlightened imperialism.' " [34]

The Roman Catholic Church was certainly vigorously anti-Communist; in the early 1950's, some prominent American Catholic clerics and some diocesan newspapers allowed their anti-

Communism to push them into unthinking extremism that often endangered civil liberties.

To Communists, the Church of Rome was a tool of Wall Street and imperialism. "With Social-Democracy . . . now greatly diminished in strength as compared with the period following World War I, imperialism leans increasingly upon the Vatican. . . . Today the Vatican shares with Social-Democracy the task of ideological mobilizer of the masses on the side of imperialism and its anti-Soviet crusade." [35] Foster, in an antireligious chapter no American Communist leader would have permitted himself in the previous decade, declared in his 1949 book, *The Twilight of World Capitalism,* that "the Catholic Church . . . is a most militant champion of capitalist reaction; it is a major force in the present attempt of Wall Street imperialism to preserve the capitalist system by setting up a fascist world under American domination." [36]

Had the Communists restricted their criticism to the Church's leaders, making a distinction between religious institutions and religious feeling, they might have made a little progress in their "struggle . . . to drive a wedge between the reactionary Heirarchy and the masses in the Church." [37] But the Communists directed their fire at religion itself as well. Foster approvingly quoted Marx on religion as "the opium of the people" and wrote that as capitalism conquered feudalism, "The capitalists quickly came to realize that . . . they had to have religion . . . to pacify so far as possible their inherently rebellious workers." Foster was as harsh toward Protestantism and Judaism as toward Catholicism. He found any religious faith a "superstition." [38]

But despite the party's antireligion, there remained, both within the party and around its fringes, a few religious people, even some ministers. There is a rather strong tradition in the United States of religiously inspired economic, social, and political reform that has at times been radical. This tradition has been strongest within Protestantism—there was a significant group of Protestant ministers in the old Debs Socialist organization—but the tradition is present also within Judaism and, to a lesser degree, within Catholicism. What strength the Communists have had among church people has been largely the tag end of this historic tendency. Others have been attracted by the party's emphasis on peace, although Communist motivation on the peace issue was hardly that of Christian pacifists. Some Negro churchmen have been in and around the party.

Religious Communists, however, have never been important leaders in the party. They have been only window dressing. Their advice and their point of view have never gained party acceptance. For example, when William Howard Melish, former rector of a Brooklyn Protestant Episcopal church who had a weakness for Communist fronts, advised that "The progressive movement has a lot to learn about the potential of a Jewish-Christian tradition," [39] his words went unheeded. Early in 1947, the editors of the *Daily Worker* stopped publishing the column of Eliot White, a Massachusetts Episcopalian clergyman and party member who had contributed a column to each Saturday edition for years.

The party did not even attempt to use religion as a weapon in the class struggle, as it tried to do with art and literature.

"ART IS A WEAPON"

In art and literature, as in other fields, the Communists went off in one direction after the war while the rest of the population went in the other. The party longed to see a rebirth of the proletarian novel, of "proletarian culture" generally, which had enjoyed a vogue in the 1930's. But no such movement developed. Most American writers, painters, and musicians turned away from social themes altogether. Since the war, writers—and readers—have concerned themselves to an unusual degree with such themes as the individual's adjustment, or maladjustment, to his environment and to his search for self. The novel has tended to become more psychoanalytic than social.

With the slogan "Art Is a Weapon" and all that this implied, the party failed badly to discern the drift of American thought. Indeed, the party failed to recognize some developments in recent cultural history that particularly concerned it. The proletarian novel, as Granville Hicks has reminded us, was not a really popular art form even at its high tide in the 1930's. These novels did not sell well, and leftist writers complained that publishers discriminated against them.[40] The party might well have heeded the reception of one of the last serious proletarian novels to be published, Ruth McKenney's *Jake Home,* which appeared in 1943.

Jake Home was published three years before Ruth McKenney was expelled from the party. She was undeniably a competent writer. Her light novel *My Sister Eileen* had been a commercial triumph, and her *Industrial Valley,* an only slightly fictionalized account of how unionism came to northeastern Ohio, had been exciting reading despite its partisanship. But *Jake Home* deserved and got a poor reception. Reading it today, one wavers between incredulity and hilarity, and readers in 1943 thought little better of it. The New York *Times* reviewer insisted upon treating the book as a burlesque. Clifton Fadiman, while commenting there was some good writing in the novel, objected to its "dated ideology." Even Browder, who was revered in the book to the point of embarrassment, thought it was "awful, simply awful." [41]

But the party leadership after the war ignored the previous reception and quality of proletarian novels and called upon Left Wing artists to rush in and satisfy the developing demand for "people's culture." Foster advised them: "The next years will show a tremendous resurgence of progressive spirit in every cultural field . . . awakening masses and peoples will increasingly demand the voice of every kind of artist in their struggle against reactionary capitalists, especially big American capital. Hence our Party must be fully prepared to play a vital leading role in the broad cultural movement of the people. . . ." [42]

Despite the changing tide of taste, Communist writers might have been able to gain a hearing if they had written works of artistic merit. The party was so insistent that "people's culture" reflect the party line exactly—as Albert Maltz soon discovered—that it sacrificed art for ideological purity.

Albert Maltz, today known as "The Pope" in the Communist expatriate colony in Mexico where he lives, had written such movies as "This Gun for Hire," "Destination Tokyo," and "Pride of the Marines," the sum of which was something less than a rich cultural experience. He had written some books which indicated talent. Early in 1946, *New Masses* published an article of his that was essentially a plea for the integrity of the Left Wing artist. He argued that a literary work must be judged on its artistic merits rather than on its ideology. He praised the writings of non-Communist and anti-Communist leftist novelists like James T. Farrell, Lillian Smith, and Richard Wright, saying that "Writers must be judged by their work, *not* by the committees they join." He deplored Farrell's committees, but said they did not detract from Farrell's stature as a writer.[43]

The reaction to Maltz's article was immediate and devastating. The party's national committee was in session in New York the week the article appeared. In giving the main report to the committee, Dennis stressed the "purity of theory [which] devolves upon every leader and member of the Party, upon every Party organization, institution and publication. . . ." Thoughts of impurity reminded Dennis of Maltz. "The need for exercising great vigilance against the smuggling of hostile ideas into our midst is brought home to us by the current issue of *New Masses,* which prints a bourgeois-intellectual and semi-Trotskyist article on the subject of the Party and the writers, an article which advocates 'citizenship' to Trotskyite writers in the camp of the Left. That this could have been published in a magazine professing a Marxist viewpoint only serves to warn us of the immensity of the task before us in the struggle we must wage against rotten-liberalism and an enemy-class ideological infiltration." [44]

Communist writers were quick to get the point. Mike Gold, a *Daily Worker* columnist with pretensions to the title of Great

Proletarian Novelist, was the first to attack. "Albert Maltz seems to have let the luxury and phony atmosphere of Hollywood at last to poison him." This was no time to be wishy-washy toward anti-Communists, because "The capitalists are plotting . . . to establish an American fascism as a prelude to an American conquest of the world." Joseph North soon joined the attack. So, too, did Howard Fast. Maltz's Hollywood colleagues Alvah Bessie and John Howard Lawson jumped on their fellow scenarist.[45]

In 1947, Maltz, as one of the "Hollywood Ten," was to stand firm in his beliefs and defy J. Parnell Thomas and his House Committee on Un-American Activities. But in 1946, he neither stood firm nor defied the attacks of his friends and the party leadership. He recanted, utterly and abjectly. He crawled. Under a particularly arty photograph of himself, with a strong light behind his head à la Hollywood, Maltz published an article, ironically called "Moving Forward," in the *Worker:* "I consider now that my article—by what I have come to agree was a one-sided, non-dialectical treatment of complex issues—could not, as I had hoped, contribute to the development of left-wing criticism and creative writing. I believe also that my critics were entirely correct in insisting that certain fundamental ideas in my article would, if pursued to their conclusion, result in the dissolution of the left-wing cultural movement." Before he concluded the article in the next day's edition, Maltz had even taken to task anyone who had defended him.[46] The "art is a weapon" campaign could now go on, purged clean of "rotten-liberalism." By the fall of 1946, this "weapon" theme had gone so far that the *Daily Worker*'s sports editor, Bill Mardo, was saying, "Yes, sports is a weapon," as he organized a basketball league for Left Wing trade-unionists.[47]

In such an intellectual atmosphere, it was not surprising that art did not develop. *New Masses* lost whatever sparkle and zest it ever possessed, and it never approached the level of ferment of the old *Masses* before World War I. When the old *Masses* advertised "Read the Masses and Enjoy the Revolution," it meant it. But *New Masses* took everything with ponderous seriousness, especially itself. In the spring of 1947, *New Masses* merged with *Mainstream* to become *Masses & Mainstream,* but it picked up no intellectual spark in the process. Its publishers estimated its circulation at 5,600.

The banality of the product that resulted from the "art is a weapon" campaign is difficult fully to describe, but a synopsis of a short story that appeared in the *Daily Worker* on Christmas Day, 1946, will suffice. The story was written by Herb Tank, a strong-armed seaman with literary aspirations who later became Harvey Matusow's bodyguard, and it was about "Jerusalem Slim and the Twelve Bindlestiffs." "A long time ago there was this Carpenter, a tall slim fellow. That's why I call him Slim. Well, this Carpenter Slim plied his trade somewhere around the Mediterranean ports. In some burg called Nazareth, I think." His career eventually alarmed "the fat boys." "The big boys over in Rome didn't like it at all. 'Got to get rid of this agitator,' they said. 'Got to put an end to this radical talk.' One of the big wheels among the fat boys put his goon squads on the job. They went fishing around the twelve bindlestiffs figuring they ought to be able to buy at least one of them off."

"Sure enough, one of the twelve bindlestiffs was ready to rat for a price. And his price was cheap, too. Then the vigilantes, the stormtroopers, turned on the radical Carpenter and they lynched Him."

This was American Communist culture in the postwar era. In 1949, this story was deemed worthy of inclusion in an anthology of the best pieces to appear in the *Daily Worker* in twenty-five years.[48]

THE PARTY AND THE NEGRO

The Communist Party after the war misread the aspirations of American Negroes as badly as it failed to detect new currents in religion and literature. The party wrongly predicted the direction

American Negroes were to take in their fight for the elimination of racial discrimination and pursued policies that tended to isolate it from the main stream of the Negro movement.

Since 1945, the Negro's fight for equal rights has been a most significant part of social history. Much, very much, remains to be done, but clearly the Negro has come a long way toward full citizenship since 1945 in the achievement of such gains as abolition of racial segregation in the armed forces, the near elimination of lynching, state fair employment practices laws, and the recognition by white politicians of the potency of the northern Negro vote. There have been important partial victories: the acceptance of Negroes in more and more fields of economic activity, the decline of racial discrimination in public transportation, and, most important, the Supreme Court's decision on racial segregation in the public schools.

The Communist Party, however, has contributed almost nothing to the winning of these achievements. (Curiously, Communists abroad have had an indirect salutary effect on the American Negro question. Part of the motivation behind white acceptance of Negro reforms is embarrassment in the ideological cold war and a desire to win the confidence of colored people in Asia and Africa.) The party, in fact, lost almost all its influence in the Negro movement at precisely the time when Negroes were making their greatest advance since post-Civil War reconstruction. In 1956, the Communists admitted as much.

The party became virtually isolated from the Negro movement, and the isolation was a disaster from the Communists' point of view, for ever since the late 1920's, they had put a major emphasis upon winning Negroes to their cause. The reason for the Communist concern for influence among Negroes is easy to discern. Here was a tenth of the population which, with perhaps the exception of the American Indians and some Latin Americans, was the most exploited and oppressed minority group in the United States, a group relegated because of its color to what a nineteenth-century Englishman would have called "the lower orders." Its attraction to Communism appeared to be a relatively simple matter. There was always some kind of an outrage against decency and democracy to which the Communists could point and say to Negroes, "Look what the white capitalists are doing to you; join us to end your degradation." That American Negroes have for the most part ignored and resisted the Communists, have refused to be an easy mark, speaks much for their common sense and their integrity.

Back in the 1920's, the American Communists had paid their Russian comrades the supreme compliment of imitation when they adopted a policy called "national self-determination for the Negro people in the Black Belt." This jargon meant that in a Soviet America there would be in the most heavily Negro populated part of the South an autonomous Negro republic, or—and here the Communists hedged a little—Negroes would be enabled to create such a subrepublic if they so wished. Stalin had developed theories on the Soviet "national question." The Soviet empire was composed of a considerable variety of nationalities, a Union of Soviet Socialist Republics, in which, theoretically, each nationality constituted an autonomous republic bound together in the union by socialist brotherhood. There was a vast difference between Stalin's theory and Stalin's practice, but the American Communists refused to see a difference. The Soviet national republics were actually considerably less autonomous than, say, Texas. But for the American Communists nothing would do but that they apply Stalin's theory to the American Negro.

Another aspect of the Communists' adoption of the slogan was that it afforded them an opportunity to point up a supposed parallel between the American Government and the Negro on the one hand and, for example, England and India on the other. The slogan was partly a device for crying "imperialism."

Needless to say, the idea of an autonomous Negro republic, with the kind of supersegregation that would involve—"Red Crow," its opponents labeled it—proved less than a howling success in attracting American Negroes to the party. Nor had the idea much appeal for whites. After the swing to the Popular Front idea in the mid-1930's, the party let the national self-determination slogan go unused, although they did not officially abandon the theory.

What attraction the party had for Negroes was a result of its "practical" Negro work, its coming to the aid of Negroes who were victims of some kind of injustice. For this kind of work, some of which was carried on quietly and unheard of among the whites and some of which received the most blatant publicity, non-Communists and anti-Communists owe the Communists due credit. If the party's purposes were cynically to capitalize on tragedy (and they were), if the party inflated instances of injustice beyond the facts of the case (and it did), and if the party made difficult the resolution of cases by its very presence and thereby added the "Red issue" to the Negro's burden (and again it did), still the party fought vigorously when too many Americans sat complacently on their hands and clucked disapproval. The Communists dramatized the Negro issue, whatever their purpose, and brought cases to attention that otherwise might never have been noticed beyond a few restricted circles.

During World War II, the Communists dropped national self-determination even as a theory. Browder explained in the party's magazine. ". . . we Communists . . . faced the possibility that the Negro people, disappointed in their aspirations for full integration into the American nation, might find their only alternative in separation and in the establishment of their own state in the Black Belt. . . . We raised this as one of the rights of the Negro people, in case the Negro people found this was the only way to satisfy their aspirations." But now, Browder continued, "The crisis of history has taken a turn of such character that the Negro people . . . have found it possible to make their decision once and for all. Their decision is for their complete integration into the American nation as a whole, and not for separation." [49]

In the 1945 reaction against Browderism, it was perhaps inevitable that the Communists should change their line on the Negro question. They changed it officially after over a year of discussion —back to the old national self-determination line.

Statements of dissatisfaction with Browder's Negro position began to appear almost immediately after the publication of the Duclos letter. James W. Ford, a Harlem Negro who had been the party's candidate for vice-president in 1932 and 1936, was one of the first to start the line in the new direction. Before the party's special convention, Benjamin J. Davis, Jr., a Negro New York City councilman elected on the Communist ticket and the party's most important Negro leader, brought back national self-determination into the discussion. Since Davis had once said that he, as a Negro, should have seen the wisdom of dropping national self-determination before Browder did, he had special penance to pay. He restored the hoary old slogan.[50]

However, the party wanted time to formulate its position. The reconstituted party's first resolution skirted the subject of national self-determination and said only that Communists had recently "glossed over the national character of the Negro question." The resolution called for the creation of a special party commission to undertake a study of Negro conditions and trends and "in the light of Marxist-Leninist theory, to formulate a comprehensive definition of Communist policy and program on the Negro question." [51]

Claudia Jones, a young New York Negro originally from the West Indies and since deported, first endeavored to prove that the "Negro people in the Black Belt constitute a nation." The Black Belt, by her definition, was a wildly shaped territory that "stretches contiguously westward from the Eastern shore of Maryland, and lies within" every Southern state except Kentucky, Missouri, and Oklahoma. Others on the commission accepted her definitions. She took her criteria of what constituted nationality from Stalin in his *Marxism and the National and Colonial Question*. These criteria were a common language, a common history and culture, a common territory, and a common economic life. The others accepted these, but they were not unanimously in agreement with her that the Negroes did in fact meet the criteria. By ignoring the fact that Negroes and whites together met Stalin's criteria of nationality, and rejecting other criteria, she concluded that Negroes were in fact a full-fledged nation—not a potential nation, nor a developing nation, but a here-and-now nation. Being a nation and an oppressed people, Southern Negroes bore, then, the same relationship to American imperialism as the Indonesians and the Indians bore to Dutch and British imperialism. Apparently defining "national self-determination" to mean the choice of Negroes to move either toward integration or toward territorial separation, a choice she vehemently insisted American Negroes had not yet made, she concluded that "the right to self-determination of the Negro people in the Black Belt" should be raised as a *"programmatic demand"* but not as a "slogan of immediate action." If the distinction was fuzzy, it was not uniquely so in Miss Jones's confused article.[52] Max Weiss followed with an article entitled "Toward Clarity on the Negro Question," a quality sorely needed at that point. What Weiss wanted was clear enough. He wanted a black republic, immediate redrawing of Southern electoral boundary lines, and a redivision of the land ownership.[53]

But other commission members were not so sure of the wisdom of a black republic. Francis Franklin, hardly sounding like the Left deviationist he was alleged to be some months later, warned that Negroes *"definitely do not want even to hear"* about any kind of separation. Their *"passionate desire"* was for equality and integration. Yet Franklin did not reject national self-determination in all circumstances.[54] Doxey Wilkerson, easily the best-qualified member of the commission by his experience and education, held a master's degree from the University of Kansas and had been a professor at Virginia State College and at Howard University. As a trained Negro social scientist, he had been an assistant to Gunnar Myrdal when Myrdal had done the work for his important book on the American Negro question, *An American Dilemma.*[55] Wilkerson wrote that consideration of American Negroes as a nation offered only "political insights," arguing that they had the characteristics of a nation only "in rudimentary form." "The overwhelming majority of the Negro people," he warned, "abhor and reject any proposal that they separate—in any form whatever, even temporarily—from the American nation as a whole." To revive self-determination in the Black Belt as a slogan or to affirm the idea as the party's theoretical position "would be theoretically incorrect and . . . tactically disastrous." [56]

In a few years, Wilkerson would be in a position to say, I told you so, but in 1946 he fought a losing battle. People with considerably more stature in the party than he—Wilkerson had not been a member for long—made it clear that Wilkerson was "incorrect." James S. Allen, a white man widely respected as a party theoretician, led the campaign against Wilkerson. Perhaps part of the reason for the sharp attack on Wilkerson was that he had written his article after Foster had already published an article on the subject taking the opposite side of the argument.[57]

In December 1946, the party's national committee adopted a resolution on the Negro question that recognized the national self-determination idea. "In fighting for their equal rights, the Negro people are becoming more unified as a people. Their fight for liberation from oppression in the Black Belt . . . is a struggle for full nationhood, for their rightful position of full equality as a nation." Negroes might even achieve full nationhood before America became "socialist." However, "The Communist Party does not attempt to impose any specific solution in advance of the form in which the right of self-determination will be exercised; nor does it prematurely raise self-determination as an immediate slogan of action." [58] The step back to the old party position was now complete.

One can only speculate upon the leadership's motivation in reviving this ideological relic. Foster recognized that the idea had not been popular among Negroes in the past; he even conceded that the "lack of response" had amounted "in many cases to vigorous opposition." Yet he was for national self-determination. Probably a large part of their motive was to "turn the clock back" to a time before Browder had identified himself with a Negro line. Evidence for this hypothesis lies in the frequent criticisms of Browder that sprinkled the debate on the Negro question. Another possibility is that the leadership wanted to reaffirm its orthodoxy to the international movement. Stalin, who undoubtedly knew less about American Negroes than the worst-informed American party member, was cited as the supreme authority several times in the discussion. Foster and Jones were particularly fond of quoting "that great expert on the national question, Stalin." [59]

And it is possible that the new Negro line was an attempt, although a clumsy one, to exploit both the movement for integration and the strain of Negro nationalism that does exist in black America. A reader of the general Negro press cannot fail to detect a current, although not a strong one, of color nationalism. This may have been a foggy idea in the back of Foster's head when he wrote that "the orientation of the Negro people is first, toward full participation of their national consciousness." [60]

Whatever their motivation, the policy of national self-determination, even if not waved "as an immediate slogan of action," proved again to be a soggy dud in the Negro community. The Communists could truthfully deny that their resolution said anything about segregation into a black republic, but the precise nature of the party's position was too abstract, too much like walking an intellectual tightrope, to be popularly understood. And the Negro community hated anything that smelled the least bit like separation. Whatever attraction the party had for Negroes after the war was because of its practical work and despite its theoretical position. In other words, what success it had was due, ironically, to a pragmatic attitude rather than to Marxist-Leninist-Stalinist orthodoxy.

In one other respect, the party hurt itself among American Negroes. It attacked respected and popular Negro leaders with all the calumny it could muster. The Communists' favorite target was A. Philip Randolph, once a Norman Thomas Socialist. At various times, Communists called him a "demagogue," an "imperialist," a "saboteur" of FEPC, and a "secret ally" of Senator Theodore Bilbo. Dr. Ralph J. Bunche was not held in respect among Negro Communists. A Negro columnist for the *Daily Worker* wrote that

Bunche had won the Nobel peace prize only "for his services to the western imperialist warmongers." [61] Comments such as these would have been better calculated to win friends in the Mississippi Democratic committee than to attract support in Harlem and in Chicago's South Side.

Nor did the party's open effort to capture the N.A.A.C.P. advance its purposes. The effort merely drew counterattacks from N.A.A.C.P. leaders, who speak for American Negroes with more authority than any other group. Seldom have the Communists allowed to appear in print such an open statement of intention to infiltrate an organization as was Henry Winston's advice to the party on the N.A.A.C.P. [62]

As if all these tactics were not enough self-inflicted wounds, the party began even during its 1945 crisis to forge a weapon with which in just a few years it would create havoc in its own ranks. Ben Davis started it all in July 1945 with one sentence: "We have relaxed vigilance against white chauvinism even in our own ranks for which we are paying dearly." [63] "White chauvinism" was Communist jargon for prejudice against Negroes. Davis's idea grew quickly. "The Present Situation and the Next Tasks" called for "a vigorous struggle to root out every manifestation of open or concealed white chauvinism in our own ranks." The following winter, Dennis ordered the members "to burn out the infamy of white chauvinism" among them, and the resolution on the Negro question of December 1946 repeated the cry: "By its own actions, the Communist Party must set an example before the whole labor movement . . . white chauvinism within its ranks, whether it manifests itself openly or in concealed form, must be systematically combatted and expunged." [64] All this talk of white chauvinism, the term Communists invariably used, within the party itself must have made Negroes a little wary about what kind of people the Communists were. The results were to become worse from the party's own point of view. In 1949, the campaign to stamp out white chauvinism within the party was to become a full-fledged witch hunt, a purge with disastrous results.

The reconstituted Communist Party's postwar line on America did not serve it well. The Foster leadership badly misjudged the health of the American economy, had to go on the defensive in the labor movement, offended many Americans' religious sensibilities, saw its cultural program lapse into banality, and flew in the face of what it itself recognized to be the temper of the Negro movement. Here and there, individual party members saw the way things were going and protested—or just quietly quit the party.

The top leadership, however, insisted it was right. "There are . . . those," said Henry Winston to the national committee in 1947, "who draw the conclusion that our Party is moving against the stream. . . . Can it be said that such is the situation today? . . . it is not true that our Party is moving against the stream. Indeed, the very opposite is true. Our Party is moving with the great body of democratic-minded Americans. . . . It is only by thus correctly estimating the situation in our country today that we can be in a position to speak to the rank and file, to the millions, and win them for the program of our Party." [65]

THREE: PARTY ORGANIZATION, PARTY STRENGTH, AND PARTY LIFE

L/ike other organizations in the United States, the Communist Party had an elaborate constitution, which, if carefully examined and explained, reveals a great deal about the party's structure and methods. The party's zeal for organizational efficiency and its tendency toward bureaucracy were so great that it frequently ignored the letter of its constitution. Nevertheless, making due allowances for operational deviations, the constitution is basic to an understanding of the party.

Few rank-and-file members had more than a slight familiarity with the party constitution. In the summer of 1956, during the party's great crisis over the downgrading of Stalin, one member wrote the *Daily Worker* suggesting that it print the constitution in full since few members had ever possessed a copy of it and many had never read it. Several days later, he wrote again, repeating his request, adding that when his party unit had decided to have a discussion of the constitution it had been unable to obtain a copy even when members went to the next higher party echelon.[1]

The constitution began, conventionally enough, with a preamble of generalities.[2] The preamble described the organization as "the political party of the American working class, basing itself upon the principles of scientific socialism, Marxism-Leninism." The party attached itself to the American democratic tradition, to the "traditions of Jefferson, Paine, Lincoln and Frederick Douglass, and the great working class traditions of Sylvis, Debs and Ruthenberg." In actuality, the party was far closer to Ruthenberg than any of the others. Ruthenberg was a Cleveland office worker who helped to split the Communists off from the Socialists in 1919, later became the party's number one leader, and was buried in the Kremlin wall in 1927. The preamble also pledged the party's support to a number of reforms which most liberal Republicans and Democrats would support, but declared that American problems could be solved finally only through socialism, "the highest form of democracy." The preamble described the party's mission as the education of the working class for socialism through its everyday struggles.

The party constitution made a vague and ambiguous disclaimer of revolutionary intent and advocacy of violent overthrow of the United States Government. Article II stated that the party's purpose was "the establishment of Socialism by the free choice of the majority of the American people," but the document said nothing on the question of whether this "free choice" was to be exercised by the ballot and other constitutional means or by the use of force outside of law. In the discussion of "different roads to socialism" that developed in the party's 1956-57 crisis, in which some Communists urged that the party renounce revolutionary force, the implication was clear that theretofore the party had not envisaged constitutional methods. The constitution also declared that "adherence to or participation in the activities of any clique, group, circle, faction or party which conspires or acts to subvert, undermine, weaken or overthrow any or all institutions of American democracy" was grounds for immediate expulsion from the party. The party, however, never used this clause. The clause could have been invoked against the left deviationists who were expelled, but, instead, those leftists were always charged with rejection of party discipline.

Most of the party constitution pertained to organization. The basic unit in the party was the club, which sometimes was still called by its older names, the "branch" or "local." The Communists did not use the term "cell" after the 1920's. With a few exceptions, all members belonged to a party club. The exceptions were a few members at large, or "floaters." Not even rank-and-file members knew who the floaters were.[3] There were three categories of party clubs: community clubs, shop clubs, and industrial clubs. The community club was to provide leadership in such community problems as housing and education, but it was to do so in such a way as to perform its primary "task of promoting the systematic socialist education of the people." In other words, community clubs exploited local problems as a way to propagandize.[4]

To the party leadership, the shop club was the most important basic unit. Composed of party members who worked within a single factory or plant, "It [provided] the best method for the Party to keep in constant touch with the most important section of the working class and to defend the economic and political interests of labor and the nation." The industrial club was a special and infrequently used device. Members of industrial clubs were workers within a number of shops in the same industry. If Communist membership in the industry increased sufficiently, a number of shop clubs superseded the industrial club.[5]

The national leadership was eager to increase the number of shop clubs and thereby increase its influence in industry, especially basic industry, vital to any revolutionary organization. National organization secretaries hammered away at this "concentration policy" in their reports, emphasizing its importance and complaining about its relative lack of success. In November 1945, for example, John Williamson, the national organization secretary until he became national labor secretary in mid-1946, proposed that "six of our most experienced and leading comrades" be sent as special organizers to work in the basic industries of Youngstown, Gary, Flint, McKeesport, Toledo, and Kansas City. Where the concentration policy had a measure of success, the party considered the results gratifying. It claimed that if it had not been for Communists on the New York waterfront, the 1945 longshoremen's strike would have been lost in a day or two. "Instead, it was able to last eighteen days and as a result forced economic concessions . . . and organized a force for democracy within the union and against [Joseph P.] Ryan." The party asserted that the concentration policy stimulated labor militancy. During the 1946 steel strike, Williamson declared, "In Indiana Harbor, where we had a live and active mill branch, the vote for the strike was 18 to 1. In South Chicago, in the big mill where we have long had influence and today have a branch that functions fairly well, the vote was 12 to 1. In Gary, however, where we were slow in organizing mill branches and in developing Party work, the strike vote was only 5 to 1." [6]

Above the clubs were the state organizations and whatever other levels between the state and the local the party wanted to create. The larger state organizations, the New York and the California, for example, had two and sometimes three levels of organization between themselves and the club. New York had city, county, and section organizations. In the Coney Island area of Brooklyn, for example, there were several clubs, which together constituted the Coney Island section, which was part of the Brooklyn or Kings County organization. The county organization, in turn, had the city organization between itself and the state party. So many links in the chain of command, of course, made it extremely difficult for a club to exert influence upward through the rest of the organization. But a centralized corps of professional party workers, or "cadres," made command efficient from the top down.

The area embraced by a party club or section depended upon how densely concentrated was the membership. Particularly in New York City, a club might embrace only a neighborhood; but in smaller cities there might be only one club in the community. In some parts of New York there were enough party members in one apartment building to constitute a club. Isadore Begun, Bronx County chairman, gloated over one building in which there were ten members: "Just think, if you want to call a meeting all you have to do is knock on the steam pipe." [7]

The party constitution empowered the national organization with authority to create districts from two or more state organizations. Thus, the national body created the New England district, of which the Massachusetts party was the most important. National headquarters also, without express constitutional authority, divided the Pennsylvania organization into two districts, one centered in Pittsburgh, the other in Philadelphia.

In theory, the highest authority in the party was the national convention, but in fact, it was the national secretariat of four or five leaders at national headquarters. The top leaders displaced the convention through a variety of techniques. One was to ignore the constitutional injunction for a national convention every other year. A national convention met in July 1945 to reconstitute the party and adopt the constitution, but three years elapsed before the next convention, in August 1948. Another convention met in December 1950, but after that there was none until February 1957. However, even the conventions were routine meetings under the top leadership's direction. At no convention until that of February 1957 was there any important dissent from the views of the national leaders, and then the dissent came because the national leadership itself was divided. Moreover, sometimes national headquarters simply ignored or reinterpreted resolutions passed by the national convention.

Each national convention elected a national committee, composed of members from all over the nation, who were expected to meet at least three times annually. The national committee elected a national board, later called the national executive committee, formerly called the political bureau, or politburo, to act in its behalf between meetings. The constitution made no provision for a secretariat, but this smaller group of the national board actually ran the party's day-to-day activities. Thus, there were three levels of leadership at the national level besides the national convention. In 1945 and early 1946, the secretariat was composed of Foster, Dennis, Thompson, and Williamson. In July 1946, Henry Winston, a thirty-five-year-old Negro veteran, born in Mississippi, who joined the party in Kansas City in 1930, moved up into the secretariat.[8]

The party's high degree of centralization was entirely in keeping with established Communist practice and theory. Grigori Zinoviev in 1920 laid down "democratic centralism" as one of the "Twenty-one Conditions for Admission to the Communist International," and centralism, if not "democratic" centralism, has been an essential feature of the American Communist Party ever since. The constitution of 1945 used the words "democratic centralism" only once, and then in a manner that emphasized democracy rather than centralism: "In accordance with the principles of democratic centralism . . . Communist Party members shall be involved in the formulation of major policies and shall have the right and duty to examine the execution of policies."

Theoretically, democratic centralism was a system of organization in which each party echelon elected the next higher echelon and agreed to abide by the decisions of the higher body. In practice, elections by lower bodies were minimized and control was emphasized. In other words, the Communist Party was organized from the top down rather than the bottom up; it was centralized rather than democratic. A textbook for new party members put it this way: "The Party is one unified whole. . . . Once a decision is made, the minority is subordinate to the majority in its execution. . . . The lower organizations must carry out the decisions of the higher organizations." [9] In this respect, the party was organized more like a military organization than a political party.

The Communist Party differed importantly from other parties, even other leftist parties, in the amount of power granted to party employees. In the Socialist Party of Eugene V. Debs, for example, the most important and powerful men in the party were not on the party's payroll. Those who were on the payroll, the national office force and the organizers, were functionaries, in the pre-Communist sense of the word, rather than policy makers. But the reverse was true in the Communist Party. The people who made all the major decisions were on the party payroll. The most important Communists were full-time, professional revolutionaries, making their living at party activity. This fact had important implications for the operation of the party.

For one thing, professional direction of the party tended to make the party the most centralized and bureaucratic organization in the history of American politics. The fact that a Communist official's salary came from party headquarters on the ninth floor of 35 East Twelfth Street, New York City, made him realize that the party's real power resided there, no matter what the constitution said about the party club. He realized that to differ with the ninth floor on any important matter might mean expulsion or dismissal, and for an expelled party functionary the economic road was rocky indeed.

The fact of centralization of authority in the hands of a few professionals also affected the decisions of the party. Had the power distribution within the party been more nearly like that of other political groups, and had leaders of the so-called "mass organizations" or Communist trade unions exercised real power within the party, its policies might have been somewhat different from what they were. But the trade-union leaders exercised little if any power in the party. Quite the reverse: they either followed the professionals' desires in political matters, and to a lesser degree in strictly trade-union matters, or they bolted the Communist movement altogether. The professional party leaders insisted that they be followed, and they offered no alternative but withdrawal from the party. The party might have been able to hold on to its trade-union following in the postwar decade if it had followed the will of the Communist trade-unionists rather than insisting upon the reverse.

Finally, the fact that the party's top leaders were not really dependent upon popularity, even acceptance, in the rank and file tended to separate them from the membership. To a politician of the major parties, nothing is so important as broad support within his party, but not so in the Communist Party. Communist leaders mend no fences. In the party upheaval of 1956, a Negro woman member from the Bronx described the relations of the top leaders with the ordinary membership rather eloquently if inelegantly: "How many of you have been introduced to a leader of the party for about a dozen times and have him or her look at you and smile each time and say so nice to know, so nice to know [?] You know after the second or third time you begin to wonder if there is something wrong with you, but after the sixth or seventh time you begin to wonder, period . . . it's not that they see so many people, it's because they don't see and know the membership. . . . I think that communist leaders are the worst snobs I have ever known." [10]

Another important characteristic of the Communist Party's organization was the high degree to which the party's professional personnel could be shifted about over the country for a variety of functions. In theory, and to a considerable degree in practice, the party was as efficient, as flexible, as capable of manipulation as a commando battalion. The analogy to military organization is one that Communists themselves used in such terms as "united front" and "cadre." In military usage, a cadre is a permanent staff of trained soldiers around which new units may be built. In Communist usage, a cadre was a trained party employee, a "full-timer," a standardized part at least theoretically capable of functioning well in any community or task.[11]

For all their power, party leaders were poorly paid. No one ever got rich, or even economically comfortable, as a professional Communist. When the federal Social Security Administration in 1956 attempted to revoke old-age benefits based on Communist Party wages, it revealed that the highest salary Foster ever received from the party was $73 a week. His annual party salary in the period after the war ranged from $2,340 to $3,180. Perhaps he also supplemented his salary by the sale of his books, which the party press touted shamelessly. *Daily Worker* staff men received the minimum American Newspaper Guild wages, $60 a week just after the war, later raised to $75 and then to $85. New York

State leaders and most national leaders received about the same pay or a little more than the *Daily Worker* employees. Leaders in states where the party was weak received less. All in all, Communist leaders lived very modestly. Many of them were able to get along only because their wives worked. Surely it was not financial gain that induced men to make the party their career; nearly all of them could have made better incomes in business or the professions.[12]

Above the whole complex party structure stood the international Communist movement. That the national leadership was subservient to international Communism, ultimately to Moscow, will be demonstrated time and again in this book. But there is some question as to just how the international leadership made its wishes known to the American party. Until the party, officially at least, withdrew from the Communist International, or Comintern, in 1940, to meet the letter of the Voorhis Act, there is no question but that there was a Comintern representative, in common party speech the "Comintern rep" or "CI rep." [13] There may have been CI reps to the party, or their equivalent, since 1940. Soon after Louis Budenz dramatically quit the party and the managing editorship of the *Daily Worker,* he charged that Gerhart Eisler, a German, was the post-Comintern equivalent of a CI rep. The party, of course, was extremely secretive about its international connections, and Eisler denied the charge. After some complex criminal litigation, Eisler jumped bail and went to East Germany. Since the Eisler case, there have been no official charges of the presence of a CI rep, but this negative evidence by no means proves that such a representative has not existed. Budenz charged also that Dmitri Z. Manuilsky, a Soviet representative to the United Nations, had acted as an international representative to the American party in 1945.[14]

Actually, however, whether there has been a CI rep or the equivalent in the United States since 1945 is an academic question. The precise means of communication between the Soviet Union and the American Communists are not so important as the fact that there was communication. In nearly all circumstances, a CI rep, a courier, or an "open wire to Moscow" was unnecessary, and there is not conclusive evidence in the public record that such means of communication have existed since 1945. American party leaders in nearly all cases had no real need for direct communication with the Soviets; there was sufficient information about Russian policy in Communist Party newspapers and magazines from abroad and in other publications accessible to them and to anyone else who made an effort.[15] Apparently, American party leaders on more than one occasion relied upon the United States "bourgeois press," particularly the New York *Times,* for information about Soviet developments.

Was there—is there—a party "underground"? Both informed and uninformed persons have made such charges. The Communist "underground" has been used to mean: 1) the "review commissions," both national and state, intended to expose police agents in the party and to maintain party discipline; 2) espionage or sabotage activities connected more or less directly with Soviet intelligence services; 3) secret party activities that do not necessarily involve espionage or sabotage; and 4) the method of party organization adopted in 1949 and 1950 in an effort to minimize the effectiveness of Federal Bureau of Investigation agents. The last will receive further attention in Chapter VII.

The review commissions played the role of the party's "internal security" agency and have therefore been compared to the Soviet Cheka or NKVD. Indeed, the NKVD and the review commissions had the same function if not the same power. Communist Party members could be charged with many offenses, and, if found guilty, they could be censured, removed from leadership, or expelled. The offenses ranged from "conduct unbecoming a member of the Party" to "personal or political relations with enemies of the working class and nation." The party club was to sit in judgment upon an accused member, and the accused had a constitutional right of appeal to the next higher echelon. In practice, only rarely did a club find a member innocent, and appeal was futile.

Charges by a review commission nearly always resulted in the disciplining of the party member. The party did have a problem. Court trials had proved that the F.B.I. had agents among the Communists, and the party had no recourse but to try to discover them. Yet to be effective, the review commissions had to operate secretly at least part of the time.

The most important kind of underground was engaged in espionage or sabotage in the service of the Soviet Union. There is overwhelming evidence in the public record of Soviet espionage in the United States before and since 1945. The most publicized cases had to do with espionage before or during World War II, notably the Alger Hiss, Klaus Fuchs, and Julius and Ethel Rosenberg cases. But three other convictions dealt with espionage committed since the end of the war: the Coplon-Gubichev case, the Soble case, and the Abel case.

On the night of March 4, 1949, F.B.I. men arrested Judith Coplon and Valentin Gubichev in New York City as Miss Coplon was in the act of passing to Gubichev some reports she had prepared based upon information she had gleaned from F.B.I. documents in her position with the Department of Justice in Washington. Miss Coplon, a graduate of Barnard College, was a United States citizen by birth. Gubichev was a Russian national, a New York employee of the United Nations. Miss Coplon was tried in 1949 for stealing documents from her government department; she and Gubichev were tried together in early 1950 for conspiracy to commit espionage. The core of Miss Coplon's defense was that she was having a love affair with "Gubie," as the tabloid newspapers insisted upon calling him. Gubichev was living in New York with his wife, also a Russian national. Juries in each trial found the defendants guilty as charged. At the request of the Department of State, Gubichev received a suspended sentence requiring that he leave the United States within two weeks. Apparently, the Department of State hoped for reciprocity for American nationals who had been convicted of espionage in Communist countries. Two months after her second conviction, Miss Coplon married one of her attorneys. In December 1950, a higher court reversed the decision against her on technical grounds. She had been arrested without a warrant, and information obtained by illegal wire-tapping had been used against her. The higher court's decision was concerned only with due process of law rather than with the facts of the case, upon which two juries had found Miss Coplon guilty.

In January 1957, the Department of Justice brought indictments against Jack Soble, his wife, Myra, and Jacob Albam for espionage committed since the war. Each admitted his guilt. In June 1957, the Immigration and Naturalization Service, at the F.B.I.'s behest, arrested Colonel Rudolf Ivanovich Abel of the Soviet secret police. Abel was tried and convicted of espionage.[16]

These cases make clear that there has indeed been Soviet espionage in the United States since World War II. They do not, however, establish a direct connection between the American Communist Party and espionage for the Soviets. None of the convicted had been a member of the Communist Party of the United States. Gubichev and Abel were Soviet citizens. The Sobles and Albam appear to have been coerced into espionage by fear for the safety of relatives in Russia. Judith Coplon was the only American convicted for postwar espionage that was apparently the result of ideological conviction, but there was no evidence at her trial to indicate she had been a member of the Communist Party.

This is not to say that there was no link between the American Communist Party and Soviet espionage apparatus in the postwar period; it is only to say that such a connection has not been made a matter of public record. The detection of espionage is a police function, the responsibility particularly of the Federal Bureau of Investigation. The F.B.I. quite understandably does not reveal all it knows or suspects, for to do so would jeopardize its opportunities to investigate further. Public statements of federal officials responsible for the detection of espionage indicate that considerable Soviet espionage has existed which has not been made public. In 1953, the head of the Internal Security Division of the Department of Justice revealed that his office had under investigation 766 espionage and 261 sabotage cases, and F.B.I. Director J. Edgar Hoover told reporters that year that "Enemy espionage rings are more intensively operating now than at any other time in the history of the country." [17] But beyond such statements as these and the above-mentioned convictions, there is no further evidence of espionage in the United States in the public record.*

During and before the war, the party served as a recruiting ground for espionage agents. This is clear from the public record. Whittaker Chambers and the Rosenbergs went into espionage work directly from the party. Judith Coplon apparently had friends who were party members, and she was on the periphery of the movement herself. The other people convicted for postwar espionage evidently had no connection with the American party. There is some evidence to indicate that if confidential sources were available it could be documented that the party has continued to serve as a recruiter since World War II as it is known to have done before 1945. In his 1958 book, *Masters of Deceit,* F.B.I. Director J. Edgar Hoover wrote that "by the early 1940's there was a definite lessening of direct Soviet dependence on the U.S. Party for espionage assistance." He also made the point that the party's "most important" contribution to Soviet espionage was recruit-

---

* On September 28, 1956, in a letter to Louis Nichols, Assistant to the Director of the F.B.I., I asked for what information the F.B.I. could give me about the Communist Party, both its underground and the open party, that was consistent with national interest for me or any other citizen to know. J. Edgar Hoover's reply, dated October 5, 1956, was as follows:

Dear Professor Shannon:
   The letter dated September 28, 1956, with enclosure which you wrote to Mr. L. B. Nichols has been brought to my attention.
   Although I would like to be of assistance, I feel sure you will appreciate the situation which prevents me from doing so when it is explained. The FBI is strictly a fact-gathering agency, and we are not empowered to divulge information from our files since they are confidential and available for official use only.
   The rules governing this phase of our operations are not flexible, of course, and this situation precludes me from complying with your request.
                                        Sincerely yours,
                                        [Signed] J. Edgar Hoover

ment. But, using a source apparently not a matter of public knowledge, he also wrote, "In one major apparatus detected by the
FBI . . . twelve of seventeen participants had been Party members." [18] Certainly, if one may speculate, it would seem that Soviet
intelligence officers would look to the United States Communist
movement for recruits as a matter of convenience; a Communist
or party sympathizer might be assumed to have the emotional and
intellectual motivation necessary. On the other hand, once recruited, a spy seems to sever all connection with American Communists and to work only with other Soviet agents. From the point
of view of both the Soviets and the American party, it would seem
only common sense to keep spies away from known Communists
to minimize the possibility of detection.

To summarize, there has clearly been Soviet espionage in the
United States in the recent past. We must presume that it continues. There is no documentation in the public record of a direct
connection between the party and espionage in the postwar period,
but such a connection may well have existed. In view of the party's
ideological commitment to the Soviet Union and of the known
record of Soviet espionage in the United States and elsewhere,
those responsible for the internal security of the United States
are wise to keep a vigilant eye on Communist activities.

Concerning the third kind of underground, activities that were
secret but not necessarily related to espionage, again there is little
evidence. It has been charged that the party operated an "underground business empire" to raise money and to further its interests within the business community. The "empire" was headed by
Robert William Weiner, usually called William Weiner, who from
1938 to 1940 was the party's financial secretary. In 1940, Weiner,
under his original name, Warszower, was convicted of passport
fraud along with Earl Browder. Because he had a serious heart
condition, the federal government did not imprison him, fearing
he might die in prison and become a party martyr. In May 1950,
the federal government moved to deport him as a subversive alien,
but both Russia, Weiner's country of birth, and France, the nation

from which he last embarked for America, refused to accept him. The Immigration Service did not intern him, again for fear of his dying while in government hands. Weiner's business investments for the party, it has been alleged, extended into many kinds of enterprises—from a night club (Café Society Uptown) to export-import houses—in a complex series of firms.[19]

Earl Browder has stated that while he was the party's head, Weiner did indeed make financial investments for the party. The organization had excess funds in the late 1930's and during the war, and Weiner invested these to get a better return than could be obtained from conventional management of organization funds. That these investments involved the party in bourgeois enterprise does not seem to have bothered the leadership. On the other hand, Browder maintained that the business operations were not extensive and that the published charges were grossly exaggerated. He did not know what happened to the investments after he was removed from leadership in 1945, but he presumed that they had been liquidated as the party became increasingly hard-pinched for money in the late 1940's. It seems quite unlikely that the party had extensive investments as late as the mid-1950's, when there was much evidence, such as the closing of party schools and the decline of its press, to indicate that it was in desperate financial condition. Yet as late as January 1959, the party expelled a Brooklyn party leader who was reported to have absconded with perhaps as much as $250,000 and gone abroad. Such a large sum probably would have been in investments of some kind.[20]

BROADENING THE PARTY'S INFLUENCE

If the party had never been able to radiate influence beyond its own membership, it would not have been a significant force in American life. But it was always able to reach certain non-Communists, mobilize them to an extent, and manipulate them for the party's advantage. The party had three main kinds of institutions for extending its influence: front organizations, party schools, and the party press.

There were many kinds of party fronts. Some were important (the International Workers Order) and some were not (the Quad City Committee for Peace). Some were more or less permanent (the Civil Rights Congress) and some were temporary (Committee for the Defense of the Pittsburgh Six). Some had broad and general objectives (American Slav Congress) and some were very limited in their purposes (American Committee for the Settlement of Jews in Birobidjan, Inc.). Some were created by the party (Veterans of the Abraham Lincoln Brigade) and some were established by non-Communists and subsequently captured by Communists (North American Committee to Aid Spanish Democracy). Besides the fronts proper, there were organizations that were only partially infiltrated by Communists. Some of the target organizations were able to repel Communist infiltration and influence (American Veterans Committee, National Association for the Advancement of Colored People, American Civil Liberties Union); other targets proved more vulnerable but were never completely captured (Southern Conference for Human Welfare). All kinds of fronts and target organizations had one thing in common, however: they provided an opportunity for Communists to mobilize people outside the party for support of one or more of the party's aims. Party fronts were by far the most important device the Communists had for the magnification of the party's influence.

A brief examination of the International Workers Order (I.W.O.), an organization primarily for immigrant workers and easily the largest Communist front in the postwar period, reveals the advantages that fronts had for the party. The party founded the I.W.O. in 1930, when Communists and other Left-Wingers split off from the Workmen's Circle, a Jewish social-democratic fraternal organization. Recognizing the opportunity to reach vast immigrant groups, the Communists pushed I.W.O. work hard. The I.W.O. became a powerful organization through the sale of life-insurance policies (incidentally, they were excellent ones), agitation against prejudice toward minority groups, and the exploitation of immigrants' interest in their country of origin and their cultural nationalism. At the I.W.O.'s high tide in 1947, it had 184,398 members holding insurance policies in the sum of $122,234,513. There were fourteen constituent organizations of various nationality groups in the I.W.O., of which the largest by far was the Jewish Peoples Fraternal Order. There were also 261 general lodges for English-speaking members, most important in the Negro communities of New York and Chicago, and to a lesser degree among French, Norwegians, and Chinese.[21]

The I.W.O. held many advantages for the party. Most importantly, it afforded the party a degree of access to foreign-language groups, which together form a significant part of the American working class and which, because of their relative isolation from anti-Communist American culture, seemed to the party to be a fruitful field for activity. The insurance policies brought the immigrants into the organization, and once there the Communists could go to work on them ideologically, developing sympathizers and even recruits. I.W.O. leaders spread the Communist line as clearly at the organization's meetings as ever did the *Daily Worker*.[22] The I.W.O. provided the party with mailing lists, which was no insignificant matter when one considers that nearly a million people were associated with the I.W.O. at one time or another. The party used the I.W.O. to give a distorted impression of support for its line. When I.W.O. conventions passed resolutions supporting the party's position on various matters, the Communists pointed to the resolutions and said that here was the view of 185,000 people. It was nothing of the sort, of course, because most I.W.O. members were apolitical people who had no understanding of the resolutions and who were in the I.W.O. solely for its capitalistic insurance benefits.

Important, too, was the financial aid the I.W.O. gave the party. Most front organizations were a drain on the party's financial resources, but with the I.W.O. the situation was reversed. The I.W.O.

subsidized the Communist press, which chronically pleaded for more money, with frequent large advertisements. During the period 1944-46, the I.W.O. paid the *Daily Worker* over $30,000 for advertising, and over $35,000 to the *Freiheit,* sometimes called "the Yiddish *Daily Worker.*" In 1946 alone, the I.W.O. spent $37,570.48 for advertising in various Communist periodicals.[23] Furthermore, the I.W.O. paid Communist cadres the best wages in the Communist movement, and thereby relieved the party of a financial obligation. It is also quite probable that the party collected salary kickbacks from Communist cadres in the I.W.O., as it was known to do in the 1930's. All in all, it was a dark day for the party when in 1950 the State of New York rescinded the I.W.O. charter and took over the administration of the insurance program itself.

An individual's membership in a party front may mean any number of things, including almost nothing at all. All kinds of people belonged to Communist fronts and for a vast variety of motives. Many were party members. Many were fellow travelers, people who were sympathetic with some or all of the party's aims but for some reason—fear, inertia, a principled reservation about the party, unwillingness to accept party discipline, or a calculated design to escape the stigma of actual membership—did not actually join the party. But the important front groups contained thousands who were neither party members nor fellow travelers. Many went into front organizations with at least a dim awareness that Communists were active in the front but feeling that the Communists' presence did not present a serious matter. To some people on the Left, the party represented the extremity of their own leftist tendencies; they were not willing to follow their own tendencies, but they were willing to co-operate with Communists on matters that were important to them. Other front members were even mildly anti-Communist but thought the effectiveness of the front in some cause or other outweighed the handicap of the Communists' participation. Still others joined front groups utterly unaware of Communist activity in the front, believing that these people sometimes accused of being Communists were actually genuine progressives being smeared by reactionaries. Some people stayed in organizations after they had become fronts in order to fight the Communists.

The party's incessant cry of "Red baiting" tended to keep non-Communists in front organizations. Any kind of criticism of the American party, of the Soviet Union, or of anything Communist, even if temperate, inevitably brought from Communists the charge of Red baiting. The Communists argued that all criticism of Communists or Communism was "fascist," asserting that it divided the opponents of fascism and thereby strengthened reaction. Since Hitler and Mussolini had indeed done what Communists accused all critics of the party of doing, the Communist Red-baiting cry, which amounted to "fascist baiting," had some effect.

The various "schools of Marxist studies" were one of the Communists' most effective devices for recruiting and propagandizing. Immediately after the war, there were several of these schools, five of them in the metropolitan New York area alone: the Jefferson School of Social Science, the School of Jewish Studies, the George Washington Carver School in Harlem, the Walt Whitman School of Social Science in Newark, and the Tom Paine School of Westchester. Others were the Samuel Adams School in Boston, the Tom Paine School of Social Science in Philadelphia, the Ohio School of Social Science in Cleveland, the Abraham Lincoln School in Chicago, the Joseph Weydemeyer School of Social Science in St. Louis, the Michigan School of Social Science in Detroit, the Pacific Northwest Labor School in Seattle, and the California Labor School in San Francisco.

Of these schools, the Jefferson School was the biggest and most important. Started in 1944, when two smaller institutions merged, the Jefferson School had more than 45,000 students in its first four years. Its building at Sixth Avenue and Sixteenth Street was so busy that the directors opened another "campus" in the Brownsville section of Brooklyn in 1946 and conducted extension courses all over the New York metropolitan area.[24] Ostensibly, the school had no direct connection with the party, but actually the relationship was very close. Instructors and other officials were party members, and the fact that instructors were dismissed when they got into difficulty with the party indicates that party conformity rather than academic distinction was the primary criterion for faculty membership. Surely, the illusion that the Jefferson School was independent of the party was difficult to retain when national party headquarters moved into the school's building in the early 1950's.

In some respects, the Jefferson School was only an adult-education center with a Communist slant. There were courses in art appreciation, American history, trade-unionism, philosophy, health, and literature. But there was also in the school an Institute of Marxist Studies, which taught a three-year course in Communist theory. The institute was part of the training of members for party leadership.

Besides the more or less permanent party schools, the party occasionally established temporary schools for the ideological indoctrination of new party members. In 1947, for example, there were at least two such temporary schools in Harlem, the Harlem Leadership Training School and the Maceo Snipes School. Most Negroes who joined the party did so because of the party's practical work for Negro rights rather than for any Marxist reasons. Consequently, when Negroes discovered the true nature of the party, they very commonly dropped out, thereby causing a more rapid membership turnover rate for Negroes than for the membership as a whole. In order to keep Negroes in the party, ideological indoctrination was a necessity, and the Harlem schools tried to provide it through fifteen hours of instruction in basic Communist ideology. These schools made no pretense of being adult-education centers.[25]

The party press served many functions: it propagandized among non-Communists, it provided an instrument for party building, it educated party members, it served as a bulletin, and it even, on rare occasions, served as a forum for discussion of divergent opinion. To American leftist groups, a newspaper or periodical is indispensable. Indeed, some leftist groups are hardly anything more than a list of subscribers to a fugitive journal. The party recognized the importance of its press and made sacrifices to keep it going and strengthen it. The party poured a great deal of money into the *Daily Worker,* which never was able to support itself after the war. In 1947, for example, the party budgeted $222,000 to make up the paper's deficit.[26]

Curiously, as important to the movement as was the *Daily Worker,* the party was never able to get even a majority of members to subscribe to it. Nearly all Communists read the *Worker,* the *Daily*'s Sunday edition, available by separate subscription, but the total circulation of the *Daily* was usually about one-third of the party's membership. Federal postal laws require that publications using second-class mail and appearing more frequently than monthly publish a sworn statement of their circulation in the first issue to appear in October. The *Daily* did not always observe this law closely—from 1946 through 1948, it did not publish its circulation—but the law forced it to publish some useful data. In 1945, the *Daily*'s average circulation was 22,220. It grew to 23,400 in 1949. The Sunday *Worker* had a circulation of 67,066 in 1946, 67,566 in 1947, and 64,348 in 1948.[27] The primary reason for the failure of most of the membership to read the *Daily* was probably that as a newspaper it was sadly deficient. It could not hope to compete with the general press in news coverage and features, although it tried. And as a propaganda sheet, the *Daily* was usually abominably dull. Anyone familiar with the party's position, as were most of its readers, seldom found anything in it that was surprising. The *Daily* was as predictable as the tides. Communists not only did not read the *Daily,* but they were openly critical of it. In 1946, the editor complained that he had "even heard of discussions in Party organizations where the paper was actually condemned as if it were a paper belonging to the enemy." [28]

The *Daily* had internal difficulties, too. For years, it did not have really effective editorial management. Browder had been the editor in chief, but actually he had little to do with the paper's day-to-day activities. When Louis Budenz was managing editor, much of the political direction came from Jack Stachel, a national committee member, but Stachel did not bother himself with journalistic routine. There had not been a *Daily* editor who was both an able journalist and a top political figure in the party since the days of Clarence Hathaway in the 1930's.

When Budenz left the party in October 1945, the *Daily* staff asked the ninth floor for the appointment of someone with party power who was really interested in journalism. Dennis in time appointed Morris Childs, whose qualifications were meager on both scores. The staff grumbled about Childs's appointment, but, typically, it did nothing but grumble. Childs's appointment did not sit well, either, with the extremely "hard" leadership of the New York State organization, Thompson and Davis. Childs's health was not good, and he knew he was looked upon with disfavor. When he returned from covering the Moscow foreign ministers' conference in early 1947, he asked the ninth floor for a leave of absence. At the June 1947 meeting of the national committee, Dennis announced Childs's leave of absence and moved the appointment of John Gates, a national committee member and the head of the party's veterans commission. Gates did not have journalistic experience, although he proved to be a capable editor, but he did have a stronger position in the leadership than either Budenz or Childs. The *Daily* staff was satisfied with his appointment.[29]

The *Worker,* somewhat larger than the *Daily,* containing even a magazine section in the years just after the war, was considerably more useful to the party. Its news columns summarized some of the more important stories that had appeared in the *Daily* the previous week, and the columnists saved some of their better material for it. But as important as the *Worker*'s content was its method of distribution. Though copies were sold by mail and on newsstands, the party worked hard at personal delivery to make contact with non-Communists. Every party club was expected to order a bundle of *Worker*s each week. Then, on Sunday, the club would hold a "Sunday mobilization" to distribute the papers, selling them from door to door, hoping to interest new people. "We look upon the Sunday mobilization not only as a means of selling papers but as a means of getting the Party into homes of the community." Conscientious Sunday mobilizers carried subscription blanks and recruiting cards with them.[30]

On the West Coast, the party's paper was the *Daily People's World,* published in San Francisco. The *World* tried to maintain the fiction that it was not a party paper, but only a Left Wing labor sheet. It is true that the *World* did not concern itself as much with strictly party matters as did the *Daily Worker,* but the difference was due partly to the fact that the California party in general tended to look inward at itself less than did the party in New York. But the *World* was the party's paper, nevertheless. It carried the *Daily Worker* columnists, and staff men moved back and forth between the two publications. Periodicals intended only for Communist eyes frankly disclosed the connection of the *World* to the party. In 1946, a party organization report praised the California party for having the *World* "on the agenda for every meeting," and another periodical announced that "The Communist Party of California has just launched a drive for 10,000 *People's World* subscriptions and renewals in the next four months." [31]

In 1947, the party began a weekly paper in Detroit, the *Michigan Herald,* but the venture soon failed, and the party fell back upon the device of a special Michigan page in copies of the *Worker* mailed to that state.[32] The special page for local matters was also used at various times for New England, eastern Pennsylvania, western Pennsylvania, the South, Ohio, and Chicago (the DuSable edition).

Some foreign-language newspapers followed the Communist line. Of these, the *Morning Freiheit* of New York, a Yiddish daily published in the same building that housed party headquarters and the *Daily Worker,* was the most important. Its circulation in 1947 was 20,911, roughly the same as the *Daily Worker*'s.

The party also had a few magazines. The party itself published

Political Affairs, a monthly devoted to Communist theory and official definitions of party line. As a monthly, *Political Affairs* was not required by law to publish its circulation figures, but in 1946 it conducted a drive to raise its circulation to 12,500.[33] *New Masses,* later *Masses & Mainstream,* followed the party line in literary and general cultural affairs, trying to reach a broad audience. *Jewish Life,* which once had been published by the New York State organization, was an English-language periodical devoted to Jewish culture. There were also the organs of the various front organizations, notably *Fraternal Life,* published by the I.W.O. and the *American Slav,* published by the American Slav Congress.

The party maintained two firms, International Publishers and New Century Publishers, for books and pamphlets. The party established International in the 1920's, partly with money given by A. A. Heller. Heller, a Communist and a successful businessman, had recently sold his air-reduction firm to a larger competitor. This Communist publishing house, founded with capitalist profits, specialized in Marxist "classics." New Century, headed by Weiner, specialized in party pamphlets. Both firms were very busy. In 1946, the Communists published through these houses over two million copies of their publications, and midway through 1947 they were running ahead of 1946.[34]

INDICATIONS OF PARTY STRENGTH

The best single index of the party's strength is the number of members it had. Fortunately, the size of its membership rolls at different times can be determined with reasonable accuracy. To determine Communist influence precisely is another matter. We can only note indexes of Communist strength or weakness and generalize from them.

Earl Browder has stated that when he was removed from leadership in the summer of 1945, there were from 75,000 to 80,000

C.P.A. members, and John Williamson roughly verified Browder's estimate in a report in late June 1945. The year 1944 had been a banner year for recruiting. The Communists that year enrolled an average of 4,275 new members a month. Many of these new converts soon quit, but there is no record of how many did so.[35]

Apparently, however, this large party was not well organized and efficient. Dues payments were irregular. Before the war, dues payments had averaged 85 per cent, but they declined to 71 per cent in the last six months of 1944 and to 58 per cent in the first five months of 1945.[36] The leadership complained about the lack of effectiveness and the ideological backwardness of many members. "In Detroit, where two-thirds of the membership is less than a year in the organization, and where not even 10 per cent has been in the organization for a number of years, many of the tasks handed down to the clubs are either not tackled at all or inadequately fulfilled." In Detroit, "the cadres are not only without previous experience as club leaders . . . they are in the majority new members themselves. Most of the club leaders in Detroit are not ten steps ahead of the members, and the average member differs little in political development from a progressive trade unionist." Chicago and New York, where there were over 5,000 members of long standing, who had been in the party for years, had another kind of difficulty: in those centers, the experienced members tended to do all the work, leaving the recruits untrained.[37]

Inevitably, many members left the movement during the 1945 upheaval. Some sided with Browder and quit. Others were formally expelled, and still others were informally dropped. Browder estimated that between 20,000 and 30,000 left the party in the first few months after the upheaval, and his estimate again is borne out by other evidence.[38] In late 1945, the party conducted a membership registration, the best way for the organization to do its membership bookkeeping. The registration showed the membership to be about 53,000. But in 1946, the Communists conducted a vigorous recruiting campaign and enrolled about 20,000 new members during the year, bringing their total to about 73,000, only slightly less than there had been in the C.P.A. before the Duclos letter.[39]

Foster's boast in January 1947 that the party had then more members than ever before in its history reflected more a pride in his leadership than a scrupulous regard for fact, but the party was undeniably vigorous. In April 1947, Communists made 110 local radio broadcasts and two national network broadcasts. In March and April, they distributed 4,500,000 leaflets.[40]

The party was also quite successful at raising money. When, in March 1947, Secretary of Labor Lewis B. Schwellenbach proposed outlawing the Communist Party, the party responded with an "Operation Fighting Fund" and hoped to raise $250,000 in twenty-five days. It obtained that sum in only twenty days, whereupon it set a new goal, $300,000 higher.[41] San Francisco Communists collected $6,667.95 at a mass meeting called on three days' notice, and they were especially proud of their ability to get "regular contributions from non-Party contacts." [42] All in all, early 1947 appears to have been the high tide of Communist strength in the postwar period.

The party enabled itself to grow in 1946 and early 1947 by exploiting every possible grievance of any significant group. The housing situation was particularly acute at that time, and the Communists capitalized on the situation to the hilt.

For example, there was the case of Michael Gorglione, a resident of New York's Greenwich Village with no particular political convictions. He and his wife, each of them elderly, had a rent-free apartment in exchange for his services as superintendent of the fifteen-tenant building. In April 1946, the landlord fired Gorglione and, without a court order, had the Gorgliones' furniture moved into the street. The couple, who had a son in the Navy, had nowhere to go. A small crowd of Villagers, apparently not Communists, saw the eviction, became angry, and moved the furniture back into the apartment. At this point, the Communist Party moved into the situation. Mrs. Clarina Michelson, the local section organizer, "mobilized" the neighborhood. She prepared and distributed leaflets explaining the case, rallied the support of fifty neighborhood leaders, including the Gorgliones' priest, and persauded the landlord that the tenants were satisfied with Gorglione's work. The landlord consented to rehire the elderly Italian and to let the couple continue to live in the building. The Gorgliones were naturally grateful for the party's work in their behalf, which had some similarity to the kind of "social work" Tammany Hall had once been famous for, and Mrs. Gorglione expressed her thanks at a public meeting of the Greenwich Village section. At the meeting, two young Italian-Americans joined the party because of the Gorglione episode, and scores of others became more kindly disposed toward the Communists.[43]

Even more successful was the party's exploitation of the deplorable housing situation in the Harlem tenements. In May 1946, the Abe Lincoln party club of Harlem staged a mass meeting on housing at the corner of Lenox Avenue and 117th Street, in the heart of Harlem. From this meeting there grew the United Harlem Tenants and Consumers Organization, operated by Communists but with a considerable non-Communist following. Tenement dwellers were happy to join the organization if it promised to improve their housing conditions, and, once in the tenants' group, they were likely targets for Communist recruiters. The party got all twenty-three tenants of one particularly bad building into the tenants' organization, and recruited fourteen of these into the party. Similar tactics were successful in the Bronx. Joe Jackson, Chairman of the Melrose club of the Bronx, reported that the party had done extensive recruiting through a tenants' organization. "Two houses are solidly Communist, from cellar to top floor. Concentration, brother." The Chicago party had similar but less spectacular results in the heavily Negro South Side.[44]

Other issues proved fruitful to the party. Many employers in the Bedford-Stuyvesant area of Brooklyn, a Negro neighborhood, refused to hire Negroes. With only a few people, the Communists there in 1947 began a campaign to change the employers' minds. The issue was popular in the neighborhood, and non-Communists did much of the picketing of offending stores. Many shop owners capitulated, and in the process the party got thirty neighborhood recruits. The party also did its utmost to capitalize on the wave of strikes in 1946. The Jefferson School sent a chorus around to picket lines to sing party songs and distribute free copies of the *Daily Worker,* and John Williamson urged members to exploit strikes to the fullest, to "understand that now is the time to recruit." [45]

The party's organizational secretaries were careful to avoid revealing much in their published reports about the party's membership composition, but they let slip quite a bit at times. We can, for example, determine the party's geographical distribution with considerable accuracy. The party was overwhelmingly urban, and it was strongest in the very big cities. The bigger the city, the more concentrated was Communist strength. An estimated one-third or a little more of the national membership was in New York City alone. The borough of Manhattan in June 1947 had 11,080 party members, more than any industrial state, such as California, Illinois, Ohio, Michigan, or Pennsylvania.[46] In June 1946, the *Worker* inexplicably printed a table showing the extent of recruiting done in the first five months of the year, with a breakdown by states and regions. The New York party acquired over 6,000 new members. California was next with 1,598, and Illinois next with 1,175. Texas recruited more than western Pennsylvania, 276 to 174, and Louisiana more than Wisconsin, 125 to 111, but, in general, the South did not have much of a movement. Montana recruited only three, Utah only eight, and North and South Dakota, New Mexico, Arizona, and Wyoming none at all.[47]

Good statistics on the class or occupational composition of the party are not available, but it is obvious that the membership was not strong among those who toiled in mines, mills, and factories. The Communists tried hard to expand their working-class membership. In recruiting drives, it set itself quotas of industrial workers—Ohio in 1946, for example, was to fill three-fourths of its recruit quota of one thousand with industrial workers—but the party had to admit, "In such states as New York and California [the two most important] . . . the present membership is not pre-dominantly working class in composition. . . ." [48]

Nor is it possible precisely to describe the party's ethnic com-position. In the years just after the war, Negroes proved relatively easy to recruit. Rose Gaulden, a Harlem party leader, reported that a few people even walked into Harlem party headquarters without any previous contact and said they wanted to join. One-third of the 1946 recruits were Negro. But, once recruited, Ne-groes did not stay. "We attract the Negro people because of our militant fight on issues which concern them. But we have not yet found the medium to train and hold our new members." [49] The Communists had some strength, but not much, in the New York Puerto Rican community. Puerto Rican migration to New York increased tremendously after World War II, but Communist strength among these people declined just as they were becoming a significant part of the New York population. In November 1952, the party regretfully announced "a drop of 80% [among Puerto Ricans] in the past few years." Typically, the party put the blame for the loss on Browder. [50] A significant proportion of the member-ship was Jewish, although statistics are not available. The Yiddish *Freiheit* had almost as much circulation as the *Daily Worker,* but this fact does not mean much—many readers of the *Freiheit* were not party members and there were unquestionably many Jewish *Daily* readers. Nor are there statistics on the numbers of party members who were immigrants or of recent immigrant background. It is likely that there was a higher proportion of immigrants in the party than in the national population, but it is questionable that the proportion was higher than that of the cities where the party was strongest.

Strong as the party was in 1946 and 1947, it had a great deal of "fat" in it; it had the same kind of organization problems it had had in 1944. The organization secretary complained con-stantly about the failure of many members to behave in an ac-cepted Bolshevik manner. Winston regretted that in building mass movements too many party members became so deeply involved in whatever struggle there was at the moment—housing, the campaign against passage of the Taft-Hartley Act, strikes, or whatever—that they slighted their strictly party duties. "There is a tendency . . . to place the Party in the background. In practice, the Party becomes a secondary matter; everything else is primary and the Party is secondary." And many members were quite inactive. The Negro members were especially lax about party work. Winston even asserted, "The bulk of the [Negro] membership we never see from one registration to the next." [51] Very significantly, the rate of dues collection was poor. In the first quarter of 1947, slightly less than half the party members were up to date in their dues payments.[52]

In late 1947 and early 1948, the party's membership began to shrink rather seriously, and the party was never able to reverse that downward direction. The Communists reached the pinnacle of their postwar influence in the Wallace movement of 1948, but their own organizational strength had already begun to wane. When the party met in its fourteenth national convention at New York in early August 1948, Organizational Secretary Winston had to report a decline in membership to slightly more than 60,000, a net loss of roughly 13,000 in eighteen months.[53] Neither the Communists nor their opponents realized it at the time, of course, but the long, slow ebb tide of the American Communist Party had begun.

THE COMMUNISTS AT THE POLLS

The Communist Party ran candidates for public office on its own ticket in several elections in the first few years after the war. These elections give the kind of statistics a historian likes to have, but it is difficult to determine precisely what the significance of a Communist vote is. When a Communist identified as such on the ballot made a poor showing, then obviously the electorate did not have significant Communist sympathies. But when a Communist made a good showing at the polls, what is signified? It possibly could mean that those who voted for the Communist candidate endorsed his position. It possibly could mean that many voters had a vague sympathy for the party's aims. And it possibly could mean that many voters were dissatisfied with the major-party candidates and voted Communist only because they had no other way to express their dissent. But it is clear that when a Communist running on his party's ticket received many votes those who voted for him, at the least, were not so anti-Communist that their attitude toward the party overrode other considerations.

A vote for a Communist or a pro-Communist on the ticket of some other party—New York's American Labor Party, for example—or in a nonpartisan election, such as many school-board elections, does not necessarily indicate support for the candidate as a Communist, because the voter might not have been aware of the candidate's Communist connection. Ohio Communists rejoiced in 1947 when A. R. Krchmarek polled 64,264 votes in the nonpartisan Cleveland school-board election even though he lost. Krchmarek was not widely known as a Communist then and was not identified as such on the ballot. It is probable that his Slavic name reaped him more votes than his party affiliation, since he was the only candidate on the ballot who had an East European name. Similarly, an Oakland, California, Communist named Emma Stanley received 23,087 votes to her opponent's 33,176 in a 1947 school-board election, but she was not identified as a Communist on the ballot. Another California school election is the best example of this kind of Communist electoral success. In 1950, when the popular mood of the nation clearly was anti-Communist, Bernadette Doyle, chairman of the Communist organization in San Diego County but not labeled as a Communist on the ballot, polled 605,-393 votes, 26 per cent of the total, for the post of state superintendent of public instruction. The fact that she was a woman and had a distinctly Irish name probably was the reason for her strong showing.[54]

Not surprisingly, the Communist Party made its best voting rec-

ord in New York City, and New York was the only city in the
nation to elect Communist officials after the war. From 1937 until
1947, New York had a complicated proportional-representation
system of elections to the city council, and under this system the
Communists enjoyed a measure of success. In 1937, Peter V.
Cacchione, of Brooklyn, ran for the city council and missed election by only about 300 votes. He won election in 1941 and again
in 1943, when Benjamin J. Davis, Jr., of Harlem, also won on
the Communist ticket. Each was re-elected in November 1945,
Cacchione by the largest vote possible under the proportional-representation system. Two candidates of the American Labor Party
(A.L.P.)—Mike Quill and Eugene P. Connolly—also won city
council seats in that election. When Cacchione died in office in
1947, the party and the city council engaged in a spectacular has-
sle over his council seat. The New York City charter provided that
when a councilman died his political party would name his suc-
cessor for the balance of the deceased's term, but in New York
one could not enroll with the election board as a Communist, and
Cacchione had not enrolled as a member of the A.L.P., as had
most Communists. Through this technicality, the council refused
to seat Simon Gerson, whom the Communists named to take
Cacchione's place. In November 1949, after Davis had been convicted under the Smith Act, the council ousted him under the city
charter provision that prevented convicted felons from holding
office. New York's voters in a 1947 referendum abolished pro-
portional representation, and after that the party never again made
a significant showing.[55]

In the 1946 Congressional and state elections, the New York
Communists supported A.L.P. candidates, but they ran two candidates for state office on their own ticket—Robert Thompson for
state comptroller and Davis for state attorney general. Thompson
received 85,088 votes and Davis 95,787. An analysis of their votes
reveals about what one would expect: the overwhelming majority
of their vote came from the poorer neighborhoods of New York
City. In Manhattan, the assembly districts with a significant Com-

munist vote were the Lower East Side, Harlem, and the extreme northern West Side. In Brooklyn, the Coney Island area, East New York, and the poorer parts of Flatbush turned in the highest Communist votes. The heaviest Bronx Communist vote came from the assembly districts just to the east of Webster Avenue, and the only Queens district to report a significant Communist vote was the area along the East River just north of Newtown Creek. But nowhere were the Communist candidates a threat to the major-party candidates. The Communists ran best in East New York, where they polled 3,495 votes. Democratic candidates customarily poll about 40,000 there.[56] All the neighborhoods with a significant Communist vote were low- or lower-middle-income areas with a high proportion of Negro or immigrant inhabitants.

No other part of the country returned such large Communist votes, but Boston's twelfth ward, Roxbury, a generally poor neighborhood with a considerable Negro and immigrant population, was a source of many Communist votes immediately after the war. In 1946, William Harrison ran for the Massachusetts General Court, the lower house of the legislature, on the Communist ticket and polled 3,124 votes, one-sixth of the total. The following year, a Communist candidate for city council from that ward received one-fourth the vote cast.[57]

California was the only other area to poll an important Communist vote. In 1946, the Communists conducted a write-in campaign for Archie Brown for governor, and he received 22,206 votes. Governor Earl Warren, with both the Republican and Democratic nominations, under the California cross-filing system, polled over 2,300,000, but Brown's total for a write-in candidate was fairly strong. The distribution of Brown's vote indicated where California Communist strength lay: he received 13,949 votes in Los Angeles County and 6,842 votes in San Francisco and Contra Costa Counties, both in the Bay area.[58]

Elsewhere in the country, Communist candidates did very poorly. The Communist candidate for governor of New Jersey in 1946 received only 4,031 votes from a total of 1,414,527 cast, and over three-fourths of his vote came from the counties adjacent to New York City. Michigan's Communists in 1946 nominated an extensive slate, but their most successful candidate, Abner W. Berry, a Negro comrade later to be a *Daily Worker* columnist, polled only 3,120 votes for secretary of state. In Indiana, in 1946, none of three statewide Communist candidates polled as many as a thousand votes, running behind Socialist and Prohibitionist candidates. Colorado Communists in 1946 made a frank bid for the Negro and Mexican vote by nominating one of each for their only candidates, but each polled only about 2,000 votes.[59]

Many conclusions might be reached from this quick survey of Communist voting power, but one that stands out is that except for a few large cities, notably metropolitan New York and Los Angeles, the Communists were unable to poll enough of a vote to cause majority-party candidates to look twice. Obviously, even in the two years of its relative strength immediately after the war, the party would have been hopelessly naïve to have entertained ideas of coming to power under its own name by the ballot box or of influencing any significant part of the electorate through its candidates' electoral activity. This the party realized, and it put its electoral emphasis upon creating other political parties in which it could work for its own ends. The high tide of this "coalition" policy was to come in 1948, and a former vice-president of the United States was to be the stalking-horse.

THE PARTY AND THE TRADE UNIONS

No survey of Communist strength would be complete without some attempt to estimate the number and influence of party followers in the trade-union movement. As noted in Chapter II, most of the trade unions in which Communists were influential were in the C.I.O.

The unions ultimately expelled from the C.I.O. as Communist

dominated and thus followers of policies inimicable to the labor movement were the following: United Electrical, Radio, and Machine Workers of America (U.E.), easily the largest of the "left" unions, and the third largest C.I.O. union, with a 1947 membership of about 500,000; Farm Equipment Workers (F.E.), about 65,000 members; International Longshoremen's and Warehousemen's Union (I.L.W.U.), the Harry Bridges union, with 75,000 to 100,000 on the West Coast waterfront and in the Hawaiian pineapple and sugar industries; American Communications Association (A.C.A.), a union of about 10,000 members with contracts in the telegraph field; International Union of Mine, Mill and Smelter Workers (Mine, Mill), 108,000 members in 1947, most of them in the Rocky Mountain nonferrous-metal industry but with some significant contracts in the eastern brass industry; Food, Tobacco, Agricultural, and Allied Workers of America (F.T.A.) with a membership in 1947 of 46,700; National Union of Marine Cooks and Stewards (M.C.S.), led by Hugh Bryson, about 7,000 members, mostly in Pacific shipping; International Fishermen and Allied Workers of America, a West Coast union of about 10,000 members; International Fur and Leather Workers Union, usually called the Furriers, Communist dominated since the mid-1920's, about 85,000 members; United Office and Professional Workers of America (U.O.P.W.A.), about 45,000 members in 1947; and the United Public Workers of America, another white-collar union, about 85,000 members.

There were four other important C.I.O. unions in which Communists had considerable power until the unions ousted the Communists from leadership or the leaders themselves broke with the party: National Maritime Union (N.M.U.), Joe Curran's union, which broke from the party in 1946-47; United Furniture Workers, which defeated a Communist-supported slate of officers for the first time in 1950; the Transport Workers Union (T.W.U.), the union of the fabulous "Red Mike" Quill, which broke in 1948; and the United Shoe Workers of America, which defeated the Communists in a 1946 struggle.

A few unions had a significant Communist caucus that could not fully control the organization. Most important of these was the United Auto Workers (U.A.W.). Until 1947, the R. J. Thomas–George Addes–Richard Leonard faction, which had the support of the Communists, controlled the U.A.W.'s executive board, although the anti-Communist Walter Reuther became U.A.W.'s president in 1946. The United Retail, Wholesale, and Department Store Workers Union had a noisily anti-Communist national leadership, but its large District 65 in New York, headed by Arthur Osman, was firmly in the Communist camp until well into the 1950's. Other such unions were the United Gas, Coke, and Chemical Workers of America, the United Packinghouse Workers, and, briefly, the Amalgamated Clothing Workers, for whom John Abt, in the 1950's to become the party's most heavily worked attorney, was counsel immediately after the war.

The Communists also controlled some of the state and city C.I.O. councils. Of these, the most important were the ones in New York City and California, but the party's followers were in every significant state and local council and had effective control in such places as Milwaukee, St. Louis, Detroit, and Minneapolis. The party's main purpose in these councils was to exploit the C.I.O.'s strength and prestige for party-line resolutions.

The party had its followers in the C.I.O. national office until 1947-48, when the C.I.O. began to clean house. Most important of these were Leonard Howard ("Len") DeCaux, a New Zealand-born graduate of Oxford, editor of the *CIO News,* and director of the publicity department, who resigned his post July 15, 1947, and Lee Pressman, who resigned as C.I.O. counsel in February 1948. Soon after the outbreak of the Korean war, Pressman testified before the House Committee on Un-American Activities that he had been a party member in the 1930's, and he clearly was close to the party after he was no longer a dues-paying member.

No A.F. of L. international union was under the control of Communists, but in New York City and Los Angeles there were strong locals under Communist domination. In Los Angeles, pro-

Communists or Communists controlled several of the numerous "Hollywood unions." In New York, the Communists controlled the painters' local, had considerable power in the local of the Hotel and Restaurant Employees' International Alliance, and had influence in the International Typographical Union local. There were many Communists in the International Longshoremen's Association—the party recruited 120 from the Brooklyn docks in the summer of 1947—but they never exercised any real power in the organization.

Not all or even most of the union leaders the Communists liked to call the "Left-Progressives" were members of the party. Among those who freely announced their party membership were Ben Gold and Irving Potash, of the Furriers, and Hal Simon, of U.E. Many of the Left leaders were more or less open about their activities around the edge of the party but did not assert actual membership. For example, Lewis Merrill, president of U.O.P.W.A. was until 1947 a trustee of the Jefferson School and a contributing editor of *New Masses,* and Max Perlow, general secretary-treasurer of the United Furniture Workers, was an open supporter of *Daily Worker* money-raising campaigns. Still others—R. J. Thomas, of the U.A.W., was a conspicuous example—were not Communists and did not accept the party's views but did accept the support of Communist fractions in their unions. Some union leaders were Communist in every respect but actual dues-paying membership. Harry Bridges is a case in point. In the many deportation proceedings against Bridges, the prosecution was never able to prove its contention that Bridges was a party member. He probably was not. But, for all practical purposes, his union was Communist led.[60]

The question of how much control the Communist Party could exercise over the Left union leaders was another matter, for the Left leaders were frequently torn between what the party wanted and what their union membership would allow. Not even in the most Communist of the C.I.O. unions was there ever a majority of members who were sympathetic to the party. Most union members were usually unconcerned with their leaders' political activities, but were anti-Communist when their political passions became aroused. The Left union leaders, therefore, had to tread softly, had to be careful lest their membership get the impression they were marching to the beat of the Twelfth Street drum. Sometimes, also, the leaders' loyalty to the party conflicted with their loyalty to their union. Mike Quill, for example, had his differences with the party over the five-cent subway fare in New York. The *Daily Worker* constantly battled against proposals to increase the fare, calling an increase a tax on the poor instigated by the real-estate interests,[61] but if Quill were to get a significant wage increase for his union members, there had to be an increase in the fare. What particularly irked Quill was that Gold and Potash, of the Furriers, old hands at extracting wage increases for their well-paid members at the expense of consumers, were against a fare increase. Finally, after differences with the party on other issues, Quill denounced the Communists in early 1948.

Still another factor preventing the party from using the Left trade-unionists as effectively as it could manipulate its political cadres was that some of them were using the party, rather than the reverse. In some unions, one could not rise in the union leadership unless one were a Communist or a pro-Communist, and some young men on the make joined for opportunistic reasons with no real ideological commitment. A disgusted former maritime worker in California summarized the situation well in labor slang: "After the unions were organized and put on a paying basis, then the scramble began for pie-card jobs. It was common knowledge in some unions that the only way to get elected to office was to get the support of the Left. So a lot of petty larceny opportunists, or just plain wishy-washy pie-cards, joined the Left and got themselves elected with criminal consequence later on."[62] The loyalty of an opportunist was as easily lost as it was gained.

Evidence that the party could not control the Left union leaders as it wanted to is seen in the frequent complaints of John Williamson, who became the party's labor secretary in mid-1946. Although Williamson tried to direct his forces at national C.I.O.

conventions from caucuses in his hotel room,[63] he was unable to get all the Left leaders consistently to toe the mark. In his reports, he complained bitterly about the Left leaders' behavior, attributing it to "Browder revisionism [which] left deep imprints in the thinking and practices of our trade union cadres." [64] Very likely the Left union leaders did yearn for the Browder period, when the party line had more frequently coincided with the beliefs of their union members.

The party's main handicap in the C.I.O., however, was that even if it could have made the Left union leaders behave like automatons it still would not have rallied a C.I.O. majority. Since the Communists were a minority, they had to accomplish their ends through co-operation with, or at least with the tolerance of, the non-Communists. They had to build and maintain what they so fondly called the "Left-Center coalition." The center, symbolized by Phil Murray, just would not go along with the Left when the party pressed for C.I.O. endorsement of its position on the Marshall Plan and the Wallace candidacy. In other words, the Communists' trouble was in their line. The non-Communist center in the C.I.O. steadily became the anti-Communist center, and, later, the results for the party were disastrous.

"THE LIFE OF THE PARTY"

A consideration of the special problem the Communists faced just after the war of how to handle returning Communist servicemen reveals a great deal about "party life." About fifteen thousand Depression-generation Communists went into the armed services during the war, and it was important to the party that these thousands return to the fold. The Communists created a special veterans committee, which put out a pamphlet to explain the Browder upheaval to the returning soldiers. They ran special classes for veterans. They had each club compile a list of returning party veterans, send the list to national headquarters, and call personally upon each veteran to "integrate" him back into the organization as quickly as possible. In May 1947, they sponsored the First (and last) National Encampment of Communist Veterans of World War II in Washington. But their special efforts failed. When an estimated one-third of the Communist veterans were back home, Robert Thompson confessed, "It is clear that a large percentage of these already discharged Party and YCL [Young Communist League] veterans are not being reached." [65]

The basic reasons why the party failed to recover many of its returning servicemen were very much entangled with two other basic party problems, neither of which the party ever fully faced nor even clearly recognized. The first of these problems was the dilemma of immersion into "party life" versus contact with people outside the party and the Left Wing movement. The second problem was that of the postwar drift—perhaps rush is a better word—to middle-class ways of life, such as the urban migration to the suburbs.

Active party members in the big cities lived a special kind of life, by the party's design somewhat isolated from the main stream of American life. To be an active member in New York, for example, was not just to be affiliated with a political group; it was to become fully involved, immersed, in a movement that permeated almost every aspect of life. Members read party literature and frequently not much else; their social life was largely limited to other members; nearly all their free time was taken by some kind of party work; when they went to the movies, they went to a Russian film at the Stanley rather than to see the neighborhood theater's Hollywood product; their cultural interests became the studied and synthetic folk culture of Pete Seeger and the hootenany, the self-conscious proletarianism of the *New Masses,* and the muscular primitivism of Hugo Gellert. The party spirit even entered family relationships, and such phrases as "a progressive marriage," to indicate the marriage of two Communists, and "a Communist home" were common.

The term "Communist home" requires special explanation. Two items from the *Daily Worker* in one 1947 month reveal the meaning clearly. A letter to the editor began, "We are a group of children, 10 to 11 years of age, who call ourselves the Roosevelt Club after a great man. Since there are many anti-labor bills, we feel it is our duty to help support the Daily Worker in fighting fascism. . . . We are enclosing with this letter $22.15 which we hope you will accept." [66]

The other item deserves full quotation:

If our Party-building drive can use a mascot, I hereby nominate the four-year-old daughter of the Hy Wallachs. This incredible daughter of the veteran section organizer is a Quiz Kid with a social conscience, the vanguard of the infant masses.

Vicky has invented a game called "Section," which all the kids on the block play. The game starts with 'lections to the Section "exec" (Vicky's always chairman) and lesser committees. Dire is the threat of being removed from the "exec" for scratching a playmate or other unsociable conduct. They have assignments of leaflet distribution (any scraps of paper will do) and Sunday mobilizations. The grown-ups are somewhat bewildered by some of Vicky's terms. A neighbor recently called on Mrs. Wallach to find out what Vicky had in mind when she called her daughter "undisciplined."

While "Section" is a game of fascinating words and forms, it is not entirely without content. After a brief "Section" meeting, the kids dispersed to their homes to urge a boycott of the anti-Negro film Song of the South.[67]

The reason that Communist leaders stimulated this kind of a Communist home and urged this special kind of party life was that it was a powerful force against backsliding and contamination by non-Communist ideas. It deepened the commitment of party members. To leave most organizations is a relatively simple matter, but to leave the Communist Party was to wrench one's very roots, to change one's whole life, to lose one's friends, to become an outcast.

While this kind of isolation had certain advantages for the party, it also had real disadvantages. Because most of their life was within the party and they had relatively little experience with outsiders, Communists were often unqualified for "mass work," for recruiting, and for co-operating with non-Communists in such "mass orgs" as the P.T.A., the co-op, or the union. It was terribly difficult for a non-Communist to respect the parents of a little Vicky. Furthermore, when a Communist did establish real contact with the outside world and with normal people—a phrase Communists themselves sometimes used [68]—the gap between the reality and their preconceptions, nurtured by years of party propaganda, was great. The release from isolation that Communists gained when they went into the armed forces was an important factor in the party's failure to regain its veterans.

Many Communist servicemen had never had friendships with non-Communists before the war, at least in their adult lives. They had never known anyone—or at least never lived with anyone —who associated the term "party line" with rural telephones rather than with ideology. The experience was disillusioning. They became aware for the first time that the "masses" were a good bit more "backward" than they had ever realized, but that the "backward masses" threw up some good specimens of humanity despite their ideology, or lack of it. Furthermore, as they saw how the workingmen of Europe and the majority of Asians lived, they began to wonder whether the lot of the workingman under American capitalism was so bad after all. Military service gave these Communists an opportunity to make a break with their pasts, and thousands of them seized it.

And the United States the veterans returned to was not the United States they had left, just as the Foster party many of them did not return to was not the Browder party they had left. The veteran had left a depression; he returned to an expanding economy. He had left a relatively stagnant society; he came back to social changes of bewildering rapidity. Thousands of young families packed off to the suburbs, to housing developments that grew almost overnight on what had been tilled fields. Families moved all over the nation. One-fifth of America's families changed their address each year. Each report of the census bureau was more startling than the last. In the general prosperity, couples who never thought they could afford children produced a crop of babies unprecedented in recent American history. Thousands of young men left home to go to college under the G.I. Bill of Rights and to begin an ascent at least part way up the social and economic ladder. This direction of American life had its effects upon the Communist party, especially upon the veterans and their generation.

"I can point to at least five couples of my acquaintance," wrote one Communist observer of social change in 1946, "who, before they had children, were active party members. When they had the first child, it became necessary to move from the city because 'you can't bring up a child in the city.' Then they lived too far out to participate in party activities. But that was not the real reason. The real reason is that they bought their home; they began to skimp here and there; mother had to do her own washing which took much more time than sending to the laundry and it saved a couple of dollars each week. The thing that happens to father is worse by far. Constantly his family needs more money. . . . He is an intelligent man . . . he has the experience to work in an administrative capacity and so he leaves the ranks of the workers. Don't tell me this is imagination. It is what I see happening all around me." [69] But the writer's plea to stay in the city and live the "party life" and create "Communist homes" fell upon many deaf ears. The Levittowns broke up most of the Communist neighborhoods of New York, where a child learned to read the *Daily Worker* at home and where a family that voted for Norman Thomas was considered reactionary. The trend that the complaining observer saw in 1946 was to grow to mammoth proportions.

PART TWO

THE
UNPOPULAR
FRONT

The present party line follows the broad path towards the people's front and people's democracy types of government now to be found in Eastern Europe. . . . Some liberals believe that a united front coalition would introduce a regime of "progressive capitalism," but this is a naive and dangerous illusion.

—WILLIAM Z. FOSTER, *The Twilight of World Capitalism*

FOUR: CREATING GIDEON'S ARMY—THE
PROGRESSIVE PARTY

A month after the end of World War II, readers of *Political Affairs* got their first hint of the political plans of the top Communist leadership. An article on American politics was nearly as critical of President Harry S Truman and his five-month-old administration as it was of the most conservative wing of the Republican Party, and it ended with a preview of what was soon to become the party's official policy: "The progressive forces will have to find other political alternatives if the only choice narrows down to a hide-bound reactionary Republican Party with fascist overtones and a Democratic Party which refuses to make a real stand for a progressive program and is constantly in retreat." [1]

Party chairman Foster opened a meeting of the national committee on November 16, 1945, with a routine flailing of Browder and then yielded the floor to Eugene Dennis for the main report. The first part of Dennis's speech, a harangue against "American imperialism" and a prediction of depression, contained nothing unexpected. But soon he raised the question of a third party. He professed to see in the C.I.O., among Negroes, "among the followers of Wallace in the Democratic Party," and in the Fiorello La Guardia–Newbold Morris wing of the New York Republican Party, "a growing minority sentiment for building a national third party." One of the basic errors of the Browder line, he told the committee, was acceptance of the two-party system. Dennis did not propose establishing a third party immediately, "or even necessarily during the course of the 1946 elections," but something would have to be done before the 1948 Presidential elections. "The American people must have an alternative to the two-party strait-jacket; they must be in a position to have a choice in 1948 other than between a Truman and a Dewey or a Vandenberg." Then came the order: *"This is why it is necessary from now on to create the conditions and base for organizing a major third party nationally."* The Communists, however, must be cautious because a "majority of the labor and progressive movement still has to be convinced and won over for a third party . . . it is essential that the advocates of a third party do not weaken their cooperative relationship with those anti-fascists who do not yet favor a third party." Communists must not "abandon the struggle to mobilize the people to exert . . . mass pressure which can influence the course of the Administration," even if Truman is quite hopeless. Should Truman advance any progressive proposals, the party should support them but *"without entertaining any illusions, and without entering any long-term alliance with the Administration."* In other words, get what you can from Truman, but build a third party to defeat him in 1948.[2]

Thus, three years before the 1948 elections, over two years before Henry Wallace announced his Presidential candidacy, before Truman disappointed many liberals in 1946, even before the cold war was well under way, the Communist Party determined its 1948 electoral policy in rough outline. How the policy should be applied, the Communists had yet to decide. When, where, how, and around whom to form a third party were still open questions. Another open question, and apparently one on which there were differences of opinion among the party leadership, was whether the third party should be similar to the American Labor Party in New York, endorsing many of the Democratic candidates, including the Presidential nominee, or a completely independent third ticket. The Communists' pressure for a third party waxed and waned in 1946 and 1947, but the party leadership never swerved from this third-party goal decided upon immediately after the war.

Party hacks ground out copy urging a break with the two-party system. At times the pressure was relatively slight, and at times it was intense, but it never ceased. The associate editor of *Political Affairs,* V. J. Jerome, invoked Lenin's approval of a third party, the highest possible authority in Communist eyes. Jerome's argument was so involute and his style so verbose, even flatulent, that it is doubtful that many readers had the patience to unravel it, but his conclusion was clear: there must be a third party, "although every care must be taken against premature actions. . . ." [3] Dennis certainly was careful in a public address at Madison Square Garden in January 1946. He only touched the issue, saying the American people "can rely only on their independent strength . . . to promote independent political action of labor and all progressives in the struggle for a truly democratic domestic and foreign policy." [4]

Dennis was more explicit at the party's next national committee meeting. The party would not try to establish a third party for the 1946 elections, but "if possible—and it is preferable—steps toward forming a third party should be taken early in 1947." The question of whether the third party would endorse the Democratic nominee was still open.[5]

The party had already begun a little experiment to test the idea. Early in 1946, Samuel Dickstein, congressman from Manhattan's Nineteenth District, resigned to accept a state judgeship. The district scheduled a special election for the balance of his term. The A.L.P. first nominated an unknown, and the Democrats put up a Tammany district leader. But the Democrats soon withdrew their first man to nominate Arthur G. Klein, who had been in Congress back in the 1930's and had a good New Deal voting record. After Klein filed, the A.L.P. put in another new nominee, the well-known radio news commentator Johannes Steel.

The Communists freely announced why they got the A.L.P. to nominate Steel and make a real race. The district, running up Manhattan's East Side from the Battery to Fortieth Street, was a working-class area with a large Jewish and immigrant population, "a district well suited to test the burning issues of the day; and to register what new alignments may be in the making in the political arena." [6] Because Klein was such a strong New Dealer, Steel's candidacy was particularly significant.

There is no question that Steel was close to the Communist Party. At that time, he was a columnist for the *Daily People's World,* and he wrote for that paper throughout his campaign. He was invited to speak at I.W.O. conventions, where he peddled the straight party line.[7] In 1947, the Soviet Union gave Steel a visa to cover the Moscow foreign ministers' conference, breaking its own rule to grant visas only to the thirty-five American journalists approved by the American Government.[8]

Steel ran a very strong race. The New York C.I.O. endorsed him. So did the National Citizens Political Action Committee and the Independent Citizens Committee of the Arts, Sciences, and Professions. So did Secretary of Commerce Henry Wallace and former Mayor Fiorello La Guardia. On February 19, Klein polled 17,360 votes to Steel's 13,421. The Republican candidate, William S. Shea, received only 4,314. The election results elated the Communists.

In the fall of 1946, there was one important political development in the third-party plans. In September, Secretary of Commerce Wallace resigned under pressure after his famous foreign-policy speech at Madison Square Garden.

The Communists had always had a rather uncertain attitude toward Henry Wallace. During Wallace's first several months as Secretary of Agriculture in Roosevelt's first term, the Communists had regarded him as just another bourgeois politician—this was their view of Roosevelt and all the New Dealers—but they warmed up to him considerably during the Popular Front period after 1935. During the war, Wallace, as Vice-President, made several speeches full of the popular clichés and sentiments of the war-time Left, and the Communists began to portray him as something of a hero. They reprinted some of his speeches in their periodicals; they were delighted with his statements on his good-will tour of the Asian areas of the Soviet Union in the early summer of 1944.[9] Yet Browder never cared much for Wallace, and he had indirectly notified Wallace's personal political adviser, Howard Young, that the Communists would do no more to support Wallace's renomination for the vice-presidency than the trade unions would, and Browder did not think the unions were prepared to fight to the bitter end over the issue.[10]

Jacques Duclos, however, in his famous article of April 1945, had kind things to say about Wallace. Duclos implied that Wallace had a better record of opposing American monopoly than Browder had. After berating Browder, Duclos wrote, "In the United States the omnipotent trusts have been the object of violent criticism. It is known, for instance, that the former Vice-President of the United States, Henry Wallace, has denounced their evil doings and their anti-national policy." And then again: "The former Vice-President of the U.S., Henry Wallace, present Secretary of Commerce, said rightly that one cannot fight fascism abroad and tolerate at home the activity of powerful [reactionary] groups." [11]

American Communists were still ambivalent toward Wallace, however. In January 1946, Alexander Bittelman, a veteran second-echelon leader, regarded Wallace as the only hope of the Truman administration, praised his book, *60 Million Jobs,* and declared that Wallace "is destined to play a great role . . . if he can shed his illusions. . . ." But later in the year, the Communists were not optimistic. At a dinner meeting of the A.L.P., the *Daily Worker* said, Wallace "gave comfort to reaction. Wallace evaded the actual facts as they exist. His words were . . . a whitewash of the present imperialist course of the administration." The editorial ended: "Wallace's advice will scarcely be taken seriously by the workers and other progressives in the nation." In June, Wallace wrote an article for the magazine published by the Democratic national committee, arguing strongly against third parties, and the *Daily Worker* swarmed with protest.[12]

On September 12, 1946, Wallace delivered a speech on foreign policy at a Madison Square Garden rally sponsored by the National Citizens Political Action Committee and the Independent Citizens Committee of the Arts, Sciences, and Professions. The speech came to be of historic importance, although no one expected it to be at the time. The public that night was under the impression that Wallace's speech had the approval of President Truman. In the speech, Wallace said, "And just two days ago, when President Truman read these words, he said that they represented the policy of the administration." Before Wallace spoke, Truman had told reporters the speech had his approval.*

What Wallace actually said in his September 12 speech soon became remarkably twisted in the memory of both the American Left and the Right. Wallace stated his conviction on the necessity and possibility of peace, and he condemned a "get tough with Russia" foreign policy. But the heart of his speech was a plea for what a decade later would be called "peaceful coexistence." "Russian ideals of social-economic justice are going to govern nearly a third of the world. Our ideas of free-enterprise democracy will govern much of the rest. . . . By mutual agreement, this competition should be put on a friendly basis, and the

---

* There later developed a considerable controversy over the facts of Truman's "approval." Two days after the speech, Truman told reporters his earlier statement had been misinterpreted, that he had only approved Wallace's right to deliver the speech. Years later, Truman wrote in his memoirs that he had not read the speech at all before it was delivered and that Wallace had only referred to it briefly at the end of a conference on other matters on September 10. Wallace directly controverted Truman's memory. He said that he and Truman had gone over the speech page by page, that Truman "didn't have a single change to suggest," and that Truman had positively stated his approval of the speech's ideas. The question of which man's memory, if either, is accurate is interesting but not vital to this book. At the time of the speech, the public impression was that the Wallace speech had Truman's endorsement.[13]

Russians should stop conniving against us in certain areas just as we should stop scheming against them in other parts of the world." At another point in the speech, he referred approvingly to "practical regional political reservations," or, in other words, political spheres of influence.

The Madison Square Garden audience was unmistakably Left Wing. It booed and hissed when Wallace said anything it construed as critical of the Soviet Union. At one point he said that "we may not like what Russia does in Eastern Europe. Her type of land reform, industrial expropriation, and suppression of basic liberties offends the great majority of people of the United States." After this sentence, the hissing was so loud that Wallace's shouted extemporaneous remark could be heard over the radio but not in the Garden: "I'm talking about people outside New York City when I say that. Every Gallup poll will show it!"

Thereafter, because his radio time was rapidly expiring, Wallace omitted several sentences that might have drawn further vocal protest. Among them was this one: "The Russians should stop teaching that their form of communism must, by force if necessary, ultimately triumph over democratic capitalism—while we should close our ears to those among us who would have us believe that Russian communism and our free enterprise system cannot live, one with another, in a profitable and productive peace." [14]

The next morning's *Daily Worker* roundly damned Wallace. A news story, replete with editorial opinion, reported, "He attacked Republican reaction in the international field, and then proceeded to back the Truman administration, which is united with the Republicans in that field. . . . He advanced views . . . which covered up American imperialism's aggressive role." Senator Claude Pepper, of Florida, who also spoke at the Garden meeting, got the headline and favorable coverage. An editorial, entitled "Wallace Evades Issue," was quite harsh. "Wallace repeated the major fallacies advanced by most apologists for American imperialism and designed to cover up administration policy. . . . The Soviet Union should not interfere in the west, he said, and we should give her a free hand in eastern Europe. The entire concept is a false one. The struggle is between the aggressive Anglo-American imperialists who want to dominate the world and the democratic, antifascist, peace-loving peoples of the world. . . . The 'bi-partisan' foreign policy followed by the administration and now generally endorsed by Wallace is one of imperialist intervention." The next day's editorial was not quite as critical, but it declared that "Wallace glossed over the responsibility of American imperialist policy." [15]

The Communists were very unhappy with Wallace's speech; so was Harry Truman, as it soon developed. Two days after the speech, Truman told reporters he had not approved the speech. On September 18, Truman and Wallace had a conference, at the end of which Wallace told the press he would make no further statements or speeches on foreign policy until Secretary of State James Byrnes returned from the Paris peace conference. On September 19, Truman and Byrnes had a teletype conference, in which Byrnes said, in effect, either he or Wallace would have to resign. The next morning, Truman asked Wallace for his resignation, and Wallace readily submitted it. [16]

After Truman's September 14 statement to reporters, the *Daily Worker* staff had executed a quick about-face. The staff was in trouble with the ninth floor. In Dennis's words, "the Party leadership quickly, immediately, and unitedly overcame this particular, unpardonable mistake." [17] An editorial of September 15— five days before Wallace's resignation—was a little warmer toward Wallace. On September 16, James S. Allen hailed Wallace for refusing "to be browbeaten by the reactionaries into silence or into accepting . . . the program of encircling and isolating the Soviet Union." On September 17, a *Daily* editorial told the readers, "The labor and progressive movement . . . has the job of welcoming and supporting Wallace's initiative." Thereafter, the Communists were all out in their support of Wallace. By Christmas, few Communists remembered they had hissed him in the

Garden and in their newspaper. By Election Day in 1948, American conservatives had forgotten it, too.

From the very beginning of Communist third-party talk, there was a difference of emphasis between some of its harder, more leftist leaders, typified by Foster, "the old man," and more practical types, typified by Dennis and the *Daily Worker* staff. There appears to have been nothing even dimly suggesting a split, but Dennis and the *Daily Worker* staff were prone to emphasize a national third party in the image of the A.L.P., which would both co-operate with the liberal Democrats and pressure the Democratic Party to pursue "progressive" policies and nominate the kind of candidates the Communists might support. They were concerned lest they alienate independent liberals and labor leaders who were not ready to support an independent ticket. Foster, on the other hand, did not seem to care whether he alienated independent liberals and labor or not.

In two *Daily Worker* articles, Foster denounced "lesser evilism"—party jargon or "Communese" for the tendency, for example, for liberals to regard Truman as a lesser evil than Dewey. To Foster, a Truman was more dangerous than a Dewey precisely because he appeared more sympathetic to traditional labor aims, was more likely than a Dewey to attract the working class, but was fundamentally as committed to capitalism as a Dewey.[18]

But Dennis said the party could not afford to ignore the differences among major-party figures, and he clearly believed such Democrats as Wallace, Pepper, and Adolph Sabath were "lesser evils" than Truman. *Daily Worker* staff men declared it "a dangerous tendency" to see no difference between the Democratic and Republican candidates for governor of New York in 1946 —James M. Mead and Thomas E. Dewey.[19]

Eventually, the Russians resolved the difference in Foster's favor, as we shall see later, but until the fall of 1947, one could not be sure whether the Communists were for or against lesser evilism. After that, lesser evilism clearly was a kind of political leprosy.

Following the Democratic debacle in 1946, when the Republican Party won the Congressional elections for the first time since 1928 and swept most of the state elections, too, the differences between Foster and Dennis became even more noticeable. The Republican victory confirmed the necessity of a third party in both Foster's and Dennis's minds. Foster declared that the Democrats "will undoubtedly strive to put in the field a conservative Presidential candidate, but one with just enough liberal coloration, they hope, to fool the workers. . . . The only possible chance (a faint one at best) to get a progressive candidate from the Democratic Party leaders will be precisely by holding over their heads the threat of a new party." [20] Dennis was more sanguine. "It is possible, actually possible, for the third-party movement to facilitate the election of a progressive presidential ticket in 1948. Such a victory will be possible if this movement is so organized and broadened as to bring about a situation in which there can be a coalition candidate, backed by the independent and third-party forces, running as a Democrat." [21] Foster could agree with Dennis that the party "must move heaven and earth to create a united, progressive front . . . a coalition party," [22] but they disagreed as to whether such a party should or could pressure the Democratic Party or should declare a three-cornered race immediately.

But while Dennis and Foster preached their different emphases, there were developments on the non-Communist Left that were soon to puncture both their grandiose dreams.

NON-COMMUNISTS AND ANTI-COMMUNISM

The typical anti-Communist propagandist before the war was as much an opponent of social security or trade-unionism as of Communism. Indeed, he often thought social welfare legislation was Communism. Often as not, the anti-Communist propagandist was a superpatriot, like some of the leaders of the Daughters of the American Revolution or the American Legion. The typical anti-Communist congressman had close ties with the business community or represented a poll-tax district or both. The activity of these conservative anti-Communists, despite their intensity and shrillness, was quite ineffective. The Communist Party's strength and influence grew fastest in the late 1930's, when conservatives had the anti-Communist field almost to themselves.

The reasons for the ineffectiveness of conservative prewar anti-Communism are not difficult to discern. The primary reason was that the conservatives' anti-Communist message did not reach liberal and labor organizations, where the Communists naturally concentrated their efforts. In the organizations in which conservatives predominated, such as the D.A.R. and the Legion, Communist efforts were negligible, and in the organizations in which there was an opportunity directly to combat Communist influence, the conservative anti-Communists were without influence. The conservative anti-Communists were in no position to do any infighting against Communists; they could only swing at them from afar. Another reason for conservative failure was their usual "shotgun" technique. They did not aim truly at the Communists; they aimed at everything they considered left of center, and the center was to them a point somewhere among the conservative elements of the Democratic Party. Thus, for example, they occasionally called Roosevelt a Communist and frequently charged that Rexford Tugwell and other "brain trusters" were Kremlin agents. So many of their charges were ridiculously extreme, that many people tended to dismiss all anti-Communist criticism as the product of the Right lunatic fringe.[23]

There was one major exception to the conservative complexion of the anti-Communists—the Socialists or social democrats—and one small group of minor exceptions—the ex-Communist Party splinter groups. These Left Wing anti-Communists and their publications, especially the *Socialist Call* and the *New Leader,* provided more accurate and balanced accounts of the Communists than anything emanating from the conservatives, such as Elizabeth Dilling's *Red Network*. But they were few in number and insignificant in their national influence, and the fact that they were both anti-Communist and anticapitalist at the same time seemed unfathomable to the man in the street.

Few though they were, the Socialist critics of Communism were significant historically, for they created and kept alive an anti-Communist Left tradition, and from their nucleus was to grow after World War II a liberal anti-Communism of major proportions. From this tradition sprang the Americans for Democratic Action (A.D.A.) and the Liberal Party of New York.

In the spring of 1944, a group of social-democratic and liberal trade-unionists and intellectuals, led by David Dubinsky, president of the International Ladies Garment Workers Union and a former Socialist Party member, bolted the A.L.P., charged it with Communist domination and direction, and organized the anti-Communist Liberal Party. At first very small, despite their good poll for Roosevelt in 1944, the Liberals gained steadily in vote and influence. In the postwar decade, they became a potent force in New York politics, in some cases holding a balance of power between the major parties. The Liberal Party serves as a pressure upon the New York Democratic organization by providing independent liberal voters a "conscience line" on the ballot. It usually, but not always, nominates the Democratic ticket. As the liberals' anti-Communism increasingly gained followers, the A.L.P. went downhill and eventually died.

More important nationally was the founding of A.D.A. If one had to choose a date that represents a watershed in the recent history of American liberalism, one could do worse than to select January 4, 1947, when A.D.A. organized in Washington. From that day forward, American liberalism became increasingly anti-Communist, and this development had important effects upon the history of American Communism. One of the important factors in the Communist Party's isolation from the main stream of American life in recent years is the development of the *non*-Communist Left into the *anti*-Communist Left.

The development of liberal anti-Communism had been a slow, sometimes painful, and frequently bewildering process. Part of the style of American liberalism in the Roosevelt era was a soft-heartedness (and soft-headedness) toward the Soviet Union and an abhorrence of Red baiting. This frame of mind could not change overnight. Indeed, there are still some non-Communists with these values and assumptions. But they are comparatively few in number, and they have become fewer each year since 1945.

A brief account of recent left of center organizations will serve to describe the evolution of the division over the Communist issue in American liberalism. To begin with the political activities of the C.I.O., in July 1943, the C.I.O. executive board created the C.I.O. Political Action Committee (C.I.O.-P.A.C.), with Sidney Hillman, of the Amalgamated Clothing Workers, as chairman, to rally the labor vote for Roosevelt and other New Dealers in the 1944 elections. The following summer, the C.I.O.-P.A.C. set up the National Citizens Political Action Committee (N.C.-P.A.C.) to raise funds and mobilize liberals outside the trade unions, largely from the kind of people who in 1952 became known as "eggheads." Although originally intended to be only a temporary operation, the N.C.-P.A.C. decided in the spring of 1945 to become permanent and loosen its ties with the C.I.O.-P.A.C. Elmer Benson, former governor of Minnesota, became national chairman, and C. B. ("Beanie") Baldwin, who had served with Wallace in the Department of Agriculture, became executive secretary. Until 1947 and 1948, people with all sorts of political convictions were in the C.I.O.-P.A.C. and the N.C.-P.A.C. There were outright Communists, pro-Communists, liberals neutral on the Communist issue, mild anti-Communist liberals, and vigorously anti-Communist socialists of various kinds. Within the C.I.O.-P.A.C., the Communists were no more important than they were in the C.I.O. itself—a noisy and sizable minority—but Communist influence in the N.C.-P.A.C. was greater. Earl Browder had said that Minnesota's Communists worked closely with Benson in that state's politics,[24] and Baldwin remained as a top official in the Progressive Party after 1950, when almost all who were not Communists or fellow travelers had left the organization.

There was still another of the Left and labor political groups, the Independent Citizens' Committee of the Arts, Sciences, and Professions (I.C.C.A.S.P.), one of the strangest groups in the history of American politics. Founded to provide money and glamour for the cause of Roosevelt's 1944 candidacy, the I.C.C.-A.S.P. was filled with Broadway and Hollywood people and professional artists and writers; it could claim a record among political organizations for physical beauty, creative talent—and for political innocence. The political thought processes of the late Hollywood actor Humphrey Bogart are a case in point. In 1946, Bogart told a *Time* reporter he had joined I.C.C.A.S.P. because he had voted for Roosevelt in 1944 and wanted Harold Stassen for president in 1948. But if some of the members were babes in the political woods, the leaders were not. They knew precisely what they were doing. In 1946, a few members complained that the organization was rapidly becoming a Communist front. When a reporter asked I.C.C.A.S.P.'s chairman, the sculptor Jo Davidson, if this charge were true, Davidson replied, "Have you stopped beating your wife?" When Hannah Dorner, the executive secretary of the organization, who affectionately called the members "glamour pusses," was asked the same question, her reply was revealing: "Says who and so what? If the ICCASP program is like the Communist line, that is purely coincidental." [25]

Soon after Secretary of the Interior Harold Ickes resigned in February 1946, because Truman nominated oilman Edwin W. Pauley to be under-secretary of the Navy, he became executive chairman of I.C.C.A.S.P. The "Old Curmudgeon" was less than happy with his new associates, but it is significant that in 1946 I.C.C.A.S.P. could attract someone of his stature at all. He tried to resign in August, but was persuaded to remain until the 1946 elections. He quit very soon after the elections, but not before one final insulting frustration. Ickes had given a speech at Chicago in which he had said that the Soviet Union was creating international tension. The sponsors of the meeting found their mimeograph machine had conveniently broken down, and Ickes's speech was not distributed to the press. After leaving I.C.C.A.S.P., Ickes called Communism "a nonassimilable political ideology. A true progressive movement has no chance of success unless it rigidly excludes communists." [26]

On December 29, 1946, the N.C.-P.A.C. and the I.C.C.A.S.P. merged to become the Progressive Citizens of America (P.C.A.). The P.C.A. clearly was bent on a third party from its first meeting. Wallace spoke at the first meeting, and although he was still publicly committed to the Democratic Party and had campaigned for a few Democratic candidates in the recent elections, he told the new organization, to its delight, "We have less use for a conservative, high-tariff Democratic Party than we have for a reactionary, high-tariff Republican Party. If need be we shall first fight one and then the other." But when Wallace said, "We should have no allegiances outside this country," the audience was noticeably cool. The preamble of the P.C.A.'s program raised the question of a new party: "We cannot . . . rule out the possibility of a new political party. . . . We, the people, will not wait forever—we will not wait long for the Democratic Party to make its choice." And it did not wait long—exactly one year—before the P.C.A., with its claimed 36,500 members (18,000 from the N.C.-P.A.C., 18,500 from the I.C.C.A.S.P.), became the nucleus of the Progressive Party. The P.C.A.'s cochairmen were the former heads of the merged organizations, Dr. Frank Kingdon and Jo Davidson, but the executive vice-chairman, the man who actually ran things, was "Beanie" Baldwin, later Wallace's campaign manager.[27]

The division among liberals over the Communist issue was becoming sharper. In early 1946, the struggle between the Reuther and Communist caucuses in the U.A.W. was in the nation's headlines. The same year saw a fight between Joe Curran and the party in the N.M.U. In November 1946, the C.I.O. adopted its "resent and reject" resolution, and state C.I.O. organizations here and there went much further. The New Jersey C.I.O. convention adopted by overwhelming vote a strong anti-Communist resolution, and the Massachusetts organization banned Communists from its offices.[28]

A National Conference of Progressives held at Chicago in September 1946 indicated two simultaneous trends in the liberal community: liberals were disappointed with the Truman administration and the alliance of northern Republicans and Southern Democrats in the Seventy-ninth Congress and were eager to revive the New Deal spirit; and they were becoming increasingly divided over the question of Communism, both at home and abroad.

The Chicago conference embraced a wide range of political and economic opinion. The C.I.O.-P.A.C., the N.C.-P.A.C., and the I.C.C.A.S.P. issued the call to the conference, which was signed also by Philip Murray, James Patton, of the National Farmers' Union, Walter White, of the N.A.A.C.P., A. F. Whitney, of the Railroad Trainmen, and Clark Foreman of the Southern Conference for Human Welfare. Among others involved in the conference were Hannah Dorner, Henry Morgenthau, Jacob Potofsky, of the Amalgamated Clothing Workers, the vigorously anti-Communist C.I.O. Secretary-Treasurer James Carey, and pro-Communist John Abt. A few months later, one would wonder that such a diverse collection ever could have assembled in the same room. But a common anxiety about the way affairs were going in Washington pulled them together. It must be remembered that it was not until mid-1947 that Truman appeared as a champion of liberalism, after a Republican Congress afforded him a conservative backdrop. The Democratic record on price control and inflation had been poor, housing was a mess, and Truman had even asked Congress for power to draft strikers in government-seized industries into the armed forces. In 1946, it seemed to the liberals that Truman would undo everything Roosevelt had gained.

If a common anxiety pulled the conference delegates to Chicago, the Communist issue blocked their unity. Angus Cameron, then of the publishing firm of Little, Brown and later to become an independent publisher of leftist books, moved that the conference go on record urging Henry Wallace to carry on his fight. The Wallace-Truman dispute was contemporaneous with the conference. The motion passed unanimously. No one moved that the conference declare itself for a third party, for third-party advocates knew that to raise the issue would only divide the group. The Communist issue could not be suppressed despite efforts to do so. Phil Murray departed from his prepared text in his speech to say he did not want any "damn American Communists meddling in our affairs."

Murray personified the confusion of liberals on the Communist issue. His course toward anti-Communism was hesitant and painful. After his Chicago remark, he disclaimed to reporters any intention of a Communist purge in the C.I.O. Yet in a few weeks, he raised the Communist question at the C.I.O. convention and pushed through the "resent and reject" resolution. And a few weeks after that he appeared to change direction again when he requested C.I.O. officers to join neither the P.C.A. nor A.D.A. Even in 1948, when he eased Lee Pressman out of the C.I.O., he arranged for Pressman to get a lesser job.

Confused as the picture was, the differences among liberals were sharpening quickly. The Chicago conference was the last major gathering of pro- and anti-Communist liberals. The Chicago meeting appointed a "Continuations Committee" to give the conference the semblance of permanence and to call a second conference in January 1947. A second conference never materialized. By January 1947, the split in American liberalism had taken organizational form with the establishment of the P.C.A. at the end of December and the founding of A.D.A. the next week.

A.D.A.'s origins trace directly to the social-democratic anti-Communism of the prewar period. In May 1941, a group of social-democratic and liberal intellectuals organized the Union for Democratic Action. U.D.A.'s first chairman was the theologian Reinhold Niebuhr, a former Socialist Party member, and its first executive secretary was James Loeb, Jr. U.D.A. never represented more than a handful of people, and in the spring of 1946, Loeb proposed that U.D.A. sponsor a conference aimed at broadening the organization. From Loeb's proposal and U.D.A.'s support came A.D.A., progressive and as opposed to Communists as to any other totalitarians.

Many liberals, most of them Democrats, were ready to join with those who believed in a socialist democracy and in a progressive anti-Communist movement. When U.D.A. called its conference, after first carefully seeing that no Communists or pro-Communists received invitations, many of the "big names" of American liberalism responded. In the new A.D.A. were such labor leaders as David Dubinsky, Walter Reuther, James Carey, George Baldanzi, and Emil Rieve. Among former New Dealers were Eleanor Roosevelt, Leon Henderson, Wilson Wyatt, and Paul A. Porter. Several young Democratic politicians, such as Hubert Humphrey, Franklin D. Roosevelt, Jr., and Richardson Dilworth, all soon to make their marks in politics, attended the meeting. Among the intellectuals were Reinhold Niebuhr, Elmer Davis, Bishop William Scarlett, Stewart Alsop, Robert Bendiner, Marquis Childs, Morris Ernst, A. Powell Davies, Louis Fischer, John Kenneth Galbraith, Saul Padover, Arthur M. Schlesinger, Jr., and James A. Wechsler.[29]

The Communists perceived the danger to them should A.D.A. and its kind of thinking grow, and their attack was immediate. Their first argument was to deny that, by definition, it was possible to be both liberal and anti-Communist. When this failed to impress many, they fell back upon their hoary devil-conspiracy theory. The whole thing was a "social democratic plot," instigated by "Wall Street" to prepare the way for "fascism." By citing the affiliation to A.D.A. of such people as Dubinsky and Professor George S. Counts, they claimed to document an association of A.D.A. "with the top reactionaries of the country." Dubinsky and Counts were no less than "Red-baiting Loreleis trying to lure liberals into reaction's swamp." [30] The Communists persuaded few. A.D.A. grew, and Left anti-Communism gained steadily.

The Communist Party set itself two main tasks in 1947, to be accomplished simultaneously. It had, first, to build a third-party movement; and, second, to persuade Henry Wallace to accept the leadership of the new party. At both tasks the Communists were successful.

Foster kicked off the 1947 program: "The Communist Party, which played an important role in the events leading up to the big C.P.P.A. campaign [one of many historical distortions about the 1924 La Follette movement in his *Political Affairs* article], must play a much more important one in the 1948 political struggle and in the building of the third party. . . . We must . . . make the question of building the new party our major task and leave no stone unturned for its realization." The job would not be easy, but it could be accomplished if "We . . . master every detail of the complicated general strategy and tactics necessary to lay the foundations for victory and the new party in 1948." [31]

The difference between Foster and Dennis over whether the third party should be a third ticket or a lever against the Democratic Party remained until later in the year, and in the summer of 1947, the Communists played a rather tricky double game. The Communists were fearful that if they pushed the third-party idea too hard in New York they might split the A.L.P., which still contained the Amalgamated Clothing Workers and other C.I.O. elements with primary political loyalty to the Democratic Party. So, as Robert Thompson explained they must, [32] the Communists played the third-party tune softly in New York, never saying more than that the A.L.P. should strengthen itself as a lever on the Democrats, saying nothing about an independent third Presidential candidacy. Simon Gerson explained the whole strategy after the critical A.L.P. county conventions and state C.I.O. convention were over. "Within the A.L.P. and the progressive labor movement in New York there are people who wholeheartedly support the principle of a third party but are not convinced about the necessity for a third ticket now. It was this central issue that had to be resolved if the unity of both the A.L.P. and . . . the State C.I.O. was to be maintained. . . . How was it resolved? By the two groups—the pro-third ticket forces and those who favored a third party but not a third ticket in 1948—agreeing on the necessity of building the A.L.P. as labor's political arm in New York while deferring for future consideration the question of a third ticket. It was on the basis of this policy that the A.L.P. county organizations remained united . . . [which] would have been impossible had the Wallace-for-President issue been placed before the convention for a vote." [33]

In California that summer, the Communists played a different game. While New York Communists lay low on the issue, California's Communists went all out. New York had the A.L.P., but California had no counterpart to it. The Communist task was to create a new party so that it could either pressure the Democratic Party from the outside, consistent with Dennis's emphasis, or strike out on its own as a third ticket, as Foster desired.

The convention of the Marine Cooks and Stewards at San Francisco passed a resolution calling for the establishment of a national third party, and Hugh Bryson, the M.C.S. president, circulated unions all over the country urging similar action. Communists and other "left progressives," including many on the staff of the Bridges union, tried to get their policies adopted first by the California Democratic committee meeting in late July, but they failed utterly. In fact, the Democratic statement on foreign policy equated Communism with fascism, called for a strong military-defense program, and endorsed the Truman Doctrine and the Marshall Plan. After this defeat, Bryson, later to be convicted for perjury for swearing in a Taft-Hartley affidavit that he was not a Communist, issued a call for a conference to be held in Los Angeles on August 24.

This conference, composed mostly of California Left union

leaders, a few Left Wing Democrats, and some followers of the Townsend old-age pension plan, including old Dr. Francis E. Townsend himself, listened to Bryson harangue against Truman's foreign policy. After a great deal of vacillation in the Townsend group, the conference declared itself the founding convention of the Independent Progressive Party (I.P.P.). California had the equivalent of the New York A.L.P. Bryson held the office of organizer and temporary chairman. He brought Elinor Kahn, who had been a lobbyist for the maritime unions, back from the East to be the state director when he moved up to be permanent chairman.[34]

Getting the I.P.P. on the California ballot was a difficult matter. California law required about 300,000 signatures to a petition, and gathering signatures became the I.P.P.'s first item of business. Foster and Pete Cacchione went to California to help out their West Coast comrades, and with hard work and thorough organization, the necessary signatures were obtained. As Foster put it, "Comrades, that was a major achievement." [35]

Things were progressing well for the Communists. The third-party program was on schedule. As late as September 1947, the plan was still to use a third party as a lever against the Democratic Party. In fact, Cacchione and Vito Marcantonio talked about a fight in the Democratic primaries and state conventions for Wallace delegates to the 1948 Democratic national convention.[36] Near the end of the month, the *Worker* published excerpts from a speech Dennis had given at Madison Square Garden earlier in September. "We Communists are not adventurers and irresponsible sectarians. We are not going to isolate ourselves. We never did and do not now favor the launching of premature and unrepresentative third parties or independent tickets. Such moves can only succeed and serve the camp of progress when they arise out of the collective decision and united action of a broad democratic and anti-war coalition." [37]

Such a tone from a Communist leader would not be heard again for a long time. For at that moment, Russian Communists were laying down a new line which the American Communists would note and then press ahead for Wallace's independent candidacy. The Russians appeared to support Foster's point of view. The changed emphasis of the party in the fall of 1947 is one of the clearest examples in the postwar period of the American Communists following the Russian lead, even when the American Communists themselves recognized the disastrous effect the Russian direction could have on their own party. "We are not going to isolate ourselves," said Dennis just before the news came of the formation of the Cominform. But we did isolate ourselves, Dennis would tell the party membership nine years later, and Dennis admitted that one of the major factors in the party's isolation was its 1948 electoral policy.[38]

THE RUSSIANS, THE COMINFORM, AND AMERICAN POLITICS

On October 5, 1947, *Pravda* revealed that at the end of the previous month there had been a secret conference in Poland of representatives of the Communist parties of nine European nations. The Russian leaders at the meeting were Andrei A. Zhdanov and Georgi M. Malenkov, both of whom were very close to Stalin. Others were Milovan Djilas and Edward Kardelj from Yugoslavia, Vulko Chervenkov and V. Poptomov from Bulgaria, Anna Pauker and George Gheorgiu-Dej from Romania, M. Farkasz and Joseph Revai from Hungary, Wladyslaw Gomulka and H. Minc from Poland, Jacques Duclos and Etienne Fajon from France, Rudolf Slansky and S. Basztovanski from Czechoslovakia, and Luigi Longo and Eugenio Reale from Italy. The subsequent careers of these delegates reflect much of the recent history of international Communism, and another meeting of those still alive today would be an interesting event. But in 1947, they listened united to a speech by Zhdanov, next to Stalin probably the strongest figure in the Russian party.

The precise content of Zhdanov's speech did not become known to the rest of the world until *Pravda* published it on October 22, but on October 5, *Pravda* published the texts of the resolutions adopted at the meeting in Poland. When Zhdanov's speech appeared, it was obvious that the resolutions were no more than a condensation of his speech; they even lifted some of his phrases word for word.[39]

The conference of the nine Communist parties was to have the greatest importance for the development of international Communism—indeed, for the history of the world—for the next few years. The conference established the Communist Information Bureau, or Cominform, composed of the parties represented at the conference. The Cominform's headquarters were in Belgrade until the Tito blowup in 1948, and then in Bucharest. Its establishment symbolized a new direction in world Communism. When the Comintern dissolved in 1943, the Communist parties of the world, at least ostensibly, had been cut loose from Russian direction. That the tie was not actually severed is indicated by, among other things, Browder's removal from leadership in 1945 upon orders from abroad. But with the Cominform's establishment, the "road to socialism" to be followed by the Communists of various nations was to be the one indicated on the Russians' ideological maps.

One of the Cominform's immediate purposes was the defeat of the Marshall Plan. The conference's manifesto declared that "the imperialist camp and its directing force, the United States of America, show a growing aggressive activity. . . . The Truman-Marshall plan is only a farce, a European branch of the general world plan of political expansion being realized by the United States of America in all parts of the world. The plan of . . . subjugation of Europe through American imperialism is complemented by plans for the subjugation of China, Indonesia, and South America." Therefore, the Communist parties of the world were to "place themselves in the vanguard of the Opposition against the imperialistic plans of expansion and aggression in all its manifestations." Zhdanov was even more explicit: "A special task devolves upon the fraternal Communist Parties of France, Italy, England and other countries."

The Communist parties of Western Europe were quick to execute the order. The Paris Communist newspaper, *L'Humanité*, fairly bristled with references to *"l'impérialisme américain."* [40] The French and Italian parties conducted several strikes over the next several months in an effort to hamper the economic recovery of their nations and prevent beneficial effects from the European Recovery Program.

Much weaker than their European comrades, the American Communists also did what they could to effect the same ends. They spurred on the third-party movement, gained effective control of it, and used it in an attempt to provide propaganda for overseas anti-Americanism. Foreign Communists could point to the American third party and assert that the United States was not united behind the Marshall Plan and the rest of American foreign policy, that American policy was only the result of insidious Wall Street machination.

With the publication of the texts of the conference's resolutions, the American Communists determined to push ahead with a third-party ticket, as distinct from just a third party, come what may. The conference manifesto had a clear meaning on East Twelfth Street: "In consequence the Communist parties should . . . unite and coordinate their efforts on the basis of a common anti-imperialistic and democratic platform as well as gather around themselves all democratic and patriotic forces in their respective nations." The manifesto also declared, "The main danger for the working class at this moment lies in the underestimation of its own strength and overestimation of the force of the imperialist camp." Zhdanov was equally clear and pertinent to the American Communists: "Communists should be the leading force in the cause of drawing all anti-fascist, freedom-loving elements into the struggle against the new American expansionist plans for the enslavement of Europe." [41] Within the American framework, this could only mean a third party with a third ticket.

The American Communists understood the meaning. The issue of the *Daily Worker* that carried the text of the Cominform resolutions declared in an editorial on the formation of the Cominform that "every American who is fighting mad at the profiteering trusts here at home" should welcome "this overseas resistance to the same crowd which is rooking him and his family and trying to wreck his unions and democratic liberties. . . . The nation urgently needs a strong anti-monopoly, anti-war coalition based on the Roosevelt-Wallace line." [42]

For another two weeks, the party leadership held off from revealing to anyone, even its most trusted followers in the C.I.O., that it had determined for a third ticket as well as a third party. The reason for the delay was that revelation of the plans might endanger the Communist position in the C.I.O., which was to meet in its annual convention in Boston October 13 to 17. If one of the Communist C.I.O. leaders knew of the decision, he might inadvertently reveal too much at the convention and touch off an anti-Communist explosion. The tactic worked well. Although Secretary of State Marshall addressed the C.I.O. convention, and Murray personally favored the Marshall Plan, the C.I.O. Left managed to prevent the C.I.O. resolution on foreign policy from supporting the plan explicitly. Furthermore, the Communists at the convention prevented the question of reaffirming the previous year's "resent and reject resolution" from even being raised. [43]

The day after the Boston convention, the Left union leaders in the C.I.O. had the new line on the third ticket explained to them at a meeting in New York City. In 1950, Mike Quill, who had broken with the party in early 1948, told the details of this meeting to a C.I.O. committee in Washington when the C.I.O. was about to expel the Bridges union:

> On Saturday, October 18th, 1947, the day after the [CIO] convention closed in Boston, I attended a meeting with Harry Bridges and Eugene Dennis, the General Secretary of the Communist Party, and John Williamson, Robert Thompson, the State Chairman of the Communist Party, and several others at the headquarters of the Interna-

tional Workers Order on 5th Avenue, New York City. There Eugene Dennis told us in very blunt language to disregard everything that happened at the CIO convention in Boston, and he especially said to disregard the Political Action resolution because the national leaders . . . have decided to form a Third Party led by Henry Wallace, and that Wallace would come out in the next few weeks and announce that he was a candidate for President of the United States on the Third Party ticket. The Communist Party was asking all the left-wing controlled unions to start to petition and campaign now, to start the publicity, to line up endorsements for Wallace as soon as he announced himself on the radio. . . . There was no use trying to reason with Eugene Dennis. He was going through. So I discussed it with Gerhart Eisler, and Eisler told me it was in the best interests of the Soviet bloc that the Third Party should be headed by Wallace and made it very clear to me that that was the only reason why the Third Party ticket was gotten up.

There were no lawyers at this C.I.O. hearing to determine whether or not the Bridges union should be expelled for Communist domination, although the witnesses were sworn, and Bridges himself was soon given the opportunity to cross-examine Quill. The result was real drama, Quill insisting in his Irish brogue upon the veracity of his testimony, and Bridges, curiously never directly denying it, playing innocent and trying to get Quill to contradict himself:

Q. [Bridges] Is it true you testified that at that meeting Dennis, Williamson, Robertson [of the Bridges union] and several others gave instructions to disregard the entire program of the CIO convention, at least the political program?
A. [Quill] That's correct. Dennis gave the instructions.
Q. Did he only mean the political program or was there additional phases?
A. There was other items came up. . . .
Q. You couldn't be mistaken on that meeting?
A. No, I couldn't, Harry. That was something that stuck in my mind.
Q. I see. Couldn't be anywhere else or any other date? It couldn't be another year or something like that, could it?
A. No, it couldn't. It was in the afternoon of Saturday October

18th, and the God damned thing dragged out until late at night. I never heard so much talk in my life at one meeting.

Q. How did you get to the meeting?

A. I was invited there.

Q. By whom?

A. By Williamson before I left Boston.

Q. Did you invite anyone else there?

A. No.

Q. Do you recall who else was there outside of you and I, Williamson, Dennis, Bob Thompson?

A. Oh, sure I can.

Q. Let's see how many you can recall.

A. Matles, Emspak [both of the U.E.]—that fellow that screwed up the strike in the Packinghouse. What was his name? Herbert Marsh. He was there. Jim Durkin; Selly; another representative of the Communist Party, Hal Simon.

Q. Who?

A. Hal Simon. He was from UE.

Q. S-i-m-o-n?

A. Yes. I believe that's the way you spell it.

Q. Anyone else?

A. Arthur Osman; Gold and Potash and Abe Feinglass from Chicago, I don't remember any more.

Q. But there were more, you think?

A. Yes, there was. It was a big room.

Q. Do you remember anything else that was decided or on which instructions were given outside of the one thing you have mentioned?

A. No, the big thing was Wallace. I don't remember anything else.

Q. It was the program of Wallace?

A. Yes. . . .

Q. Was there any discussion of how it was to be carried out or anything like that?

A. Oh, there was a tremendous amount of discussion about setting up a labor committee of CIO and A.F. of L., getting the petition campaign carried on, getting radio time, getting the unions on record as far as possible behind them. It took a long, long time.

At another point in the cross-examination, Quill said that at the meeting "Williamson came to me and said, 'This is ours; we created it; get busy and support it.' " [44]

At the same time that the Left trade-unionists were getting the new line at I.W.O. headquarters, six hundred Communist leaders from the East and South were similarly instructed at a meeting elsewhere in the city. At this latter meeting, Henry Winston and Foster gave the new line on the third ticket.[45] The following Monday, Foster spoke on "The Meaning of the 9-Party Conference" at a well-advertised meeting at New York's Manhattan Center. He attacked the Marshall Plan, hailed the formation of the Cominform, and concluded by saying that it was time for the American Left to "open its eyes politically, unite its split forces, cleanse its ranks of Hitler-like red-baiting, cut loose from the leading strings of the Democratic and Republican Parties, and launch a great mass, anti-monopoly, progressive peace party of its own." [46]

Gone now was all thought of trying to pressure the Democratic Party into the kind of program and candidate the Communists wanted. Gone now was all idea of an A.L.P. kind of party on a national scale. An independent third ticket was now the order of the day.

The Communists' next immediate goal was to persuade Henry Wallace to declare himself an independent candidate for the Presidency of the United States. October 1947 would have been a most appropriate time for Wallace to have strengthened his ideological defenses, but, to his eventual regret, he did not.

PERSUADING HENRY WALLACE

To understand the relations of Henry Wallace and the Communists, some things about Wallace the man, one of the most puzzling figures in twentieth-century American politics, must be understood. A man of peace, he became a world figure as vice-president of a nation at war. He had a rural background and was interested primarily in agricultural problems, but his support during and after World War II came mostly from urban people. A man who became embroiled in intense political conflicts, he shrank from personal battles and tried to ignore, or forestall, or compromise strife about him. Of all Roosevelt's cabinet members, he became the symbol of radicalism, to both his friends and his opponents, yet he actually did relatively little to warrant the reputation. A man whose fame was established by his rhetoric, he was, however, quite awkward and wooden on the public platform. Strongly committed personally to a Keynesian "progressive capitalism," he became a manipulated instrument of the Communists, to whom Keynesian economic thought was anathema and to whom "progressive capitalism" was a contradiction in terms. Widely considered, with some justification, as an impractical dreamer and even a mystic, he was intensely interested in the practical and mundane subject of hybrid corn and other utilitarian genetic experiments. A cabinet member for nearly a decade and vice-president for four years, he was still remarkably innocent of American political realities and of the ways of people seeking their ends through political activity.

Henry Wallace was no Communist, and he was not sympathetic to the Communists' basic aims. But he was a relatively easy mark for the Communists. They were able to manipulate him for several reasons: he was astonishingly unknowing about Left Wing politics and methods; he was devoted to the cause of peace and sincerely believed the Truman administration to be headed toward war; and he had in his intellectual baggage many of the beliefs of liberals during the Popular Front period, particularly a fear of being charged with Red baiting, which he could not discard as easily as did many other liberals when international and domestic conditions changed after the war. Furthermore, Wallace was himself so lacking in Machiavellism that he found it difficult to recognize duplicity in others. He was a likely victim for political "con men."

Wallace's lack of knowledge about the Left often led him to make poor judgments. When he endorsed Johannes Steel's candidacy in early 1946, an action that he conceded a decade later had been unwise, he did so because he thought Steel had been an effective anti-Nazi in his radio broadcasts. He did not know that Steel's Democratic opponent had previously served in Congress and had a good New Deal voting record. He did not know that Steel was a columnist for the *Daily People's World,* and, indeed, he had only the vaguest idea of that newspaper's nature.[47]

When conversation turned to practical politics, Wallace was prone to let his mind wander to some other subject, perhaps to agriculture. Michael Straight, publisher of the *New Republic,* tells a story of a meeting of Wallace advisers with Wallace in Straight's home in the early fall of 1947. A sharp argument developed between Straight and "Beanie" Baldwin over a critical detail of organization, and in the exchange Straight took the position that if the Wallace camp could not gain better trade-union support than it had, it would fail dismally. When Straight turned to Wallace to see which side of the argument he was taking, he saw that Wallace, who had not seemed tired when the meeting began, had fallen into a sound sleep.[48] With such disinterest in, even distaste for, practical politics, Wallace was dangerously naïve.

In December 1946, Wallace became editor of the *New Republic,* then published in New York. He wrote a weekly column with the aid of an assistant, and lent his prestige to the magazine, but his position was actually more honorific than functional. The *New Republic* presented Wallace a stage on which to play the role of liberal public figure.

In March 1947, Wallace first hinted broadly that he had a third party in the back of his mind. In a speech at Garden City, Long Island, he recalled that liberals under Wilson had succeeded in winning the Democratic nomination in 1912, but that Theodore Roosevelt that year had not won the Republican nomination and had bolted the G.O.P. to run on an independent ticket. He concluded his brief review of political history with the sentence, "Liberals wonder which of these experiences will be repeated today." In May, he told newsmen at Olympia, Washington, that he would lead a third ticket if he thought doing so would help prevent war.[49]

Through the spring and summer of 1947, however, Wallace's

emphasis was on working within the Democratic Party rather than on forming a new party. After he returned from his highly publicized and criticized trip to England and the Continent in the spring, during which Congressman J. Parnell Thomas urged that Wallace be indicted under the Logan Act of 1799 for activities abroad contrary to the American national interest, Wallace and his advisers made a long trip throughout the United States. On this trip, made after the announcement of the Truman Doctrine but before the Marshall Plan proposal and Truman's veto of the Taft-Hartley Act, Wallace spoke to large and enthusiastic audiences. His aide "Beanie" Baldwin was active during the tour trying to line up local Democratic leaders sympathetic to Wallace, or at least opposed to Truman, and at the end of the trip, he thought he had about 120 votes for Wallace for the 1948 Democratic convention.[50] As late as September 1947, Wallace said publicly he would continue fighting within the Democratic Party to "prevent it from committing suicide," but he warned that if the Democrats continued in their present direction "the people must have a new party of liberty and peace."[51]

One cannot but wonder how much the Communists influenced his public statements. Wallace, like most other active figures in politics, relied heavily on ghost writers, increasingly so in 1948 when he was giving as many as a dozen speeches a day. From early 1947 until just before the 1948 elections, Wallace's principal ghost writer was Lewis Frank, Jr. Michael Straight brought Lew Frank and Wallace together, an act that he was soon to regret. Frank, a personable and likable young man in his late twenties, the son of a well-to-do Detroit manufacturer, had been Sidney Hillman's protégé in the New York N.C.-P.A.C., and to Straight that was recommendation enough. Straight had also known Frank in the American Veterans Committee, which was then having a sharp internal fight between Communist and anti-Communist factions. Frank had been among the Left-Wingers in A.V.C. battles and had led the pro-Communist caucus at the Michigan A.V.C. convention in the fall of 1946. Straight then thought him to be an independent leftist, not unsympathetic to the Communists but not under their discipline. In the A.V.C.'s bitter struggles, Frank aligned himself clearly with the Communist caucus in the organization's national planning committee.[52] Wallace did not then and does not now suspect Frank of being a Communist, but he was never fully comfortable in his relationship with him. In retrospect, he disapproves as "too extreme" many things Frank wrote into his speeches.[53] James A. Wechsler, now editor of the New York *Post,* who traveled with the Wallace campaign party for ten months in 1948, reported that Wallace's extemporaneous speeches to small groups were quite different in tone and content from his prepared addresses for large meetings, a fact that underlines the critical role that Frank and other speech writers played.[54]

Wallace certainly was not careful to protect himself from Communist influence, either direct or indirect. Indeed, he almost made it a principle not to ascertain if any person were Communist. Michael Straight had conversations with Wallace about the fight over the Communist issue in A.V.C. In these talks Wallace disapproved of an organization's trying to keep out Communist individuals, because such a policy would necessarily involve investigation into each individual's beliefs.[55] Wallace's responses to newsmen's questions revealed his attitude toward relations with Communists. In May 1947, in response to a query if he would accept the support of known Communists, he said, "Anyone who will work for peace is okay with me. . . . Folks have found out they don't have to be scared of the word 'communism.' We've seen folks smeared and called red. This word 'communism,' this word 'red,' seems to lose its terror." When asked if the Communists were attempting to overthrow the government, Wallace replied, "I'm no expert on the Communist Party. But the Communists I've met have been very good Americans." And in December 1947, he told a meeting of U.E. shop stewards, "I am not following their [the Comunists'] line. If they want to follow my line I say God bless 'em. I admire their utter devotion to a cause they think is just." [56]

The Communists responded warmly. May Day marchers in 1947 carried a fifty-foot photograph of Wallace through New York's streets. Speaker after speaker at the I.W.O. national convention praised Wallace, and the delegates responded with applause.[57]

Wallace also had many admirers who were not Communists or fellow travelers by any stretch of imagination. Wallace's popularity was a function of Truman's unpopularity, and Truman was a very unpopular president in early 1947. Millions of people who voted for Truman in November 1948 disapproved of him early the previous year. Thousands who later approved of the Marshall Plan denounced the Truman Doctrine, and Truman's first domestic policies compared badly with what people remembered of the ferment of the New Deal era. In the spring of 1947, a P.C.A. official in Chicago made a tour of downstate Illinois to sound out Wallace sentiment among local trade-union leaders of both the A.F. of L. and the C.I.O. His wishes may have biased his findings, but he reported, "People whom we have considered to be 'conservative' trade unionists tell me that if their choice in 1948 is between Truman and a Republican, they just would not vote. They indicated . . . that if Mr. Wallace is ever ready to declare himself, they would support him." [58] Anti-Wallace observers reported similar conditions. In the early summer of 1947, James Loeb, Jr., of A.D.A., reported to his organization after a trip through the West. Many liberals, he said, who were quite opposed to Wallace's position on many issues were supporting him anyway because they regarded him as a symbol of opposition to reaction, which they felt was growing rapidly. He further reported considerable dissatisfaction with the Truman Doctrine.[59]

And the idea of a third party was clearly in the minds of many who were not Communists or pro-Communists. As early as December 1945, some Socialist leaders had discussed the possibility of a labor party to regroup liberals and laboring men who had supported Roosevelt. The Socialist discussion brought consternation among the Communists, who thought the Socialists were preempting their own domain. The Socialists thought there was not enough mass support for such a party and let the matter drop.[60] By mid-1947, however, third-party sentiment had grown considerably. For example, in June, sixty-seven Northwestern University professors addressed an open letter to Wallace urging him to form and lead a third party. They based their plea on the premise that Truman was betraying the Roosevelt tradition, and certainly Truman was not yet the "give-'em-hell Harry" he was to become the next year.[61] As late as April 1948, the anti-Wallace editor of the *Progressive,* Morris H. Rubin, wrote, "Much as I hate to admit it, I must say that there are tens of thousands of good American progressives who aren't even faintly fellow-travelers who are lined up with Wallace." He divided these Wallace followers into four categories: liberals who find "peace of mind in any haven that doesn't belong to the major parties"; pacifists; Wallace's personal partisans; and those who were thoroughly disgusted with Truman but could not bring themselves to vote Republican.[62]

The story of Truman's gaining the confidence of the American people, particularly of the liberals, is one of the most exciting chapters of recent political history. His popularity began to grow in June 1947, the month of Marshall's Harvard commencement address and his vigorous, but overridden, veto of the Taft-Hartley Act. From that month until Election Day, eighteen months later, Truman's popularity grew steadily. And as Truman's stock rose among former F.D.R. supporters, Wallace's declined.

After the announcement of the formation of the Cominform in October 1947, the Communists intensified their pressure on Wallace, and now their object was to get him to announce his independent candidacy. Wallace slowly yielded. He had told a Labor Day audience at Detroit that his main purpose was to keep Truman from having a "blank check" from liberals. And after a speech in mid-October in which he charged that Secretary of Defense James Forrestal "and others in the Truman cabinet" constituted a "war party" leading America to destruction, he replied when asked his party affiliation, "I'm a Democrat." He predicted, however, that if Truman received his party's nomination, he would not carry ten states.[63]

Wallace moved closer and closer to a clear announcement of third-party intentions after the C.I.O. convention. In early November, he told a visiting delegation of Italian Communist women, led by Mrs. Palmiro Togliatti, that a third party would be formed "if the peace requires it." In early December, he told Cornell University students that "if it is apparent that the Democratic Party is a war party, I shall do all I can to see that there is a third party." Two days later, he said that the "people must have a choice between progress and reaction." [64] Wallace was beginning to respond to thoroughly manipulated pressure from the Communists.

Throughout the fall of 1947, delegates from Communist Party fronts and Left-led unions called upon Wallace at the *New Republic*'s offices. In the words of the magazine's publisher, "there were steady deputations led in to see Henry. Phil Murray would criticise the Third Party—on the following day a 'rank and file' delegation from some painters or auto workers local in New York or New Jersey would troop in to tell Henry that Murray did not speak for the membership." Another *New Republic* editor complained that the offices were "like Grand Central station." Wallace's anteroom frequently overflowed into the hall.[65] One group from New Jersey that came to Wallace to urge him to run was typical. It was headed by the non-Communist pacifist James Imbrie, chairman of the New Jersey Independent Citizen's League. Also in the delegation were a non-Communist publisher and a Baptist minister. But others in the group were the secretary of the American Slav Congress of Greater Newark, and local officers of Mine, Mill, C.I.O. Packinghouse, and U.E. Wallace told these groups he would run if he thought he could get three million votes on the peace issue.[66]

The problem for the Communists, then, was to persuade Wallace that he would receive strong support. In the fall of 1947—before the Soviet coup in Czechoslovakia, before the Berlin blockade, before the antics of the Communists at the Progressive Party convention, before Truman's aggressively liberal 1948 campaign—it was not difficult to convince Wallace that he had three million supporters, for at that time he probably had a great many more. If Wallace could have run for the Presidency a year earlier, he undoubtedly would have polled a much better vote than he did.

In the Chicago judicial elections in November 1947, a new local Progressive Party received a substantial vote. Twenty-one judgeships on the Cook County Superior Court were up for election. Of the approximately 700,000 votes cast, 113,000 were straight Progressive, and one Progressive candidate, Professor Homer F. Carey, of the Northwestern University Law School, received 313,000. The Communists were greatly excited by the election—3RD PARTY VOTE ROCKS CHICAGO, POLITICOS STUNNED was a *Daily Worker* headline on November 6—but actually the significance of the Progressive vote for the 1948 national elections was more apparent than real. The Chicago issues were not the main Wallace issues. Two major factors in the Chicago election were dirty politics and Jim Crow. The major parties there had for years refused to nominate a Negro for the Superior Court, and the Progressives had nominated well-qualified Negro attorneys. Carey's strong showing resulted from the revelation that his bipartisan opponent was a close friend of a famous Chicago gangster's lawyer. All the Chicago newspapers supported Carey after the association became known. The election results, rather than the conditions behind them, impressed Wallace and the men around him.[67]

The Communists and others working with them, fearful that Truman might make a liberal address to Congress in January and thereby reduce third-party sentiment, did their utmost to get Wallace to declare his candidacy in December. The I.W.O. handled the immigrant-group pressure, and the Left trade-union leaders promised labor backing. On December 12, 1947, Albert E. Kahn, president of the Jewish Peoples Fraternal Order, the I.W.O.'s largest constituent organization, wrote to Louis Adamic, the leftist Yugoslavian-American writer:

Will you join Zladko Balokovich [President of the American Slav Congress], Vito Marcantonio, myself and others in the signing of the enclosed letter?

We feel that it is of the utmost importance at this time that every encouragement be given to Henry Wallace in getting him to run for the presidency in 1948.

I'd appreciate your wiring me collect—c/o Jewish Peoples Fraternal Order, IWO, 80 Fifth Avenue, New York, N. Y.—as we want to get the message to Wallace at the earliest opportunity.

The message to Wallace will not be sent in the name of any organization but will come as a personal message from the signatories.[68]

In mid-December, the Progressive Citizens of America's national committee met in Chicago, and there was a hot debate over whether to ask Wallace to declare his independent candidacy. The principal opponents of an independent candidacy on the committee were Frank Kingdon, a cochairman of the P.C.A., Bartley C. Crum, a San Francisco attorney, and Robert W. Kenny, a former California attorney general. Those most vocal for Wallace's candidacy were Vito Marcantonio, the A.L.P.'s East Harlem congressman, John Abt, and the then Communist writer Howard Fast. The third-party advocates won the fight, whereupon Kingdon and Crum resigned from the P.C.A.

At this point, the Left trade-union leaders shifted their Wallace endorsement program into high gear. Already several Left unionists had declared for Wallace, among them Bryson of M.C.S., who was actively getting signatures to Wallace nominating petitions in California. On December 18, Kenneth Sherbell, A.L.P. state senator from Brooklyn and public affairs director of the Communist-led District 65 of the Distributive Workers, announced that forty-five New York C.I.O. and A.F. of L. local leaders had signed a letter to Wallace urging him to run. Most of the labor leaders were from the painters, the furriers, and the C.I.O. city organization. A few days later, a group of Communist Negroes in Philadelphia joined with Local 30 of the Furriers to ask Wallace to declare. On December 27, the national executive board of the Bridges union endorsed Wallace and a third party, as did two locals of the rubber workers at Akron. The next day, Ford Local 600, the largest U.A.W. local and the last one to have a strong Communist caucus, wired Wallace, "Declare yourself as a candidate for President." [69]

On Monday, December 29, Hugh Bryson and Elmer Benson, along with other P.C.A. leaders, conferred with Wallace in Chicago. After the conference they issued a press release which summarized their activities of the past two weeks: "Ever since the executive committee of the Progressive Citizens of America urged Wallace on Dec. 16 to run as an independent he has been visited by a stream of similar delegations from Eastern states." [70]

That night, Wallace, on a national radio network, announced his candidacy for the Presidency. He ended his speech with these words: "We have assembled a Gideon's army—small in number, powerful in conviction, ready in action. We have said with Gideon, 'Let those who are fearful and trembling depart.' For every fearful one who leaves there will be a thousand to take his place. A just cause is worth a hundred armies. We face the future unfettered by any principle but the general welfare. We owe no allegiance to any group which does not serve that welfare. By God's Grace, the People's Peace will usher in the Century of the Common Man."

Would Wallace have run for the Presidency in 1948 if the Communists had not exerted pressure to persuade him to run? if the Communists had opposed the idea of a third ticket? Would there have been a national third party if there had been no Communist Party? These are legitimate subjects for speculation, but only for speculation. History cannot be written in the subjunctive.

One reason to think that there would have been a third party even without the Communists is that Wallace had considerable non-Communist support when he first announced his candidacy and for a few months thereafter. Indeed, he still had the support of many non-Communists on Election Day, although he had lost many thousands during the campaign. On the other hand, there was no national organization with a third-party goal that was not dominated by Communists or people working closely with Communists, and Wallace had to have some kind of a vehicle, such as the P.C.A., from which to throw his hat in the ring. Timing must be considered in this speculation. It is unlikely that Wallace would have decided to run so many months before the Democratic national convention if the Communists and their allies had not pressured him, and in the first half of 1948, Wallace's popularity among non-Communists started to wane. But Wallace lost support among non-Communists partly because he was identified with the Communists. Certainly if there had been no Communist Party or if the Communist Party had opposed a third ticket, the situation would have been different from what it was. How different is anyone's guess.

FIVE: PROFESSIONAL SOLDIERS IN A CAMPAIGN THAT FAILED

T he Communists greeted Wallace's announcement of his independent candidacy with enthusiasm. His decision to run for the presidency was "an historic challenge to a vast and sinister conspiracy against the true interests of the United States," said a *Daily Worker* editorial. A *Daily Worker* columnist went so far as to suggest that in New York the third party "may well" become the "major party."

But these same *Daily Worker* articles revealed that Communists were sensitive and defensive about Wallace's candidacy—defensive against Wallace critics who charged his candidacy would only elect a reactionary Republican, and, shrewdly, sensitive to the possibility that Wallace's advocacy of "progressive capitalism" might corrupt his Communist supporters.

The Communist counter to the argument that Wallace was insuring Republican victory was confused. Their usual reaction was to cry "lesser evilism": it made no difference whether Truman or Vandenberg, Dewey, or Taft were president. This was the argument taken in the *Daily Worker* editorial hailing Wallace's announcement: there are "only two parties now facing the electorate—the war party of the bi-partisan Truman-GOP coalition [and] the peace party of the new people's movement." But a *Daily Worker* columnist argued that Truman was so unpopular he could

not win even if there were no third party, an argument that did
not contest the basic point of Wallace's critics that Truman's
election was desirable.[1]

Liberal Democrats in 1948 occasionally charged the Communists with deliberately seeking the election of a conservative president and Congress in the hope that the economic policies of
such a government would plunge the United States into a depression and thereby improve the Communists' position. The Communists always denied the accusation, and to deny was all they
could do with an allegation about their intentions.[2] The charge
was probably wide of the mark. Both before and after 1948, the
Communists supported legislative proposals that would have a
salutary economic effect.

Having embraced Wallace for immediate political advantage,
the Communist leadership took measures to prevent the membership from embracing Wallace's ideas, which were not Communist, or even Marxist. They saw the possibility that, in the heat
of a campaign, Communists might begin to believe everything
Wallace said. Wallace's "progressive capitalism" bothered the
Communists a great deal, and they tried to offset whatever influence Wallace might wield within the Communist Party by
starting a big anti-Keynes campaign. Foster declared in January
that "We Communists must take up the cudgels energetically
against all the Keynesian theoretical nonsense," and the comrades
took up their pens, if not their cudgels, to write a whole series
of anti-Keynesian pieces. By spring, a casual reader of *Political
Affairs* might have reasonably wondered if the Communists were
for or against Wallace. Every issue but one in the first seven
months of 1948 contained at least one anti-Keynes article.[3]

Although Wallace's Keynesian views disturbed the Communists
more than anything else about the former vice-president, they
were critical of some of his expressed views on foreign policy
as well. In May 1948, Wallace published *Toward World Peace,*
a short book about his views on international relations.[4] Max
Weiss wrote a twelve-page review of the book praising Wallace

for his criticisms of American foreign policy but taking him severely to task for writing that the Soviet Union and the United
States were "equally responsible" for the danger of war. "The
danger to peace comes from one direction," wrote Weiss, "from
the expansionist drive by American imperialism. . . ." He was
also critical of Wallace for saying "that the [Russian] proletarian dictatorship suppresses political democracy. On the contrary,
the proletarian dictatorship . . . was from the start a thousand
times more democratic than the freest of the bourgeois democracies. . . ." [5] Actually, Weiss made the same kind of criticism
of Wallace that the *Daily Worker* editorial writer made the day
after Wallace's Madison Square Garden speech and which got
him in trouble with the ninth floor. But that episode, of course,
happened before the Communists had Wallace installed as the
front man for the new "antifascist coalition."

More important in the long run than the ideological differences
between Wallace and the Communists was the effect that Wallace's candidacy and the Communists' support of it had upon the
Communist unions in the C.I.O. The Communists' support of
Wallace shattered the "left-center coalition" in the C.I.O.; for
the Communist unions, the Wallace movement was the beginning
of the end.

The coalition began to dissolve almost immediately after Wallace's announcement. A.L.P. leaders in New York hailed Wallace's decision, and within three days, the Amalgamated Clothing
Workers and other non-Communist C.I.O. unions in New York
left the A.L.P.[6] At the national level, the alliance of the Murray
group and the Communists broke down completely at the January
meeting of the C.I.O. executive board in Washington. This was
one of the historic meetings of American labor. The Left union
chiefs caucused in Communist labor secretary John Williamson's
room in the Hay-Adams Hotel the night before the meeting.
Among those present were Mike Quill, Harry Bridges, Abe Flaxer,
Ben Gold, Irving Potash, Donald Henderson, Joseph Selly, John
Santo, and James Matles. Williamson instructed them to try to

get a pro-Wallace resolution passed at the next day's meeting. The meeting ran over into a second day, and, at a second caucus in Williamson's room the night between the board sessions, the Left unionists reported it highly unlikely that such a resolution would pass. Williamson directed them to stall, to try to get the C.I.O. to take no position at all on the third party for another month. In about a month there was to be a special Congressional election in the Bronx in which the Communists expected the Wallaceite A.L.P. candidate, Leo Isaacson, to make a strong showing, and Williamson hoped that if the C.I.O.'s decision could be postponed, the Bronx election would influence it. At the next day's session, however, the Left unionists lost the motion to postpone. Then the board went ahead and voted 33 to 13 to condemn the Wallace candidacy. It also passed a resolution supporting the Marshall Plan.[7]

By fostering and supporting Wallace's candidacy, the Communists had brought the Communist issue to a head in the C.I.O., and they had lost the battle. But the worst for the C.I.O. Communists and pro-Communists was yet to come. Within two weeks after the January board meeting, Lee Pressman was forced to resign. In March, Murray fired Bridges as C.I.O. regional director for northern California. In two more years, the Left unions were expelled from the C.I.O. altogether, and in eight more years, there would be almost no Left unions in existence. The price to the Communists for their support of a third party proved to be very high. The Communists lost almost everything in the labor movement and gained nothing.

There appears to have been some division in the Communist Party's leadership over how hard to fight for Wallace support in the C.I.O., over how much to endanger the Left unions' position. As usual, Foster was the most extreme. Mike Quill testified: "To follow up the fear that I had of what the Communist Party were doing within the CIO, I discussed this new line with William Z. Foster . . . in the month of January, 1948. I expressed to him fears that this move will split the unions, and weaken our position locally and nationally against the employers. He said the Communist Party have decided that all the unions that it can influence within C.I.O. are to go down the line behind Wallace if it splits the last union down the middle." [8] There is other evidence to confirm Quill's testimony. Foster himself hinted that such was his position in an article that blasted Murray and other C.I.O. leaders as "labor-imperialists" who have "abdicated the working-class leadership." And John Williamson, who was close to Foster, told the Communist national committee in early February, "We Communists have always supported the idea of a united trade union movement because it is in the general interests of the workers. However, different conditions dictate different approaches. . . . It is impossible to think in terms of trade union unity on the basis of support of Wall Street's imperialist program and two-party system." [9]

Dennis, however, did not go along with Foster and Williamson on this point. He told the same national committee meeting that "we . . . oppose any sectarian tendency to convert the political struggle within the trade unions in behalf of Wallace and the new people's party into a movement to split or withdraw from the established trade union centers." [10]

Neither point of view became final party policy. Foster, according to Quill, advocated "a Third Federation of Labor" in early 1948, "carved out of the A.F. of L. and the C.I.O. in order to implement the Henry Wallace movement." [11] Such a federation was never founded. Nor did the Communist unions bolt the C.I.O.—although they were later expelled. They left the C.I.O.-P.A.C. only when the C.I.O. endorsed Truman. Neither did Dennis's view prevail, if Dennis intended that the Left unions should not go so far in their Wallace support as to evoke retaliation from the C.I.O.

The C.I.O.'s alliance with the Democratic Party was so firm and mutually advantageous that to have severed it would have been disastrous to both. The C.I.O. Communists and pro-Communists went ahead and tried to break the alliance. The result, perhaps the inevitable result, was that they soon found themselves outside what they themselves had called the "mainstream" of labor.

In February 1948, the Communists had no regrets about their third-party decision. Quite the contrary. For on February 17, in the Twenty-fourth Congressional District in the East Bronx, A.L.P. candidate Leo Isaacson won the special election by a nearly two-to-one majority. Isaacson received 22,697 votes to the Democratic candidate's 12,578. The Liberal Party candidate received 3,840 votes, and the Republican ran a poor last, with less than 3,000.[12] This February 1948 election was the high tide of the Wallace movement.

The Twenty-fourth Congressional District was poor and ethnically mixed. It was about two-fifths Jewish, but some parts of it were primarily Irish. There was a considerable Negro and Puerto Rican population.[13] The Communists exploited the dissatisfaction of these groups for their own advantage.

The election came before Israel's independence or Truman's quick recognition of the new state, and many of the Jewish voters of the district considered Truman's Palestine policy one of appeasement of the British. In early 1947, the Communists themselves had advocated a binational Palestine and urged the Jews to come "to an agreement with the Democratic Arab forces, and even with the Arab states as such"[14]—surely an unpopular position in the Jewish community—but their line had changed along with that of the Soviets late in the year, and they now supported Palestine's partition and independence.[15] Isaacson's Communist and A.L.P. workers rallied hundreds of Jewish votes with a pamphlet, published in Yiddish, charging that "Truman spills Jewish blood for Arab oil."[16]

Isaacson polled a fairly good vote in the Irish Catholic neighborhoods. In 1946, the A.L.P. had received only one vote in ten in the predominantly Irish election districts, but in the special election, Isaacson carried five Irish neighborhoods and did not do badly in others. Samuel Lubell, a political analyst who advances the interesting "urban frontier" thesis, attributed the increased Irish vote to anxiety over the changing ethnic character of the area.[17]

Isaacson carried the Negro and Puerto Rican vote by sheer hard work. There were between 800 and 1,000 Communist Party members living in the district, who worked with typical party energy, and each day the A.L.P. sent over 300 campaigners into the area. On Election Day, Isaacson had 2,000 people working for him.[18]

An election eve Isaacson rally was typical of the campaign's ethnic approach. Wallace was the main attraction at the meeting, and in his speech he concentrated on denouncing Jim Crow and Truman's Palestine policy. Other speakers were Vito Marcantonio, who had a strong Puerto Rican following in his congressional district; Paul Robeson, who pointed out that Southern white supremacists were Democrats; Isaacson himself, who is Jewish; and a young Negro veteran who had been the victim of a brutal Southern policeman. Mike Quill was on hand to plug for Isaacson in an accent that no one could mistake.[19] By thus playing for the support of minority groups, which in New York City are majority groups, the Wallace forces gained an overwhelming victory.

The Isaacson election caused jubilation in the Wallace camp and alarmed the Democrats. Two days after the Bronx election, Senator J. Howard McGrath, chairman of the Democratic national committee, in a radio speech, all but invited Wallace to return to the Democratic fold.[20] The next week, Democratic Senator Glen Taylor, of Idaho, a singing-cowboy type, cast his lot with Wallace, announcing that he would seek to be Wallace's running mate. Even to outside observers, Wallace seemed to have great strength; not enough to win the Presidency but enough to split the Democratic Party, much as Theodore Roosevelt had split the G.O.P. in 1912. The Wallace group was confident and optimistic. Many non-Communist Wallace supporters were gratified with the organizational job the Communists could produce, and the Communists were pleased with Wallace's apparent appeal.

Wallace's speeches in late 1947 and early 1948 reflected the Communist line more accurately than they ever had before. The opening for the Communists was the inadequacy of two young people.

Lew Frank, Wallace's pro-Communist principal speech writer, was a young man. He was called upon constantly to write about subjects that a more experienced and learned person would have found difficult to handle. The Marshall Plan as it was developing in Congress in the winter of 1947-48 and the Communist coup in Czechoslovakia, which occurred immediately after the Isaacson victory, were two cases in point. Frank needed help.

Help arrived in the form of a young newspaperwoman named Tabitha Petran. Miss Petran had been on *PM,* and on *Time* before that. For *PM,* she specialized in foreign affairs. Her politics is indicated by her subsequent career: after the 1948 elections, she joined the staff of the fellow-traveling *National Guardian,* and in the 1956 crisis of world Communism, her point of view was less critical of the Soviet Union than that of many *Daily Worker* writers.[21] But Miss Petran did not feel adequate to the Wallace task either. For intellectual counsel, she helped organize a "research group," which met at the Manhattan home of the wealthy Frederick Vanderbilt Field.

The research group met each week, usually on Wednesday nights, to discuss the general content of what should appear in Wallace's speeches. The group contained some people of intellectual ability. Field was an expert on East Asia and had written on that subject for *Political Affairs.*[22] Among other members of the group were Marion Bachrach, later a Smith Act defendant; Victor Perlo, once an economist for the War Production Board and the Department of Commerce; David Ramsey, a contributor to the *Communist* as early as 1936, a collaborator with Perlo in criticizing the Marshall Plan, and a person with good grounding in economics; and an expert on German affairs, Walter Schlieper, a German refugee who wrote under the name Maximillian Scheer for the Overseas News Agency, a respectable non-Communist press association. In late 1948 or early 1949, Schlieper-Scheer left the United States to work in East Berlin. In the words of the Alsop brothers, who wrote a column on the research group in March, after which it no longer functioned as a body, "Mr. Wallace thus provides the voice. Mr. Frank provides the words. But the select company to which Mr. Field plays host provides the ideas." [23] Certainly the ideas of some people in the group found their way into Wallace's speeches and other public statements.

Wallace testified against the Marshall Plan before the House Committee on Foreign Affairs in the morning of February 24, 1948. He came to the hearing with a prepared statement, which was extreme in its language and point of view. His main point was that the Marshall Plan had undergone a change since Marshall made the original proposal in June 1947, that "militarists and bankers" had converted it to a program that "could convert western Europe into a vast military camp, with freedom extinguished." The European Recovery Program (E.R.P.) would bring neither real relief nor recovery to Europe, would revive German militarism, and would cause repression and union-busting in the United States. It had already, Wallace charged, postponed the plans of the British Labour Party government to nationalize the steel industry, a charge that Jennie Lee (Mrs. Aneurin Bevan), a Labour member of Parliament, later denied. In place of E.R.P., he proposed the "Wallace plan," which envisaged American-Soviet co-operation and an expansion of the principle of the defunct United Nations Relief and Rehabilitation Administration. To a congressman's objection that such a plan would be at the mercy of a Russian veto in the U.N. Security Council, Wallace replied that the Soviets would not want to veto such a plan.

Wallace's criticisms of E.R.P. and his own recovery plan were precisely the ideas that two members of the research group—Victor Perlo and David Ramsey—had made the previous month in a *New Republic* article. The Perlo-Ramsey article had been more restrained in its language than the Wallace statement, but the ideas of the two documents coincided exactly.

That Wallace was reading someone else's words, and words with which he did not entirely agree, was indicated by his responses to questions from congressmen after he read the prepared statement. In one exchange, for example, Wallace granted that Communism was totalitarian and "a system of desperation" of hungry people. At another point in the questioning he said, "I do not think that the present administration at any time entertained any idea of imperialism of the type you are talking about—that is, world domination. . . . I don't think our military ever envisioned anything of that sort and to suggest anything of that sort is—only a madman could entertain a thought of that kind." [24]

But the Marshall Plan testimony was not the last time that the ideas of Wallace's ghost writers were to lead him into situations he would in time regret. At the time he was testifying before the House Foreign Affairs Committee, the Russians were directing events in Czechoslovakia about which he could not keep silent.

On February 19, 1948, Soviet Deputy Foreign Minister Valerian A. Zorin arrived in Prague by plane. He stayed in the city for six days, by which time the Communists had successfully accomplished their *coup d'état*. Within a fortnight, Jan Masaryk, the Czech foreign minister and one of the most respected and popular statesmen of Europe, committed suicide. American public opinion was outraged. Wallace had to comment on the Czech crisis. The position he took, Wallace was to say four years later, was "my greatest mistake." [25]

Wallace knew Czechoslovakia. He had been there in the late 1920's, and he was related by marriage to a Swiss diplomat who had served in Prague for years. Obviously, he determined much of his position on the Czech coup himself. But at the same time, he echoed the sentiments of the Communists so promptly that it is apparent he also continued to let others put words in his mouth.

In a Minneapolis speech on February 29, Wallace blamed the Czech crisis on the Truman Doctrine, saying the Soviets were merely reacting to American aggression.[26] A few days later he told newsmen essentially the same thing but characterized the whole affair as "unfortunate." This was too much for the *Daily Worker.* "But why does Henry Wallace view the advance of the people's democracy against intriguers as 'unfortunate?' Unfortunate in what respect? . . . surely this is not unfortunate." [27]

Two days after Masaryk's suicide, a *Daily Worker* columnist wrote: "Let [Americans] remember another suicide—of John Winant's, who found that postwar America was not what he hoped and expected . . . and could not endure the strain of it." Four days later, Wallace, who was then living in Winant's former home, told the press, "Maybe Winant had cancer, maybe Masaryk had cancer. Maybe Winant was unhappy about the fate of the world." [28]

In a press conference on March 17, Wallace accused the American ambassador to Czechoslovakia of having attempted to stage a "rightist coup" in Prague. The Communists had merely beaten the reactionaries to the punch. The accused ambassador categorically denied the charge, pointing out that he was not even in Czechoslovakia until after the crisis began. The Communist Party had the same position on the coup that Wallace had.[29]

Wallace has said that he arrived at his position on Czechoslovakia partly from having heard indirectly from a Czech he had long admired, Joseph L. Hromádka, the outstanding Protestant theologian of East Europe.[30] Three months before the coup, Hromádka had written in a Czech periodical, "If the reactionary elements in America were to gain complete victory, then I . . . would feel constrained . . . to stand on the side of the East." A month after the coup, Hromádka, who had been a close friend of Masaryk, wrote, ". . . we fear nothing. We look to the days ahead with hope and peace." [31]

Hromádka had fled from the Nazis in 1939 and come to the United States, where he served as Stuart Guest Professor of Apologetics and Christian Ethics at Princeton Theological Seminary. He returned to Czechoslovakia in 1947. While in America, he published *Doom and Resurrection,* a "crisis-of-our-age" sort of volume with Protestant theological overtones. The book's dedication read, "To Henry A. Wallace. A man of deep social and spiritual vision." In 1958, Hromádka received a Lenin Peace Prize from the Soviets.[32]

One cannot but wonder if another European influenced Wallace's public statements on Czechoslovakia. A man named Hermann Budzislawski told his Communist friends that he had persuaded Wallace to his position on the Czech coup. Budzislawski was a friend of Schlieper-Scheer and his colleague on the Overseas News Agency. Budzislawski wrote for the agency under the name of Donald Bell, and appeared in several important and respected American newspapers. He also was an occasional member of the research group. Budzislawski-Bell was something of a poseur, but an able man. During the war, he was Dorothy Thompson's research assistant until she discovered his Communist affiliations. He claimed to be her ghost writer, which she denied. In the late summer of 1948, Budzislawski-Bell accepted an appointment as professor of sociology at the University of Leipzig in East Germany, the institution that subsequently appointed Gerhart Eisler to its faculty.[33]

Budzislawski-Bell was known to have exaggerated his importance in the past, and it is difficult to know how much credence to give his story about Wallace. Wallace does not remember him under either of his names.[34] Budzislawski-Bell, however, may very well have influenced Lew Frank, which would not have been especially difficult, given Frank's predilections and Budzislawski-Bell's obvious familiarity with European politics.

THE PROGRESSIVE PARTY CONVENTION

Some of the Communists' official and published statements called attention to their connection with the Progressives. In the draft resolution for the fourteenth national convention of the Communist Party, published and available to the general press in late May, appeared these sentences: "The Communist Party, from the earliest days after the end of the war, understood that its traditional fight for a new people's party . . . had once more been placed by events as an immediate, practical question. . . . Because of its correct line, the Party was able to carry on effective mass work and make significant contributions to the . . . forging of the new political alignment and people's coalition." [35] The nation's press, almost unanimously opposed to Wallace, picked up this expression of self-congratulation and made the most of it. William Z. Foster, in his keynote speech to the Communist convention, held a week after the Progressive national convention, declared, "They are brazen liars who charge that the Communist Party is trying to dominate the new party or to claim the credit for its formation," [36] but the damage was already done. Furthermore, no unusual powers of observation were required to perceive that at the Progressive convention the Communists had not only tried to dominate the proceedings but had been quite successful in their effort.

Charging Communist control, liberals began to leave the Wallace camp in significant numbers even before the Progressive Party convention. Most of these defections were in the western states. When the Colorado Progressives began intensively organizing in June, the Communists made their power in the new party obvious. In early July, two prominent Denver Progressive leaders resigned from the Wallace movement, and there were more withdrawals after the Colorado Progressives named their delegates to the national convention. Among the delegates elected were Robert

Trujillo, who had run for state office on the Communist ticket in 1946, and Mrs. Arthur Bary, wife of the Communist district organizer. Another Colorado delegate was Graham Dolan, national educational director of the Mine, Mill and Smelter Workers, who himself admitted he did not know how he became a delegate, since he had not been elected. At this point, the state's most prominent Progressive, Charles Graham, a former regional chairman of the War Labor Board, quit the movement. He was to have been a member of the national platform committee, but he did not even go to the convention.

In other western states, the Communists played similar tricks with similar results. At Nevada's state convention, the Progressive state chairman, George Springmeyer, insisted the convention go on record as opposed to fascism, Nazism, and Communism. Elinor Kahn, California leader of the Wallace party, and Charlotta Bass, publisher of a Los Angeles Negro newspaper, neither of whom was even a delegate, since they were from another state, denounced Springmeyer's attitude as Red baiting. When his motion lost, Springmeyer resigned and stalked out of the hall. In South Dakota, the Progressive state committee itself criticized Wallace for "playing into the hands of the Communists and the fringe elements." [87]

The Progressive Party met in Philadelphia in late July for its first national convention. When the convention was over, the Communists had eliminated doubt about their role in the Wallace movement, and disillusioned non-Communists dropped out by the thousands. Minor party conventions are usually quiet and staid affairs. The Progressive meeting was anything but quiet or staid. For organized enthusiasm and synthetic folksiness, no political conclave was ever its equal. Pete Seeger, People's Songs, Inc., amateur folk singers, and community song leaders set the convention's tone, and their spirit reached a climax when the beaming Vice-Presidential candidate, Glen Taylor, gathered his children about him, whacked his guitar, and sang "Friendly Henry Wallace" over three national radio networks. Ten thousand New

Yorkers, brought to the convention by special trains and under effective Communist Party discipline, supplied a cheering section. Many of these people had responded to a notice in the *Daily Worker* for "all members on vacation to return immediately, and all planning vacations to temporarily cancel them. . . . Our new and urgent tasks require the fullest mobilization of all our members." [38]

But the Philadelphia convention was more than noise and folk songs. The meetings of the convention's committees and the debates over the committee's reports on the convention floor were serious matters, and they showed the extent to which the Progressive venture was a Communist operation.

The first news from Philadelphia had to do with the deliberations of the platform committee. Rexford G. Tugwell, then of the University of Chicago, was the committee's chairman; Lee Pressman was its secretary. There were seventy-two other members of the committee and several "staff assistants."

An unofficial advisory subcommittee of the platform committee had already met in New York the weekend of July 17-18 and begun work on the platform. Working under Pressman's general direction, David Ramsey, Tabitha Petran, and others prepared what became known as the "New York draft." When the full platform committee met at Phiadelphia on July 20, before the convention opened, it accepted the New York draft as a basis for its further work. The committee then conducted hearings on the platform. The high point of the hearings was the rude reception given A.D.A.'s James Loeb, Jr., when he came before the committee and challenged it to criticize Communism. [39]

The full committee appointed a five-man drafting subcommittee to make desired changes in the New York draft. Martin Popper, Executive Secretary of the National Lawyers Guild, was chairman of the drafting subcommittee. Other members were Louis Adamic, Mrs. Paul Robeson, Dean Joseph E. Johnson, of Howard University, and Professor Frederick L. Schuman, of Williams College. Schuman was ill and did not actually serve. Sitting with the subcommittee as "staff assistants" but informally functioning as members were Petran and Ramsey again, Professor Richard Watt, of the University of Chicago Law School, Paul Sweezy, and Leo Huberman.[40]

The Communist issue in various guises divided the platform committee from the beginning. Before the convention, Tugwell had discounted charges of Communist infiltration in the Progressive movement as the inevitable reaction of hostile politicians, but he began to change his mind when he saw men he knew to be Communists operating at the convention. He began a withdrawal from the Wallace movement at this point. Technically, his appointment as platform committee chairman was provisional, and when the full committee met for the first time, his first act was to ask for nominations for permanent chairman, saying he did not wish to be nominated. Popper objected and nominated Tugwell, arguing that if Tugwell did not serve as chairman, the press would interpret the action as evidence of dissension. Tugwell declined and asked for further nominations, but there were none. Tugwell backed down and served as chairman.[41]

Early in the committee's work, Cedric Thomas, a Maine realestate man, dropped a bombshell by urging that the platform make clear that the Progressive Party was not Communist. Charles Rohrer, Progressive candidate for lieutenant governor of Indiana, supported Thomas, saying, "To the average man, Communism still stinks." The reaction to these statements was tumultuous. Thomas retreated a little and formally moved to include in the platform a statement Glen Taylor had made to the effect that the Progressive purpose was to make the economy function so well that Communism would interest no one. This was no less than Red baiting, declared Popper and Mrs. Robeson. In a maze of parliamentary technicalities, the committee defeated Thomas's motion.[42]

But Thomas was not through yet. The New York draft contained the sentence "The Progressive Party will fight for the constitutional rights of Communists and all other political groups to express their views . . ."—a plank of immediate pertinence, since the first indictments of Communists under the Smith Act had been returned just the previous week. Thomas moved that the sentence be amended to read simply "the constitutional rights of all political groups," omitting direct mention of the Communists. Red baiting again, said Popper, and the original statement won by a large majority.

Communists and those close to the party were not a majority of the platform committee, but there were enough non-Communists who agreed with some parts of the party line to allow the Communists and their close allies to write most of the platform. Had there been an organized non-Communist caucus in the committee, the platform could have been quite different. On just one point was the Communist position defeated without an appeal to higher authority or a threat to bolt. The New York draft contained a plank calling for confiscatory corporation taxes. Sweezy, a Marxist economist but not a Communist, opposed the plank, saying it was poor economics. Popper and Petran opposed him strenuously, but a majority voted with Sweezy. However, the non-Communists did not agree among themselves enough to vote together on all issues. When the non-Communist Schuman offered a long and detailed substitute on monopoly that avoided a pledge to nationalize specific industries, Sweezy opposed him, and Schuman lost.[43]

The bitterest fight in the platform committee came over the issue of Puerto Rican independence. Independence for Puerto Rico was a frequently repeated Communist demand, for the Communists hoped to make it appear that the Puerto Ricans suffered under the yoke of American imperialism. Foster had been in San Juan in March to whip up support for independence.[44] The New York draft contained a plan for Puerto Rican independence, and Tugwell vigorously objected. A former governor of Puerto Rico, Tugwell asserted there were not five hundred people on the island who were for separation from the United States. After all, New York had proved to be Puerto Rico's best safety valve, and that valve would close with independence. Tugwell proposed a plank calling for self-determination for Puerto Rico, with the Puerto Ricans free to choose either independence or full American statehood. Vito Marcantonio argued vociferously for outright independence. The East Harlem congressman declared, among other things, that "Self-determination is a term of the imperialist demogogues." The Left, of course, stood with Marcantonio, except for one amusing exception. Mrs. Robeson, perhaps getting the matter confused with "national self-determination for the Negro people in the Black Belt," came out for Puerto Rican self-determination. Looking dismayed when she saw who was for independence and who was not, she quickly changed her mind, saying she was "for independence, period." Tugwell was adamant. The committee meeting ended before the dispute was resolved. Before the next meeting, Wallace appealed to Marcantonio to yield on the issue, and Marcantonio offered no more opposition on that issue. The final platform did not contain an independence plank.[45]

There was one last battle in the platform committee. Schuman was disappointed with the final draft for its thorough condemnation of American foreign policy and its silence about Soviet policy. He prepared an amendment which read, "We demand that the United States stop sacrificing the cause of peace to industrial profits and military ambition. We demand that the Soviet Union stop sacrificing the cause of peace to territorial aggrandizement and power politics." However, someone told Schuman, correctly or not, that if this statement were offered to the convention, Paul Robeson would object from the floor and declare the second sentence untrue. Schuman thereupon modified the proposal, making it read that the threat to world peace was the "joint responsibility of the Soviet Union and the United States." Very early the next morning, Schuman and three other men saw Wallace in his hotel room and asked his support of the Schuman amendment. Wallace agreed with Schuman and told Baldwin, Frank, and Albert J. Fitzgerald, the convention's chairman and president of U.E., that he wanted the Schuman amendment in the platform. He told Baldwin to notify Pressman of his position, saying that Pressman was "the only one likely to object." The platform committee held a special session just before the platform was to be presented to the convention, and Pressman supported the Schuman amendment. Popper and several others protested vigorously for some time before Baldwin came into the meeting and said that Wallace demanded the amendment. At this point, the opposition ceased. On the convention floor, Pressman read the amendment as a "correction" to the platform draft which had already been mimeographed and distributed to the delegates.[46]

On the convention floor itself, the Communists and their close followers made their influence felt. The keynote address, delivered by Charles P. Howard, an Iowa Negro, had been written by a radio writer named Allan E. Sloane, who described himself to a Congressional committee in 1954 as a former party member and fellow traveler. Sloane also testified that he had written Wallace's acceptance speech with the aid of Millard Lampell, another radio writer, whom Sloane described as a Communist. Several weeks before the convention, Sloane told the Congressional committee, he had received a telephone call from Hannah Dorner, who said that Wallace's acceptance speech was "terrible" and asked Sloane to write another one. Sloane went to Progressive Party headquarters in New York and there encountered Lampell, his former roommate, who had recruited him into the party in 1943. Lampell said Wallace's speech was "a dog," and they proceeded to write another one.[47]

Not everything went smoothly for the Communists. There were three important incidents on the convention floor itself in which non-Communists unsuccessfully challenged the party machine: a dispute over the composition of the Progressive Party's national committee; a quite improbable and embarrassing farce over a platform plank on the Macedonians; and the so-called "Vermont resolution" on foreign policy.

The convention's rules committee, technically headed by Marc-

antonio but actually run by John Abt, proposed a party-organiza-
tion scheme that would practically insure Communist minority
domination of the party machinery. The rules committee suggested
a national committee of 180 members, one-half of which would
constitute a quorum. Each member could vote proxies. The feature
that brought the fight on the convention floor was a device that
allowed the Communists and fellow travelers from the so-called
"functional divisions," such as the youth division and the labor
division, to pack the national committee. The functional divisions
were loaded with Communists. Hugh Bryson had proposed in the
rules committee that these divisions be given sixty seats on the
national committee. The non-Communists, who had "Beanie"
Baldwin's support in this matter, scaled the number down to
forty. But even forty of these committee members, if they were
faithful to the Communist line, would assure the Communists almost a quorum majority, not counting proxies and party-line
followers among other members of the national committee.

James S. Martin, cochairman of the Maryland delegation and
a former New Dealer, spoke against this committee-packing proposal on the convention floor and moved to recommit the section
to the rules committee for reconsideration. During the debate,
Scott Buchanan, former dean of St. John's College, made a short
speech in which he said, "This article allows for minority control
of this party. If we want to do that, I think there'll be some of us
walking out of this party." When the delegates finished booing
Buchanan, they defeated Martin's motion to recommit. But the
battle was not quite over. Leonard Stein, an assistant dean at the
University of Chicago, moved that the sentence about the forty
divisional representatives be deleted. Chairman Fitzgerald ruled
his motion out of order, Stein appealed the decision of the chair,
and parliamentary confusion became rampant. The upshot was that
the convention adopted the rules committee report as originally
presented.[48]

The Macedonian dispute was hilarious farce. The Macedonians
were scattered among three nations—Greece, Bulgaria, and Yugo-

slavia—and some kind of support for Macedonian unification, aimed to discredit anti-Communist Greece, was a standard item in Communist statements of what the world should be. But since Tito had been excommunicated about a month before the Progressive convention, the Macedonians had allied themselves with the Tito heresy. Macedonian unification now became anathema to the Communists. But someone slipped. The New York draft contained this sentence: "We support the aspirations for the unified homelands of traditionally oppressed and dispersed people such as the Irish, Armenians and Macedonians." Someone caught the slip just before the convention adopted the platform.

The platform had been read to the convention, and the delegates had the document in their hands. Pressman got the microphone to present several "corrections" to the platform. Among them was the deletion of the Macedonians from the sentence about "oppressed and dispersed people." A delegate from New Haven, a man named Spodick, tried to get the floor to ask the reason for the deletion. Chairman Fitzgerald ruled him out of order. The press and radio men, sensing that something was afoot, began to watch closely and to ask questions. Spodick asked for the floor again, and Fitzgerald relented. Spodick wanted to know what was wrong so suddenly with the Macedonians. He had been for Macedonian unity last month, he was still for Macedonian unity, and why wasn't the platform committee? Fitzgerald looked puzzled and turned to Pressman. Pressman looked helpless. Finally, Louis Adamic, an expert on Balkan problems, came to the rescue. Adamic became a Titoist before he died, but he was anything but a Titoist then. He talked for a few minutes in language so vague that no one understood his meaning. James Wechsler reported he might as well have been speaking his native Balkan tongue. Spodick was not persuaded by Adamic's double talk. He moved that the sentence stand as originally written. Fitzgerald did not even put the motion to a vote. Very few of the delegates understood the background of the squabble, and the convention allowed the Macedonians to be "corrected" out of the platform.[49]

The most dramatic and best-publicized dispute at the convention occurred when James Hayford, chairman of the three-member Vermont delegation, arose and proposed that the following sentence be added at the end of the foreign-policy section of the platform: "Although we are critical of the present foreign policy of the United States, it is not our intention to give blanket endorsement to the foreign policy of any other nation." "Beanie" Baldwin, who was in another room dealing with another matter but keeping one eye on the television set, rushed back to the platform. He was too late. Other speakers were seconding Hayford's motion and receiving applause as well as cries about Red baiting. Pressman and others pointed out that the platform already declared the danger of war the "joint responsibility" of the Soviet Union and the United States—itself a last-minute concession. One anti-Vermont delegate declared that the amendment was "an insinuation against a friendly ally of the United States" and received greater applause than those who spoke for the amendment. After enough debate for the radio audience to understand the significance of what was going on, the convention overwhelmingly defeated the amendment by a voice vote. There was only one conclusion the radio audience could reach: the Progressive platform did give blanket endorsement to the foreign policy of another nation.[50]

The most highhanded acts of Communist manipulation at Philadelphia occurred at the convention of the Young Progressives of America (Y.P.A.), which met immediately after the main convention adjourned. Christine Walker, of Detroit, and Alvin Jones, a Negro honor student at Southern University Law School in Baton Rouge, were cochairmen of Y.P.A. Miss Walker was a member of U.O.P.W.A. and of the Wayne County Industrial Union Council, from which non-Communist locals had resigned. Jones was prone to make slips of the tongue. When he introduced Leo Isaacson to the Y.P.A. convention, he referred to him as "Comrade, no, I mean Congressman Isaacson." Later in the convention, he called for order by saying, "Comrades, comrades, quiet, please." The executive director of Y.P.A., with whom day-to-day power actually lay, was Seymour Linfield, associate general counsel of U.E., on loan to the Wallace movement for 1948.

The non-Communists in Y.P.A. were better organized than their elders. When Linfield presented the report of the convention arrangements committee, which had been delegated to suggest the convention rules and methods of electing convention officers, several delegations created a storm. They protested that the industrial states, where Communists had the greatest strength, were overrepresented on the convention committees. The proceedings bogged down in parliamentary confusion, with cries of "Point of order," "Point of information," and "I call the question" from all over the hall. In the general hubbub, Miss Walker called for a voice vote on the arrangements committee's report. The result was indecisive. She called for a show of hands, after which she announced the report was adopted. In the words of one observer at the convention, at this point "all hell broke loose on the floor. One group began to chant 'rollcall, rollcall,' while another chanted 'We want Wallace, We want Wallace.' " Then the lights went off, throwing the room into darkness, and an offstage voice introduced Glen Taylor.

The lights came on, and Taylor spoke briefly. At the end of his speech, the United States senator from Idaho accompanied himself on his guitar and sang a parody of "The Isle of Capri," a popular song of the 1930's. The parody told the story of a man who went swimming with a nude woman, encountered her husband, and left his false teeth on the Isle of Capri. After this cultural phenomenon, Wallace gave a brief speech and Paul Robeson sang.

The next day's session came to a more dignified but similarly abrupt conclusion. When a dispute arose the next afternoon, the chairman announced that the convention was presented with a choice of adjourning the session or paying the proprietors of the hall an additional fee of nearly $2,000 an hour. The convention voted to grant the Y.P.A. national council power to act as the convention's agent on all unfinished business, and the convention adjourned without even adopting a platform.[51]

The Progressive Party convention was almost a total victory for the Communists. They gained almost every objective they had sought. Some Progressives, including even those at the convention but not on important committees, failed to perceive the extent of Communist influence. Most planks of the platform and most of the speeches would have been acceptable to non-Communist liberals with only a little revision. Yet the Communists left Philadelphia with warranted satisfaction. The main reason for their victory was that they were organized and the non-Communists were unorganized and divided. There was no Progressive of stature willing to organize and lead a non-Communist caucus.

Wallace, of course, was the most prominent non-Communist in the Progressive Party, and he refused to act against the Communists. After Tugwell recognized party members working at the convention, he personally appealed to Wallace to repudiate them. Wallace did not give Tugwell a direct reply. A few hours later, Tugwell encountered William H. Lawrence, of the New York *Times,* who asked Tugwell when Wallace was going to repudiate the Communists. Tugwell replied that he was trying to persuade Wallace to reject them. Lawrence gave Tugwell a clipping that described Robert M. La Follette's strong stand against the Communists in the Progressive movement of 1924. Tugwell later showed the clipping to Wallace, saying that in his opinion La Follette had taken the true liberal position. Wallace answered, "If they want to support me I can't stop them." Yet Wallace knew the danger to his candidacy that the Communists represented. Before the Progressive convention, he had said in a New Hampshire speech, "I'm never going to say anything in the nature of red-baiting, but I must say this: If the Communists would run a ticket of their own this year, we might lose 10,000 votes, but we would gain 3,000,000." [52]

THE CAMPAIGN FAILS

After the convention, a wave of non-Communists withdrew from Gideon's army. Within a week, six New Mexico Progressive leaders, including the state treasurer and organizer, quit the movement. The same day, the chairman of the Colorado convention delegation announced his resignation. A Progressive rally in Denver attracted only two hundred people, many of whom were open Communists, and several of this small body left before the meeting was over. In early August, twelve Progressive leaders in San Mateo County, California, publicly resigned from the party, saying the defeat of the Vermont resolution had been too much for them. Thousands of other Wallaceites just quietly withdrew. Among them was Tugwell. He told a Baltimore *Sun* reporter in August, "I am an uneasy member of the Progressive party. I hope its organization and program will develop in a way that will permit those of us who are old-fashioned American progressives to go along with it." He soon decided that his hope was futile. Because of his long friendship with Wallace, he made no public statement when he left the Progressives.[53]

Apparently even some Communists saw what was happening to the Progressive Party, saw that what they had so carefully nursed along was rapidly becoming a kind of big party front rather than a real third party. But the Communist leadership persisted in its policy. "A wrong theory exists, which even permeates Left circles, that the Progressive Party reached its high point during or before its Philadelphia convention," said John Williamson at the Communist national convention in early August. Firm in its belief that the decline of the Wallace movement was a "wrong theory" rather than a demonstrable fact, the Communist convention reaffirmed positions that already were having disastrous effects from the Communists' own point of view. There was nothing wrong with the "fundamentally correct line," said Foster. The trouble was "weaknesses and mistakes . . . of a Right-opportunist character" in applying the line. As for the party's increasing isolation from the labor movement—a month later, the C.I.O. would endorse Truman and even U.E. would fail to endorse Wallace for fear of a union split—Foster only fulminated against labor's delay in recognizing "the increasingly reactionary, pro-war line of the Murray forces." [54]

The Communists had gained effective control of the Progressive Party, and they had reaffirmed their hard line at their own national convention. Given these two facts and the realities of American politics, there was only one direction the Progressive Party could go thereafter: down. As more and more non-Communists left the Wallace movement, the Communists increased their control. By October, the Communists were even trying to sell the *Daily Worker* at meetings where Wallace spoke, including, of all places, Houston, Texas. Pro-Wallace I. F. Stone had to admit in one of his columns, "The Communists are doing a major part of the work of the Wallace movement, from ringing doorbells to framing platforms. Okay if you want it that way, so they 'dominate' the party. So what? I'm just a poor dupe who can't take either Dewey or Truman." [55]

In the fall of 1948, Wallace began to suspect that the Communists were deliberately embarrassing his candidacy in order to keep the Progressive Party small and easily controlled. Josiah Gitt and Louis Adamic came to see Wallace to warn him of this possibility. Adamic was convinced that the Communists were more interested in control of the party after the election than in getting Wallace a good vote. Wallace told Baldwin of his suspicions, but Baldwin pointed out that the Communists were serving a useful organizational function at the local level. Nevertheless, in October, Wallace hired a new ghost writer whose ideas more nearly matched his own. [56]

Certainly the Communists had no desire to see the Progressive Party mushroom so that they would lose control of it, but there was little likelihood of that. The Communists actually worked as faithfully for the Wallace campaign at its end as at its beginning, and there is no evidence to support Wallace's suspicions. The Communist attitude toward Wallace and the Progressives did not change essentially in 1948. Wallace was just slow to realize—and then only dimly—what co-operating with the Communists involved. If anything, the Communists at the very end of the campaign softened their position a little. At the last minute, they acceded to the decision to withdraw some of the several Progressive Congressional candidates who were running against liberal Democrats.

These Progressive Congressional candidacies particularly irritated the anti-Communist Left. In California, the Progressives put up candidates against several liberal Democrats, among them Helen Gahagan Douglas, Chet Holifield, and Frank R. Havenner, when these Democrats refused to crossfile with the Progressives. In New York, the Progressives ran Lee Pressman against Abraham J. Multer, and in New Jersey and Pennsylvania, Wallaceite candidates ran against Charles Howell and Frank Buchanan, both Democratic liberals with labor support. In Illinois, where Progressive candidates could receive only write-in votes, Grant Oakes, President of the Left Wing Farm Equipment Workers Union, opposed Adlai Stevenson for governor, and Professor Curtis MacDougall, of Northwestern University, opposed Paul Douglas for the United States Senate. Late in the campaign, the Progressives withdrew some of these candidates, including all of them in California.[57]

The primary reason for the decline of the Wallace movement was the Communists, both at home and abroad. The American public became highly aroused against Communism during the course of 1948, and the electorate, with justification, identified the Wallace Progressive Party with the Communists.

A series of events in 1948 intensified American anti-Communist sentiment. Indeed, if foreign Communists had deliberately tried, they could not have done much more than they did to hurt the Wallace campaign. In late February came the Communist coup in Czechoslovakia. In June, the Russians began their blockade of West Berlin, and the United States Air Force retaliated with the airlift. In late June and early July, the Soviets and the Cominform excommunicated Yugoslavia's Tito. The sensational Kasenkina affair in New York occurred in August. Oksaka Stepanova Kasenkina, a teacher for the children of Russian diplomats in New York City, had defected and gone to the farm for Russian refugees operated by the Tolstoy Foundation. The Russians kidnaped her and returned her to the Soviet Consulate. On August 12, she jumped from a third-floor window of the consulate, successfully escaped, and told the whole story. That same month, Whittaker Chambers began his revelations about Soviet espionage. By Election Day, the electorate was in no mood to vote for a party it associated with Communism.

But it was not only Communist activity in the Progressive Party that diminished Wallace's following; Harry Truman played no small part in the desertions from Gideon's army. Truman conducted a campaign designed to minimize the Wallace movement. Tugwell exaggerated in his postelection analysis when he wrote, "As fast as [Wallace] occupied a forward trench, he found Mr. Truman in it with him . . ." but certainly Truman did move toward the Left during the campaign. Without attacking Wallace directly, Truman made it clear, especially before labor audiences, that a vote for Wallace was a half-vote for Dewey. He capitalized on the fear of reaction that had only a few months earlier stimulated the Wallace movement. In Detroit, for example, the president told a Labor Day audience in Cadillac Square that Taft-Hartley was "only a foretaste of what you will get if the Republican reaction is allowed to continue to grow. . . . If you let the Republican reactionaries get complete control of the Government, the position of labor will be so greatly weakened that I fear not only for . . . wages and living standards . . . but even for our democratic institutions." [58]

Furthermore, the Dixiecrat revolt hurt Wallace and helped Truman in the North. When Truman's civil-rights position was too strong for the Dixiecrats to stomach, it appealed more than ever to northern Negroes. Wallace's tour of the South, in which he refused to speak before segregated audiences and was the target of several rotten eggs, was clearly intended to gain Wallace votes in the North. But it failed of its objective. Southern recalcitrance on the race issues, symbolized by Strom Thurmond's Presidential candidacy, boosted Truman rather than Wallace.

On November 2, Harry S. Truman, "the man who couldn't win," surprised the political experts, the press, the public, and Thomas E. Dewey by winning re-election. The experts were nearly as surprised by Wallace's poor showing. Wallace received only 1,156,103 votes.[59] In April, Wallace had spoken optimistically of twenty million votes, and he had been generally conceded two or three million down until Election Day.[60] Probably, the mechanics of vote counting being what they are, there were many Wallace votes never officially reported. But even if only half the Wallace votes were counted—and the count was surely more honest than that—Wallace still ran a miserable race.

Of Wallace's total vote, well over half came from New York City and California. His total New York State vote was 501,167; in California, he received 190,381, of which 101,085 came from Los Angeles County, 21,492 from San Francisco County, and 16,853 from Alameda County (East Bay).[61] Other states with significant Wallace votes were Massachusetts (38,157), Michigan (38,955), New Jersey (42,683), Ohio (37,596), Pennsylvania (55,161), and Washington (29,745). If all Wallace voters in New York, Maryland, and Michigan had voted for Truman, Truman would not have lost those states. In Illinois, one could vote for Wallace only with a write-in, and Ohio's ballot carried only the names of Wallace electors without mentioning Wallace or the Progressive Party. Had the Progressive ticket been fully on the ballot in those states, Truman might well have lost them too.

Wallace carried only thirty of the nation's precincts. Seven of these were in Tampa, around Ybor City, inhabited largely by Cuban cigar workers. Five were in Los Angeles; the other eighteen in New York City—eight of these in Vito Marcantonio's bailiwick, which sent him back to Congress. Wallace also carried two election districts in the East Bronx, where there was a large workers' co-operative apartment house, started by Communists in the 1920's and later known as "little Stalingrad." [62] Wallace, the *Daily Worker* complained, did not even carry some of the traditionally A.L.P. "Jewish working class districts." The Democrats in those districts increased their vote more than did the A.L.P.[63]

What were the end results of this Communist venture into third-party politics? Most were on the debit side of the Communist ledger. The Communists almost completely sacrificed their position in the C.I.O. They brought to a head a crisis over Communism in the non-Communist liberal community, and the election results showed that the progress of the Left from non-Communism to anti-Communism was well developed. The Communists had bet a great deal on the establishment of a popular leftist party, and they lost the wager.

The Communists had little on the credit side of the 1948 ledger. The third party had given international Communism a propaganda weapon, an opportunity for foreign Communists to point to the Progressive Party and say that the American masses were grumbling under the yoke of their Wall Street masters.[64] The Communists had gained a little influence among some non-Communists and through them had broadened the audience for their propaganda. The party even acquired some new members from the Progressive Party, especially young people—Elizabeth Gurley Flynn reported that she had recruited four Amherst boys and five Boston students within a week [65]—but it is not likely that the recruits stayed in the party long. Total party membership declined during the year.

The Communists stuck with the Progressive Party for another four years. They saw nothing mistaken about the Progressive venture when they surveyed the 1948 election returns. On the contrary, the Communists declared, "the basis for a mass, potentially powerful, anti-imperialist coalition was created." The election results *"reinforce the view that the foundation of a national Third*

Party, capable of successfully challenging the reactionary program of American monopoly, was laid in this campaign." [66]

William Z. Foster in 1949 candidly described what Communists expected from such a third party. In a book confidently dedicated to his great-grandson, "who will live in a Communist United States," Foster spelled out what he hoped would happen if the third party had won:

The present party line follows the broad path towards the people's front and people's democracy types of government now to be found in Eastern Europe. . . . First, we propose the regular election of a democratic coalition government, based on a broad united front combination. . . . Second, our party contends that such an anti-fascist, anti-war, democratic coalition government, once in power, would be compelled either to move to the Left or to die. With state power in its hands, it would be forced to pass over from the more or less defensive program upon which it was elected to an offensive policy. . . . Third, a democratic, anti-fascist, anti-war government, under the violent attacks of the capitalists and in its efforts to find solutions to the burning economic and political problems, if it were to survive, would necessarily move leftward, toward socialism, much as the People's Democracies of Eastern and Central Europe are now doing. Some liberals believe that a united front coalition would introduce a regime of "progressive capitalism," but this is a naive and dangerous illusion.[67]

In view of revelations Communists themselves would make in 1956 about life in the "people's democracies," the judgment of the American people in 1948 in rejecting Foster's "united front coalition" acquires a new significance. In 1956, even Communist leaders would admit publicly that their third-party venture had been a stupid mistake.

PART THREE

YEARS
OF
SUSPICION

Comrades, we are heading into some big storms.

—EUGENE DENNIS, *August 1948*

SIX: THE PARTY AND ANTI-COMMUNISM

In 1949 and 1950, the disillu-
sion, frustration, and anxiety that had been building in the United
States over the Communist issue at home and abroad burst into
full, angry reaction. Each year since the war was one of shock,
but 1949 and 1950 were traumatic even for that trying era.

By then the world was clearly divided into three camps—the
Communist world, led by the Soviet Union; the Western world,
led by the United States; and the "neutralist" Afro-Asian bloc—
and the cold war was sharp. Some events of 1949 led many Americans to think they were losing the cold war, and many people
thought the reverses were as much the result of internal betrayal
as of foreign Communist strength.

In the spring of 1948, Chiang Kai-shek had controlled about
three-fourths of China's territory and two-thirds of its population.
The next year, Mao Tse-tung's Communist forces drove Chiang
and his Nationalists to Formosa. Shanghai obviously would not
now become what Senator Kenneth Wherry had so wildly predicted—"just like Kansas City." [1] In September 1949, President
Truman announced that the Russians had exploded an atomic
bomb. It was now apparent that Soviet bombers could destroy the
industrial centers of the Western European nations, which had
been brought into a military alliance with the United States earlier

in the year. Further than that, as many an American recognized when he awakened in the night at the sound of an airplane over his home, it was possible now for the Russians to bring nuclear destruction to the United States itself.

Americans were bewildered, angry, and resentful. A few years earlier, when their fascist enemies were near defeat, the chances of postwar peace and international harmony had seemed bright. But there was no real peace, no harmony, and now another hostile dictator had power to hurt America such as Hitler had never possessed. Assured by some military leaders and others in 1946 that only American technology and science were capable of discovering the "secret" of atomic fission, many people now leaped to the conclusion that only Communist espionage, disloyalty, treachery, and a bungling, "soft-on-Communism" administration could account for the Russians having the bomb. And when Klaus Fuchs confessed to atomic espionage and the Rosenbergs were convicted, these dark conclusions were confirmed in some people's minds.

In 1946, there had been a spy sensation when the Canadian Government exposed an espionage ring which had operated during the war. In 1947, there had been the confusing Eisler case. Contemporaneous with the revelation of the Russian bomb was the story of Judith Coplon's passing classified information to Valentin Gubichev of the Soviet Embassy. The biggest headlines about espionage at the time, however, concerned the affair of Whittaker Chambers and Alger Hiss.

The Hiss case marked the end of one era and the birth of another. The whole Hiss story as it slowly unfolded was so bizarre—involving microfilms hidden in an abandoned dumb-waiter and a pumpkin, Oriental rugs, an old Woodstock typewriter, a Model A Ford, and two very strange men—that one would reject the story as too wild if one read it as mystery fiction. The evidence in the case was extremely complicated, but the main point is that relatively few Americans formed their judgment of Hiss and Chambers—at least their first judgment—on the basis of the evidence. The personalities and appearances of the two men, their careers, and the kinds of people they symbolized, rather than the evidence, influenced the judgment of most people—that, and whether one regarded himself as a friend or an opponent of the New Deal.

The Hiss case began during the 1948 campaign, when Chambers, once a Communist and a Bohemian writer, later a spy for the Soviets, and later still a senior editor of *Time,* charged that Alger Hiss, to all appearances the prototype of the young, competent, well-educated, idealistic, and liberal lawyer and junior New Deal administrator, had been a member of the Communist Party from at least 1934 to 1938. Chambers made his charges before the House Committee on Un-American Activities, whose chairman then was J. Parnell Thomas, of New Jersey. But the most prominent member of the committee in the Hiss case was a young politician-on-the-make from southern California, Richard M. Nixon. Nixon was a freshman congressman at the time, having defeated the veteran liberal Democrat Jerry Voorhis in the 1946 Republican landslide.

Faced with a libel suit brought by Hiss, Chambers broadened his charges against him, asserting now that Hiss had helped him covertly transmit classified State Department documents to agents of the Soviet Government. He produced the "pumpkin papers," and a New York grand jury indicted Hiss for perjury, the statute of limitations preventing an indictment for espionage, and early in 1949 the case went to trial. The trial ended in July with a hung jury, eight to four for conviction. A second jury found Hiss guilty, and he received a five-year sentence.

More important to us here than the details of the Hiss case was its impact upon American public opinion. The case brought to the public in a dramatic way a realization of the strength of Communism in America in the previous decade, and the contemporary political implications of the case tended to exaggerate Communist influence in 1949. President Truman during the 1948 campaign referred to the Hiss affair as a "red herring" designed to distract voters from the inadequacies of the "awful Eightieth Congress," and the public came to see the case as a struggle between Nixon, the symbol of aggressive Republicanism, critical of all things New Deal, and Hiss, the symbol of the bright young New Deal intellectual. When more evidence was brought to light and Hiss was finally convicted, more was at stake than his own career. The New Deal and the kind of liberalism it represented were now suspect to many a person who had voted for Roosevelt; and some New Deal critics, always ready to impute the worst to "that man" and what he symbolized, now felt vindicated. Then Secretary of State Dean Acheson, dapper, urbane, suspect in some quarters anyway because of his Ivy League polish, in an impolitic but compassionate statement said he would not "turn my back on Alger Hiss." Many people concluded that subversion was still rife in the federal government.

The jury found Hiss guilty on January 21, 1950. On February 3, Klaus Fuchs confessed in London. On February 9, at Wheeling, West Virginia, Joseph R. McCarthy, then a relatively unknown first-term senator, asserted he had "here in my hand" a list of 205 —or 57, as later speeches put it—names who were known to Acheson to be Communist Party members and who were nevertheless still working in the State Department. The era of McCarthyism was born. It was a violent child, destined to live about a half-decade.

McCarthyism was a whole complex of attitudes, some of them contradictory. It was militant anti-Communism, but it was also unreasoning fear and hysteria about Communism, both at home and abroad. It was exploitation of popular fear and frustration about Communism for partisan political advantage, but it was also a more general political irresponsibility. It reflected isolationist attitudes toward Europe—but not toward Asia—yet played upon the nationalist feelings of European immigrants whose homelands were behind the Iron Curtain. It was anti-intellectual, both in the sense of exalting the irrational and in the sense of animosity toward intellectual and cosmopolitan people. It appealed to the prejudices and frustrations of the relatively poor as well as to the fears of the *nouveaux riches,* particularly Texas oil millionaires. Above all, McCarthyism was an acceptance of the idea that the end justifies the means, the end being power and the eradication of the Communists, who themselves believed that the end justifies the means.

Senator McCarthy did not invent McCarthyism, and his abrupt political decline after his repudiation by the Senate in December 1954 did not absolutely end the phenomenon. Nevertheless, McCarthy—as did Hiss—came to symbolize more than he actually was. The years of the height of McCarthyism saw many wild and improbable developments. The American people swung frantically with an anti-Communist bludgeon. They used the rapier very little. The bludgeon hurt the Communists, but it hurt a great many anti-Communists too. In the effort to save democracy and liberty from Communism, the American people outraged democracy and liberty themselves. At both popular and official levels, Americans violated both the spirit and the letter of the Bill of Rights.

The federal government, under the administration of both Truman and Eisenhower, pursued an extensive campaign against Communism at home and abroad. The Truman administration instituted a security program to root out subversives from government, and the Eisenhower administration widened its scope. Congressional committees investigated almost everything and received many headlines. Congress passed new anti-Communist legislation, for example the McCarran Internal Security Act of 1950, which among other things provided for concentration camps for the internment of Communists in the event of war. And the Department of Justice brought many prosecutions under the Smith Act of 1940. By the end of 1954, ninety-two Communist leaders had been indicted and tried under that act. Four others were indicted but were fugitives at the time of their trials. Of this total of ninety-six, only three were acquitted. One died during trial, and five others had their cases severed because of poor health.

State and local governments and the people generally were also active in the anti-Communist crusade. A few states prosecuted Communists under "little Smith acts." Many instituted non-Communist oaths as a condition of public employment. At the state level, officials were apt to be extreme, even sometimes a little silly, in their anti-Communism. One member of the Indiana Textbook Commission, for example, wanted to ban school readers that included Robin Hood stories, perhaps on the theory that the Sherwood outlaw was an anticapitalist precursor of Marx and Lenin. Indiana also required professional boxers to take a non-Communist oath before practicing their trade in the Hoosier State. But government officials were only a little wilder, if any, than the public at large. The Cincinnati Reds became the Redlegs. Social clubs ostracized members who were suspected of Communist sympathies. An association of chess players expelled an officer thought to be a Communist.

American public opinion had been hostile to the Communists ever since they came into being during and just after World War I. Apparently, however, the experience of being a wartime ally of the Soviet Union softened that hostility, and immediately after World War II, American Communists enjoyed greater good will— or, rather, less ill will—from the public at large than ever before or since. A 1940 public-opinion survey indicated that nearly three-fourths of the population favored a law to forbid membership in the Communist Party. In 1946, fewer than half the people favored such action. But soon public opinion was to change again. By the early 1950's, Americans were unwilling to tolerate Communists. A careful survey made in the early summer of 1954 revealed that about three-fourths of the people favored stripping admitted Communists of their citizenship, and about one-half thought they should be jailed.[2]

All this anti-Communism hurt the Communist Party. The party suffered badly. Hampered by legislation, vulnerable to prosecution, and the object of the public's intense hostility, the Communists were in no position to advance their political program nor to expand their organization. In this climate of opinion, the opportunities for an actual, living, active Communist were limited indeed. Forces and conditions outside the party, in the real world—what Communists call the "objective situation"—put the American Communists on the defensive. The Communists had to be more concerned with their party's survival than with its advancement, and they quite naturally tended to isolate themselves from the harsh world.

Yet it was not the "objective situation" alone that brought the Communist Party to a moribund and feeble condition. When Communist parties die, or nearly die, a large part of the final illness is self-inflicted. Not even the "objective situation" of Hitler's Germany killed the German party. Years of intellectual malnourishment and ill-advised self-medication with magic rituals, complete with incantations and exorcism of demons, take their toll.

EXPECTATIONS OF FASCISM AND WAR

The Communists had two closely related ideas about the immediate future during the years of McCarthyism that underlay their line and activities on almost all matters. These basic assumptions were that the United States was on the verge of fascism nationally and on the precipice of total nuclear war internationally.

The villains, of course, were "American imperialism," "Wall Street," "the monopolies." The twin dangers of war and fascism were but two sides of the same imperialist coin. Imperialism, "especially American imperialism," was "incurably warlike." But the American masses—"labor and progressive-minded Negro and white masses"—opposed war, as did, of course, the Communist Party, the "vanguard" of the working class. The imperialists, according to Communist writers, then, had to make America fascist to put over their war program: ". . . the purpose of the fascist trend is to hasten the preparation for a war seeking Wall Street's world domination." [3]

The Communists deluded themselves with the thought that they were in actual fact the vanguard of the working classes and that they were so regarded by "Wall Street." From this delusion arose their belief that all measures directed against Communists or the party were but the opening wedge of fascism, of a program of imperialism to destroy American democracy, annihilate the labor movement, reverse the direction of the Negro toward full equality, and coerce the population to an acceptance of total war. "The anti-Communist drive cannot and will not be limited to Communists," wrote the veteran Communist Will Weinstone in 1950. "The Communists are singled out for attack first of all because they are staunch fighters for peace against a ruling class gone war mad; because they are unyielding battlers for democracy against a bourgeoisie which is turning to fascism and hates and fears every vestige of democracy. . . . But while the main edge of the onslaught is directed against the Communists . . . the anti-Communist crusade is seeking to speed the destruction of all working-class, militant, progressive organizations, and to gag all decent people." The Communists thus saw themselves in the heroic posture of the Dutch boy with his finger in the dike. If they faltered, if they were defeated and silenced, all was lost, not only for them, but for "all decent people."

The party leadership's position on whether or not war and fascism were inevitable was another of their several Scylla-Charybdis constructions. The "correct" line was that the party must sail between the Scylla of underestimating the danger the imperialists represented and the Charybdis of considering war and fascism inevitable. The consequences of Scylla were obvious, and Charybdis "can only lead to paralysis in action, to waiting about and even to feelings of hopelessness, and to attempts at liquidationism of the Party in practice." [4]

In actual practice, as apart from what they said, the party's leaders operated on the assumption that war and fascism were extremely likely if not inevitable. Their arguments admitted of no other logical conclusion. If the imperialists had their way, they would bring war and fascism. If their drive for world domination were blocked by the Soviet "peace camp," they would make war out of frustration. Either successful or unsuccessful in their expansionist program, the imperialists would bring fascism and war. The Communists had themselves in a tight intellectual box. While exhorting the membership not to let up the fight against war and fascism, which the membership might do if told the twin evils were inevitable anyway, the leadership instituted internal party reorganizations based upon the premise of the extreme likelihood of war. Surely the party's internal purges and the decision to go "underground" (to be described in the next chapter) were designed to ride out the storm of an imminent war and accompanying fascism.

There is more than a little irony in the denouement in the mid-1950's. By then the danger of war had subsided—because of changed Russian leadership and policy—and McCarthyism had declined to relative insignificance. But the American Communists, huddled in their storm cellars, talking only among themselves, had nothing to do with this outcome. All in all, the Communists' campaign against war and fascism was quite ineffective. Their worst fears—indeed, their expectations—did not materialize. The Communists were ineffective because they alienated non-Communist opponents of war and reaction and because the insincerity of their posture as civil libertarians and defenders of freedom was transparent.

A few examples will illustrate. Labor leaders, Communists thought, should be their allies. But Foster called C.I.O. and A.F. of L. leaders "blatant supporters of the current employers' program . . . splitting unions and breaking strikes at the behest of the State Department . . . tools of the warmakers." Will Weinstone called Phil Murray a "slanderer" pursuing "a craven policy." [5] Negro leaders also felt the Communist lash. Communists attacked Dr. Ralph J. Bunche "for his services to the Western imperialist warmongers," and called the anti-Communist George Schuyler "a true lackey of the monopolists." [6] Nor were Communists likely to get sympathetic understanding or co-operation from the liberal wings of the Democratic and Republican parties, which the Communists attacked more vigorously than they did those parties' conservative wings. When Truman vetoed the Mc-Carran Act, Will Weinstone said that Truman was just as bad as McCarran and did not really want to defeat the measure. His veto was "only for the record and to 'appease' and deceive the masses."[7] And back in 1946, Wisconsin Communists in the U.A.W. West Allis local had supported McCarthy, then an unknown conservative circuit-court judge, against the liberal Senator Robert M. La Follette, Jr., in the open Republican primary. The *Daily Worker* was clearly delighted with La Follette's defeat.[8]

The Communist effort to pose as defenders of the Bill of Rights was ridiculous to anyone who knew their record on freedom within the party, let alone Communist unwillingness to grant civil liberty to their enemies. When the Supreme Court announced its decision in the Dennis case, upholding the constitutionality of the Smith Act, the party's national committee issued a statement which among other things urged the American people to "speak out together in defense of the Constitution and the Bill of Rights" and declared the party would "not capitulate to the bookburn-ers."[9] The appeal had a hollow ring to people who remembered that the Communists had supported the prosecution of the Minneapolis Trotskyists under the same Smith Act in 1942 and had reaffirmed that position in July 1949 even while the first Communist Smith Act trial was in progress.[10] In 1946, the party had tried to get what it called "poison books" removed from the library shelves of New York's public schools. The *Daily Worker* was particularly opposed to an allegedly anti-Negro novel called *Lanterns on the Levee,* by William Alexander Percy.[11]

In fact, the Communists had several times used precisely the same kind of illiberal tactics and methods that the McCarthyites used. In 1946, the Communists heard that old White Russian General Anton Denikin had been admitted to the United States. They demanded that the Immigration Service explain itself and deport the man.[12] And they had pushed the guilt-by-association device to extreme lengths to smear an enemy. A *Daily Worker* story in 1946 by William Allan, a Detroit U.A.W. Communist, about Walter Reuther is a case in point. Reuther, as head of the U.A.W. committee on social security, had negotiated on a group-insurance plan with "one Leo Perlman, former Czech social Democrat, who likes to be called a doctor and an insurance actuary, though he is neither." Perlman's firm was the Trade Union Casualty Co., which had associations with another insurance firm called Continental Assurance Co., which was "connected through interlocking directorates with the Chicago packing houses, Elgin Watch Co., the large Illinois banks and International Harvester." There was thus a link between Reuther and Chicago capitalists. But Allan pushed the association one step farther. On the board of Continental Assurance was the uncle of the first national secretary of America First. Thus Reuther was also consorting with Nazis. This tenuous commercial and avuncular relationship was "evidence" for Communist support of the Thomas-Addes faction of the U.A.W.[13]

The Communists invoked the memory of Jefferson and Madison when the court upheld the Smith Act. The tragedy was that the times called for genuine, rather than cynical, defenders of the Jefferson-Madison tradition of civil liberty.

THE SMITH ACT CASES

In 1940, during the period of the Nazi-Soviet pact, President Roosevelt signed the Alien Registration Act, generally known as the Smith Act, for its sponsor, Representative Howard Smith, of Virginia. The measure's Title I forbade, upon pain of fine up to $10,000 and imprisonment up to ten years, "knowingly or willfully" advocating, abetting, advising, or teaching the "duty, necessity, desirability, or propriety" of overthrowing or destroying by force or violence the United States Government or American state and local governments. Title I also forbade organizing or attempting or helping to organize "any society, group, or assembly of persons who teach, advocate, or encourage the overthrow or destruction of any such government by force or violence; or becomes or is a member of, or affiliates with, any such . . . [organization], knowing the purposes thereof." The act had first been invoked in 1942 against eighteen Trotskyists. The Eighth Circuit Court of Appeals upheld the conviction and the Supreme Court denied certiorari. Also, during the war there had been an indictment of thirty alleged Nazi sympathizers under another section of Title I, pertaining to inciting disloyalty in the armed forces. The presiding judge died after seven hectic months of trial, and the case was dropped, only to be revived in 1945. In November 1946, the District of Columbia Court of Appeals dismissed the indictment.

One other relevant background case involved William Schneiderman, chairman of the California Communists. The case was a denaturalization proceeding not involving the Smith Act. In 1943, the Supreme Court ruled that the government had not proved by "clear, convincing, and unequivocal evidence" that the Communist Party in the five years before 1927 had advocated violent or forceful overthrow of government.[14]

Then on July 20, 1948, the Department of Justice sought and obtained from a federal grand jury in New York City an indictment against the twelve members of the national board of the Communist Party under Title I of the Smith Act. The twelve national board members were: William Z. Foster, Eugene Dennis (born Francis X. Waldron, Jr.), John B. Williamson, Jacob Stachel, Robert G. Thompson, Benjamin J. Davis, Jr., Henry Winston, John Gates (born Israel Regenstreif), Irving Potash, Gilbert Green, Carl Winter, and Gus Hall (born Arno Gust Halberg). The specific charges against them were that they had conspired with one another "and with divers other persons to the Grand Jury unknown" to dissolve the Communist Political Association and to reconstitute the Communist Party of the United States, "a society, group, and assembly of persons who teach and advocate the overthrow and destruction of the Government . . .

by force and violence," and then knowingly and willfully had caused to be taught and advocated such overthrow and destruction by force or violence. The indictment did not allege the defendants had committed any overt revolutionary act—only teaching and advocating. In other words, they were not charged with a conspiracy to overthrow the government; they were charged with conspiracy to form a party to teach and advocate overthrow of the government. The twelve defendants were arrested without incident in July and were released upon bail. At the beginning of the trial, the case against Foster was severed because his health was frail.[15] Since then, the government has occasionally reconsidered trying Foster, but each time it has let the matter drop because Foster's health has deteriorated further.

The trial opened January 17, 1949, before Judge Harold R. Medina in the federal court building, Foley Square, New York City. The trial lasted nine months, dragging through an exceptionally hot summer, and did not end completely until October 21. It was, in the words of one constitutional historian, "certainly among the most turbulent and hectic in American court annals." [16] The defendants engaged five principal attorneys: George W. Crockett, Richard Gladstein, Abraham J. Isserman, Louis F. McCabe, and Harry Sacher. Dennis acted as his own attorney. In the words of Judge Augustus Hand, the conduct of the defense attorneys at the trial was "wilfully obstructive." Despite several warnings from Medina that their conduct was contemptuous, the defense attorneys persisted in baiting the trial judge and accusing him of seeking publicity, of partiality toward the prosecution, and of racial prejudice. In June, Judge Medina declared defendants Hall and Winston in contempt, and the party organized a demonstration of pickets on Foley Square and a Union Square rally of protest. At the trial's end, Judge Medina cited the defense attorneys for contempt, found them guilty, and sentenced them to imprisonment without giving them an opportunity to reply. The Court of Appeals, by a 2 to 1 vote, upheld the contempt conviction, as did the U.S. Supreme Court, by a vote of five to three. Justices Black, Douglas, and Frankfurter dissented, and Justice Clark did not participate.[17]

It was clear from the beginning of the trial that the Communists' strategy in the courtroom was to use the case as a sounding board for its general position and program and to attempt to portray American justice as a sham. For the first several weeks of the trial, the Communists challenged the validity of the jury panel, asserting that the method of selecting jurors systematically excluded Negroes, the poor, and working people. The open purpose of this unsuccessful gambit was, in Foster's words, to put "the Government, not the Communists . . . on trial." [18] But the courtroom strategy was only part of a larger strategy: to arouse mass protest against the government's case in order to pressure the administration to drop its prosecution and actually to build the party and the movement in the process.

Soon after the trial opened, the Communist national committee made a full-page announcement in the *Worker*. The headline was "THE HERESY TRIAL HAS BEGUN." A subhead continued, "But this 20th century Political Inquisition is not proceeding according to bipartisan plan. In the courtroom the accused have become the accusers." In a box on the page was an outline of general strategy: "HERE IS OUR PLAN FOR A NATIONWIDE CAMPAIGN TO QUASH THE HERESY INDICTMENTS AND PRESERVE THE BILL OF RIGHTS: 1) Speak To the People, For the People Will Decide. . . . Get All Within The Sound of Your Voice to Pass Resolutions And Send Telegrams To Attorney General Tom Clark. . . . 2) Give The People Something To Read And Pass On To Others. . . . 3) Show The People How To Act Together. . . . 4) Ask The People To Pass The Ammunition. . . . 5) Build While You Convince." A few weeks later the veteran party war horse Elizabeth Gurley Flynn wrote in one of her frequent "pep talk" articles, "There is no more telling offensive to defend the leaders of the Party . . . than for the Party to grow right now in the very period of the court trial." [19]

The party's strategy did not work. The defendants and their

counsel did not present the kind of a case to persuade a jury, and the party's activities outside the courtroom neither helped the party grow nor aroused public opinion in the defendants' behalf. Indeed, the party could not even count on its usual friends. The party had difficulty raising money for trial expenses. One of the party fronts, the Civil Rights Congress, began a campaign in the summer of 1948 to raise $250,000. By the following February, it had collected only $74,095.45. (The way this sum was spent is further evidence of the party's strategy: only $25,592.05 went for legal defense; the balance was spent on "mass agitation, tours, conferences, printing, etc.") [20] The party's defenders complained of public apathy. As "The Thin Man," Dashiell Hammett, put it, "We had a lot of people going around saying, 'I don't care how it comes out just so they get it over with.' " He blamed the "imperialist press" for this apathy.[21]

The prosecution in the trial presented a three-pronged case. It dealt at length with the circumstances under which the party had been reconstituted in 1945; it introduced as evidence of intent to overthrow the government several "classics" of Marxism-Leninism-Stalinism published or taught by the party; and it presented thirteen former Communists and F.B.I. "plants" who testified that the "classics" had been taught or that the defendants had otherwise taught and advocated overthrow of the government.

The Communist strategy not only failed in the courtroom, it failed also to arouse any widespread concern in the public at large for the civil-liberties issues involved in the case. Indeed, the Communist antics in the court tended to prevent such general concern. Their tactics certainly were not well calculated to attract non-Communists and anti-Communists to the defense of free speech for Communists, though the Supreme Court ruled in 1957 that the case did involve principles of free speech.

Perhaps the most important aspect of the trial was Judge Medina's charge to the jury. The prosecution had concerned itself only with evidence about Communist speeches and publications, the advocacy of overthrow of government, rather than overt action leading to such overthrow. Yet the first amendment to the Constitution clearly guarantees free speech and a free press, which has been judicially construed to mean no limitations unless the speech or publication presents a "clear and present danger" to the safety of the republic. Judge Medina bridged the gap between illegal action and constitutionally guaranteed speech by charging the jury that the defendants could be found guilty if they found that the defendants intended to overthrow the government by violence and force "as speedily as circumstances permit." And he removed the clear-and-present-danger issue from the jury's consideration by stating that, as a matter of law, "there is sufficient danger of a substantive evil."

The jury found the eleven defendants guilty as charged. Judge Medina sentenced them to $10,000 fines and five years' imprisonment, except for Robert Thompson, whose record of heroism in the army prompted the judge to reduce his imprisonment to three years. The defendants appealed, and in 1950 the Court of Appeals, Judge Learned Hand writing the opinion, upheld the conviction. The Supreme Court granted certiorari, and, in June 1951, found the Smith Act constitutional and upheld the convictions. Justices Black and Douglas dissented, and Justice Clark did not participate.

The Supreme Court's decision in the Dennis case is an extremely important one in the nation's constitutional history, but it need not detain us here. Suffice it to say that the opinions were varied and complicated and that the vote of the court represented an unprecedented judicial approval for restriction of speech. It is interesting to note that Justice Douglas's dissenting opinion referred to the Communists as "miserable merchants of unwanted ideas," and that two of the majority justices, Frankfurter and Jackson, wrote that the Smith Act, while constitutional, was an ill-advised and ineffective method of combating Communism.[22]

The Department of Justice sought and secured indictments of many other Communist leaders after the Supreme Court upheld the convictions of the top eleven leaders. On March 10, 1952,

Philip Frankfeld, his wife, and four other Maryland Communist leaders were brought to trial in Baltimore. All were found guilty and sentenced to $1,000 fines and from two to five years' imprisonment. Ironically, the *Daily Worker* announced Frankfeld's expulsion from the party and his wife's removal from leadership just three days before the trial began. The party's leadership accused him of "defeatism," of writing and circulating among the membership a pamphlet counter to the line of the party, and "moral degeneracy and corruption . . . double-dealing and deception." [23] Such charges certainly smacked of the party's own "thought control."

In a trial in Los Angeles beginning on February 1, 1952, and ending August 5, William Schneiderman, Oleta O'Conner Yates, Dorothy Healy, and eleven other top California Communists were convicted under the Smith Act. Although convicted, the California Communists conducted quite a different kind of defense from the one in the first trial. These defendants, in June 1957, became the first Smith Act group to receive a favorable decision from the Supreme Court.

The most widely publicized of these "second-string" prosecutions was *United States* v. *Elizabeth Gurley Flynn, et al.,* sometimes known as the "second Foley Square trial." In this trial, thirteen Communists were convicted, but a new development was Judge Edward J. Dimock's directed acquittal of two of the defendants, Isadore Begun and Simon W. Gerson, on the grounds that insufficient evidence had been presented to connect them to the indicted conspiracy. Subsequently, the convictions of two other defendants, Alexander Trachtenberg and George Blake Charney, were set aside and new trials ordered when the testimony of the principal witness against them, Harvey Matusow, was revealed to be questionable at best.

Prosecutions and convictions of "second-string" and even "third-string" Communist leaders continued through 1953 and 1954. Seven were convicted in Honolulu, five in Pittsburgh, four in Seattle, six in Detroit, five in St. Louis, and nine in Philadelphia. In all these cases there was but one acquittal.

What were the effects on the Communist Party of all these prosecutions, convictions, and imprisonments? (The question of the wisdom of the Smith Act prosecutions, which involves an assessment of their impact on civil liberties, is another question.) Certainly prosecutions under the Smith Act did not kill the party, for it was still a going concern after the frequency of new indictments declined about 1955. In that year, the F.B.I. estimated the party had 22,663 members.[24] Membership strength shrank considerably after the 1949 trial, but the party's most important membership loss did not come until 1956 and 1957, after the Smith Act prosecutions had almost ceased.

It is impossible precisely to measure the various factors causing the decline of the Communist Party in the early 1950's and say that this or that causal factor was responsible for x percentage of the party's deterioration. Smith Act prosecutions were only one among many actions and conditions that hurt the party. Among others were the further deterioration of Russian-American relations during the Korean war, the continued health of the American economy, and, perhaps most important, the ill-advised actions of the Communist Party itself.

The prosecutions obviously hurt the party. It was forced to spend for legal defense a great deal of money it would otherwise have spent for offensive, rather than defensive, activity. The trials consumed a great deal of the Communists' time and energy, which they would have preferred to use otherwise. It has been asserted that the Smith Act convictions "beheaded" the party, leaving the rank and file without effective leadership. Unquestionably, the imprisonment of the abler and more experienced leaders damaged the party's efficiency, but the most important party leader, William Z. Foster, actively led the party despite the poor health that prevented the government from pushing his prosecution. There is no reason to believe that the main direction of the party would have been different had the imprisoned leaders remained active in the leadership. The party's decision to go "underground" in 1949 and 1950, related of course to the Smith Act prosecutions, probably damaged party efficiency more than the leaders' imprisonment. It is unlikely that a considerable number of Communists severed their party connection because of fear of prosecution. Only one of the convicted Communists, Barbara Hartle, convicted at Seattle in 1953, renounced the party before the Communists' 1956 crisis, and she related that her indictment prompted her to stay in the party longer than she would have otherwise. It may even be true that the prosecutions led members to resolve to stick with the party, come what may.

"PEACE" AND WAR

In the late 1940's and early 1950's, the most prominent feature of the American Communists' outward face was their "peace crusade." "Peace," by which the Communists actually meant unstinting agreement with the foreign policy of the Soviet Union, had long been a prominent Communist demand. But in 1949 and early 1950, "peace" became the ideological hook upon which all else hung.

Foster expressed the notion of the centrality of the "peace" issue clearly in a message to the party's national committee. "Under no circumstances should we neglect the mass struggles over wages, unemployment, Negro rights, and fascism: but we must recognize that these are all bound up with the fight against war. Everything depends upon our success in this all-inclusive key struggle. To mobilize the masses to fight for peace should be the very center of the work." Then, in a passage that illustrated the party's ambiguous position on the inevitability of war, he advised that the "peace crusade" must be a long-term campaign, if not one of indefinite duration. "Regardless of any agreements that may be made to soften the cold war . . . the war danger will continue to exist. . . . That is because of the incur-

able warlike character of imperialism, especially American imperialism. The war danger will last as long as capitalism does,
and we must orientate upon this realization . . . the fight for
peace must be in the center of all our Party's work." [25]

The party's first big peace project was the Scientific and Cultural Conference for World Peace, usually called the Waldorf
Peace Conference, in March 1949. An organization called the
National Council of the Arts, Sciences, and Professions, composed of former Progressive Citizens of America members for
the most part, officially sponsored the conference, but the Communists actually organized the affair. The conference attracted an
impressive list of intellectuals as participants, indicating that as
late as the spring of 1949 the influence of Communists in the
non-Communist Left was far from extinguished.[26] In October,
the party inspired the formation in Chicago of the National Labor Conference for Peace, and in December, it was behind a
weekend peace rally in New York City's Manhattan Center.[27]

The Communist peace campaign began in earnest in the spring
of 1950; the immediate occasion for the stepped-up program was
the job of getting American signatures to the so-called Stockholm
Peace Petition. In March, the Permanent Committee of the World
Peace Congress met at Stockholm and drafted the appeal. The
chairman of this committee was the French scientist and Communist Frederic Joliot-Curie, now dead; the vice-chairman was a
non-Communist former assistant attorney general of the United
States, O. John Rogge. Other American delegates were Albert
Kahn and Johannes Steel. The petition itself was an innocuous
condemnation of the use of atomic bombs, which several million
Americans might have endorsed had it not been for the petition's
international Communist sponsorship. It did not call for the abolition of nuclear testing. The Russians still had a lot of testing to
do.

O. John Rogge's story was interesting. Rogge had criticized
both American and Russian imperialism at a peace conference
in Mexico City in 1949, and the Communists called him a slan-

derer. In early March 1950, before the Stockholm meeting, he agreed to serve as legal counsel for Tito's Yugoslavia in the United States, and he registered with the Department of Justice as required by the Foreign Agents Registration Act of 1938. Still he went to Stockholm. At a meeting of the World Peace Conference in Warsaw in November 1950, Rogge gave a speech in which he vigorously condemned Soviet imperialism. His speech caused a scene of memorable proportions. An American delegate, Charles P. Howard, who had given the keynote speech at the 1948 Progressive convention, called Rogge "not only a lawyer for Tito but . . . the advocate for the slaveholder Jefferson Davis . . . and of King George III." The staff of the Cominform's newspaper was violent in condemnation of Rogge.[28]

In order to reach their goal of five million signatures to the Stockholm petition by October 24, United Nations Day, the Communists staged the kind of organizational campaign at which they once excelled. They used their influence in the trade unions they still dominated; they created new front groups (Harlem Women's Committee on Peace, Veterans for Peace, U.S. Youth Sponsoring Committee for the World Peace Appeal); they organized conferences with noble titles; and they exploited their old front groups, like the American Slav Congress. But their effort failed to achieve the goal. At the end of the campaign, the Communists claimed only two and one-half million signatures, and that figure was unquestionably padded.[29]

Before the petition campaign was over, the United States was actually engaged in armed conflict with Communists in Korea. Early in the morning of June 25, 1950, North Korean troops crossed the thirty-eighth parallel, the boundary between the American and Russian occupation zones set by the Potsdam Conference, in a large-scale, obviously long-planned invasion of South Korea. Almost immediately, the United States, independently and through the United Nations, went to the aid of the South Koreans; within a matter of days, American soldiers were being killed as the North Koreans pushed on south.

The American Communists now faced a new situation, but the fundamentals of their position on the Korean war had already been decided. As early as 1947, the party press had begun to publish paeans to the Soviet-supported North Koreans and condemnations of the American-supported government of Syngman Rhee in South Korea. The North Koreans were peaceful and democratic; Syngman Rhee was a reactionary puppet of Wall Street.[30] Curiously, there had even been foreshadowings of some of the details of the party line on the Korean war. On the first anniversary of V-J Day, *New Masses* had carried an article on bacteriological warfare with ideas that would in time come to fruition in such *Daily Worker* headlines as "REPORT U.S. PLANES DROP MORE GERMS ON KOREA," "BACTERIOLOGICAL WAR CRIMINALS," and "EYEWITNESS DESCRIBES GERM BOMB." [31]

The Communists claimed that the whole Korean affair was part of a conspiracy of Wall Street and its agents in Washington and Seoul. In a "plot . . . as thoroughly planned as . . . the Japanese seizure of Mukden in 1931," Wall Street had entrusted Syngman Rhee to arrange the incident. John Foster Dulles was "the trigger man." The party secretariat issued a statement that even had Dulles "standing in the front lines of the puppet government trenches, giving them their marching orders." Dulles was indeed an awful person in the Communist press. The Cominform called him, under the headline "JOHN FOSTER DULLES, BANKER, SLAVEOWNER, WARMONGER," "one of the more sinister members of the imperialist gang of misanthropic fiends." [32] According to the Communists, North Korea had not invaded South Korea. Quite the reverse. Troops of "the quisling South Korean government" had "crossed all along the 38th parallel and penetrated one kilometer into North Korean territory." [33]

The purposes of the whole Wall Street plot, the Communists maintained, were the "colonial enslavement" of all East Asia and the establishment in Korea of "powerful bases from which to make war upon the new China and the Soviet Union." [34] The North Korean "guards," as the party press first called them, had foiled the imperialist plot with strong resistance. Then they counterattacked. Within six weeks, they controlled nearly all the Korean peninsula, and the "guards" became "Korean people's liberation forces." How the North Koreans were able, without previous planning and careful and extensive preparations, to launch such a major offensive was a military question the Communists did not answer—or even consider. The intervention of American-U.N. forces on a large scale, the subsequent expulsion of the North Korean army from South Korea, and the carrying of the war north of the thirty-eighth parallel only served to confirm for the Communists their interpretation of the whole conflict.

Almost from the beginning of the Korean war, there was a difference of opinion about war aims and strategy between President Truman and General Douglas MacArthur, commander of the U.N. forces in Korea. Truman wanted no more than a limited war; he tried to restrain his colorful and outspoken general, who was for more adventurous policies even should they risk involvement for the United States in a general war with Communist China or the Soviet Union. The Truman-MacArthur differences became impossible to ignore or compromise in the spring of 1951, and in April, the president removed the general from command.

The MacArthur ouster prompted a few Communists to reassess their interpretation of the Korean war, as well it should have. If the Truman administration were bent on a war of conquest in the Far East, why should it risk political disaster with the removal of the bellicose and politically important MacArthur? No important Communist, apparently, at that time prepared any thorough critique of the whole party position on war, imperialism, and American foreign policy. But at least one, Joseph Starobin, foreign editor of the *Daily Worker* and secretary of the party's commission on peace activities, quietly and privately expressed his doubts to party leaders about the validity of the party line. Neither Starobin nor anyone else led any large-scale agitation in the party. The rank and file and most leaders had no knowledge of any dissent in the national office.[35]

Lest anyone else should develop heretical ideas about the party's line, Eugene Dennis wrote a letter to the party membership on the MacArthur affair, in which he upheld the old line in no uncertain terms. The Truman-MacArthur controversy was of no real significance, wrote Dennis. The differences between the president and the general were only over tactics and pace. "The Truman Administration continues to move in its own aggressive way and at its own pace toward a global war . . . under the guise of opposing a 'third world war,' of waging a 'limited war,' the Truman Administration continues to pursue Wall Street's aggressive war policy, a criminal policy which . . . if unchecked, can only lead . . . to a third world war." The party must not relax, must not let up the struggle against a general war. Henceforth, ordered Dennis, every item *"of every Party agenda in every leading committee and club must be linked with . . . an all-out struggle and campaign against the Truman and MacArthur war policies."* [36]

The Communists failed to modify their position on Korea in the slightest. Through the long truce negotiations, conducted intermittently from July 1951 until the armistice two years later; through a Presidential election in which Foster called General Eisenhower "Wall Street's speed-war candidate"; [37] through the gradual but steady fading away of old soldier MacArthur, the Communists incessantly maintained that Washington was about to launch a new world war of imperialistic conquest. Even when the final armistice was signed, the party's national committee declared that the peace was only a partial victory over "the plans of Wall Street to establish its world domination through war." Foster, never one to allow a fact to upset his theory, found little solace in the armistice. The "Wall Street planners of a third world war," he told his readers, "have been trying (and still are) to make another Spain in Korea." The State Department will yet "try to sabotage the [Korean] peace." [38]

The most important effect of the party's whole peace crusade in the long run was that it further contributed to its isolation from the publics it needed for sustenance. Besides all their work in especially constituted peace organizations—they scorned the established peace organizations such as those of religious groups and the Fellowship for Reconciliation and were in turn scorned by them—the Communists tried to use their influence in organizations founded for some other purpose. In trade unions, for example, the Communists regarded a leader's position on foreign policy as a touchstone. "A labor leader is a progressive to the degree that he stands for peace . . . and co-existence with the Soviet Union. He is a reactionary to the extent that he stands for . . . the war drive of U.S. imperialism and its anti-Soviet foreign policy. No matter how militant . . . on other questions, to the extent that he supports the war drive, he is a reactionary." [39] Communists applied the same test to Negro leaders. When the national leaders of the N.A.A.C.P. supported the Korean war, the Communists accused them of selling out for "a few paltry jobs [in] the operation of Point Four in Africa." [40] And, as will be seen in greater detail later, the Communists in the Progressive Party insisted on their position on Korea, precipitating a crisis in the Progressive organization that left it without a prominent non-Communist leader. The root of the matter was that the party accorded conformity to the international Communist line a higher priority than its own viability.

A few Communists dimly perceived the effects of the party's parochialism. There was even a guarded and fuzzy warning in the party's official magazine.[41] But warnings from their own ranks did not change party policy. The Communists were not fully to realize the consequences of their sectarianism until they were jarred by events in the Soviet Union.

With a more astute peace program, one less obviously a reflection of Russian foreign policy, the Communists might have gained some strength or at least slowed their decline. For there was widespread opposition to war in the United States as well as widespread opposition to Communism. A large part of the population was anxious and frustrated about the Korean war. Ironically for the Communists, popular desire for peace expressed itself in the election of a Republican administration, an administration headed by a war-hero five-star general and a Vice-President who made his mark in politics as a professional anti-Communist.

THE LAST DAYS OF THE PROGRESSIVE PARTY

After Wallace's showing in the 1948 elections, the Communists were slow to lose their illusions about the Progressive Party being a "mass party of the working class." Communists deplored the electorate's commitment to the major political parties and tried to convince themselves that sentiment for the Progressive Party's program was growing even if the party was not. But in 1950, they had to admit that "there is not yet a mass third party in America." [42]

Despite the ineffectiveness of the Progressive Party and despite the fact that any realistic appraisal of its future would not indicate growth, the Communist Party continued until after the 1952 elections to support and dominate the Progressive Party. The Communists, too, continued their relationship with the A.L.P. in New York, which supported the Progressives in national elections. With each group, the Communists continued their support because these "progressive" political organizations represented the best instruments then available to the Communists for amplifying the general Communist program. Within the Progressive Party and the A.L.P., there were still some leftist non-Communists, residues of the popular frontism of the mid-1930's, who would tolerate the Communists and respond to such general slogans as "Peace, Democracy, and Socialism."

Early in 1950, Henry Wallace belatedly tried to change the popular impression that the Communists controlled his party lock, stock, and barrel. At the second national convention of the party, in Chicago, Wallace said that the failure of the first convention to adopt the "Vermont resolution" denying blanket endorsement of the foreign policy of any nation had been a mistake. He went on to warn that Progressives should not take any positions that would give observers "the slightest, legitimate reason for believing that any working member of our Party puts Rome, Moscow or London ahead of the United States." [43] The convention went on to declare in one of its resolutions that the United States and the Soviet Union had both "made mistakes" in foreign policy.

This was mild enough. Neither Wallace nor the convention seriously criticized Soviet foreign policy or began any movement to remove Communists from influence within the Progressive Party. The Communists, nevertheless, refused to overlook the Progressives' slight reproach to Communist orthodoxy. The *Daily Worker* took the Progressive convention to task. "What happened at the Progressive Party convention," National Committeeman Gil Green instructed his comrades, "cannot be condoned." [44] Thus bucked up, the Communists in the Progressive Party were in no mood to compromise when the outbreak of war in Korea came.

Within a few days after the administration's decision to go to the aid of the South Koreans, the executive committee of the Progressive Party called a meeting of the full national committee for July 15. The smaller group then began on July 6 a series of sessions in preparation for the meeting of the full committee. In these meetings it became obvious that the differences over the Korean war between Henry Wallace on the one hand and the Communists and pro-Communists on the other were too great to be compromised.

There were five meetings of the executive committee before it finished drafting a statement on Korea. Not all members of the committee attended all the sessions. The members most consistent in attendance were C. B. Baldwin, Progressive Executive Secretary; James Durkin, President of the Communist-dominated United Office and Professional Workers of America; the playwright Lillian Hellman; Vito Marcantonio, the A.L.P.'s congressman; John McManus, Editor of the *National Guardian;* Paul Robeson; Arthur Schutzer, Executive Secretary of the A.L.P.; Alfred K. Stern; Henry Wallace; and Walter Wallace, who has since testified that he was then a member of the Communist Party.[45] Others who attended meetings but were not committee members were John Abt, Vaughn Albertson, Louis Burnham, Lydia D'Fonseca, and Mrs. Martha Dodd Stern.[46] After the Sterns refused to return to the United States from Mexico in the spring of 1957 to appear before a grand jury investigating espionage, Boris Morros, an American counterspy, implicated Mrs. Stern in espionage. The daughter of the late Professor William E. Dodd, American Ambassador to Germany in the 1930's, and her husband then fled to Czechoslovakia.[47]

There was a wide gulf between Henry Wallace's estimate of the Korean conflict and that of the rest of the executive committee, but Wallace's dissent from the statement drawn by the committee was not stated clearly and decisively in the committee's meetings. At the end of the July 10 meeting, according to the minutes, Wallace even expressed "provisional agreement" with the drafted statement but would reserve final decision until the next morning. The next morning, he telephoned Baldwin to say that he could not agree to the statement unless it contained four major modifications. These modifications would have changed the entire direction of the statement. The committee declined to make the changes, and thus, on July 11, 1950, Wallace severed his connection with the Progressive Party.[48]

On July 15, the entire Progressive national committee met, and by a vote of 32 to 2 adopted the statement with which Wallace could not agree. The two dissenters were Clark Foreman, of the Southern Conference of Human Welfare, and Thomas Emerson, of the Yale University law faculty. Henry Wallace did not attend the meeting because he had already in effect left the party. The statement condemned Truman's directive commanding the fleet to defend Formosa, urged that Communist China be admitted to the United Nations, and urged the U.N. Security Council to "issue appropriate orders and adopt measures" to end the hostilities and then increase economic and technical assistance in Asia. On the same day, Wallace issued a statement to the press in which he put responsibility for the conflict on the Soviet Union. "We must continue our fight . . . in South Korea until such time as Russia is willing to use her influence to stop the fighting and start . . . UN negotiations. . . . I say that Russia could stop the fighting now if she wished to do so." [49]

From the summer of 1950 on, the strength of the Progressive and American Labor parties steadily waned. The Korean war polarized political opinion: the general public more and more identified the policies of these parties with sympathy for the Soviet Union, and the Communists and fellow travelers in these parties were less and less inclined to compromise. The Progressives and Communists in California, for example, condemned Mrs. Helen Gahagan Douglas vociferously in her race against Richard M. Nixon in 1950 because she supported the war.[50] In the same election, Vito Marcantonio made "peace" the main issue of his campaign and was defeated by a fusion candidate. The 1952 Progressive Party national candidates—Vincent Hallinan for President and Mrs. Charlotta Bass for Vice-President—were almost unknown. Hallinan, a cousin of Ireland's Eamon de Valera, was a wealthy San Francisco Left Wing lawyer; Mrs. Bass had worked closely with the Communists.[51] The Hallinan-Bass ticket received only 140,023 votes, about one-fifth of 1 per cent of the total vote. Well over half the Progressive vote came from New York City, Los Angeles, and the San Francisco Bay area.[52]

After the 1952 election, it became obvious to the Communists that to continue their third-party gambit was fruitless. The "mass party of peace" had become just another Left Wing sect, only slightly larger than the Communist Party itself. The extent to which the Communists controlled the Progressive organization and the American Labor Party is seen in the subsequent history of those parties when the Communists pulled out: the Progressives disappeared altogether, and the A.L.P. failed to get enough votes in 1954 to stay on the ballot.

THE C.I.O. EXPULSIONS

The C.I.O. began in a small way to expel the Communist-controlled unions the very month Truman trounced Dewey and Wallace. The end of the road for the C.I.O. Communists was in sight after the Portland, Oregon, C.I.O. convention in late November 1948. The convention summarily ended the jurisdictional dispute between the Left-led Farm Equipment Workers (F.E.) and the U.A.W. by ordering F.E. to merge its 65,000 members into the Reuther organization within sixty days. When the F.E. leaders refused, the U.A.W. raided F.E.'s members, and F.E. disappeared anyway. At the Portland convention, President Murray gave three small Communist unions a stern lecture on their inadequacies as trade unions and threatened to deal with them more harshly in the future. These unions—the United Office and Professional Workers, the United Public Workers, and the Food and Tobacco Workers— had organized only a tiny fraction of the workers in their industries.[53]

The Communist unions did not stand together at the Portland convention. The leaders of the Food and Tobacco Workers, the Furriers, and the Marine Cooks and Stewards, all with much stronger Communist support in the rank and file than most Left unions, fought back at the anti-Communist C.I.O. leadership. They submitted and voted for a set of resolutions that sounded like a summary of the Communist line.[54] But the leaders of the bigger Left unions, more vulnerable to attack from their non-Communist rank and file, tried to compromise. Delegates from U.E., I.L.W.U., and the Furniture Workers voted for the C.I.O. majority resolution and even for the resolution rescinding the charter of the Communist-run New York City C.I.O. Council—to the exasperation of the Communist labor secretary.[55] Albert Fitzgerald, President of U.E. and the presiding officer of the Progressive convention four months before, voted for a resolution endorsing the Marshall Plan in the C.I.O. executive board and delivered a self-effacing speech on the convention floor: "I tell you frankly I do not give a damn for Russia. . . . Vishinsky and Molotov are engaging themselves in saber rattling and war mongering. . . . If President Truman makes a sincere effort to carry out his promises . . . I will tell the Progressive Party to go to hell." [56] Through such tactics, Fitzgerald managed to postpone C.I.O. action against his union and even remain a C.I.O. vice-president—for another year.

After the convention, the party's leadership stiffened the resistance of the C.I.O. Left unions. Early in January 1949, delegates of eight Communist unions met in New York and announced a "rank and file unity plan." [57] In the spring, the Communists refused a compromise in the Transport Workers Union, which, according to Mike Quill's account, would have given them a large minority on the union's executive board and the post of national secretary-treasurer. The party preferred to fight it out with Quill for a majority of the executive board. Quill utterly routed the Communists after this challenge. At the next national convention of the T.W.U., the Communists won no national offices and not a single seat on the executive board.[58] In May, the officers of nine Left unions voted as a bloc against the C.I.O. executive-board decision to withdraw from the World Federation of Trade Unions.[59] In June, the Communists, in an effort to give better co-ordination to the Left unions, started a new monthly magazine, the *March of Labor*.

Perhaps the best example of the Communists' decision not to compromise—even to counterattack and take the consequences— was in U.E., by far the most important of the Communist-controlled unions. The Communists had effectively controlled U.E. since 1941, when they elected James Matles and Julius Emspak to national office. The slow-moving and slow-thinking Albert Fitzgerald, President of the union, was not a Communist; he was only a "front man" for the Communists who ran the union. At U.E.'s national convention in Cleveland in September 1949, the Communist leadership encountered for the first time an effectively organized anti-Communist opposition, led by James B. Carey. The Carey forces represented most of the big U.E. locals, but Matles and Emspak had a majority at the convention through their control of the many small locals. The Communists got their slate of national officers elected and their resolutions adopted. Then they counterattacked. They began a purge of the anti-Communists by amending the union's constitution to empower the general executive board to bring charges against and expel individual members. The amendment empowered the Communist national U.E. officers to eliminate their opponents even when their opponents had the support of their locals.[60]

Even after the C.I.O.'s Portland convention, the Communist unions might have been able to survive in the C.I.O. if they had behaved circumspectly. After the Communist activities in 1949, however, the C.I.O. leadership resolved to make quick work of them. At the Cleveland C.I.O. convention in November 1949, the national C.I.O. majority effectively ended all Communist influence in the national body. By a large vote, the convention amended its constitution to make Communists or those who consistently followed the Communist line ineligible for C.I.O. national office, including membership on the executive board. The convention itself then expelled U.E., saying that it was no more than "the Communist Party masquerading as a labor union." The convention then amended its constitution again to empower a two-thirds majority on the executive board to expel "or take any other appropriate action against" any union whose policies and activities "are consistently directed toward the achievement of the program or purposes of the Communist Party." [61]

Soon after the convention, the C.I.O. executive board, through a series of subcommittees, began hearings on charges against the Left Wing unions. The pattern in all the hearings was to prove that the union, through its publications and resolutions, had consistently followed each turn in the Communist party's line, a relatively easy matter to prove. The C.I.O. did not try to prove that the union leaders were members of the Communist Party, a task which would have been considerably more difficult, if not impossible, but would have been irrelevant anyway. By the late spring of 1950, the C.I.O. executive board had expelled nine Communist-led unions. Communist influence in the C.I.O. was all but completely eliminated. Any Communists left were either rank and filers or, at most, local officers who thereafter could sing the party tune only softly.[62]

Being cut off from the rest of the labor movement was a severe handicap for the Communists and the unions they controlled, but worse was to come. The C.I.O. granted charters to new unions to compete with the expelled unions or allowed established C.I.O. unions to raid the Communist unions' membership. Within a few years, the Communist unions, assaulted by raid after raid, had dwindled away. By 1956, the only Communist unions with anything like their strength before expulsion were the Bridges union and Mine, Mill. A new union in the electrical industry, the International Union of Electrical, Radio and Machine Workers (I.U.E.), the Machinists (I.A.M.), and the A.F. of L.'s International Brotherhood of Electrical Workers had all but eliminated the once-powerful U.E.[63] The Bridges union and Mine, Mill were able substantially to retain their old strength because of special circumstances. Harry Bridges, despite, rather than because of, his politics, is a popular figure among West Coast dock workers. His generation of dock workers will not forget his heroic role in the 1934 dock strike, and Bridges runs a union that "delivers" in the Gompers "bread and butter" sense. There are two reasons for Mine, Mill's survival. It has a heritage of radical rhetoric that goes back to William D. ("Big Bill") Haywood and the Western Federation of Miners, for one thing, and employers prefer Mine, Mill to unions, such as the United Steelworkers, that might give them greater opposition at the bargaining table. Thus, Mine, Mill is a peculiar combination of a Red and a company union.[64]

In Communist theory, the workers in basic industry are supposed to be the core of their party's strength, the revolutionary proletariat. Until 1949-50, the Communists looked at the two million members in the unions they controlled and, with a bit of optimistic self-delusion, saw themselves as the vanguard of the working class. But by the mid-1950's, the membership of Communist-controlled unions had shrunk to about 200,000, about one-tenth of the former membership, less than 1 per cent of total American trade-union strength. Any group that professes to speak in the name of the working class with as little power in that class as the Communists have demonstrated speaks with a hollow ring indeed.

THE ROSENBERG CASE

The exclusion of Communist influence from the main stream of the American labor movement, the prosecutions under the Smith Act and other governmental anti-Communist programs, the deflation of the Progressive and A.L.P. popular fronts, and the general anti-Communist sentiments of the public, together with certain internal activities of the Communist organization, considerably reduced the strength of the Communist Party. Any index of the party's health shows a sharp decline from about 1949 to about 1953. In early February 1950, F.B.I. Director J. Edgar Hoover testified to a Congressional appropriations committee that there were at that time 54,174 members of the Communist Party. In 1953, he reported that party membership was 24,796, more than a 50-per-cent decline in three years.[65] In 1950, the general manager of the *Daily Worker* in his annual sworn circulation statement reported his paper's average circulation as 20,336, and the Sunday edition (the *Worker*) as 67,199. In 1953, these figures had fallen to 10,443 and 28,822 respectively.[66]

Despite the party's weakened organizational strength, despite the almost universal disapproval of Communist doctrines by the American people, despite the inhibitions upon Communists when they operated in public, the Communists still were able in the early 1950's to make of the Rosenberg affair one of the biggest, noisiest, and most successful propaganda campaigns in Communist Party history.

In early February 1950, Klaus Fuchs, a German-born physicist who as a naturalized British subject had worked in the United States during the war on the atomic-bomb project, was arrested for espionage. Fuchs confessed to the English authorities and told them what he knew of espionage. His testimony implicated Harry Gold, an American, who soon confessed to his role as a courier for a spy ring. Gold pleaded guilty in the Philadelphia courtroom of Federal Judge James P. McGranery, and was sentenced to thirty years' imprisonment. This sentence was the maximum imprisonment; the law provides for "death or imprisonment for not more than thirty years." Gold told the F.B.I. all he knew about the ring and implicated Julius Rosenberg, a Communist engineering graduate of the City College of New York; Julius Rosenberg's wife, Ethel; Ethel Rosenberg's brother, David Greenglass, a skilled machinist; Morton Sobell, a college classmate of Rosenberg; and Anatoli A. Yakovlev, a Russian national then presumably in the Soviet Union. When Gold's arrest was announced to the press, the *Daily Worker,* under the headline "FBI WHIPS UP NEW 'ATOMIC SPY' HOAX," declared, "By an obvious 'coincidence,' the arrest of Gold was timed to knock off the front pages the return tomorrow of United Nations Secretary-General Trygve Lie and his anticipated report of Soviet proposals to end the cold war." [67]

Greenglass confessed and revealed all he knew, as had Fuchs and Gold before him. The Rosenbergs and Sobell were indicted in August 1950, and their trial began in New York City in the court of Federal Judge Irving R. Kaufman on March 6, 1951. The burden of the prosecution's case was the testimony of Harry Gold and David Greenglass. The revelations of these two witnesses were partially confirmed by the testimony of others. The Rosenbergs denied everything. Ethel Rosenberg, when asked before the grand jury if she knew Gold and Yakovlev, had declined to answer on the grounds that her testimony might be self-incriminating. At the trial she denied she knew Yakovlev or had ever seen Gold before. Sobell pleaded not guilty, but did not take the witness stand at all; he said nothing to the jury whatsoever. The trial consumed three weeks. On March 29, 1951, after deliberating seven and one-half hours, the jury announced its verdict: the Rosenbergs and Sobell were guilty as charged. The Rosenbergs' attorney, Emmanuel H. Bloch, thanked the court, the prosecuting attorney and his staff, and F.B.I. members for their courtesies during the trial. He told the jury he was satisfied that it had examined the evidence "very carefully." Judge Kaufman sentenced the Rosenbergs to death and Sobell to thirty years' imprisonment. David Greenglass received a sentence of fifteen years' imprisonment.

The Communist press did not carry one word about the Rosenbergs until after they had been found guilty and had been sentenced. A person in the unenviable position of receiving news only from the *Daily Worker* would not have known until the day after they were sentenced that the Rosenberg case even existed. Nor did the party's Civil Rights Congress come forward to raise bail for the Rosenbergs after their arrest. When the Communists finally mentioned the case, they did not deny the Rosenbergs' guilt. The first mention, a news story, asserted that the Rosenbergs were being made scapegoats for the Korean war. An editorial three days later took the position that the sentence was what one would expect from a government "which is refusing to negotiate peace in Korea." The whole case, according to the editorial writer, was an effort "to turn the hatred of 57,000 American casualties away from the war makers in Washington toward Jews and Communists. Not since the days [of] the Czars . . . and Nazis . . . has this pogrom tactic been so brazenly used." But there was no accusation of a judicial frame-up.[68] No newspaper asserted that the Rosenbergs were innocent until four months after the end of the trial, and the charge that the Rosenbergs had been framed came then, not from the Communist press, strictly speaking, but from the fellow-traveling *National Guardian,* a publication of the New York A.L.P. begun for the Wallace movement in 1947.[69]

Why the Communists were so reticent about the Rosenberg case at first is an interesting subject for speculation. It seems likely that the Communists were quiet about the case until they were confident that the Rosenbergs were not going to confess to espionage, as had Fuchs, Gold, and Greenglass before them. To have organized and launched a big amnesty campaign and have it undermined by a confession would have been disastrous.

On November 8, 1951, seven months after the Rosenberg trial, while the case was being appealed, a group that called itself the National Committee to Secure Justice in the Rosenberg Case opened a bank account in New York City. The committee did not announce its formation until almost two months later. The president of the organization was Louis Harap, Editor of the Communist magazine *Jewish Life*. The chairman was Joseph Brainin. The most active directors of the committee were its executive secretary, David Alman, and his wife, Emily, who served as national treasurer. Alman had been a paid staff member of the New York Civil Rights Congress and the American Peace Crusade. The sponsors of the committee were a mixture of active party members, such as Herbert Aptheker, and intellectuals with several past associations in party fronts, such as W. E. B. DuBois, a few of whom enjoyed national prominence.[70] This committee organized and co-ordinated the pro-Rosenberg campaign throughout the country.

For its first several months, the Rosenberg committee's effort failed to generate much excitement except among small leftist groups in a few big cities ever ready to respond to such appeals. In the late fall and early winter of 1952, the committee stepped up its activities with more mass meetings, delegations to Sing Sing, where the Rosenbergs were imprisoned, and pickets outside the White House gates. Simultaneously, Rosenberg committees appeared in Paris and London. From then until the Rosenbergs' execution on June 19, 1953, the campaign operated at fever pitch.

Circumstantial evidence indicates that there was a relationship between the intensification of the Rosenberg campaign both in the

United States and in Europe and the case of Rudolph Slansky in Czechoslovakia. Slansky and thirteen other defendants were tried in Prague, November 20-27, 1952, and eleven of the defendants were hanged six days later. All but three of the fourteen were Jewish, and there were distinctly anti-Semitic overtones to the prosecution. Among other things, Slansky was charged with "Jewish bourgeois nationalism." The Communists everywhere were quick to deny they were anti-Semitic—they were only anti-Zionist, they asserted—but they clearly linked the Rosenberg and Slansky cases in an apparent attempt to divert attention from the Prague trial. Jacques Duclos, the French Communist leader, went so far as to say, "The conviction of U.S. atom spies Julius and Ethel Rosenberg was an example of anti-Semitism but the execution of eight Jews in Czechoslovakia last week was not." [71]

The French Communists achieved much more spectacular results with their pro-Rosenberg campaign than did their American comrades. Exploiting the legacy of the Dreyfus case of more than a half-century before, the French Rosenberg agitation emphasized the assertion that the couple were victims of anti-Semitism, a charge the major American Jewish organizations consistently rejected. Such prominent non-Communist French leaders as Cardinal Feltin, Archbishop of Paris, Edouard Herriot, President of the National Assembly, four former premiers of France, and Vincent Auriol, President of the Republic, took part in appeals for the Rosenbergs.[72] Undoubtedly, the Rosenberg agitation in France heightened anti-American sentiment, as it was intended to do.

In the last frantic days of the American pro-Rosenberg campaign, which featured motorcades, special "Rosenberg trains" from New York to Washington, and "round-the-clock vigils" outside the White House, there occurred a little-publicized incident that indicated that the Rosenberg committee and the Communists were determined to run the clemency campaign entirely by themselves and wring from it the greatest possible propaganda value. The incident involved Irwin Edelman, of Los Angeles, an erratic leftist expelled from the Communist Party in 1947. In November

1952, Edelman published a pamphlet entitled *Freedom's Electro-cution,* which quite agreed with the Communist line on the Rosenberg case except that it was critical of the conduct during the trial of the Rosenbergs' counsel, Emmanuel H. Bloch. Soon after the pamphlet's publication, Edelman was expelled from the Los Angeles Rosenberg Committee.[73] The *National Guardian* refused to accept an advertisement for the pamphlet, and a letter in the *People's World* urged that Edelman be ignored.[74] Edelman interested two lawyers, Fyke Farmer, of Nashville, and Daniel G. Marshall, of Los Angeles, in his indictment of Bloch and in his suggestion that the Rosenbergs should have been tried under the Atomic Energy Act of 1946 rather than under the Espionage Act of 1917. Under the 1946 act, the death penalty or life imprisonment may be imposed only when intent to injure the United States is proved and only by recommendation of the trial jury. Using Edelman's argument, Farmer and Marshall, on June 13, 1953, five days before the Rosenbergs' scheduled execution, filed with Judge Kaufman a petition for a writ of habeas corpus. Bloch declined to co-operate with Farmer and Marshall and wired Judge Kaufman to state his refusal to be associated with the petition. Judge Kaufman denied the petition on June 15. Bloch refused again to co-operate with Farmer and Marshall when they tried to interest the Supreme Court in their argument. On June 17, two days after the Supreme Court had recessed for the summer, Justice William O. Douglas granted a stay of execution after hearing the Edelman argument. The court reconvened in extraordinary session the next day. The following day, June 19, the court vacated Justice Douglas's stay of execution. That evening, shortly after eight o'clock, the Rosenbergs were executed.[75] The Communists and the Rosenberg committee had been determined to keep the Rosenberg case activity in their own hands, where they could control it, even if this end meant rejection of a legal argument that had sufficient merit to persuade a justice of the nation's highest court to call the court into extraordinary session.

The primary motive of the Communists in the Rosenberg agitation in the United States was to broadcast the Communist opinion, central to their whole political line, that the government of the United States was controlled by "fascists" who sought to involve the nation in war, destroy the labor movement, abrogate civil liberties, eliminate dissent, and persecute minority groups. For Communists, already persuaded to the party's line, the Rosenberg case served as confirmation, and the defense agitation served to deepen personal commitments. And non-Communists moved to sympathy for the Rosenbergs by humanitarian considerations afforded the Communists an opportunity for indoctrination. From the first editorial on the Rosenberg case to the blast when the couple was executed, the Communists hammered away with the argument that the Rosenbergs were sentenced to death as a step toward outright fascism. The facts of the case itself got short shrift in Communist pages. The Rosenberg affair, the Communists repeated, was a device to channel "the hatred of the American people for the Korean war, for the 'inevitable atomic war' line of the atombomb maniacs . . . against the working-class vanguard, the Communists, the Negro and Jewish people, the labor and progressive forces generally." The Rosenbergs' trial and conviction was nothing but "a political plot to assist in advancing the McCarthyite pro-fascist reign of fear in the United States, to brutalize the population, and get it to accept the further fascization of the United States without resistance." Thus, the Communists asserted, to defend the Rosenbergs was not only humanitarian, but it was self-defense against fascism, essentially patriotic protection of American democracy. "There must be a halt to the Hitlerization of America by the Eisenhower-Brownell-J. Edgar Hoover forces working hand in glove with the swastika-minded McCarthy and his goons." [76] The opening-wedge-of-fascism theme dominated appeals directed to organized labor and to Jews, both groups that had good reasons to fear fascism. The theme permeated even the sentimentally murky poems and songs of the Rosenberg campaign.[77]

Why was it that the Communist Party, declining in size and power even while it led the Rosenberg agitation, was able to create such a big amnesty campaign and then bombard the campaign's followers with the usual Communist propaganda line? Why was it that thousands of non-Communists came sincerely to believe that the Rosenbergs had been framed, despite a trial at which defense counsel expressed no complaint about procedure and despite over two years of appeals, motions for retrials, petitions for habeas corpus, and applications for reduction of sentence which were heard seven times by the Court of Appeals and seven times by the Supreme Court? Part of the answer lies in the fairly widespread opposition to capital punishment. And a large part of the answer lies in part of the American heritage. There were skeletons in America's closet. There had been cases of injustice in the courts and discrimination against minorities. It was not difficult to persuade some people that what had happened before was happening again. Had there been no Sacco-Vanzetti case and no Mooney-Billings case and had no American Jew ever suffered persecution, it is not likely that the Rosenberg defenders would have received a serious hearing. This the Communists realized, and they worked mightily to inflate the Rosenberg case into an American Dreyfus affair. Therein lies the real tragedy in the Rosenberg case. The sins of the past are not easily lived down.

This, then, was the outward face of the Communist Party in the late 1940's and early 1950's. It clearly was in retreat. American public opinion had reached an unprecedented pitch of opposition to Communists and their ideas. The government's prosecution of Communist Party leaders and the kind of defense that the party elected to make against the prosecution had resulted in an important handicap to the party's efficiency. The manner in which the party conducted its "peace" campaign had further isolated it from the non-Communist Left and from the movement for Negro equality, and the Communists' "hard" line had contributed to the decline of the Progressive Party and the elimination of Communist influence in the decisions of the C.I.O.

Facing attack from government, from the trade unions, and

from the public in general, the Communists endeavored to appear as militant advocates of freedom and justice, as defenders of the Jeffersonian tradition of civil liberty. They sought to be regarded as the innocent victims of a society that had lost its restraint and that had forgotten a noble tradition of due legal process and fair play toward dissenters from majority attitudes. The Communists and their organizations obviously were the victims of a reaction that was sometimes disrespectful of the highest traditions of law and justice, but they were hardly innocent victims.

SEVEN: THE PARTY'S INTERNAL SECURITY

I n the trial of the top eleven leaders of the Communist Party, the prosecution brought to the witness stand F.B.I. agents who had been accepted in the party as bona fide members. In 1950, Congress passed the McCarran Internal Security Act and the Korean war began. All these events the Communists interpreted as the beginning of American fascism, which might well end in an American equivalent of the German Third Reich.

The Communists had to assume there were still other F.B.I. "Communists," as yet unrevealed, and it began immediately to strengthen its defenses. There is a bitter humor in the fact that the measures the party took to safeguard its "internal security" against its enemies were in many ways similar to the measures that federal and state governments and American society in general took to protect itself against the Communists. Both instituted loyalty checks. Both became irrationally suspicious of behavior and thought that did not conform to its norms. Both expelled and ostracized suspected individuals. Both infringed freedom in the quest for security, although the party never had afforded freedom to its own members. Both injured innocent people—that is, those who were not actually working for the enemy. One is reminded of a sentence of Edmund Wilson's in the early 1930's when he described a battle between police and Communists in New York's City Hall Park: "A gray flight of pigeons rises from the park, the only free living things in sight." [1] There were differences between the two internal-security systems, of course, and the differences were important. The Communist society had almost no restraint upon authority.

The Communist Party's system of internal security can be described under two categories; first, organizational measures to eliminate or minimize the effectiveness of police agents, or to establish an underground apparatus for a refuge in the event an open party proved impossible; second, the strengthening of ideological defenses so that the party would be intellectually pure —lean, hard, invulnerable to the erosion of outside ideas, 100 per cent Communist, not "soft on capitalism."

THE "LOYALTY" PROGRAM

The party made its first important organizational change for security early in 1949 when it stopped issuing party membership cards and quit keeping central membership lists. Soon thereafter, alarmed by their new awareness of F.B.I. agents in their ranks, the Communists launched what J. Edgar Hoover described as a "loyalty check." The party's review commissions at all party levels investigated the loyalty of every party member. There even was a subcommittee of three members of the national executive committee to investigate their fellow committee members. J. Edgar Hoover knew of the existence of this high-level subcommittee; its establishment reflected apparently well-founded suspicions.[2]

In 1950 and 1951, the party reorganized itself thoroughly in an effort for maximum security. The party clubs, the party's basic unit, had typically been composed of twenty-five to fifty members. In order to prevent a member's knowing many other members, each club broke down into several with a membership of from three to five. Written communications were kept to a minimum.

Rather than use mimeographed documents, which might find their way to F.B.I. files, party units used the blackboard extensively, erasing the messages as soon as possible. There were standing directions to destroy after reading whatever written communications were necessary.[3] The whole effort proved to be a farce and a serious impairment of party efficiency. The small clubs did not prevent members from identifying other members, because they had already known their comrades from the days before the security reorganization, and, in many cases, members of different clubs continued to see one another socially. Thus, the purpose of the system was not achieved, and the new arrangement sacrificed efficiency. Communications often became garbled in their clandestine transmission. Moreover, there were not enough dedicated and efficient Communists to lead the expanded number of party units. As a result, many clubs failed to meet regularly, had inadequate planning for their meetings, and displayed—to quote a survey of organization problems in New York—a distressing "lack of ideological and political content." [4] In sum, many ordinary rank-and-file members proved to be inept conspirators.

Another aspect of the party's security program was purposely to reduce the party's size, weeding out the suspect, the unenthusiastic, and the easily frightened. Clearly, many of the expulsions were the result of hysteria over party security and reaction to nonconformity, but a large part of the pruning of the membership was deliberate and calculated. According to the sworn testimony of a former Communist official, at one time William Z. Foster, ever an extremist, proposed reducing the membership of the party by 90 per cent and sending the remaining 10 per cent underground.[5] How many members were dropped by design is impossible to say —probably the party's top leadership itself does not know—but the organization secretary of the New York State organization in the party's self-appraisal in 1956 reported that in his state "For 'security reasons,' we also dropped a few thousand members, and so exaggerated the fascist danger by this and other security measures, that we actually menaced the continued existence of our

Party." Some members—an estimated "many, many hundreds"—were expelled on trumped-up charges.[6] Others did not have to be expelled. They read the words of the national organization secretary, Henry Winston, and accepted his not too subtle invitation for the uninterested to leave the party. Winston warned that the party's situation "makes necessary a qualitative strengthening of the work of our Party" before he explained how easy it was to leave: to join or leave "the ranks of the Communist Party has at all times been a voluntary individual action based on conviction. We will continue that concept of organization. Only those who have been registered by the Party in the current registration [to last another thirty days] will carry the great honor that goes with membership in the Communist Party." Thousands already looking for a way out grasped the opportunity. Still others, especially those thought to be fainthearted or those who might be compromised because of something in their past, were simply informally dropped. They were not notified of meetings nor assigned to any tasks.[7] These people did not quit the party; the party quit them.

The underground was one of the most important of the organizational methods adopted in quest of party security. Scores of important party leaders left their homes, assumed new names, and lived a clandestine existence. There were two reasons behind the decision to go underground: to obstruct F.B.I. agents and to form the nucleus of a party for the future should the maintenance of the regular above-ground party prove impossible.

Those who went underground—or became "unavailables," as they were commonly called within the party—were important leaders but not from the very top leadership. The most important leaders were too well known for the anonymous underground, and lesser leaders at the club level were not trusted enough for such assignments. But when the very top leadership went to prison in 1951 under the Smith Act, many of the unavailables automatically moved upward in the party bureaucracy.

Those in the underground lived hard and unpleasant lives, away from their families and friends, writing for the Communist press under pen names, traveling a great deal, and delivering messages and attending secret meetings in the accepted Hollywood spy-film fashion.[8] But the hardships of the "unavailables" did not strengthen the party. Indeed, the whole underground venture tended to make the party more inefficient, more isolated, and more bureaucratic than it had been in the late 1940's. Clearly, the underground had important ill effects upon the party as well as for the people in it.

The Communists always denied that there was such a thing as the underground, but a published organizational report in late 1953 indirectly admitted as much. The report, itself written by someone in the underground under the pen name Alex Parker, declared that a "fairly large section of the leadership" must "work and live in a new way, under conditions . . . which guarantee the protection of the Party members and organizations." [9]

The Parker report defended the decision to go underground but obliquely revealed some of the harmful consequences of the decision. One admitted difficulty was that secrecy prevented the degree of contact between upper and lower party echelons necessary for efficiency: "Formerly, when we were able to see each other daily, use the phones at will, we never gave much thought to the content of our association. Our National Committee must . . . find ways to guarantee closer and quicker connections between the various levels of organization." Another admitted disadvantage was that the underground "bred an 'inner type' of party functionary who is often disconnected from the masses. . . . Such people are often shipped around the country from post to post by 'mail order,'" unable to give "leadership to mass work." But the unavailables became not only isolated from the "masses" but also from the party membership, thereby making the party more bureaucratic than ever. Instructions appeared as if by magic from somewhere in the underground. Much of the leadership was truly invisible, truly "unavailable," and no organization with such an isolated and yet powerful leadership could maintain even a semblance of democracy.[10]

Inefficiency, isolation, and bureaucracy were perhaps not so harmful to the party as the adverse opinion the public in general took toward the underground. Conspiracy is a dirty word in American politics, and the Communists with their underground tactics behaved very much like the conspirators their opponents said they were. Certainly the Communists did not constitute any ordinary political party in the days of the underground. Clearly, part of the reason the Communist Party came very close to being an illegal organization was that it behaved like an illegal organization.

The pursuit of men's motives is a precarious occupation at best, but it seems altogether likely that the decision for underground and other clandestine activity was not altogether rational. There was in the Communist Party a strong strain of radical romanticism that lent the underground member an aura of leftist glamour. It was not difficult for the underground Communist to identify himself with the French Communist underground against the Nazis or with the early twentieth-century Bolsheviks conspiring against the czar. Furthermore, the underground was "an opium of the Communists," a release into another world for people thoroughly frustrated by the real political world. It was natural for a romantic Communist, given his interpretation of the world about him and his frustration by it, to believe that as part of the underground he would live as a hero in Communist pages or that as a fugitive he was a modern Jean Valjean. How else can one explain the story of the four Smith Act fugitives?

In June 1951, the Supreme Court upheld the conviction of the first eleven Communist Smith Act defendants. The defendants had no further recourse in law and were to begin their sentences. Seven of them entered prison, but four became fugitives from justice: Robert Thompson, Gus Hall, Henry Winston, and Gil Green. All were married and had children. To become a fugitive meant separation from wife and family for an indefinite period, undoubtedly longer than it would take to serve their five-year sentences. (Thompson, as a war hero, had received only three years.) It does not seem likely that each of the four fugitives made his decision independently, but someone made such a decision, and it was one that would be difficult to defend on rational grounds. As fugitives hunted by police, they could have been of very little if any value to the party. The party gained nothing; the four sacrificed much. The first to be caught was Gus Hall, apprehended in Mexico in October 1951. In September 1953, the F.B.I. seized Robert Thompson in a cabin in California's Sierra Nevada mountains, along with Sid Stein, who was by then a fugitive from another Smith Act trial. Winston and Green were never caught. In 1956, when the party was in the biggest uproar of its history as a result of Khrushchev's disclosures about Stalin, they surrendered separately to federal officers in New York City. The two men never disclosed publicly where they had been. Had they gone to prison in 1951, they would have been already released. As it was, they were sentenced to additional terms for contempt of court. The decision to become fugitives doomed them to separation from their families for at least ten years. Back in 1950, when the first Smith Act case was under appeal and Green was temporarily imprisoned, Mrs. Eugene Dennis had written a lament about the longing of one of Green's children for her father. "I hold close the memory of little eight year old Josie Green . . . sitting in a corner, holding locked in her arms her father's soiled shirt just as it had been sent home from the West Street Jail; and she sat there, rocking back and forth, crooning to herself, holding that shirt in her arms." [11] There was no such political exploitation of a child's tragedy after Green had been bailed out and then holed up as a fugitive.

The fugitives and their families were not the only ones who suffered from the Communist "loyalty program." Expulsion and rejection caused unhappiness for hundreds. Expulsion is not a matter to be taken lightly for a dedicated member who has spent years in the Communist movement. To be expelled is to be abandoned by one's little society, to receive the "silent treatment" from associates of years' standing, to suffer rebuff and execration from old friends. For party functionaries and frequently for members of Communist-led unions, to be expelled meant to lose one's job.[12] Furthermore, the former Communist has a difficult time adjusting to non-Communist society. Suspect in some quarters unless he goes through the accepted rites of expiation, and suspect in other quarters if he does, the expelled Communist lives a lonely life between two worlds. Hundreds, perhaps thousands, of Communists were banished to this twilight purgatory in the early 1950's.[13] To combat expulsion was useless. The defendant in expulsion proceedings had no rights. The organ of the New York State party itself declared, "Each 'prosecutor' at an expulsion knew full well that there were a series of standard charges . . . to be put into each case . . . anti-leadership, undisciplined, anti-working class, and for the poor soul who would dare to attempt to argue his or her case, the cardinal crime of breaking the unity of the Party and . . . wanting it to degenerate into a debating society." [14] Two cases in which the party mistakenly and unfairly ostracized members whose lives had been devoted to the movement illustrate a great deal about the party's methods and devotion to the Soviet Union as well as different reactions to party rejection.

Anna Louise Strong's association with the Communist Party went back to the party's earliest history. She became a party specialist on Asia, and for thirty years her articles appeared in the party press. In early 1949, Miss Strong was in the Soviet Union, writing a series of articles under the title "Tomorrow's China," which were published in late January and early February in the *Daily Worker*. Then, for reasons never explained, the Russians arrested her as a spy and on February 21 deported her to the United States. The American Communists, embarrassed at having published her articles almost until her arrest, tried to atone for their sin by vilifying her. The first Smith Act trial was then in progress, and Miss Strong sent the Civil Rights Congress a check for $1,000 for its defense fund. She endorsed the check, "For the American Communists who are getting as raw a deal from American justice as I got from the USSR, from a fellow victim of the cold war." At the "request" of Eugene Dennis, the Civil Rights Congress returned the check. Dennis said, "The noteworthy efforts

of the CRC [Civil Rights Congress] to defend the Bill of Rights
. . . would be harmed, not helped, by tainted money." A few days
later, Elizabeth Gurley Flynn, who had the reputation in the party
of the "rebel girl" mellowed into a kindly grandmother, attacked
Miss Strong as "arrogant and egotistical." It was, said Mrs. Flynn,
"no wonder the Russians were at the end of their many years of
patience with the erratic highhanded Miss Strong, about whom
they obviously know more than they are telling." [15]

Miss Strong, grown old in Communist service, took her calumny
without retaliating. She settled down in California to await a better
day, still devoted to Communist principles. Seven years later, when
the Russian leaders themselves said that Stalin had been a criminal
paranoiac, the American party leaders again accepted the single-
minded and patient Miss Strong.[16] And she again accepted the
American, Chinese, and Russian Communists.

John Lautner did not accept his own treatment from the party
so quietly. Lautner was born in Hungary and came to the United
States when he was eighteen. He became a naturalized citizen in
1926 and a Communist Party member in 1929. From 1930 to
1932, he worked in the party's national group activities in Cleveland and Detroit. Early in 1933, he became a full-time party functionary as a section organizer in New York City, where he remained
until he moved up to district organizer of West Virginia. Late in
1940, the party sent him to its National Training School, and
when he finished he became the national secretary of the party's
Hungarian National Bureau. In 1942, he went into the army and
stayed three years, the last year of which he served in the army's
psychological-warfare program in Italy. After the war, he resumed
his life as a professional Communist and worked up to greater
positions of power. In May 1947, he became head of the New
York review commission, charged with the administration of the
party's internal security. In September 1948, the party added to his
duties by making him a member of the national review commission.[17]

In September 1949, in Budapest, the Communist Hungarian

Government tried a Communist leader, Laszlo Rajk, on charges of espionage in behalf of Tito, the United States, and Great Britain. The trial in Budapest was to have repercussions on the American party and to bring about the expulsion of John Lautner. When Lautner had been in Italy during the war, there were a few members of the British army attached to his unit, among them a Hungarian named Charesyez. Charesyez "confessed" at the Rajk trial that he was an agent of Tito and testified that Lautner had first introduced him to Titoists in Italy during the war. Thus, Lautner was suspected of being part of an anti-Communist spy ring. In 1956, the Hungarian Communists themselves confessed that the entire Rajk case had been a frame-up, and they restored Rajk to their list of heroes—posthumously.

Lautner was not aware of the testimony in Budapest concerning him until January 1950. The American Communists devoted a great deal of attention to the Rajk case; the *Daily Worker* of October 4, 1949, used four full pages to reprint part of the trial record, and *Political Affairs* carried a favorable review of a collection of documents relating to the case published by the Hungarian Government.[18] But these accounts did not mention Lautner. There were, however, American Communists who knew that Lautner had been implicated, and they were determined to get rid of him. They took as further "evidence" of Lautner's guilt the fact that, as head of the New York review commission, he had not detected that Angela Calomiris, who testified for the government in the first Smith Act trial, was an F.B.I. spy.

In December 1949, Louis Weinstock, a Communist leader for years, approached Lautner, who was still unaware of the suspicions about him, at a *Daily Worker* fund-raising bazaar at the St. Nicholas Arena in New York. Weinstock suggested that Lautner should go to Hungary. Lautner said he could not afford such a trip, and Weinstock replied that he would raise the necessary money and get Lautner a trade-union job in Hungary. He urged Lautner to get a passport. A few days later, Robert Thompson also urged Lautner to get a passport, and Lautner made application for one. The

State Department denied the passport because of Lautner's Communist affiliation.

In later years, Lautner told the following story under oath in a number of trials and hearings. In January 1950, after Lautner had been out of circulation with a brief illness, the party treasurer, Jack Kling, told Lautner they had some work to do in the Midwest. Lautner wrote his mother in Youngstown, Ohio, that he would see her Sunday afternoon, January 15. He left New York by train Friday night, January 13, arriving in Cleveland the next morning. Early that afternoon, he met Kling at Cleveland's Union Station. Lautner and Kling spent the afternoon at a show, then were picked up by a car and taken by a circuitous route to a house in the Kingsbury Run section of Cleveland. Kling told Lautner to go down to the basement. In the basement were two men, whom Lautner did not know, armed with guns, knives, and rubber hoses. They ordered Lautner to undress, and the men searched his clothes. Then Kling came downstairs with the driver of the car, Saul Wellman, a Detroit Communist leader, and Joseph Brandt, a leader of the party in Ohio. They had a wire recorder and a device they said was a lie detector, which they strapped to Lautner's arm. They asked him if he were a C.I.A. agent, what his relationship was to Noel and Herman Field, and to whom he had talked about underground plans. They shook a Hungarian newspaper in his face and said, "We know you." In Lautner's words, "I was threatened time and time again that if I don't come clean I will never leave that place." When they learned that his mother was expecting a visit from him the next day and that he had registered at a Cleveland hotel, Kling, Wellman, and Brandt went upstairs. When they returned in a few minutes, their attitude had changed. One of the men originally in the basement put a gun to Lautner's ribs, and Kling told him to write down what he dictated. Lautner wrote in pencil Kling's dictated "confession" that he was a paid anti-Communist spy and that he had received a fair hearing on the espionage charges. Brandt insisted the statement be rewritten in ink. Lautner rewrote it. Kling then announced that the "hearing" would continue the next day, Sunday, and that Lautner should meet them at the Mayfair Restaurant on Euclid Avenue. Kling and Brandt departed. Lautner complained that he was cold and asked for his clothes. When he got them back, he found that fifteen dollars, his gloves, and the State Department letter refusing him a passport were missing. He was then taken by car to a city bus stop.

Such was Lautner's loyalty to the party and his intelligence that he thought the whole affair in the basement "was a way of testing me or something like that." The next day, he actually went to the Mayfair Restaurant and waited for Kling for an hour and a half. When Kling failed to appear, Lautner went to Youngstown to see his mother. He returned to New York, Monday, January 16. The next morning, Lautner read in the *Daily Worker,* "The National Review Commission approves the recommendation of the subcommittee which examined the case of John Lautner and hereby expels him from the Communist Party as a traitor and enemy of the working class." Not until then did Lautner realize what had happened. Still he wanted to remain in the party. A few days later, he wrote a letter to Alexander Trachtenberg, chairman of the national review commission, to protest his expulsion and ask for a hearing. To insure delivery of the letter, Lautner had his brother take it to Trachtenberg personally. Trachtenberg never replied.

It took months for Lautner to get his bearings. When he did, he was not as patient with the party as Miss Strong was. He was angry for being falsely accused and expelled. "I was not a revisionist. I was a loyal and devoted Party member up to the time I read my expulsion." In September 1950, eight months after his expulsion, Lautner wrote to the F.B.I. volunteering to tell what he knew about the Communist Party.[19] Subsequently, he became a most effective witness for the government in trials and hearings involving Communists.

All in all, the Communist organizational defense methods were disastrous from the party's own point of view. An exaggerated estimate of the danger of American fascism, blind adherence to the methods and style of foreign Communist parties, and a romantic emotional predilection for the bold, heroic stance combined to produce, in the end, a shrunken organization, inefficient and isolated. The process left a trail of personal tragedy and bitterness, some of which was to be effectively directed against the Communists. But the underground and mass expulsions were no more disastrous for the party than the other aspect of its defense mechanism, the campaign for ideological purity.

THE CAMPAIGN AGAINST HERESY

At a meeting of the state committee of the Communist Party in New York in the spring of 1956, after Khrushchev's speech denouncing Stalin had triggered a crisis in the American Communist movement, one of the committee members found release from years of party suppression in a vigorous condemnation of the Communist Party's undemocratic and relentless smothering of intellectual dissent. He was especially critical of "the ideological purification processes which were literally brainwashing." [20] He was referring to the mental-purification program the party undertook in 1949 and 1950 as an integral part of its fortification against outside assaults. In its intensity, its intellectually repressive extravagance, its fever for detecting and routing heretics, the Communist Party's striving for purity made the contemporaneous tendency toward conformity in American society at large seem pale in comparison.

The Communists were systematically thorough in their campaign. In March 1950, Foster, in a message to the party's national committee, deplored "what I consider to be the greatest of all the weaknesses of our Party, namely its lack of systematic theoretical work." [21] Within a week, the leadership exerted pressure to enroll more party members in classes in Communist theory at party schools. Robert Thompson, leader of the New York organization, ordered that "all clubs take immediate steps to mobilize its members to take courses at the [Jefferson] School, at its annexes, and at the School of Jewish Studies." Each club should assign one additional member to attend party schools, preferably in courses on the Soviet Union, on Marxism and the Negro question, and on Marxism and labor. His injunction to the party clubs to take action was clear: "This statement should be read, discussed and acted on immediately at every club meeting." [22]

More important than the party's effort positively to develop "correct" ideology through education, however, was its campaign negatively to eliminate heresy. In this campaign, not even Foster himself was immune. Dennis related "that a number of us in the National Committee have called attention to certain faulty or unhappily formulated statements in some of Bill's writings. . . ." Such suspicion of Foster had been misguided, Dennis confessed; Foster had received the imprimatur of important foreign Communists and was obviously acceptable. "We have . . . noted that his book *Twilight of Capitalism* received very favorable comment in the great Marxist-Leninist journal, *For A Lasting Peace, For A People's Democracy!* And we took cognizance of the fact that this same book has been published in abridged form in tens of thousands of copies by our great brother Party, the Communist Party of Italy." [23]

The list of banned ideas and attitudes in the Communist index was a long one, but the two that received the greatest fire in the party's age of suspicion were Freudianism and color prejudice. The party's anti-Freudianism was interesting for its intellectual justification, and its attitude toward prejudice was noteworthy for its extremism.

There are a great many people who have reservations about the validity of Freudian psychiatry and who deplore the facile popular interpretations that have become common in this age of oversimplified Freudianism. But only the Communists interpreted the popularity of Freudianism as an anti-working-class plot of bourgeois imperialism. And only Communists had a basically conspiratorial motive for their opposition to Freudianism. Throughout the Communist denunciation of psychiatry, no matter what the explicit argument, ran the fear that Communists would go to psychiatrists and reveal secrets about the party. The anti-Freud campaign was at least partly a security measure.[24]

Criticisms of psychoanalysis began to become common in Communist periodicals in 1950. Milton Howard had a series of articles on Freudianism in the *Daily Worker* early in the year, and *Masses & Mainstream* devoted some space to the subject. The antipsychoanalysis campaign got official leadership endorsement in the March 1950 meeting of the party's national committee. Henry Winston, in his report at the meeting, condemned the "reactionary bourgois philosophy and practice which violates every principle of working-class ideology. . . . The fight to mold Communist thinking must be developed resolutely in a struggle against these subjectivist, idealistic, Freudian concepts, which, in essence, are anti-working class, anti-Communist, and tend to undermine a class struggle approach to social and individual problems." In June, Mrs. Eugene Dennis wrote, "As a mother and a Communist I reject such tripe. . . . Freud be damned!" [25] The war was on.

There is a fundamental conflict between dialectical materialism and Freudianism which Communist philosophers could have fruitfully explored and clarified. The Communists, however, fell back upon their convenient theory of capitalist conspiracy.

In the "general crisis of capitalism," one Communist article argued, "bourgeois ideologists" are forced to "invent theories which are calculated to conceal the naked brutality of imperialism's aims by giving them a 'scientific' facade." Capitalism had already degraded "social science into an ideological instrument justifying mass impoverishment, imperialist war, and fascist cannibalism." "Bourgeois psychology" was no more than another "insidious instrument at the disposal of the monopolist ruling class." "The most widespread and dangerous form of this shoddy bourgeois psychology," the argument went, "is Freudian psychoanalysis . . . [and] it is not accidental that the Wall Street dominated United States . . . has become the center for the dissemination of Freudianism."

The only answer to emotional distress was communism: "In the Socialist Soviet Union, where exploitation of human beings has been abolished . . . the source of the insecurities, the conflicts, and the mental anguish chargable to capitalism has . . . been eliminated." [26]

The task of developing an intelligent Communist critique of psychoanalysis fell to the Russians. In the summer of 1950, a group of Soviet psychologists met for a symposium. This group also rejected Freud, but they advanced the discussion by reviving the conditioned–reflex psychology of Ivan Pavlov. Pavlov offered a way to reconcile psychology with materialism. His work on the functioning of the cerebral cortex provided a materialist base for psychology; psychology became an aspect of physiology. In 1951, the Russians published the papers presented at the symposium in English,[27] and in due time the American party responded. In September 1952, *Political Affairs* discovered Pavlov, explained the implications of his work, and touted him as the new answer to Freud.[28]

After the party developed its theory of psychoanalysis as a façade for imperialism, psychoanalytic terms became anathema in Communist circles. To use such terms indicated an infection of bourgeois ideology, an infection dangerous to intellectual purity which must be eliminated. The Communist novelist Howard Fast was to learn that the use of such terms was forbidden. In his *Spartacus,* a novel about a slave revolt in ancient Rome, Fast had used such terms as "inner struggle" in his fictional glorificatio, of class struggle. For such deviation from 100-per-cent Communism, Fast was subjected to personal abuse and his book was criticized in the *Daily Worker* for, among other things, having too much "of the destructive influence of Freudian mystifications." [29]

Far more important for the development of the party and far more repressive was the party's campaign to stamp out "the virus of white chauvinism." The campaign against white chauvinism within the party became a full-scale internal witch hunt, as hysterical, as disrespectful of justice, and as ridiculously self-defeating as any hunt for Communists in non-Communist American society.

The Communist purge on the question of anti-Negro prejudice was a natural and logical development from the party's past. The Communists had long realized that American Negroes represented an opportunity and a challenge unique to a Communist party in a capitalist country. And, as related earlier, the party's line on the Negro had vacillated back and forth between a peculiarly Stalinist kind of Negro nationalism and a militant struggle for Negro rights and equality as Americans. After World War II, the party had gone back to its earlier Negro nationalism position, which tended to isolate Communists from the main stream of the Negro's movement for equality and integration. It was natural, then, for Communist energies in behalf of Negroes to become directed inward, within the party, rather than outward, against the many unhappy conditions and forces in American life that discriminated against and exploited the colored 10 per cent of the population. It was perhaps inevitable in a purification campaign that any manifestation by a Communist of prejudice against Negroes should make him suspect as a carrier of a bourgeois virus.

The metaphors "carrier" and "virus" are not invented here. These were terms Communists themselves used frequently as an integral part of their explanation of Negro prejudice. In Communist theory, the proletariat is inherently virtuous and the bourgeoisie is the source of all evil. Communists did not recognize that in the South and elsewhere lower-income groups are more vehemently anti-Negro than people more comfortable economically, but they did recognize that there was prejudice against Negroes among American workers. The Communists tried to explain away this worker prejudice, which embarrassed their basic theory, as an infection deliberately introduced by the bourgeoisie. For a party member, then, to be infected indicated that he was not really a good Communist.

The Communists' barrage against discrimination outside the party was not nearly so rewarding as their efforts had been in the

1930's. In 1950 and 1951, they made a major matter of the conviction and execution in Mississippi of Willie McGee. It is probably true that Communist support for McGee served to reinforce Mississippi's determination to execute him, but it is also probably true that if it had not been for Communist activities in McGee's behalf, the case would have been little noticed nationally. The biggest Communist effort against Negro oppression generally since the war was the petition the Civil Rights Congress submitted to the General Assembly of the United Nations charging that America's treatment of Negroes constituted a violation of the UN's convention on genocide. The petition was an obvious effort to discredit the United States in the eyes of the colored peoples of the world and to furnish ammunition for the Soviet bloc's anti-American propaganda program. Although Americans may not justifiably take pride in their Negro relations, the charge that the Government of the United States deliberately pursued a genocidal policy toward its Negroes was too fantastic to be effective among people who knew America.[30]

The party's campaign against white chauvinism got started in early 1949, at precisely the time the trial of the first Smith Act defendants began at Foley Square. Pettis Perry, Secretary of the national Negro work commission, was the director of the operation. "Pete" Perry had been born on a tenant farm in Alabama in 1897. When he was ten, he started to work picking cotton. At twenty, he left the South and bummed around the country on freight trains, working sporadically at a variety of unskilled jobs. In 1932, he settled in Los Angeles, and soon thereafter, having become involved in the defense compaign for the Scottsboro boys, joined the Communist Party. Like many another Southern Negro, his formal education had been poor, and he was only barely literate when he became a Communist. The party opened new intellectual vistas for him: "I practically learned to read by reading the *Communist Manifesto* and *Capital*." He rose steadily within the party in California as a "full-timer," becoming in the 1940's a member of the committee responsible for California and Arizona. In 1948, he moved to New York to become director of the national party's Negro work.[31] Perry was ideal as the person in charge of the campaign against white chauvinism: as one who had grown up in semifeudalism and whose only intellectual experience was in Communism, he was militant; as a true Negro proletarian as well as a Communist, a relatively rare phenomenon, no white Communist of less humble origins was in a position to challenge him.

Innocent actions or words very quickly became interpreted as manifestations of prejudice. One of the first incidents occurred at the special office the party established early in 1949 to turn out propaganda in defense of the Smith Act defendants then on trial. One night, a white girl typist who was very busy asked another girl in the office, a Negro comrade who was not then occupied, to go out and bring back coffee. The colored girl took offense at the request and brought charges of white chauvinism against the typist.[32]

Fairly important party leaders soon learned they were not immune. Isadore Begun, Bronx County party chairman and a member of the state committee, and two of his subordinates were removed from leadership in the spring of 1949 because of alleged white chauvinism. Begun had given a speech at a Harlem testimonial affair for a Negro woman trade-unionist comrade. The speech was, Robert Thompson wrote in *Political Affairs,* "devoid of any appreciation of the political significance of the holding of such an affair in honor of this Negro trade-union leader." Begun "descended to the level of telling a dirty joke, which, under the circumstances, was a chauvinist act. The nature of this act was all the more serious in its character and consequences because the offense was against a Negro woman, a member of the most oppressed section of the Negro people." [33] For this offense, the state committee removed Begun from all his party posts, reprimanded him, and assigned him to special "control tasks" in Bronx Negro work. A loyal party member for more than twenty years, Begun did not rebel. In a spirit of abject contrition, according to the *Daily Worker,* he "fulfilled his control tasks . . . with merit, achieving a greater Communist understanding of the Negro question as a national question." After doing penance for a year, Begun was restored, although his restoration apparently did not end the problem in the Bronx. Years later, a comrade complained, "The Bronx Party was paralyzed for over three years with a series of removals of the County leadership on charges of white chauvinism." [34]

The party disrupted itself in several districts over these charges. The vice-chairman of the Wisconsin party, Fred Blair, was suspended because of "weakness in combatting 'white supremacy' ideas." Southern white Communists were more than usually suspect. Charges against leadership in Louisiana and Texas "almost wrecked" the party there, and in Georgia the party disappeared altogether in a white-chauvinism controversy. [35]

The campaign led the party to absurd lengths. The party forbade members to take vacations in Florida and thus earned the antagonism of a considerable number of formerly friendly members of the Furriers' Union and District 65 who had been accustomed to Miami vacations in the off-season. [36] In the summer of 1951, the party moved its national headquarters away from the *Daily Worker* building, just below Union Square, to the heart of Harlem. [37] Publishing a drawing of a Negro minister "with distorted features" was found to be white chauvinism, and for this offense the editors of the Sunday *Worker* publicly apologized. They also apologized for publishing a drawing of a nonsegregated dance which had shown Negro men dancing with white women but had failed to show white men dancing with Negro women. [38] Howard Fast was forced to write a public apology for allowing one of his characters in *The Proud and the Free,* a novel of the American Revolution, to use the term "nayger." To use the words "boy" or "girl" in referring to Negroes became suspect, and some Communists even objected to the use of "black" and "dark" as in such phrases as "black despair" or "dark future." [39]

Obviously, things had got out of hand. The effort to eliminate white chauvinism had become a spasm of hysterical suspicion which damaged the party's effectiveness. Still, the party did nothing to call off the farce so long as Pettis Perry remained in command. In 1950, he had been elected to the national committee, and in 1951, when the Supreme Court ruled in the Dennis case and the top eleven leaders either went to prison or took off for the woods, he and Gurley Flynn and Foster became the party's ruling triumvirate. Not until Perry's conviction as one of the "second-string" leaders in early 1953 did any top leader try to correct the excesses of the white-chauvinism spasm. Finally, in July 1953, Foster himself acted.

He published in *Political Affairs* an article on "Left sectarianism" in the fight against white chauvinism. He by no means condoned any white-supremacist thought in the party, but he did assert that "our Party must achieve a more realistic definition of what constitutes white chauvinism than is now the case." He also pointed out that there was such a thing as "Negro bourgeois nationalism." To make sure his new definitions of what really constituted white chauvinism and what constituted "Left sectarianism" on that issue were understood, he ended his article with a series of textbookish study questions.[40] The wilder aspects of the white-chauvinism campaign soon disappeared.

The hysteria ended but it left its mark upon the party. By 1953, there were fewer Negroes in the Communist Party, both in absolute numbers and in percentage of total membership, than there had been any time since 1937.[41] Instead of making the party more attractive to Negroes, the furor had actually driven them out. A 1956 survey by the New York State organizational secretary concluded that "gross distortions in the fight against white chauvinism in the Party . . . tended to create an unreal estimate of rampant white chauvinism in the Party. What Negro would want to associate with such a Party?" [42]

In fact, the entire party defense program—underground, small and secret clubs, and emphasis on ideological purity—backfired. Recruitment of new members all but ceased. The party was more interested in apprehending heretics in its ranks than in recruiting.

By 1953, only 43 per cent of the membership had been in the party less than ten years and 60 per cent were between the ages of thirty-five and forty-five, the Depression generation. For reasons that are obscure, the party had also driven out more men than women. In 1953, women party members outnumbered their male comrades, and in community organizations of the party, as opposed to industrial organizations, women constituted three-fourths to nine-tenths of the membership. And, finally, the party's emphasis on security tended to isolate the Communists. Instead of working among non-Communists, party members huddled together where they felt more secure, either entirely within the party or in front organizations where party membership was no handicap.[43]

In 1953, it became obvious to the party leaders that some changes had to be made. Furthermore, after the nineteenth congress of the Soviet party late in 1952 and Stalin's death a few months later, Russian emphases were changing. The American party, however, modified its approach only gradually. It failed to make any major and dramatic changes until there were major and dramatic developments within the Soviet bloc, and nothing really dramatic happened until February 1956, when Nikita Khrushchev addressed the twentieth congress of the Soviet party on the sins of Joseph Stalin.

PART FOUR

THE
AGE
OF
KHRUSHCHEV

"Humanity has lost the greatest man of our time. . . . Stalin meant that a new era had dawned for mankind. . . . As humanity bids him farewell, his vision will grow brighter with the generations." —Daily Worker *editorial, March 6, 1953, the day after Joseph Stalin died.*

"Stalin was a very distrustful man, sickly and suspicious. . . . The sickly suspicion created in him a general distrust even toward eminent Party workers whom he had known for years. Everywhere and in everything he saw 'enemies,' 'two-facers' and 'spies.' Possessing unlimited power he indulged in great willfulness and choked a person morally and physically. . . . And how is it possible that a person confesses to crimes he has not committed? Only in one way—because of application of physical methods of pressuring him, tortures, bringing him to a state of unconsciousness, deprivation of his judgment, taking away of his human dignity. In this manner were 'confessions' acquired."—NIKITA KHRUSHCHEV *to Twentieth Congress, Communist Party of the Soviet Union, February 24, 1956, as reported in the* Worker, *June 10, 1956.*

EIGHT: SLOW THAW IN THE COLD WAR

In October 1952, the Nineteenth Congress of the Communist Party of the Soviet Union met at Moscow, the first such meeting since the 1930's. Stalin had just published his *Economic Problems of Socialism in the U.S.S.R.* and set a slightly modified line for the congress to ratify. Stalin played down the conflict between the "socialist" and capitalist camps, suggesting "peaceful co-existence," and emphasized "contradictions" between the capitalist nations which, he hoped, would bring acute conflicts among them. There seemed to be a shift from "cold war" to "cold peace." Following the congress, Communist parties of Western Europe became increasingly hostile toward American influence in their countries and tried to form popular fronts for "peace" in an effort to intensify the "contradictions."

Stalin died March 5, 1953. The Russians had no constitutional or traditional arrangement for succession to the real seats of power, and the next several months saw a series of top officials rise and fall before Nikita Khrushchev emerged as the new Russian dictator. Khrushchev, thus far at least, has been more moderate and restrained than was Stalin in his last twenty years or so. Even while the struggle for power within the Soviet Union was in progress, there was the beginning of a "de-Stalinization" process. Overt terror declined. In July 1953, the Russians announced the removal—and subsequently the execution—of Lavrenti P. Beria, chief of the secret police. Many political prisoners from the Stalin era were released. Clearly, a greater degree of personal security for Russian Communist leaders and other important Russians began to develop soon after Stalin's death. The new leaders, especially Khrushchev, displayed more flexibility and a relative moderation, both in foreign and domestic affairs.

There were changes, too, in the United States. The strength of the American "radical right" began to wane in the spring of 1954 when the Army-McCarthy hearings were televised into millions of homes. Senator McCarthy finally hanged himself on the plenitude of rope which the "modern Republican" administration allowed him, and before the televised hearings had ended, comedians were making jokes about "point of order." A few months later, the Senate of the United States formally repudiated the junior Wisconsin senator, and McCarthyism faded as a major political force.

With something of a thaw in both the U.S.S.R. and the U.S.A., relations between the two countries improved a little. In July 1953 came the signing of the Korean truce, and the war that was not a war (but that killed 25,000 American soldiers, nevertheless) at last came to an end. In May 1955, East and West finally agreed to a peace treaty for Austria, and that summer Khrushchev and President Eisenhower conferred at Geneva. Their "summit conference" brought no new agreements, no new era of East-West harmony, but the mere fact that the American and Russian executives had met indicated that the cold war had eased somewhat. Observers noted a "Geneva spirit." The summer of 1955 also saw the visit of a delegation of Russian agricultural experts to the lush cornfields of Iowa and the spectacle, unthinkable three years before, of conservative little corn-belt towns vying with one another for the opportunity to play host to Russians at Gargantuan fried chicken and ice-cream dinners.

With all these developments, it was inevitable that the American Communist Party should modify its position on a variety of matters, that there should be a change in the direction of the Communist line. Developments in the Soviet Union had never failed to make an impact upon the United States Communists; they were now to do so again. But for three years after Stalin's death, there were no dramatic and sudden changes, nothing comparable to the changes of line in 1939, 1941, and 1945. The changes were so gradual, so piecemeal, that they generated little excitement. The changing direction of the Communist Party was a slow drift rather than a fast current, hardly perceptible to outsiders at any given moment. Even party rank and filers had to look back to old landmarks and measure the extent of their drift before they realized they had moved at all.

A bare beginning of a shift in the party line came in December 1952, before Stalin's death—but after the nineteenth Soviet party congress—with a "Draft Resolution on the Situation Growing out of the Presidential Elections." Two months later, *Political Affairs* carried an article which contained the admission that "in the past few years our Party has suffered considerable isolation from the masses." In June 1953, the party leaders made sure the membership understood the importance of Stalin's last work as well as the pedigree of the draft resolution by publishing as a special supplement to *Political Affairs* a "Reader's Guide" to Stalin's book, complete with pedantic study questions and directions on how long to study each part.[1] These first deviations from the party's postwar Left orthodoxy were not in response to new conditions or developments in America or in American-Russian relations, for there had not as yet been any important new developments. They were in response to the nineteenth congress and to a recognition—but only a dimly perceived recognition—that the party's postwar line had led it into a blind alley.

The draft resolution, as published in late 1952, even contained an admission of error from the party's leaders, the first time the leadership under Foster had granted it could have been mistaken: "It was incorrect to have favored the departure of the Wallace forces without masses from the Democratic Party. Every effort should have been made to encourage the Wallace forces to fully unfold the struggle for peace to its conclusion within the Democratic Party in a determined effort to influence the mass base of that party." In the resolution's final form, adopted in the summer of 1953, the leadership watered down its admission of error. "The mistakes made by the Party" were not now attributable to the leadership, but to "strong sectarian tendencies within its ranks." [2]

After Stalin's death, the pace of the party's drift toward greater moderation quickened a little. When Foster wrote his article calling for an end to the wild excesses of the campaign against white chauvinism within the party, he denounced "Left distortions" and "sectarianism." In September 1953, he made the flat-footed assertion that the party's "most predominant handicap is a Left-sectarianism, which . . . has tended to shrink back upon itself and to neglect mass work on various fronts." [3] With such statements as these, it was to be only a matter of time before the comrades would again reach to their bookshelves for Lenin's *Left Wing Communism: An Infantile Disorder,* a document that had lain undisturbed and forgotten since several old Bolsheviks had been railroaded out of the party on charges of Left deviation soon after the war.

The softer post-Stalin line began to jell with the publication and adoption in 1954 of a draft of a new party program, "The American Way to Jobs, Peace, Democracy (Draft Program of the Communist Party)." Both a magazine article and a pamphlet,[4] the draft program emphasized what leftists had once called "immediate demands" rather than a new social order: "the Communist Party emphasizes that the issue at the present time is not Communism. The choice before our people today is peace, security, democracy versus the grip which the monopolists have on the country and their plans of fascism and war." The document made a great effort to establish the party as "American." The name of the program itself emphasized this national approach, and the writers of the program took pains to picture their party as "the inheritor and continuer of the best in American democratic, radical and labor thought and traditions. Its devotion to the true national interests of the American people is the source of its deep and abiding patriotism." The draft program advocated "a peaceful path to Socialism in the U.S.," declared that "socialism" could be established only by the will of a majority, and denied intentions to import any social system from abroad.[5]

A subcommittee of the national committee wrote the draft program and sent it to the full committee for criticism. Five national committee members dissented in one way or another from the new program, and the fact that disagreement within the committee was made public indicated a slight departure from the postwar style of hard monolithic unity. Two national committeemen thought the draft program's new line on political action was too soft, two thought it was not soft enough, and one deplored the emphasis on immediate demands to the near exclusion of professions of socialism.[6]

The party, however, had not become democratic enough to allow these dissenters to publish their points of view in the regular party press. The whole "discussion" of the draft program was stacked in favor of the program as originally written. When the party's national election conference met in New York City in early August 1954—a substitute for a national convention—a worker in party headquarters could say that the discussion revealed "the unanimity of the Party." No one was surprised when the conference's 150 delegates unanimously ratified the program, which in its final form differed from the original draft only in some phrasing.[7]

The new Communist line, as it evolved from the draft resolution of December 1952 to the program adopted in the summer of 1954, as clarified and explained by other writings of party leaders, is best described by breaking it into various parts: policy toward political action, toward trade-unionism, and toward Negroes.

THE END OF THE AMERICAN LABOR PARTY

In the election of 1952, the national ticket of the Progressive Party, led by Vincent Hallinan, received under 150,000 votes and evoked none of the excitement, synthetic though it may have been, that had characterized Wallace's race in 1948. Organized labor supported Adlai Stevenson, whose campaign had the enthusiastic support of Democratic liberals. Plain to see, the Communists' support of the Progressives in 1952 had gained them nothing.

The Communists, consequently, reassessed their whole third-party line, which had been firm and unexamined since the formation of the Cominform in the fall of 1947. Their third-party ventures had cut their contact with the great mass of voters whom the Communists hoped to influence; labor, Negroes, and the liberals generally were obviously not going to bolt the Democratic Party in the near future. The problem for the Communists was how to go hunting for the big game within the vast coalition of political groups that constitute the Democratic Party without losing the smaller game they already had corralled within the American Labor and Progressive parties.

One method of actually abandoning third-party ventures without seeming to was to use double talk: to support Hallinan and Bass in 1952 "as the only clear voice for peace" had been "correct," but the third-party line had been too "rigid" and there had been a lamentable failure "to sufficiently unfold a policy of united front and of coalition approaches on issues and in congressional and senatorial races." [8] Another method was to reshape the A.L.P. into a combination independent party and Democratic Party pressure group by having it support some Democratic candidates and run some others under its own emblem, as it had before 1948. This tactic within the A.L.P. had something to be said for it because party Chairman Vito Marcantonio had a good organization, which in 1952 had been able to produce over 90,000 votes for Corliss Lamont in the Senatorial race.

Neither method worked. In the more than half-decade since the Communists abandoned third-party action, they have made no perceptible progress within the major parties and they have, ironically, alienated the fellow-traveling types who once followed the A.L.P. and the Progressive Party. These non-Communists, who like to call themselves "progressives" and who are sometimes referred to with some justification as "Stalinoids," can abide no alliance, even temporarily, with one of the major parties. They are too radical, too impatient, to accept the compromises inherent in working within the Democratic camp. Paradoxically, the progressives—in actuality, the *National Guardian* subscribers—are often to the "left" of the Communists, who, with their tighter organization, their discipline, and their messianic vision, are able to compromise, to accept as a temporary tactic working with groups they despise. Certainly the Communists never intended their turn toward the Democratic Party as anything more than a temporary tactic, a going back to get the "masses" within that camp and bring them out eventually into a real third party. The Communists admitted as much.[9] But the *National Guardian* crowd, a loose group of non-Communist but pro-Communist radical "socialists," centered in New York, refused even temporary alliance with the Democrats, and when the Communists scuttled the A.L.P. and the Progressive Party, the progressives wandered aimlessly in their own political never-never land, resentful of their treatment by the Communists but unable, given their firm popular-front belief that to criticize a Communist is to commit unpardonable Red baiting, to do anything to retaliate.

Both the Progressive Party and the A.L.P. collapsed quickly when the Communists changed their electoral tactics. The Progressives just quietly expired, failing to run candidates again. Hallinan displayed only minor resentment when he remarked that "the extreme left"—he could not bring himself to say "Communist Party"—"wanted the Progressive Party to lay down and die," which is what the Progressive Party did.[10]

Marcantonio's A.L.P. resisted a little more. Marcantonio and other non-Communists, who constituted a majority of the A.L.P., refused to follow the Communists' urging to support the Democratic candidate, Robert F. Wagner, Jr., in the 1953 New York City mayoralty campaign. The A.L.P. insisted upon running a candidate of its own, who, without Communist support, received only 54,372 votes. After the election, the A.L.P. disintegrated rather quickly. Marcantonio himself resigned from the A.L.P. two days after the election with a bitter and yet restrained statement. A "minority," he said—he could not bring himself to say the words "Communist Party" either—had sabotaged the A.L.P., which would have received twice the vote had the "minority" co-operated. But he "rejected the course of a purge of the minority [as] repugnant to the democratic principles to which I have subscribed throughout my political career." He predicted that the A.L.P. would become "more and more a mimeograph machine rather than a political party" and that the party would fail in the 1954 gubernatorial election to muster the 50,000 votes necessary to stay on the ballot.[11] Marcantonio's prediction was accurate: in 1954, the A.L.P. candidate for governor of New York, *National Guardian* publisher John McManus, fell short of the 50,000 minimum, and in October 1956, the A.L.P. officially folded.

After the demise of the A.L.P. and the Progressives, the *National Guardian* clientele, dimly aware that it had followed a political Pied Piper, had no electoral instrument. In the fall of 1955, the *National Guardian* urged its readers to withdraw from electoral activity altogether should they be unable to develop another independent party,[12] and in 1956, some of the progressives declared lukewarm support for Eisenhower as a "man of peace." In 1958, they organized in New York an Independent Socialist ticket with Corliss Lamont for United States senator and McManus for governor, getting on the ballot through nominating petitions. The Communists did not support them, and their ticket ran poorly.

TRADE-UNION "UNITY" AGAIN

By the time Stalin died, the Communists were as cut off from the main stream of the American labor movement as they were from the political activities of the "masses." Without influence in either the A.F. of L. or the C.I.O., the Communists and their sympathizers in the labor movement were reduced to defensive actions in the handful of Left-led unions against the membership raids conducted by competing unions in the main tents of organized labor. Defensive action against raids in the Left unions availed the Communist Party nothing, because the Communist leaders in these unions had to compromise with their anti-Communist rank and file by playing down their Communism and emphasizing their bread-and-butter unionism. At best, such methods could be only a holding action. But in fact, despite their lack of emphasis on political matters, the Communist union leaders saw their locals steadily deserting to their anti-Communist competitors.

At last, recognizing they were in a weak position which offered no prospect of improvement under their current line, the Communists changed their line on labor to one similar to their new line on political action. They slowly and awkwardly modified their position to play down their enmity to anti-Communist trade-union leaders, to make greater efforts to get within the main stream of labor, and to emphasize work within what they termed the "Right-led" unions rather than those expelled from the C.I.O. As in the political sphere, the Communists had got "too far ahead of the masses" in trade-unionism; now they determined to go back and pick up the "masses."

The party made its switch on political action more quickly and easily than its switch on trade-unionism. Indeed, the party embarrassed itself by inconsistently maintaining its old-fashioned strident leftism in the trade-union field after it had already abandoned these tactics in the political field.

In June 1953, three months after the beginning of the post-Stalin thaw in Russia and six months after the beginning of the new line on politics in the United States, there appeared in *Political Affairs* an article by Alex H. Kendrick and Jerome Golden entitled "Lessons of the Struggle Against Opportunism in District 65." Editors of the magazine indicated that the article was the first of two installments, the second of which would appear in the July issue. Kendrick and Golden blasted the leadership of District 65, the New York metropolitan area district of the Distributive, Processing, and Office Workers Union. The leaders of District 65 had once been very close to the party, if not actual members. In 1952, the top leaders of the union, David Livingston, president of District 65, and Arthur Osman, president of the International, left the comrades' cause and assumed a "third camp" position critical of both the Communists and Right Wing conservatives. Kendrick and Golden could think of nothing too harsh to say about the "renegades," who, they charged, lived a plush life on the rank and file's dues while they co-operated with the bosses against the membership, were aggressively "white chauvinist," and were guilty of "Zionism and Jewish bourgeois nationalism." Presumably, the choice vitriol was saved for the second and concluding installment.[13]

Part II of the Kendrick-Golden article never appeared. The line on trade-unionism changed between issues of the magazine. The July issue of *Political Affairs* contained a note that "pressure of space" prevented publication of Part II in that issue and that it would appear in August.[14] "Pressure of space," however, did not prevent publication of the first part of another two-part article on labor with quite a different line, one with a conciliatory tone that emphasized "unity." "There cannot be real labor unity which does not base itself on the principle of unity *despite* ideological differences and *inclusive* of these differences." There were, the author argued, "tiny, weak, young early buds of Spring" which "must be kept in mind by the Left in its work to win the Right-led unions for progressive policies and in its work to strengthen the role of the progressive Left-led unions in the struggle for a united labor movement." [15] The second installment advised against "name calling, re-raiding, and other forms of 'answering in kind' " because these tactics only solidified the "subjective reactions" of workers in non-Communist unions and made them feel their organizations were "under attack and that they must rise blindly to its defense." [16]

To buttress the new line on labor, party leaders soon found impeccable scriptural authority. They exhumed a preface written by Lenin to an edition of letters written by Marx and Engels that was beautifully appropriate to the new "unity" line, and thereby invoked three saints in one swoop: "And now we very clearly perceive the two lines of Engels' (and Marx's) recommendations, directives, corrections, threats, and exhortations. They most insistently called upon the British and American Socialists to merge with the labor movement and to eradicate the narrow and hidebound sectarian spirit from their organizations." [17] How could Kendrick and Golden, whoever they were, stand up to opposition like that?

To proclaim the new "unity" line and to apply it successfully were quite different matters. The Communists realized that the leaders of the C.I.O. and A.F. of L. unions were not eager to unite with leftist unions merely because the leftists wanted to unite and promised to behave. Non-Communist trade-union leaders would work with the Communists and their sympathizers only if they were pressured into working with them, and the way to bring the pressure, the Communists believed, was to build it from below, in the union rank and file. "The watchword for today must be *unity of struggle* . . . struggle to break through and defeat the divisive policies of the dominant labor leadership. . . . Through united front actions from below more and more advances can be made in this direction. Pressure *can* be exerted on the top leadership." [18]

The new tactic brought no results for the Communists. If there were "young early buds of Spring" for the Communists to nurture to maturity, they have not yet blossomed. There has developed within the main stream of American labor a greater degree of unity than there was in 1953. As the A.F. of L. and C.I.O. merged, along with several of their constituent international unions, the Communists became excitedly optimistic about the possibilities of new influence.[19] But the mergers have, if anything, shut the Communists out colder than ever. For example, when the Furriers merged with the A.F. of L. Meatcutters, led by Patrick Gorman, an old Socialist, the anti-Communists succeeded in keeping the old Communist furriers out of the leadership in the new organization. Merger in this case meant loss of power for the party.

In what little contact has developed between the Left unions and the central labor movement, the contact has come at the top, through the leadership, without pressure from below, and has involved some of the more disreputable trade unions. There have been "feelers" for co-operation between the Bridges union and the East Coast International Longshoremen's Association and between the I.L.W.U. and the Teamsters. These unions are natural allies economically, of course. But also involved is the ideology, or lack of it, of the I.L.A. and the Teamster leadership, which is more interested in power than politics and therefore might accept an alliance more ideological union leaders would reject. Should these "feelers" develop into an alliance between Reds and racketeers in the labor movement, the irony would be too much for the ghosts of Debs and Haywood to bear.

ANOTHER CHANGE IN THE NEGRO LINE

The Communist line on Negroes changed in the post-Stalin era in much the same direction as the change of line on political action and labor—and for the same reasons. The party's line on the Negro and its wild internal witch hunt against "white chauvinism" had thoroughly isolated the party from the movement for Negro equality. The general Negro liberation movement, led especially by the National Association for the Advancement of Colored People, enjoyed its greatest success since Reconstruction with such victories as the Supreme Court's decision against segregated schools. Communists were on the outside looking in.

Foster called a halt to the white-chauvinism spasm in July 1953, and later characterized the whole affair as "glaringly wrong policy." "The general idea that our Party was unable to fight for Negro rights until it first cleansed itself completely of all traces of white chauvinism . . . was a dangerously sectarian notion, which . . . [could] only lead our Party into distorted and fantastic conceptions of white chauvinism and undermine our fight against it, cripple the Party's mass struggle for Negro rights, and weaken its influence among the Negro masses—all of which this 'Leftist' mistake did in a very marked manner." [20]

The Communists were slower and more cautious in modifying their Negro line than in changing other aspects of their position. In the late fall of 1953, months after the Communists had decided to be conciliatory to the liberal wing of the Democratic Party and non-Communist labor leaders, a Negro Communist attacked Walter White and the N.A.A.C.P. with the old customary vehemence. White came in for criticism for an alleged "fawning attitude" toward the Eisenhower administration and for indulging in "an orgy of Red-baiting and anti-Communist slander" at the 1953 N.A.A.C.P. convention. The organization itself was guilty of "continuing subordination of the Negro workers to the bourgeoisie" and of being squeamishly superior in condeming the violence of the Mau Maus in Kenya. In December 1953, Communists organized the Third Annual Convention of the National Negro Labor Council, a party-front competitor to the N.A.A.C.P., and Pettis Perry's report of the convention was an attempt to justify the N.N.L.C.'s existence.[21]

Perry's sectarianism and his power within the party seem to have been the main obstacle to a change of line. In an article

on the draft program of 1954, which on other matters was obviously inconsistent with the party line on the Negro, Perry attacked "Negro reformists" and continued to speak about the "right
to self-determination in the Black Belt." [22] Indeed, the draft program itself, one white leader pointed out, only veiled the national-
self-determination idea in new language.[23]

Perry went to prison in January 1955, after about two years of
appeals, along with other "second-string" leaders, and the line
changed almost immediately. The tactic now was a "mass policy"
on the Negro question. The old policy of "dual unions," or
"Left centers," as the Communists preferred to call them, was now
dropped. The N.N.L.C. quietly expired as the Communists decided
that the "central task is to influence . . . in a correct direction"
such organizations as the N.A.A.C.P. and the Urban League. "The
main thing to realize," wrote Foster, "is that we must work within
the mass organizations and not isolate ourselves in separate movements." [24] Working within the N.A.A.C.P. meant, of course, a halt
to vituperation against "Negro reformists." Doxey Wilkerson's report to his comrades on the 1955 N.A.A.C.P. convention contrasted
sharply with the last Communist report on that organization.
N.A.A.C.P. leaders were now "militant fighters," and the bourgeois group had somehow within two years become "highly con-
scious . . . of the decisive importance of trade union support."
Only when the N.A.A.C.P. took a position diametrically opposed
to the Communists did Wilkerson make any criticism, and then
the criticism was mild. Wilkerson even optimistically interpreted
a slight change in the wording of the N.A.A.C.P.'s traditional
resolution against co-operation with Communist trade unions.[25]

Working "within the mass organizations" obviously meant that
party members were to bury themselves within the N.A.A.C.P. and
other Negro organizations in an attempt to mold their policies.
How many Communists have infiltrated the N.A.A.C.P. is unknown, but obviously such buried Communists have been unable
to influence the organization "in a correct direction." The national N.A.A.C.P. leaders have had sufficient experience with

Communists to be able to resist them effectively, and they know that to weaken their guard against the Communists is only to play into the hands of the Southern white supremacists, who would like nothing better than successfully to smear black with red.

As with the new positions on politics and trade unions, the new Negro policy of the party availed it nothing. Months after the decision to infiltrate the N.A.A.C.P., the Communists still complained of failure to make progress. During the party's internal crisis in 1956, Benjamin J. Davis, one of the hardest of the party's sectarians, had to note the "extreme isolation of our Party in the struggle for Negro rights." [26] And, for the Communists, failure in this field is particularly bitter. For if the Communists cannot capitalize on this spirited movement of America's most exploited and oppressed people, where can they expect success?

"THE AMERICAN WAY"

With such a new line of moderation and emphasis on contact with the masses in non-Communist groups, party members who remembered the Browder era and the fight against Browderism just after the war—and almost all remembered because there were so few new members—were bound eventually to ask an embarrassing question: Was not this new line "Browderism without Browder"? Party headquarters could not avoid the question. "Some comrades ask," said central office worker Betty Gannett in a 1954 pamphlet, "how does this type of democratic unity differ from what Browder advocated? Is there not a danger of once again becoming entrapped in revisionism?" She went on to explain that of course there was always a "right danger" to be avoided, but the new line was not Browderism at all. Of necessity, she emphasized the theoretical differences between the new line and Browderism because in their applications and, to a degree, in their style of action, they were similar. "Our party is the defender of the interests of *all* oppressed and exploited, the *whole* people. Browder had no faith in the people. On the contrary, he wanted the people to pin their faith on 'enlightened' monopoly capitalists." [27]

There were differences, important ones, between Browderism and the post-Stalin line. In their theories, the differences rested on quite contrasting expectations about Soviet-American relations. Browder had a "perspective" of harmony between the two nations, with the United States shipping to the Soviet Union a significant amount of its "surplus" industrial product, and at this time the Foster party expected nothing more harmonious than the "cold peace" line Stalin had laid down at the nineteenth congress. The main differences between the two flowed from the fact that Browder's party was considerably more successful. Browder's party had significant strength in the labor movement, a bridgehead into the Democratic Party's coalition through the A.L.P., and greater toleration if not strength in the Negro community; Foster's party was isolated and seeking the kind of alliances and influence that the Browder party had enjoyed.

Still, the similarities were sufficient to embarrass Foster and amuse Browder, now retired in Yonkers. There was, for example, the incident of the "outstretched hand" to the Catholics, a policy Browder had developed in the realization that a large part of the working class is in the traditionally anti-Communist Roman Catholic Church. The party's 1954 program declared for the same policy: "The Communist Party declares that it seeks no conflict with any church or any American's religious belief. On the contrary, we stretch out our hand in the fellowship of common struggle for our mutual goal of peace, democracy and security to all. . . ." [28] Foster hastened to qualify his personal position on the "outstretched hand" before anyone pointed out the origin of the idea. In July 1954, Foster explained, he had received a letter from an enterprising priest who proposed that Foster resume his affiliation with the Church, with which the Irishman had broken as a young man. Foster declined in a private letter quite promptly. But when the final version of the program appeared in the party's official theoretical journal in October, Foster published his letter in the same issue of the magazine. The letter reaffirmed his atheism, cited the Soviet Union as the shining example of what he meant by "freedom of religious beliefs," and criticized the conservative nature of the Church's politics. He then quoted the "outstretched hand" sentences of the party's program. The priest must have been bewildered indeed.[29]

Late in 1954, the party launched a new magazine for young people that smacked of a Browderite flavor. A pocket-sized product on slick paper with good photographs, *New Challenge: The Magazine for Young Americans* sold a lot of clever propaganda for fifteen cents. Tucked in among such articles as "How a Wonderful Day Got Started," on the origins of Mother's Day, "Duck, Men—Here Comes the Spitter," on baseball, and "Is the Mambo Here to Stay?" were party-line nuggets such as a denunciation of universal military training, "Why They March on May First," and "World Youth Set for Summer Meet." [30]

Another similarity in style between the post-Stalin and Browder periods was a revival of the "we-too-sing-America" theme, a rebirth of the peculiarly fuzzy, Whitmanesque, Popular Front "patriotism." The 1954 party program was entitled "The *American* Way" to jobs, peace, et cetera. The document emphasized that the party "has its roots deep in the history and struggles of the American people and its labor movement. . . . Its devotion to the true national interests of the American people is the source of its deep and abiding patriotism . . . sealed in the blood of hundreds of members of the Communist Party who have died in defense of our country and our people." [31]

No sooner had the party adopted this document than it embroiled itself in a humorous little public washing of dirty linen about what patriotism meant for a Communist. One Andrew Montgomery, probably a pen name, wrote an offbeat article for the summer issue of *Party Voice*. On Memorial Day, he wrote, in trying to get to the subway he was blocked by a parade. "As I stood and watched, numerous flags floated by. At first, hesitantly, and a little embarrassed, I started to salute each one. At times I looked up and down the street and hoped, inwardly, that none of my 'left' friends were looking." But then he decided that the party's new program was patriotic and that he need feel no embarrassment. "For if the Draft Program is anything it is a patriotic document. It is not, as some comrades think, a gimmick which assumes a patriotic coloration as a concession to national pride." He went on to say, "There exists in our party some trends of cultural and intellectual exclusiveness which border on snobbery and are a distinct liability to the progressive movement." Examples? "I have no doubt that there are comrades . . . who have not read a single American book outside of progressive literature in many moons but who can discuss in detail the latest Soviet book or periodical from China." Other comrades go only to foreign films, "see only the decline and fall of American culture," and have "a certain contempt for television . . . a mass media accepted by the workers." During the Olympic Games, too many Communists had rooted for the Soviet athletes rather than the American boys. And then "the question of coca-cola. It is one thing for the French people to wage a struggle against this drink which symbolized the role of Wall Street in their country. But it is an entirely different thing within the United States. Coca-cola is an accepted and popular drink here, and does not symbolize the policy of the government. Those comrades then who stop drinking it for political reasons demonstrate nothing but their own inability to understand that it is impossible to substitute internationalism for national pride at this stage of the struggle." [32] All in all, a refreshingly different article for a Communist magazine.

The candid but naïve Mr. Montgomery did not long go unanswered. The next issue of *Party Voice* carried a reply by Betty Gannett and V. J. Jerome, editor of the party's theoretical magazine. "We note with grave concern—indeed, with alarm—the distortions in the article . . . by Andrew Montgomery. . . . It is hard to understand how this article was printed in *Party Voice*— and without editorial comment." Patriotism, yes, but not the patriotism of the Montgomery article, "permeated with bourgeois-nationalism, with jingoism." "We are *of* the people, and no false charges from the enemy, or their echoings in our midst, can cut us off from our roots. The allegations and 'portrayals' in this article are figments; they reflect no reality in our Party. Dressed up as a 'critique' of sectarianism, they are utterly alien to Communist teaching and practice." The party is truly patriotic, engaged in "a struggle for a progressive concept of patriotism—*for patriotism on a higher level."* As for American culture, Communists should not forget "there is an inherent relationship between an exploitive economic system in decay and its cultural superstructure. To work among the masses and to strengthen our ties with them, we cannot adopt uncritical attitudes or glorify cultural backwardness." The most serious error of the Montgomery article was its failure to understand that "True patriotism and proletarian internationalism cannot be counterposed to each other. . . . The whole article is a rejection of the Marxist-Leninist principle of the dialectical interconnection of that which is universal, or international, and that which is nationally unique." The reply ended on a somber note: "The article reflects a current danger of weakening before the ideological pressures of the war-inciting bourgeoisie. It reflects a certain capitulation to the propaganda barrage of chauvinist nationalism and to the Big Lie about the Communist Party. . . . The serious error of publishing this article should spur us all to deepen our concern with theory, to fortify ourselves with Marxist-Leninist understanding." [38]

The "patriotism" campaign proceeded without further errors such as Comrade Montgomery's. Party intellectuals began to write on the subject, and if they succeeded in fairly well obfuscating the subject with hairline distinctions and obscure references, a close reader still could draw the "correct" conclusion that the Communists were the true patriots and the anti-Communists were unpatriotic. After the Geneva Conference in the summer of 1955, one party intellectual, James S. Allen, had a vision of the Marxist conception of national interest coming closer to the popular understanding of that interest as Soviet-American relations continued to improve. "During the period of temporary isolation of the Left in American life, with the consequent encouragement of sectarian moods, [a] broad and dynamic vision of the national tradition was dimmed, at a time when reaction was glorifying everything that was backward in our history." But now "Marxists and progressives should revive and mature these concepts of the national interest and the national tradition as an inherent part of their outlook." [34]

Between the end of 1952 and the end of 1955, the party had come a long way ideologically. The process had been slow, uneven, and hesitant, but the party line had changed in some important particulars. At the very end of 1955, even the underground operation began to come out above ground. In September, Max Weiss, who had been underground for some time, openly visited party headquarters in Harlem in the company of his wife and daughter. The F.B.I. promptly arrested him, and soon he was indicted under the membership clause of the Smith Act. In late November and December, fugitives from indictment began to surrender voluntarily. Within a week, William Norman, Fred Fine, and James Jackson, all of them important leaders, turned themselves in.[35] The "first-string" fugitives, Green and Winston, who had disappeared after the Supreme Court's decision in the Dennis case in 1951, did not surrender until 1956.

In other and important respects, the party changed not at all. Communists still took on faith everything the Russian leaders said. The June 1953 East German working-class revolt seemed to Foster a "putsch . . . organized, financed, and led in the streets by tools of the Eisenhower Government." [36] When the Russians announced the execution of Beria and denounced him as an "agent of imperialism" and an enemy of peace and socialism, the *Daily Worker* duly accepted the same explanation, never acknowledging the significance of the affair.[37] When Khrushchev tried to make his peace with Tito, the Communists accepted without blinking the Russian story that Beria had been responsible for the whole difficulty.[38] And the party still suffered from literary filiopietism with each anniversary of the Bolshevik revolution, as in this full-page paean by Sean O'Casey in the *Daily People's World:*

> Red Star shines over the Kremlin,
> The Red soldiers with their Red cavalry are on the frontiers.
> Star of Power.
> Red mirror of wisdom.
> Red health of the sick.
> Red refuge of the afflicted.
> Red course of our joy.
> Red star shine on us all!

Still the party had changed some—the *People's World* published a letter of complaint about the poem from a party worker who sold the paper every weekend and found the poem a serious handicap to sales. "Go out some time if you doubt me and try and sell this kind of copy to the people." [39]

What changes there were added up only to changes in tactics. The more change, the more the same thing. The unchanging fundamental principle of the party, as well as its fundamental weakness, was that the party molded its aims and tactics in response to Soviet conditions and requirements rather than those of either the United States as a whole or of the American working class. Dedicated Communists believed, of course, that the interests of American workers were the same as the interests of the Soviet Union, and their belief was sincere. Sincere faith was, after all, what held the party together, to the degree that it was held together.

But the faith of the American Communists was soon to receive a jolt such as it had never encountered before. Nikita Khrushchev was preparing his speech for the twentieth congress of his party.

NINE: TARNISHED HEROES: STALIN AND FOSTER

When delegates to the Twentieth Congress of the Communist Party of the Soviet Union assembled in Moscow in early February 1956, no one in the United States, the Communists included, anticipated anything out of the ordinary. The congress surely would be another dull series of economic reports and abstract statements of party line, which Soviet experts in the Western world would inspect microscopically for significant clues. The twentieth congress, one of the most important meetings in communism's history, precipitated an unprecedented crisis in the Communist world and set in motion a chain of events that all but killed the Communist organization in the United States.

On February 14, Nikita Khrushchev delivered to the congress the report of the party's central committee. This report was not the famous "secret" Khrushchev speech, which came ten days later, but even this first speech was explosive. In an obvious but unexplicit reference to Stalin's regime, Khrushchev condemned the "cult of personality" or "cult of the individual" and announced a return to the Leninist principle of "collective leadership." In the speech he also declared that the Soviet Union's goal was "peaceful co-existence" with the West, asserted that each nation of the world would have to follow its own inevitable "path to socialism," and hailed united fronts of Communists with social democrats and other popular groups.[1] The *Daily Worker* revealed no excitement over this first Khrushchev speech. Sam Russell, correspondent in Russia for the London *Daily Worker,* had a story which featured the coexistence part of the report and the promise of a shorter working day for Russian labor. The editors of the New York *Daily Worker* published nearly two pages of excerpts from the speech but omitted the sections with the implied criticism of Stalin's leadership. Editorial writers and columnists ignored the criticism as well. They put their emphasis on Khrushchev's "various-paths-to-socialism" theme and on his disclaimer of intent to export revolution, each of which was consistent with the current American party line. The *Daily Worker* was caught without a good photographic cut of Khrushchev. The one it used was obviously outdated, showing a Khrushchev twenty years younger, with hair and a thinner face.[2] The first specific mention in the *Daily Worker* of Russian criticism of Stalin appeared in a news story about a speech by Anastas Mikoyan at the congress rather than the first Khrushchev speech, but there was no editorial comment and the story appeared under the innocuous headline "SOVIET LEADER CALLS FOR NEW STUDY OF CAPITALIST TRENDS." [3]

The first reports to reach the United States about Khrushchev's "secret" speech of February 24-25 came March 16. Even before Americans knew anything about the famous account of Stalin's paranoid misrule, a few American Communists publicly revealed their anxieties about the Russian congress. Others were unruffled. James S. Allen, a veteran Communist historian, declared in his regular column in the *Worker* of March 4 that he was not disturbed: "Marxists abroad are supposed to be embarrassed by the Party Congress just concluded in Moscow, according to what I read in the newspapers. I must confess that I have no sense of embarrassment." He went on to praise the Russians' "dynamic, bold, open-minded approach to all problems" and to condemn John Foster Dulles in routine fashion.[4] The first evidence of confusion and doubt among Communists in public prints appeared in a column by Alan Max, managing editor of the *Daily Worker,* on March 13. Max, once editor of Columbia University's humor magazine, had a reputation in the party as a writer of light satire, but now he was not trying to be funny. "Any Marxist who says he has not been jolted is either not being honest with himself . . . or minimizes the extent of the developments now in progress in the Soviet Union." So much for Mr. Allen. He went on to begin an examination of the errors of the American party, as thousands of others were soon to do: "We went overboard in defending things like the idea of Stalin as infallible, in opposing any suggestion that civil liberties were not being fully respected in the Soviet Union, in discouraging serious discussion and criticism of Soviet movies, books, etc." He ended the column by asking readers to write letters about their reactions to the twentieth Congress.[5]

Three days later, Communists realized there was a basic disagreement among the party's leaders. It seemed likely there would be a party disruption which would dwarf the upheaval of 1945 when Browder was downgraded. The Friday and Sunday editions always arrived in the same mail. Sunday's *Worker,* dated March 18 but actually received March 16, contained a letter from Ring Lardner, Jr., one of the "Hollywood Ten," which dared even to point out there was a cult of personality in the American party around William Z. Foster. "I wonder if some of the rather maudlin testaments to William Z. Foster on his recent birthday are really the most mature and effective way of acknowledging the respect due America's outstanding working-class leader." Lardner had a point there. The March issue of *Political Affairs* had combined the practice and the condemnation of the cult of personality in a novel manner. All but the last feature in the issue were eulogies to Foster, "Dear Comrade Bill," on his seventy-fifth birthday, February 25, 1956, the same day that Khrushchev finished his "secret" speech. The last item in the issue was Khrushchev's first report to the twentieth congress with its condemnation of the "cult of the individual as being alien to the spirit of Marxism-Leninism." That Lardner should write such a letter to the newspaper was not particularly surprising; what was startling to people who had read the *Daily Worker*'s dreary pages for years was that the editors should print it. All the more surprising was the editorial note following the letter: "Ring Lardner's letter raises a number of interesting and important questions of vital concern to the American Left. We are happy to have his views and by the same token invite our readers to submit theirs for publication." [6]

In the other issue of the paper which subscribers received that day was Foster's first comment. Foster conceded that Stalin had made "errors," but warned the membership that its "task is neither to rush indignantly to the defense of Stalin nor to tear him to political shreds, as some in our ranks seem inclined to do." There were, Foster argued, mitigating circumstances to be remembered in Stalin's defense. With the necessity of Russian industrialization, the hostility of other powers, the war with the Nazis, and then the cold war, "it was not difficult to fall into Stalin's command methods of leadership." Furthermore, American Communists should not forget "positive" features of Stalin's regime and "must be doubly vigilant not to fall into the bourgeois trap of making a negative and destructive sum-up of the whole situation." "The Stalin revaluation" is a problem for the Russians, not the American Communists, and "Of course, they will . . . master this problem, and in the doing . . . bring forth lessons of great value for the workers of all the world." [7]

No report of a secret speech appeared in American newspapers until March 16, after the Lardner letter and the Foster column were already in the mails. The first accounts were incomplete and undocumented. The speech was so sensational that even partial news about it threw the American party into an uproar. Khrushchev was reported by the newspapers as saying that Stalin had been a madman, acutely suspicious of his colleagues, personally abusive in his relations with subordinates, and ruthless in his persecutions. He had framed thousands of innocent Communist leaders and army officers, bungled the war with Germany, and created a feeling of terror among the top leadership of the Russian party.[8]

The American Communists obviously relied upon the "bourgeois press" for their information about what happened in the Soviet Union. There seems to be no reason to believe that the party had a "private line" open to Moscow in 1956 or since. Over and again during the party's upheaval, they reacted to the news from East Europe only as the news became available to readers of the New York *Times,* but surely many times American Communist Party leaders would have given a great deal for "inside information" from the Kremlin. In March 1956, the American Communists could not dismiss as capitalist lies the reports about the downgrading of Stalin.

There was too much evidence from the Soviet Union itself, and from Communist leaders elsewhere in Europe, that the charges had indeed been made. *New Times,* published by *Trud* in Moscow in ten languages and distributed in the United States by the Four Continents Book Company, had printed a special supplement on the twentieth congress containing the Russian central committee's resolution which had mentioned "re-establishing" inner-party democracy and former "violations of socialist law." [9] Nor did Russian criticism of Stalin cease with the end of the congress. On March 28, a *Pravda* article declared that under Stalin the "cult of the individual assumed ever more monstrous forms and did serious harm to the cause." [10] The next day, Hungarian Communist leader Matyas Rakosi announced that Laszlo Rajk had been convicted upon fabricated evidence, and a few days later, Polish Communists revealed that Wladyslaw Gomulka had been released from prison and "rehabilitated." [11]

Obviously, American Communists could not duck the anti-Stalinist controversy. Their public disagreement became intensified and, more importantly, quickly shifted from the question of Stalin to the matter of their own party's record in recent years. Ordinary rank-and-file members, repressed for years, found irresistible the *Daily Worker's* invitation to express themselves. When George Blake Charney, New York State party chairman, promised in a public meeting that no member would be expelled or punished for expressing his own views, the audience, composed mostly of Manhattan active members, interrupted him with enthusiastic applause.[12] A *Daily Worker* letter from a Communist who called himself "Guido" was typical. The year before, "Guido" wrote, he and some Italian-American friends had written a series of letters to the editor which had been neither published nor discussed. Now he wanted to know what was being done to free the party of "dogmatism and bias" and wanted to ask the foreign editor, Joseph Clark, who had once been the paper's Moscow correspondent, why he had not reported the abuse of the Russians by the secret police.[13] (Clark replied that he had not been aware of the activities of the secret police when he was in Moscow but conceded, "I should have written how silly the glorification of Stalin appeared to me at that time." [14]) The energy and exhilaration of the Communists' long pent-up discussion and criticism was reminiscent of a group of children just released from the discipline of an authoritarian schoolmaster.

Before long, the letters to the editor and the writings and speeches of the leadership began to fall into a pattern. At one pole were those who were critical of Stalin and wanted a thorough revamping of the American party, and at the opposite pole were those who made only minor concessions on Stalin, opposed a full party discussion of its own problems, and wanted no essential changes in the party's program. The bulk of the membership was somewhere between these two extremes, but clearly a majority was for greater party democracy and for a flexible and moderate party line.[15] The staff of the *Daily Worker,* led by editor John Gates, came to symbolize the first tendency, while Foster symbolized the other extreme.

The extent of the division within the party was evident in any issue of the *Daily Worker.* One issue, for example, carried on opposite pages an editorial on the Rajk case, presumably written by Gates, and a column by Foster on "What Was Done to Check Stalin?" The editorial was strong. The Rajk case had been a "frame-up" and a "murder," and American Communists were entitled to know more than they had been told about the case. The editorial insisted that all connected with the frame-up be brought to justice. "We . . . demand that the investigations in Hungary and the Soviet Union shall be full and complete and shall bring to book those responsible for injustice, no matter how high their position was or is." But Foster, who would never "demand" anything of the Russians, dealt harshly with those who asked what Khrushchev and other Russian Communists did to try to prevent Stalin's tyranny. Foster absolved the Russian leaders of all responsibility on the grounds that any "organized movement against Stalin would have had to confront the prospect of a split in the Party." [16] Presumably, Foster regarded a monolithic party as more important than justice, which, of course, was good Leninist doctrine. Fear of a split in the American party troubled both the Foster "hards" and the Gates "softs," [17] although the softs wanted the kind of a party in which dissent did not imply party split.

THE TAX AFFAIR

Just when the disagreements among the Communists were getting sharp and outsiders were watching the spectacle with fascination, an agency of the United States Government intervened and nearly ended the fight. On March 27, 1956, four agents of the Federal Bureau of Internal Revenue walked unannounced into the *Daily Worker*'s offices on the eighth floor at 35 East Twelfth Street, told the newspaper staff to leave, and posted notices to the effect that all property in the office was seized as a lien against unpaid back taxes. The assets seized included, besides the battered office furniture and typewriters, the newspaper's records, morgue, and addressing machine. There were simultaneous raids at party headquarters on Sixth Avenue and at the *Worker* "offices" in Chicago, Philadelphia, and San Francisco, dingy little rooms in low-rent districts with almost no property in them, where local Communists received *Worker* mail and prepared copy for their regional section of the weekend *Worker*. The tax liens held that the *Daily Worker* owed a total of $46,049 in taxes and penalties for 1951 through 1953 and that the party owed $389,265 for 1951.[18]

Who in the federal government made the decision to make the tax raids is not clear. The Internal Revenue Office in Washington disclaimed all connection with the raids, saying that the district director for Lower Manhattan, Donald R. Moysey, had acted "entirely on his own, without realizing the implications." But *Time* observed that Moysey had been in his position for less than two months and that it appeared that the office of Attorney General Herbert Brownell had "planned . . . and directed" the raids.[19]

The *Daily Worker* staff refused to let the raid disrupt publication. The group moved downstairs one floor to the workshop of the F & D Publishing Company, an independent printing firm which printed the *Daily Worker,* and wrote their copy for the next day's issue with pencils. The issue appeared with the proud headline "OUR OFFICE SEIZED—HERE WE ARE." The next day, the staff moved into temporary offices with the *Morning Freiheit,* the Yiddish-language Communist paper on still another floor of the building. Each issue of the paper appeared on time during the several days the staff was out of its regular office.

Significantly for the battle within the party currently in progress, the *Daily Worker* kept the paper going without the help of the party's national officers. Eugene Dennis was at home writing a speech when the tax agents seized the office. Telephone calls from the *Daily Worker* to tell him what was happening only irritated him. Neither he nor Foster did anything to keep publication uninterrupted. The extent of Dennis's help was a sarcastic telegram to President Eisenhower designed for propaganda rather than for solving the immediate problem, the recovery of their offices and equipment. Whether Dennis and Foster were secretly hopeful that the federal government would unwittingly remove the Gates thorn from their sides, as many of Gates's followers believed, or whether they were so much in a mental rut of manifestoes, resolutions, and other party rituals that they were unable to act in a practical situation cannot be told. In any case, the federal government did not silence the *Daily Worker,* whether or not that was its intent, and the failure of the national office to help the paper intensified hard feelings between the two factions in the party.[20]

Notified that the Internal Revenue Bureau had assessed value of the seized office equipment in the newspaper offices and party headquarters at a total of $4,000, Communists borrowed the money, deposited it with Moysey's office, and moved back into their regular quarters in early April.[21] In order to prevent seizure for taxes on future income, the *Daily Worker* set up a special Emergency Committee for a Free Press, which received all payments for subscriptions and other income, in effect becoming the paper's financial office. Checks for subscriptions made out to the paper's publisher, Publisher's New Press, Inc., were returned with instructions to make payments to the Emergency Committee. In May, the *Daily Worker* and the party sought a federal injunction to prevent further seizure of income and property; their plea was denied.[22]

The whole tax affair was a fiasco. If the administration was seeking to shut down the paper, it failed; if someone thought the Communists could really produce over $400,000 for revenue, he was stupid. The affair served only to rally a great many anti-Communist organizations and individuals to the party's defense on civil-libertarian grounds. Several newspapers over the nation condemned the raids, giving the party the kind of favorable publicity it could not have bought at any price.[23] The American Civil Liberties Union defended the *Daily Worker* as did even the American Committee for Cultural Freedom, a group whose anti-Communism was almost unbounded.[24] All in all, the tax affair gained the federal government nothing and, by endangering the existence of the *Daily Worker,* came near to knocking out one side in the most important inner-party fight the Communists ever had.

JOHN GATES CRITICIZES

At public party meetings, it was plain that the fire of the dispute was hot indeed. The Jefferson School inaugurated a series of four meetings on the significance of the twentieth congress. At the last, John Gates, the main speaker, used blunter language than he did in his editorials; it was clear he was a Communist and a defender of the Soviet Union, but equally clear that he sought a thorough change in the American party's organization and line. Gates was obviously feeling his way, confused in his own mind about what the party should do.

John Gates, born Israel Regenstreif, grew up in the Bronx, did well in school, and went to City College. In early 1931, the Young Communist League at City College organized a campaign against the R.O.T.C. (Reserve Officers Training Corps), and several of the young Communists found themselves suspended. The seventeen-year-old Gates joined the Y.C.L., left college the next year, and went to work for the party trying to organize steel workers in Youngstown, Ohio. From the time he got off the train in Ohio until January 1958, except for his army service in World War II, Gates was a professional revolutionary, a "full-timer" for the Communist Party. He fought in Spain as a member of the Lincoln Brigade, rising to the rank of lieutenant colonel, the highest-ranking American officer in Spain. In World War II, he was a sergeant in a paratrooper division. After the war, he became editor of the *Daily Worker*. He was convicted at the first Communist Smith Act trial and spent his imprisonment in Atlanta Penitentiary, where for the first time since he left college, he read non-Communist, even anti-Communist books. Among the books he read was George Orwell's *1984,* but contrary to the stories in the party that his revolt from Communist orthodoxy dated from his reading of the book, he disliked it. He only wondered at the self-imposed censorship which had previously prevented him from even reading the works of an anti-Communist. The books that impressed him more, interestingly, were the historical volumes on the post-Civil War South by Professor C. Vann Woodward. He realized that the history of the Negro in the United States was somewhat more complicated than he had thought and that the pat Communist interpretation was inadequate. When Gates got out of prison in the spring of 1955, he was still a confirmed Communist. There were only seeds of doubt in his mind. After ten more months of imposed absence from party affairs, a condition of his parole, he went back to the *Daily Worker* as editor just before the twentieth congress convened.[25]

Gates said a great many things to his enthusiastic Jefferson School audience that would have been unthinkable at a Communist meeting only a few weeks earlier. He was strong for civil liberties, even for enemies of Communism. The party's approval of the prosecution of the Minnesota Trotskyists under the Smith Act had been "dead wrong," a position later endorsed by the *Worker*'s Virginia Gardner.[26] When "by peaceful means" a socialist government comes to power in the United States, there would be full civil liberties for all, "including those who advocate the return to capitalism." The Ford family, if it wished, would be allowed to "harangue the workers on the streets of Detroit for return of their factories." (The party's education director, Max Weiss, very cautiously and guardedly endorsed this position.[27]) But he spent most of his time arguing that the party's greatest emphasis should be "on the creation of greater democracy in the party" and on correcting "sectarian errors which resulted from self-imposed isolation from popular movements." "We stand isolated from the great popular movements, from the new merged labor movement, from the Negro movement, and absolutely isolated from the farm revolt." Just how the party could break out of its isolation, just what its program should be, Gates did not know. He knew only that Communists could not find the answers from Communists abroad. "We have to stand on our own feet, to learn to think through for ourselves, not to let others think for us, not to parrot what anybody says." Communists must study the works of non-Communists and reflect the desires of the working class. "We Marxists are not the best authorities on the United States within America. There are others more astute, more learned, have more facts. We have got to be modest, especially because we are so small, so unsuccessful, so isolated from the working class." Over and over again, he enjoined Communists to study, to think, to come up with new solutions. But he himself had no solutions to offer.[28]

Many Communists were in no emotional condition to think deeply in 1956. Some were thoroughly shaken, their faith of years shattered by the highest priests of their church. Samuel Sillen, editor of *Masses & Mainstream,* came near to an emotional collapse. One day he walked out of the *M & M* offices and never returned. A few months later, he was working as a salesman. The February issue of the magazine had to be skipped altogether.[29] Leaders of the New York State organization, mostly of the Gates tendency, were in such an emotional turmoil and fever of factional activity that their state magazine, *Party Voice,* failed to appear in March, April, and May. Many "progressive homes" were in retrogressive turmoil, husbands debating party policy with wives, sons in ideological conflict with parents. When the party tried to present a solid front to the general public for the 1956 May Day demonstrations, the results were feeble. A small and listless group assembled at the north end of the park in Union Square and listened to unknown third-rate speakers on such safe subjects as denunciations of Franco and Trujillo. Around the edge of the small crowd, a group of Trotskyists, far younger in years than those in the passive Communist audience, distributed copies of the *Militant.* The meeting was only a pallid parody of Communist May Day demonstrations of times past.[30]

SOVIET ANTI-SEMITISM

One special reason for anxiety among American Communists during the downgrading of Stalin was that the Soviets were revealed to be anti-Semitic and a large proportion of the American party was Jewish. In New York City, the party's center, perhaps one-half the members were Jewish. Many of them read Yiddish. Furthermore, even to non-Jewish Communists—and to non-Communists, too, for that matter—anti-Semitism was among the most heinous of sins. Had there been no Jewish questions involved in the international crisis of Communism after the twentieth congress, it is unlikely that the emotional impact upon the American party would have been as severe.

On April 4, 1956, *Folks-Shtimme,* a Yiddish Communist newspaper published in Warsaw, ran an article entitled *"Unzer Veitig un Unzer Treist"* ("Our Pain and Our Consolation"). One week later, *Freiheit* reprinted the article, again in Yiddish, and the *Daily Worker* very briefly summarized its contents in English. The full text of the article appeared in English for the first time in the American Communist magazine *Jewish Life,* along with a comment by the magazine's editors.[81] The Polish article praised Lenin's policy toward Soviet Jews and hailed the development of Jewish culture in the Soviet Union during the 1920's and early 1930's. But then had come the "social plague which is today known as infamous 'Beriaism' " and brought "tragic results" for Jewish culture "and for a number of [Jewish] community and cultural leaders." To put it bluntly, which the article did not do, the Soviet Communist leadership had killed them. Jewish life and culture survived the plague of the 1930's and fought against the Nazis during the war, only to be rewarded with the "destructive work of the Beria gang and the damaging effect of the cult of the individual." "How then did it happen that the spokesmen of the Jewish community . . . suddenly, and without a why or wherefore,

were liquidated and its leaders condemned to death?" Now, however, everything has been set right once more. "The CPSU, with
Leninist boldness, has penetrated to the very core of the terrible
evil, in order to tear it out by the roots. . . . It is in this victory
that we find our consolation, our hope and our certainty of the
future." The comments of the editors of *Jewish Life* were stronger.
They regarded the article "with profound sorrow and indignation"
and used words like "murder," which the Poles had avoided. They
called for more details. "Why were the crimes committed, who
were responsible? The situation calls for a documented, detailed
history of these crimes against the Jewish cultural and political
figures." The guilty must be named and brought to justice. But to
the American editors, too, there was "a beam of light" in contemporary Russia. The acknowledgment of the cult of personality
"gives promise" of the end of Soviet anti-Semitism. "Steps are
being taken in the Soviet Union to restore the rights of Jewish
culture." The editors obviously expected more.

The *Daily Worker* staff, very largely Jewish but not so con-
scious of their Jewishness as the editors of *Jewish Life,* were more
indignant. "We register our strong dissatisfaction that the Soviet
leaders have not offered any explanation of what took place," said
a Gates editorial. "What is being done to guarantee against repeti-
tion of these actions against any minorities in the Soviet Union?"
The *Daily Worker* had been "too prone to accept the explanation
of why Jewish culture had disappeared in the Soviet Union in the
late 1940's." Now it demanded a full explanation—but it never
received it.[32]

Instead, the Russian Communists consistently played down
Communist anti-Semitism in the past and denied it in the present.
Even when Ekaterina Furtseva, the only woman member of the
Soviet party's central committee, in an interview with Tabitha
Petran for the *National Guardian* tacitly admitted the existence of
a quota system for Jews in the Soviet civil service—"the govern-
ment had found in some of its departments a heavy concentration
of Jewish people, upwards of 50% of the staff. Steps were taken

to transfer them to other enterprises"—she denied anti-Semitism. "It is impossible," she said, "to speak of anti-Semitism in our country"—a sentence that admits of two interpretations.[33]

By no means were all Communists or all Jewish Communists in agreement with the *Daily Worker*'s indignant position. Many letters vigorously criticized the paper's "revisionism" and accused it of giving comfort to the enemies of communism. "The paper should not be so touchy." "It is regrettable that the paper [should be] so sensitive to wrongs committed by Parties elsewhere. . . ."[34]

The party itself, through its various resolutions and reports, took little notice of Soviet anti-Semitism. A statement of the national committee on the Khrushchev secret speech, issued in June after the full text of the speech was published in the United States, devoted three sentences to Soviet anti-Semitism.[35] By September, in its new draft resolution, the only reference was an indirect and obscure one to the effect that the American party had been "unprepared for and shocked by" the "mistreatment of certain national minorities."[36] In October, a group of twenty-six American Jewish Communists wrote a letter to Bulganin in which they cited evidence of Soviet anti-Semitism and requested a "public and authoritative statement" on Jews in the Soviet Union and expressed their "anxiety in respect to the reconstruction of Jewish communal and cultural life." No prominent party leader was among the signers.[37]

SHIFTING PARTY WINDS

The party's crusty cake of custom dictated the process by which it discussed and attempted to resolve its internal differences. The Communists had been through the process several times before, the last time in 1945. A series of reports, statements, and resolutions are always discussed at various party levels, culminating in the writing of a comprehensive statement of party principles called a draft resolution, always adopted in a routine manner at a national party convention. During performances of this ritual, outsiders who observe closely can learn a great many things about the party which have been hidden since the last such affair. The lid comes off for a while, only to be sealed firmly again when the national convention signals the end of the rites.

The upheaval after the twentieth congress lasted much longer than earlier performances of the ritual. In 1945, Jacques Duclos had published his article in April, the American party became aware of it in May, and the party convention was in late July. Actual sharp discussion did not last more than two or three weeks. But in the mid-1950's, the party crisis was protracted. Beginning in March 1956, it did not even get to the draft-resolution stage until September, and there was no convention until February 1957. And this time not even the national convention brought an absolute end to hostilities. The final blows were not struck until early 1958.

The party's national committee met from April 28 to May 1, 1956, in New York. This meeting was the first one the national committee had held since 1951 and was an "enlarged national committee meeting," meaning that important leaders who were not members of the committee were allowed to attend. The group debated vigorously and announced a party convention for December. Party secretary Dennis delivered the main report to the meeting, and Max Weiss and Claude Lightfoot submitted lesser reports on the significance of the twentieth congress and the 1956 American elections. The national committee also announced a "sixty-day pre-convention discussion," after which the committee expected intramural bickering to end. The leadership would then harmoniously write a draft resolution, to be mechanically ratified by the December convention.[38]

Dennis's report was, for him, a strong statement and indicated that a party majority had revised its thinking considerably in its first two months of turmoil. A cautious party bureaucrat with a damp finger always in the air to detect both rank-and-file and Kremlin breezes, Dennis had delayed any kind of a statement

until weeks after the twentieth congress adjourned. Not until
April 8 did he express himself publicly at all, and then his statement was so commonplace and equivocal that one could not be
sure what his position was or even if he had one.[39] After the publication of the *Folks-Shtimme* article, Dennis revealed a little
personal agony, but the most critical statement he made about the
Soviets was that Beria's treatment of the Jews was "a sad stain
upon, and wholly at variance with, the noble and inspiring record
of the Soviet Union." [40] Until the meeting of the national committee, Dennis's position clearly was in the middle, neither defending
Stalin nor criticizing him, neither defending the recent policies of
the American party nor defending them.

Dennis's national committee report, later published as a pamphlet, was a vigorous and comprehensive criticism of the party's
policies of the past few years. The party's isolation was partly its
own fault. Most of the party's errors had been "of a left sectarian
character." The party had been mistaken in thinking that total
war and fascism were almost a certainty and wrong in believing
that the United States was on the brink of a major economic depression. From these mistaken "perspectives," the party had been
wrong in not striving to prevent the C.I.O.'s expulsion of the Communist unions, had been "erroneous and harmful" in its third-
party policies, and had been in error in its Negro policy. He even
urged democracy within the party and "an end to dogmatism,"
although he did not explicitly concede that the party had been
undemocratic and dogmatic. For the future, Dennis advocated
"forging diverse labor-Negro-democratic front coalitions and alliances." [41]

Actually, Dennis had not gone far beyond the party program
adopted in 1954. He neither proposed any new policies nor criticized any past ones that had not already been tacitly dropped, but
he did criticize the party's postwar policies more explicitly and
much more vigorously than anyone in the 1954 discussions. His
report raised a great many eyebrows. Some national committee
members inferred that Dennis was critical of the party leadership

and that, since Dennis was himself number two man, he was criticizing Foster. Other national committee members thought Dennis was not far-reaching enough, was neither using a new broom nor sweeping hard enough with his old one.

Foster only "appeared briefly" at the meeting, because of his heart condition,[42] but he was there long enough to speak against the report and vote against it. He began his remarks by saying that he agreed with the report and then proceeded to tear it apart. Gates called Foster's position dishonest. If he was really against the report, as he seemed to be, he should say so. But the membership had to get the news that Foster had voted against Dennis's report from a story by Joseph Lash in the New York *Post,* which Foster later denied completely.[43] A report of the party's New York State organization stated that the national committee had debated the Dennis report for four acrimonious days, after which "most comrades came around to agree with the general direction the Dennis report was moving in, and the vote on his main line was unanimous." But, the report continued confusingly, Dennis's "hard-hitting summary which defended his main line was not unanimous. There was one against and three abstentations [*sic*], about 40 for." The report did not identify the dissenting voter. The vote against the report was Foster's; the three abstaining were Benjamin Davis, Ed Strong, and Carl Winter.[44]

Dennis had enumerated many of the party's errors and its mistaken assumptions from which the errors logically derived, but he did not even hint at the fountainhead of all the party's policies, which had isolated it: its slavish adherence to a line laid down in Moscow. Dennis did not say so, of course, but the Communists had made their decisions on the basis of the current line of the Soviet Union. And the Soviets never determined their line by any consideration of what was good or bad for the American party or for American workers.

There were Communists who dimly, but only dimly, perceived the real fountainhead of the party's isolation. To describe them as "national communists," as Yugoslavia's Tito, Poland's Gomulka, and Hungary's Nagy were national communists, is to exaggerate, but they tended in a national communist direction. That is, while remaining Communists, they wanted their party to make its decisions independently of Russian conditions. Gates was clearly thinking in a Titoist direction when he said the American party had to stand on its own feet and not "parrot what anybody says." This Titoist or national communist tendency dominated the leadership of the New York State organization in 1956.

Soon after the April-May meeting of the national committee, the New York State committee held a meeting and listened to a report by its organization secretary, Norman Schrank. Schrank's report went far beyond Dennis's in all respects, but its most significant aspect was its national communist tendency. "The influence of the international Marxist movement on our party is a source of much of our disorientation. The international Marxist movement weighed heavily on our past policies and estimates. In my opinion this influence cannot be exaggerated." He singled out Zhdanov's line at the 1947 meeting of the nine Communist parties. "We took this warning on the main danger of overestimating the strength of the bourgeoisie and underestimating the strength of the working class, and mechanically and in a doctrinaire way applied it to America—with the disastrous consequences which we are now examining in our work of the past decade. . . . What may be valid internationally, may not be valid in America, or fully valid." Schrank was close to accepting what had often been said of the Communists: they were not really Left; they were just East.

Schrank's report, actually a heretical document, became the basis of the party discussion in New York. At the state committee meeting, there was a vote on the proposal "That the State Committee approves the main line of the report by Norman Schrank as a basis for discussion." None opposed the motion, three abstained, and the rest voted in favor of it.[45] Surprisingly, much of the discussion in New York, the party's strongest state, was in fact based upon Schrank's report, and the subsequent issues of the state party magazine, *Party Voice,* were filled with the national communist heresy, vivid denunciations of the Foster-Dennis leadership, and an independence of thought extremely rare in Communist pages. Some of the statements in *Party Voice* were vigorous indeed: "I think that communist leaders are the worst snobs I have ever known." "I'm an American Communist. I don't want to be a Russian Communist." "The dictatorship of the Party and finally the dictatorship of a selected group within the Party is not and cannot become Socialism." [46]

Schrank's report even called for a reconsideration of "Browder's contribution," and this curious story justifies digression. The 1956 party crisis revived ghosts that the leadership assumed had long been exorcised. Browder, expelled from the party a decade before, received considerable attention. Even the party's ancient history produced a ghost when Charles Dirba, a leader of the "Left opposition" in 1921, which had advocated an entirely illegal Communist organization, wrote a letter to the *Daily Worker* that indicated his ideas had not changed much in the past quarter-century. [47]

In early July 1956, Earl Browder answered the door of the Yonkers apartment where he lived alone to find a man he did not recognize. The man introduced himself as Chick Mason and handed Browder a twenty-eight-page mimeographed booklet he had written entitled *Sources of our Dilemma: A Rejection of the "Right Opportunist-Left Sectarian" Explanation by our Leadership*. Browder took a quick look through the booklet and saw it was a defense of Browderism. He asked Mason if he represented an organized group or only himself, and Mason replied he was working alone. Browder asked Mason to bring him some more copies.

Mason had produced a rather confused piece of political analysis with unusually long quotations from the writings of Browder and Foster. His work certainly was not the product of an experienced Communist writer, but he managed to make his main point clear. "It is my contention that in order to understand our present isolation we will have to re-examine how we had once emerged from isolation, how we were beginning to learn to 'walk in the sun,' and what forces combined to stampede us back into the shell."

Mason returned to Browder's apartment in a few days with a few extra copies of his work. On the cover was the notation, "This article is being published serially in 'Party Voice.'" He drew a line through the announcement, apparently to indicate that *Party Voice* had reneged on a commitment. Parts of Mason's work were to appear, however, along with a disclaimer of endorsement, in the September and October issues of the New York party magazine.[48]

Mason did not succeed in his apparent objective. No organized group in the party wanted to revive Browder's ideas, and Browder himself was certainly in no mood to go back to the party wars. Yet the ghost of Browder hovered over the party during the tortured discussion of its difficulties; his name was frequently mentioned in party publications. Some Communists believed, as one member of the New York State committee put it, "It is undeniable that Browder made the first serious effort to apply Marxism to the American scene and to relate it to the American past and future," and this inevitably attracted those Communists who were groping their way toward the idea of an American party which shaped its policies without subservience to the exigencies of Soviet foreign policy.[49]

THE RUSSIANS AGAIN

In the middle of this hottest inner-party fight in Communist history, the United States Department of State released the text of Khrushchev's secret speech to the twentieth congress as it was edited for circulation among certain important Russian Communists. The Russians have never released the full text and never published any edition of it for general consumption.

American readers, though prepared by earlier reports from East Europe, found the fuller report in the New York *Times* of June 5 sickening. Khrushchev spoke of false confessions acquired "with the help of cruel and inhuman tortures." He cited chapter and verse from several cases, quoting letters from the victims of judicial murder. Stalin had been insanely ruthless. "Stalin . . . sanctioned . . . the most brutal violation of Socialist legality, torture and oppression, which led as we have seen to the slandering and self-accusation of innocent people." One of Stalin's most trusted political policemen, Rodos, responsible for the purging of several old Bolsheviks, was "a vile person, with the brain of a bird, and morally completely degenerate." Everything that capitalist critics had ever said about Stalin was now repeated by Khrushchev—and more.[50]

The Communists were jarred most severely. Many had joined the party because they sincerely saw communism as freedom, justice, and brotherhood; now they saw that Stalin's Russia was the negation of all these values. And for the party heretics, those who were struggling with Foster for a more liberal party, there was a particularly terrible realization. As *Daily Worker* columnist Howard Fast put it to a meeting of the paper's staff, "I wonder if there is any comrade here who can say now, out of what we know and have seen, that if our own Party leaders had the power of execution, he or she would be alive today." [51] They were alive because their party did not have power. To realize failure is a bitter experience; to realize that it is better to have failed is worse.

The only logical escape for the Communists was the argument that Stalinism was not socialism—the word Communists insist upon to the dismay of social democrats—but was an aberration from socialism. Many Communists wanted to believe in this escape, but they found it a little difficult. How, they kept asking themselves, if a socialist state is the best of all possible worlds, could such a fiend come to power? How could the proletariat, the theoretical womb of all economic and political virtue, bear such a monstrous travesty of "socialist justice"? Other Communists pursued less logical theories. Foster, for example, while not denying Stalin's "mistakes," a mild-enough word, emphasized the accomplishments of the Soviet Union even under Stalin. Still others hid their heads in the sand and continued to inveigh against "revisionism." And there were a few cranks, such as the woman who wrote the *National Guardian* that Bulganin and Khrushchev had "sold out to Wall Street" and would in time desert to Switzerland, where their reward, "a billion dollars apiece," had been "salted away" for them.[52]

The *Daily Worker* staff took the first of these rationalizations, embellished with a great deal of confession and breast-beating. Two editorials immediately after the publication of the speech summarized the position. "The State Department is dead wrong when it suggests that the evils of the Stalin era are inherent in socialism. . . . The exposure of Stalin's misrule, of his crimes against socialism and humanity is a measure of how much this was a departure from socialist ideas, and from what Lenin taught." But at the same time, "We were wrong, terribly wrong. We extended the proper and laudable sympathy for the world's first socialist state, and its defense against the monopolists and fascists who would destroy it, to a stupid and arrogant condemnation of those who told the truth about the violations of justice in the Soviet Union. We did not want to believe these crises could occur in a socialist state and so we refused to believe." No more such fawning approval and lack of a critical attitude toward the Russians. "We do not hesitate to state that we don't like the way Khrushchev's speech was made public. The leaders of the Soviet Union . . . should have published the speech immediately and made it available throughout the world." And why was there nothing in the speech about the "crimes . . . against Jewish culture and Jewish cultural leaders?" But still "socialism" is desirable for America. "We dedicate ourselves to helping the American working people find the American road to a complete reorganization of our society . . . a society of democratic socialism in which the civil and political rights of the individual and of groups will be guaranteed under the Constitution . . . a society in which the American people will own the resources and giant factories which they have built with their own hands and will at last, in friendship with the peoples of the whole world, determine their own destiny in their own way." [53]

Howard Fast was more eloquent. "I, for one, looked hopefully but vainly at the end of the document for a pledge that the last execution had taken place on Soviet soil. I looked for a pledge of civil rights, for the sacred right of habeas corpus, of public appeal to higher courts, of final judgment by one's peers rather than by professional judges. I looked for these things knowing full well how they have been mishandled and perverted in the courts of capitalism. . . . Instead, I learned that three more executions had been announced from the Soviet Union, and my stomach turned over with the blood-letting, with the madness of vengeance and counter-vengeance, of suspicion and counter-suspicion. . . . I think millions of human beings share my disgust at this idiotic behavior—wicked, uncivilized, but above all, idiotic." And then the *mea culpa:* "I knew that writers and artists were intimidated, but I accepted this as a necessity of socialism, even as I accepted all else that I have enumerated as a necessity of socialism." But Fast, too, remained steadfast for "socialism": "If of any value, [the Soviet Union] still has in me a friend—a man whose devotion to socialism and to social justice has not been shaken." [54]

The tide of the struggle within the party now clearly was with Gates and his supporters. Had there been a freely elected convention of the party in June, it surely would have reshaped the organization and adopted a line into some kind of "national communist" position closer to social democracy than the party had ever been. There even was some sentiment—how much will never be known— for dissolving the party altogether. Howard Fast wrote months after the fact that if there had been a party convention in June, the party would have been liquidated.[55] At the time, a party journalist, Sam Coleman, asserted in a letter to the *Daily Worker* that there were no national leaders for liquidation and few in the rank and file.[56] Obviously, hundreds of members quietly walked out on the party during the summer of 1956. To use an old radical party expression, they "voted with their feet." To these people, even Gates's national communism was a middle position.

Dennis's finger detected the stronger breeze. He wrote an article for the *Daily Worker* of June 18—the chronology becomes important here—in which he yielded a little more to that paper's position than he had before. He wrote that "The crimes and brutalities that sullied the latter period of Stalin's leadership are unforgivable" and deplored the "snuffing out the lives of more than a score of Jewish cultural figures." At the same time, Stalin's Russia had become an industrial power, had "wiped out illiteracy," and had given workers and farmers "status and dignity undreamed of under the Czars, and, in many ways, unmatched in the advanced capitalist nations." He disassociated himself from "ideas expressed in some of the letters, articles, and editorials appearing in the Daily Worker." He would not minimize the errors, but he could not "accept the viewpoint that wipes out and undermines pride and confidence in the Socialist countries." [57]

On June 24, the national committee of the party adopted and issued a statement a little stronger than earlier ones, although it had much of the on-the-one-hand-but-then-on-the-other-hand flavor that characterized the resolutions of the divided national committee. The "mistakes" in Russia "were primarily a result of wrong policies and concepts arising, in part, out of the fact that the Soviet Union was the pioneering land of socialism and was surrounded for decades by a hostile capitalist world." But on the other hand: "Khrushchev's contribution to the exposure of mistakes and to the process of correction . . . makes only a beginning in this direction. We cannot accept an analysis of such profound mistakes which attributes them solely to the capricious aberrations of a single individual, no matter how much arbitrary power he was wrongly permitted to usurp." The statement was also strong on the disclosures of Soviet anti-Semitism. "We are deeply disturbed by facts revealed in information coming from Poland that organs and media of Jewish culture were summarily dissolved and a number of Jewish leaders executed. This is contrary to the Soviet Union's historic contributions on the Jewish question. Khrushchev's failure to deal with these outrages, and the continuing silence of Soviet leaders, require an explanation." [58] The statement was a compromise between the Gates and Foster tendencies, yet it went farther in the direction of an independent attitude toward the Soviet party than any official statement ever had before.

The Communist parties of Western Europe began to kick up their heels a little, too. In an interview on June 16, Palmiro Togliatti, leader of the Italian party, went so far as to say that, although the twentieth congress "greatly aided the proper understanding and solution" of serious problems, "it is not possible . . . to consider satisfactory the position which was taken at the Congress and which today is being fully developed in the Soviet press regarding the errors of Stalin and the causes and conditions which made them possible." Quickly, the Danish, Norwegian, Finnish, and Belgian parties hailed the Togliatti interview.[59] By the end of June, the ferment of the Communist parties made itself felt in Poland. On June 28, the workers of Poznan rebelled, demanding "bread and freedom." In what was to become a pattern in East Europe, the object of the rioters' wrath was a building which housed the local state-security police. By June 30, artillery and tanks had crushed the revolt, leaving about five hundred dead in their wake.[60] The *Daily Worker* recognized the righteousness of the rebels' cause but argued that the American State Department had cynically exploited the Poles' just grievances and instigated the rebellion.[61]

At this point, the Russian party stopped short, surveyed the effects of the Khrushchev speech, and decided that matters had got too far out of hand. It had already, on June 27, in an effort to stop the heresy developing in the Western parties, published in *Pravda* a translation of Dennis's article of June 18, one of the least critical written by a Western Communist leader, deleting Dennis's adverse comments on Russian anti-Semitism.[62] (Publication in Moscow, despite the deletions, did wonders for Dennis's ego.) Now, on

June 30, as soldiers in Poznan were completing the quelling of the rebellion, the central committee of the Soviet party met and adopted a resolution "On Overcoming the Personality Cult and Its Consequences." *Pravda* published the resolution on July 2.

The central committee's resolution was remarkably like Foster's columns on the twentieth congress, although the resolution nowhere mentioned Foster and did mention and quote favorably from Dennis's article of June 18. The reactionary imperialists, said the resolution, were trying to exploit the revelations about Stalin "to undermine the trust of the working people in the first socialist country in the world." Washington had financed the "anti-people's demonstrations" in Poznan, but the Poznan "provocateurs and . . . diversionists" had lost their courage before the opposition of the Polish workers.

The main purpose of the resolution was to set aright "certain of our friends abroad" who did not fully understand the question of the cult of personality and "sometimes give incorrect interpretations of certain points." The central committee singled out Togliatti specifically for "incorrect tenets." The resolution dealt at some length with a question that had bothered many Communists: "How could the cult of the person of J. V. Stalin, with all its negative consequences, have arisen and become widespread under conditions of the Soviet socialist system?" The Russians really added nothing in reply to this question that Soviet apologists had not already written. A "besieged fortress encircled by capitalism," Russia had had to contend with enemy spies and diversionists as well as "Trotskyists, right-wing opportunists and bourgeois nationalists." In other words, Stalinism had not derived from socialism and was not the fault of the Russians; it was the result of capitalist opposition to socialism and the fault of the Western imperialists. And despite Stalin, the Soviets had performed miracles of production because they had a socialist state. Now that Stalin was dead—and it had been "impossible" to do anything about his mistakes before he died because any action against him "would not have been understood by the people"—the party was eliminating the results of the personality cult and "restoring Bolshevik norms of Party Life." Reports of a crisis of communism or confusion in communist ranks were only "fables" concocted by "bourgeois ideologists," only "malicious, slanderous attacks by our enemies." [63]

At any earlier time in the history of the American Communists, such Russian actions as the publication of Dennis's article with significant deletions and the resolution of the central committee would have brought capitulation to the Russians and an end to further dissent. But in 1956, the Russians could not silence the dissent from afar. The exhilarating effect of freer air and the fight between the hards and the softs had gone too far and too long to be stopped, despite the Soviets' obvious wishes. Foster, in an article with the significant title "Achievements as Well as Mistakes," went all the way in agreement with the Russians' resolution. He also warned the party that it was still "a worthy part of this great, constructive world movement." [64] Dennis was only slightly more reserved in his endorsement of the resolution. The central committee's action "is a most welcome development," and the resolution "goes a long way in explaining—while clearly not justifying—what has become known as the growth of the cult of the individual." [65]

The *Daily Worker* staff dissented. A Gates editorial interpreted the Russian resolution as another round in "a fraternal, critical discussion, conducted on an equal basis among Marxists," although clearly the central committee of the Soviet party had intended their statement to be the last word. "In the latest chapter of this discussion," the Soviet party "has now given its reply to some of these questions. Many Marxists will feel satisfied with the answers which the Soviet Communist Party now presents. Many will feel that the final answers still need to be found and that the discussion must continue." And to emphasize that they would continue the discussion, the *Daily Worker* staff published in the same issue a statement of the Canadian party's national committee which termed Khrushchev's explanations as "inadequate" and a column by the paper's foreign editor, Joseph Clark, which called the Russian deletion of Dennis's comment on anti-Semitism lacking in "full truth and candor." "It is a tragic fact, as Dennis put it, that 'the lives of more than a score of Jewish figures' were snuffed out. They can't be brought back to life by snuffing out a clause in an article." [66] Two days later, the *Daily Worker* printed the Togliatti interview of June 16, which the Soviet resolution had specifically indicted.[67] The paper continued to publish letters that were critical of the Russian silence on anti-Semitism and that were quite critical of Foster. One letter, from a party member of twenty-two years' standing, urged Foster to "stop parroting alibis." [68] Nevertheless, the *Daily Worker* calmed down after the publication of the Soviet resolution. It did not capitulate, and it did occasionally publish some dissenting thought; but it did not have the fire that it had in June.

The national committee of the American party met again on July 19 and adopted a statement on the Soviet resolution of June 30. The statement, not released to the press, not even to the *Daily Worker,* until July 25, represented still another compromise between the Foster "hards" and the Gates "softs"; the hards clearly had gained ground. Compared with the national committee's statement of the previous month, it was a pallid document indeed. The new statement called the Soviet resolution "a most valuable and important contribution." It denounced, as had the Russian resolution, the efforts of "certain monopolist circles" to use the discussion within international Communism for their own ends, and it declared that "nothing will ever shake [the Communist party's] firm adherence to the principle of international working class solidarity." The statement did make reservations about the central committee's resolution, although they were mildly stated: "We believe certain aspects of the origins and effects of past violations of socialist law and principle need, and will receive, further study and discussion. Among these are: the question of bureaucratic distortions in a Socialist society, as well as the happenings in the sphere of Jewish cultural institutions and their leadership."

"Bureaucratic distortions" replaced such words as "murder," and even Dennis's phrase "snuffing out" became only "happenings." Still, the statement was too strong for Foster, who would not consent to criticizing the Soviets for anything that they had not already criticized themselves. That was his consistent position throughout the crisis. He voted against the statement, but his sole negative vote was never publicly disclosed.[69]

When the New York *Times* reported, "The American Communist party, a bit grudgingly and somewhat later than its fellow parties, toed the Moscow line on post-Stalin policy yesterday," Gates took exception to its interpretation. He emphasized the "bureaucratic distortions" phrase and defended the national committee statement.[70] Not all Communists defended the statement. *Party Voice* published an anonymous criticism of the statement, presumably with the permission of the New York State organization.[71] Apparently, the statement was too strong for the Russians. *Pravda* published the statements of many of the Western parties on the June 30 resolution, but the Russians never mentioned the American party's statement.

If the Gates wing soft-pedaled on the matter of the party's relations with the Russians, it did not let up in its criticism of the hards on other matters. After the June meeting of the national committee, the party initiated a series of "discussion articles" in each Sunday's *Worker*. From this series were supposed to come the ideas upon which the draft resolution for the party convention would be written. Gates supporters, especially people in the leadership of the New York organization, dominated this discussion in every respect.

The Foster wing of the party expressed no new ideas—indeed, the hards scarcely bothered themselves at all. Benjamin J. Davis went along with Foster in a kind of "positive thinking" about the party's recent past. There had been some mistakes, yes, but these were being overemphasized and "we should not go overboard." [72] One old-timer who signed himself "Jarama" made it clear that he thought the Russians ought to do something about Gates and the *Daily Worker* staff. "It took the intercession of the Communist International to help us get rid of Lovestone & Company with his theory of exceptionalism. . . . It took the comradely advice of Jacques Duclos to break the hold that Browder . . . had on our Party." Now help was needed again. "Jarama" thought even Dennis was too unorthodox. Dennis's report in May had been called *The Communists Take a New Look,* and "Jarama" was satisfied there was nothing wrong with the old one.[73]

Week after week, the Gatesites or those who tended in his direction called for a thorough overhaul of the party. The party's organization, "borrowed hook, line, and sinker from the Communist Party of the Soviet Union" had to be replaced with a "structure conforming to a Party with a line of peaceful transition to socialism, a Party based on American democratic traditions of organization." The party must "boldly free itself from the fetters of dogmatic adherence to any political line which can be misconstrued as not reflecting the national interests of the American working class and people." New tactics, new line, new everything.[74]

The party softs, or "liberals," it was clear, had vigor and passion, and they knew precisely what they did not like about the party. But they never determined exactly what they were for. They were unable to formulate precisely what the new line and the new tactics should be. Just how and to just what purpose the party should break out of the isolation to which Foster's leadership had led it were questions they never answered.

FOSTER COUNTERATTACKS

Late in the summer of 1956, a special subcommittee of the party's national committee was busy writing a draft resolution. Party custom decreed there should be such a document, which would serve as a basis for further discussion and then be ratified at the national party convention, already postponed from December until February 9-12, 1957.

The national committee adopted a draft resolution on September 13 and released it for publication on September 23. A document of about 23,000 words, the draft resolution began with a relatively calm analysis of the problems confronting America. Prosperity was not stable, although the party did not expect an economic crisis soon. A socialist economy was "the only basic answer," but meanwhile the party endorsed and supported the "forward looking domestic and legislative proposals of the labor movement and other democratic organizations for economic betterment and social welfare." The party stated its support of peaceful coexistence with the Soviet Union and other communist countries but did not attack imperialism with its old-fashioned abandon. The document declared the party's support of the absolute abolition of Jim Crow and ended its first section with a defense of the Bill of Rights and civil liberties generally.

A section on political and economic reform did not differ substantially from what a group of militant New Dealers might have written. The party would limit the power of monopolies, cease tax favors to big business, strengthen the labor movement, and introduce such political reforms as abolition of the electoral college and gerrymandering. The party declared its faith that someday the working class would have its own political party, perhaps the Democratic Party, perhaps a farmer-labor party. Another section, on "The American Road to Socialism," had little to say about what that road was like beyond saying that socialism was not the immediate order of the day in America and that the party sought "the broadest possible unity of all socialist-minded elements," or, in other words, a united front.

The last section of the draft resolution, comprising about one-third of the total, had to do with the party's past errors and weaknesses. It contained nothing new to one who had followed the discussion. "Left sectarianism" had led the party to overestimate the danger of war and fascism and had led to its isolation from the labor and Negro movements. The party must stand with other Communist parties as brothers, mutually helpful and critical, rather than as father and son. In the past, the resolution confessed, the party had "tended to accept uncritically many views of Marxists of other countries . . . some [of which] did not correspond to American conditions." And the document urged some modifications of party structure and procedure, which if observed would reduce the party bureaucracy's power and lessen the separation between the leadership and the rank and file.[75]

The draft resolution obviously represented a repudiation of the kind of leadership Foster had given the party since 1945. On the other hand, it did not represent a total victory for Gates, the *Daily Worker* staff generally, and many of the New York party leaders, although it was closer to their position than to Foster's, because it in many places expressed the new ideas rocking the party in a compromising and weaseling way. The party only "tended" to follow the Russians. Although Left sectarianism was the "main danger," the party must "maintain its vigilance against right opportunist tendencies." The slogan of "self-determination for the Negro nation of the southern Black Belt" needed only reappraisal. Clearly, the national committee majority in September 1956, when it adopted the draft resolution, was between the Gates and Foster poles, although closer to Gates than it was to Foster.

Thirteen members of the national committee voted on the adoption of the draft resolution. Three others had been deported and six were in prison. Foster and Davis voted for the draft resolution only with qualifications, which they announced they would later publish. The others—Eugene Dennis, Fred Fine, John Gates, James Jackson, Claude Lightfoot, William Schneiderman, Jacob Stachel, Sidney Stein, Martha Stone, Ed Strong, and Carl Winter —voted yes without qualifications.[76] How the members who could not be at the meeting would have voted is a matter of conjecture. Williamson, deported to England, probably would have sided with Foster, and Green, then in a federal penitentiary, probably would have sided with Gates.

Foster voted his qualified yes only in the interests of party unity. He obviously could not have really endorsed the draft resolution; endorsement would have meant repudiating all he had written for months and admitting gross misleadership of the party. But the yes was only temporary.

On Sunday night, September 23, at about ten o'clock, the first edition of the next day's New York *Times* hit the streets. The edition carried a story by Harry Schwartz, one of the *Times*'s Soviet specialists, which was dropped from subsequent editions by space limitations imposed by later stories. Schwartz's article was about a review of Foster's *The Negro People in American History* that had just appeared in *Pravda*. The review was less of an examination of the book than a eulogy of its author. "Soviet people know Comrade Foster as a fighter for peace, democracy and socialism, as a noted figure in the international Communist and workers' movement . . . he well knows the needs and aspirations of the workers of his country. Thirty-five years of his life Comrade Foster has devoted to the struggle for the purity and unity of the Communist party of the U.S.A. against opportunists and diversionists . . . in the spirit of firm loyalty to the teachings of Marxism-Leninism." [77] Apparently, Foster first learned of his new accolade by reading the *Times* story. With this Russian feather in his party cap, Foster went back to fighting for "purity" and against "opportunists and diversionists." The next morning, he changed his vote on the draft resolution to a flat no. [78]

Foster hastened to the counterattack. The adoption of the draft resolution had been the nadir of Foster's power. After the *Pravda* review, he began a comeback. Within eight days, he had written a 15,000-word blast at the "opportunists and diversionists" for the October issue of *Political Affairs*. So eager was he to have his denunciation circulated that he released it on October 2, several days before the magazine appeared. [79] The main trouble with the draft resolution, Foster wrote, was that it "weakens seriously the Party's stand on Marxism-Leninism." It was for "firm loyalty to the teachings of Marxism-Leninism" that he had received *Pravda*'s blessing. Foster objected most strenuously to two sentences in the draft resolution: "Basing ourselves on these Marxist-

Leninist principles as *interpreted by the Communist Party of our country,* we must learn much better how to extract from the rich body of this theory that which is universally valid, combining it with the specific experiences of the American working class in the struggle for socialism in the United States. The Party must distinguish better between the additions to Marxist theory made by Lenin which are valid for all countries and those specific aspects of Lenin's writing which reflect exclusively certain unique features of the Russian revolution or Soviet society." [80] To Foster, the statement was nationalist heresy. The party should unqualifiedly endorse Marxism-Leninism; to do less would be to reduce Marxism-Leninism "to the status of a Russian Socialist philosophy, subject to a maze of national 'interpretations' before adoption." Then, in a nice revelation of his political ethics, he wrote, "If we were just forming our Party the questions of whether or not we should put the words 'Marxism-Leninism' into the Preamble would not be a too important tactical matter, but to take them out of that document . . . will be understood only as a major ideological retreat."

And the members' incessant talking about party errors irked Foster thoroughly. He conceded that the party had made some mistakes, but they had been only tactical in nature. The line had been "correct." The "Right tendency in the Party" "exaggerated," even "manufactured" alleged errors. Emphasis on errors "is . . . but a form of self destruction for the Party. It definitely originates in and feeds the plague of pessimism and liquidationism now afflicting the Party." Such emphasis must be erased from the draft resolution. The party was isolated, Foster admitted, but alleged errors had little or nothing to do with the isolation. The isolation was altogether the result of "objective conditions," pressures on the party from the outside during the cold war.

Foster injected a personal note into the party discussion. Before his article, the national party leaders had not singled out other party leaders for individual attack in their published writings, although some of the rank and file in the letters to the *Daily*

Worker pinpointed their criticisms by name. But now Foster minced no words. He was especially critical of Gates, Joseph Clark, and Joseph Starobin, a former party member and also once the *Daily Worker's* foreign editor. These people were guilty of inner-party "agitation" and "factionalism," he charged, as well as representatives of a dangerous "Right tendency." [81] Foster had taken off the gloves and put on brass knuckles. It was time for Gates and his followers to keep up their guard, for the old party chairman was a veteran at party infighting. He had won inner-party fights before Gates was out of grade school, and this experience was of considerable advantage over the party "liberals," none of whom had ever engaged in anything rougher than the relatively easy ousting of Browder in 1945. Gates was still in the army then and did not have even that experience.

Gates did not counterattack. No one fought back immediately. The *Daily Worker* concerned itself with the World Series—it was for the Dodgers, who had several Negro players and who lost— and the Presidential election—it mildly supported Stevenson and Kefauver, who ignored the Communists and who also lost. In a debate over the draft resolution at the Jefferson School on October 5, Sidney Stein, a national committee member who leaned in Gates's direction, did not even mention Foster's blast. (Incidentally, another speaker that evening, *National Guardian* publisher McManus, indicated that the fellow travelers were still to the "left" of the party; the draft resolution did not come out for socialism hard enough for McManus.[82]) There was nothing in the October issue of *Party Voice,* which, as the journal of the New York party, followed the Gates line, to indicate recognition that Foster had given the party battle a new character. Perhaps they were bemused by Decca Truehaft's recently published satire on Communist language, which applied her sister Nancy Mitford's method in her account of English upper-class and non-upper-class speech with sometimes humorous results. "Tell me not in mournful numbers / Life is but an empty dream" becomes in Communist language, wrote Mrs. Truehaft, "Do not project to me in moods

of pessimism and despair / The perspective that no positive conclusions can be drawn from the present relationship of forces." [83]
That Communists could laugh at satires of themselves indicated
there was a new mood in the movement.

Foster, however, was not able to capitalize on the lethargy of
his party enemies. Before everyone in the party could finish
reading his long October 1956 article, events in Hungary and
Poland were building up to a climax which would precipitate
another party uproar. Communists in those countries were soon
to come into open conflict with the Russians. The "fraternal"
discussion was soon to become fratricidal.

TEN: HUNGARY AND FURTHER DISILLUSION

In the history books of another generation, the year 1956 will live as a year of revolution in some ways similar to 1848. Poland and then Hungary, each with a long history of nationalism, rebelled against Russian imperialism and yet remained Communist. These revolutions staggered the American Communist Party at least as much as Khrushchev's denunciation of Stalin a few months earlier.

In mid-October, the central committee of the Polish Communist Party named Wladyslaw Gomulka to join their body. Gomulka, only a few months before in a Stalinist prison, had come to symbolize the desire within Polish Communism for greater independence from Moscow. The term "national communist" is commonly applied to Gomulka, and it shall be used here in preference to coining a new term. The term is misleading in a sense, for it implies that the Russian Communists were internationalists and that the Poles, for example, were not. Surely the Russian Communists were at least as nationalistic as the Poles, and the Russians' "internationalism" was largely only a device for carrying Russian nationalism beyond its borders. After the Polish central committee appointed Gomulka, its members resigned in order to clear the way for Gomulka's election to party leadership. While the central committee deliberated, Khrushchev and other Soviet leaders arrived in Warsaw in an attempt to prevent Polish "liberalization." In a face-to-face showdown the Poles defied the Russians and elected Gomulka. When Russian troops started to enter Poland from the East German border, Polish troops fired at them and the Russian troops withdrew. Although the Russians had the power to crush any Polish rebellion, they realized that Gomulka had popular and well-disciplined support, especially among the workers and the students, and they restrained themselves rather than precipitate a bloody revolt. The Poles, knowing they would be crushed if they pushed the Russians too far, similarly restrained themselves. The Poles gained a measure of independence nevertheless.

Before the Polish crisis was over, on October 23, to be exact, the Hungarians tried to follow the Poles' example. Thousands of national communists demonstrated in Budapest, demanding that the Russians leave. When security police fired into the crowd, the demonstrators rioted and pulled down statues of Stalin. The next day, when ten thousand Russian troops entered Budapest, Erno Gero, who had called for the Russian military force, yielded the premiership to Imre Nagy. Fighting between the Hungarians and the Russians continued until October 29 during negotiations for Russian withdrawal. On October 30, the Russians began to withdraw from Budapest, leaving the rebels in control of the city. At the end of October, the rebel national committee in both Poland and Hungary seemed to have won.

American Communists, with only some Stalinist dissent, hailed the events in East Europe. The *Daily Worker* proclaimed in bold headlines "POLES CHEER MOVES TOWARD DEMOCRACY. DEMONSTRATE FOR INDEPENDENCE, FRIENDLY TIES WITH U.S.S.R." An editorial praised the Poles for "advancing the democratization and independence of their socialist regime" and Gomulka as "the champion of the independent Polish path to socialism." Gates had strong things to say about Washington. "We strongly condemn the efforts of the Eisenhower administration" to exploit the Polish situation for its own advantage. But he was also critical of Moscow. "We believe that Pravda had a right to discuss what it didn't approve of in Poland, just as the Polish press has the right to disagree with Pravda. We are dubious, however, of imputing on a blanket scale to sections of the Polish press, the desire to restore capitalism. This sounds too much like some of the unjustified criticism made of Yugoslavia in 1948." [1] Two days later, managing editor Max further criticized "the way Pravda unjustly (in our opinion) impugned the motive of the Polish press." [2]

The first events in Hungary likewise brought approval from American Communists. When Hungarian security police and national communist demonstrators clashed, the *Daily Worker* declared that "it is doubly a tragedy that it is in a country of socialism that this violent eruption occurs," but told its readers, "There is a forward movement in Hungary . . . symbolized by the restoration of Imre Nagy to the premiership." There was a danger from "Counter-revolutionaries and outright supporters of the former Horthy dictatorship," but the *Daily Worker* editors were confident that "out of these tragic events . . . socialism will be strengthened." [3] In a series of *Daily Worker* editorials from October 29 to November 1, Gates developed the thesis that the Hungarian and Polish revolutions proved that "Stalinist repression" was not in the best interests of communism. In Poland, Gomulka "acted in time to uproot the remnants of Stalinist repression," but in Hungary, Rakosi and Gero had "relied on force and repression instead of on the democratic aspirations of the people." Their Stalinist tactics, supported by the Soviet Union, had led to the growth of anti-Communist reaction, leaving Nagy not only the problem of the Stalinists, but a problem of rightist reaction. The Hungarian revolution, wrote Gates, was not "merely a plot planned from the outside." "To persist in the theory . . . is to fall into profound error." And Gates was explicit in his criticism of the *present* leadership in the Soviet Union. "Soviet delegate [to the U.N.] Sobolev . . . flew in the face of facts when he described the Hungarian upsurge as the work of a pro-fascist underground. It was the 20th Congress of the Soviet Communist Party which registered the need for ending with Stalinism. And the Soviet Union itself is making changes in the direction of democratization. However, this process is too slow and hesitant, as the Soviet actions in the Polish and Hungarian crises demonstrate." There were, wrote Gates, deep lessons for the American party in recent East European history: "Socialism will triumph if it proves its superiority to capitalism in every respect. It cannot triumph by repression or violations of democracy." [4]

This was strong language, even for a *Daily Worker* editorial. American Communists felt very strongly about Poland and Hungary, so strongly that on November 1 the New York City residents of the party's national committee met and adopted a statement that put the committee "fully in accord" with the *Daily Worker* editorials and did some criticizing of its own. The Soviet Government in a statement of October 30 had said it was "consistently putting into practice these historical decisions of the 20th Congress, which create conditions for the further strengthening of the friendship and cooperation between Socialist countries and the inviolable basis of maintaining the complete sovereignty of every Socialist state." The national committee denied the Soviet statement: "The events in Poland and Hungary show that despite the promises of the 20th Congress which aroused great expectations, these principles are yet to be fully applied in practice."

The national committee statement was, of course, too independent for some of its members. Foster did not attend the meeting. James Jackson, an alternate committee member, voted yes only with qualifications. Dennis and Davis abstained. Three dissenting members besides Foster indicated a gain for the Foster wing of the leadership. Dennis said he agreed "with many of the views set forth"; what his agreement was is difficult to ascertain in view of his stated disagreements. The statement, said Dennis, "minimized the primary responsibility" of the Polish and Hungarian parties "for the erroneous policies they pursued." The statement also failed to "appreciate the steps being taken to rectify the previous unequal and incorrect relationships" between the satellite and Russian parties. Dennis objected, too, that the statement did not adequately express "the vital principles of international working class and socialist solidarity," was wrong in saying the Nagy government was "oriented in a democratic socialist direction," and failed to analyze the effect upon Hungary of the State Department's "liberation" policy.[5]

The national committee adopted this statement on a Thursday. Over the weekend, before the statement was even published, the situation in Hungary changed tragically. On Sunday, November 4, hundreds of Russian tanks rolled back into Budapest to quell the rebellion with massive savagery. The Hungarians, armed only with light arms, hand grenades, and home-made gasoline bombs which had acquired, ironically, the name "Molotov cocktails," fought back as best they could, but their resistance was futile. Nagy took refuge in the Yugoslav Embassy, only to be kidnaped and taken to Romania a few days later when out of the embassy on a Communist-issued safe-conduct. About 80,000 Hungarians fled across the Austrian border while others staged a general strike against the Russians. The Russian-installed regime of Janos Kadar broke the strike. By the end of November, the revolution had been lost.

Most fortunately for Communist propagandists the world over, the Soviet military action in Hungary was not the only major military action of that last tense weekend before the American Presidential elections. Earlier in the week, the Israelis had invaded the Sinai Peninsula, and over the weekend British and French troops invaded Egypt to gain control of the Suez Canal, which the Egyptians promptly sabotaged. In the United Nations, the United States and Russia voted together for a cease-fire, which Britain, France, Israel, and Egypt accepted on November 6. The Egyptian invasion gave the Communists a chance to look the other way on Hungary and scream about what the "western imperialist warmongers" were doing. The party's national committee issued on November 5, the day before Election, a statement on the Egyptian crisis that bristled with words like "brutal aggression" and "flagrant violation," that congratulated Eisenhower for "belatedly" attempting to "extinguish the fires which Dulles' brinkmanship helped ignite," and that condemned Adlai Stevenson for his criticism of Eisenhower's policy in the U.N.[6]

Not all American Communists looked the other way. John Gates began his first editorial after the second Russian intervention "with a heavy heart in view of the weekend's renewed fighting in Hungary and the use of Soviet troops there." The Soviet intervention in Hungary "retards the development of socialism because socialism cannot be imposed on a country by force." Then Gates made a sweeping proposal: "We are for the withdrawal of all troops from all countries to their own borders. We are for the right of all people, the Hungarian people as well as those of Cyprus, of Egypt, of Israel, of Kenya, of Okinawa—the list could be greatly extended—to rule themselves in complete independence." He made it clear that he included the withdrawal of United States troops from West Germany and of Russian troops from East Germany.[7] Two days later, Max and Clark took similar positions. They conceded that reaction in Hungary had grown before the second Soviet intervention and that Nagy's decision to withdraw from the Warsaw Pact—the Communist N.A.T.O.—made the Russian decision to intervene again "probably inevitable." Here Max raised an embarrassing point. "To say that such a decision was inevitable only emphasizes the tragic errors of 11 years of Stalinist rule. Think of the implications," continued Max, "of the fact that Hungary, after eleven years of a certain kind of Communist rule, faced a fascist resurgence, while West Germany after 11 years of Adenauer faces a labor-backed Social-Democratic victory in the next election!" The Soviet intervention solved nothing; it "can only bring on new woes . . . socialism cannot be imported on bayonets."[8] The *Daily Worker* reprinted an editorial from the *Daily People's World* of San Francisco written by Al Richmond. The Soviet occupation of Hungary and its support of the puppet Kadar regime, wrote Richmond, "will only further discredit socialism in Hungary, and will greatly diminish its prestige on a world-wide scale." Richmond was particularly concerned about the conclusion that rebels in colonial areas could not help but make after the Soviets had quelled Hungarian independence.[9]

Such editorials as these sharply divided the party, divided it more than had the debate over the Khrushchev speech or the disagreement over how serious had been the errors of the American party of the past several years. The division was sharper because now some Communists were criticizing what the Russian Communists were doing currently rather than what the Russians admitted had been done in the past. The *Daily Worker* had actually published editorials critical of contemporary Russian Communist leaders, an unprecedented action. The party newspaper violated the actual but unadmitted Communist Party cardinal principle that American Communists must defend the Soviet Union and follow the Russian Communist example. To refuse to support and imitate the Russians was the ultimate Communist heresy. Such heresy in *Daily Worker* columns inevitably disturbed the faithful.

Letters from outraged readers poured in. A group of Michigan Communists wrote that they were "extremely disturbed" by the paper's "overwhelmingly negative approach." One old party member called the *Daily Worker* "anti-Marxist-Leninist and anti-workingclass," declaring that it and the New York State organization were full of "the right danger." Still another accused the *Daily Worker* staff of Red baiting.[10] Leaders as well as rank and filers were alarmed. Dennis wrote a letter to the paper in which he declared that the Soviet intervention was "anti-fascist and pro-peace," condemned one of Clark's columns as reaching "a new low," and charged that the editors were lacking in "Marxist, scientific, working class outlook."[11] James Allen blasted the *Daily Worker* editorial of November 5 in a long article.[12]

Yet the paper had its supporters. The Connecticut State organization declared that it "completely opposes and condemns the intervention of the Soviet army in the present Hungarian situation."[13] Enough Communist leaders agreed with Gates and his colleagues on the Hungarian question that the second national committee statement on Hungary, adopted November 18, was a compromise between the hard and soft tendencies.

The national committee met on Sunday, November 18, two weeks after the second Soviet intervention, determined to write a statement on Hungary that would minimize the differences between party factions. The result was one of the most obviously compromised national committee statements in party history. Neither Gates nor Foster and Dennis won the day. "We do not seek to justify the use of Soviet troops in Hungary's internal crisis on November 4. Neither do we join in the condemnation of these actions. . . . On this there are different viewpoints in the National Committee and the Party. With the unfolding of events further clarity on this point will be achieved." [14] Gates indicated what he thought of the statement by printing alongside it a long article by the paper's sports editor, Lester Rodney, who stated his views on the Soviet intervention in no uncertain terms. Rodney could "not understand how we can condone in any way the forcible imposition of an unwanted government on a people by the armed forces of another country and still speak to our fellow Americans about each nation's own path to socialism." As for alleged fascism developing in Nagy's Hungary: "I am afraid I no longer have confidence in the ability of the Soviet leaders to decide when a nation is fascist or going fascist. Eight years ago we were told that Yugoslavia was fascist." [15] Foster revealed what he thought of the statement when he announced he had voted against it. [16]

The national committee's effort to compromise differences was futile. Neither side would back down. In a *Daily Worker* article as long as the national committee statement, Dennis indicated that he could never condone the heresy of criticizing the Soviets. Those who condemned the Soviet actions in Hungary, Dennis wrote, "made the mistake of looking at [the Soviet Union] through the eyes of the American imperialists." [17] And Gates indicated he would not change his position even when he was criticized in Moscow. *Kommunist,* theoretical magazine of the Russian party, declared that the *Daily Worker* had been "babbling" and said it had "equated" Soviet actions in Hungary with the invasion of Egypt. Gates replied that "we do not 'equate' the events in Hungary with the imperialist invasion of Egypt. But neither do we condone Soviet policies in Hungary or those of the Hungarian Communist Party." He requested *Kommunist* to publish his reply and his other editorials on the subject.[18]

BOLTING THE PARTY

In the fall of 1956, the strife within the party was sharp enough to end in a party split, and at any earlier time in Communist history the party probably would have divided. But now it was clear that neither side stood to gain from a split. The party was small enough—and getting smaller every day—without splintering off into even smaller sects. Each side had seen enough Communist splinter groups to recognize the futility of that kind of activity. And although the Gates wing of the party talked about organizing a new, broadly based party of socialism, they really knew the idea was a pipe dream, that the record of the Communists prevented most non-Communists from participating in such an organization. Hundreds and hundreds of ordinary rank-and-file members saw the situation as hopeless and quit. But most officials were not yet ready to take the plunge into the cold, difficult world of the ex-Communist. Most of them decided to battle on until the convention in February and try to "win the franchise."

Several prominent Communists did leave the party after the Hungarian crisis. Howard Fast, still in the emotional turmoil that characterized his column on the Khrushchev speech, left quietly without announcement. His leaving made no stir until New York newspapers discovered his resignation in February 1957.[19] John Steuben, editor of *March of Labor,* left the party after the Kadar government threatened to execute strikers, making the eloquent request that he be allowed to live out his life "in agony and silence." [20] (Steuben, who had serious heart trouble, died only a few months later. Foster, Dennis, and Davis, who had once been close to him, did not attend the funeral.) Stetson Kennedy, who never admitted to being more than a fellow traveler but who nevertheless wrote for several party publications, had been in Budapest at the time of the revolt. He fled to Belgrade with his family and denounced Stalinism.[21] Another former American Communist, John Santo, formerly organization director of Mike Quill's Transport Workers Union, left Communism in a dramatic fashion. In 1949, Santo had been deported to Hungary, his country of birth. There he had become an important government official, in charge of the meat division of the Hungarian Ministry of Public Supply. In November 1956, he and his family fled to Austria, where he denounced the "dictatorship against the proletariat." He revealed that in Hungary he had always lived in fear, keeping a small traveling bag packed to take along if the secret police arrived at three o'clock in the morning, "their favorite hour." [22] The emotion of the factional fight was sharply revealed when Mrs. Santo, an American citizen by birth, arrived at New York's Idlewild Airport from Vienna. After she told newspapermen at the airport that Communist Hungary was "no place for an American woman," a woman relative there to meet her told her to say nothing more to the press. When she tried to go ahead in her talk with reporters, she and her relative engaged in a quarrel in which they slapped one another.[23] Ideological warfare infected even family homecomings.

How many members left the party in the fall of 1956 will never be known since the Communists did not conduct a party registration until the spring of 1958. Yet party officials knew that hundreds were quietly leaving.[24] No one will ever know with any certainty how many of the members who remained in the party leaned in the Gates direction and how many supported Foster and Dennis, although it is clear that until the convention in February 1957, the liberals, or softs, outnumbered the Fosterites. These softs by no means supported Gates completely. They represented quite a range on the party's political spectrum.

There was an interesting sociological pattern to the positions adopted by sections of the party membership. Age, length of party tenure, ethnic background, and the extent of experience outside the party's own little world often determined whether one supported Foster orthodoxy or advocated considerable change within the party, whether one stayed with the party until the bitter end or quit it altogether. There were many exceptions, of course, but the younger people, those who had come into the party during the Depression, those whose contacts with non-Communists had been wide, and those who were fairly well in the main stream of American culture tended in Gates's direction.

Almost all of the *Daily Worker* staff and the leaders of the organization in New York and California, the party's strongest states, were of the party's Depression generation. They were no longer youngsters, of course—the party's average age in 1956 was over forty—but they were younger in years than the hards and they had not been in the party as long. The symbols of the two extremes, Foster and Gates, indicated the difference. Foster was born in 1881, claimed to have first become associated with Marxist movements while still an adolescent in the 1890's, and joined the party in the early 1920's. Gates was born in 1914 and joined the party in 1931.

Foster had for years been an "inside" man in the party, and Gates had looked outward. Foster, of course, had wide trade-union experience as a young man, but in 1932 he had a serious heart attack which changed the direction of his life. For five years, he was in bed most of the time, seeing only other Communists, reading mostly party literature. When he recovered sufficiently to lead a fairly normal life, his political isolation remained. Gates, on the other hand, had tried to organize steelworkers in the 1930's, had seen a great deal of non-Communists in military service, and as *Daily Worker* editor had been obligated to look at the "outside" world and interpret it for his readers in terms of the party line. With fairly few exceptions, those who labored in the party's national headquarters administering the party's internal organization resisted change within the party. Those whose experience had been in trade unions or other "mass organizations" or in party journalism were for various degrees of change in the party's line and organization.

Those who were in one or another of America's subcultures also tended to support the Foster position. The party's Negroes and foreign-language groups, of which the largest was Yiddish speaking, were relatively isolated from the "outside" world. They lived in what amounted to ghettos and worked and associated with people much like themselves. Their contacts with the general American culture were few. Furthermore, except for the Negroes, these culturally isolated Communists were at least middle-aged and with long standing in the party. To them it did not make much difference personally if the party led a viable movement or not; they were old and tired, seeking more of an ideological old people's home than a vigorous political movement. They had fought their wars. They had been the backbone of the International Workers Order and still held that defunct organization's bargain insurance policies. They had seen their children grow up as Americans, reject their immigrant background and language, improve themselves economically, and move out of the lower-class ghetto. Now these old people read the *Freiheit*—whose circulation was greater than the *Daily Worker*'s—and clucked disapproval of the storm that Gates, Fast, and the others created in the party. They wanted peace and stability in their party, not the disturbing editorials and resolutions demanding a thorough overhaul of their ideology and organization. Above all, they wanted the party to remain a party, and talk of dissolution particularly disturbed them; to dissolve the old people's home was out of the question. They were sorely troubled by the revelations of anti-Semitism in the Soviet Union, but they found some way to rationalize the uncomfortable fact. Some of them just refused to see. Others knew from first hand that, after all, the Russians had been anti-Semitic before the revolution too. You just could not expect much from the *goyem,* Communist or not.

THE 1957 CONVENTION

In the weeks immediately before the party's national convention, the question of whether to keep the party's name and form or to change it into some kind of political-action organization with a new name came to be the main issue between the orthodox and the unorthodox. The proposal for a new kind of organization, aside from its intrinsic merits or lack of them, symbolized other differences within the party, such as its relationship with other Communist parties of the world, its place in the tradition of American radicalism, its attitude toward Marxism-Leninism, and its views toward a monolithic party of the Lenin type with "democratic centralism."

In the first *Discussion Bulletin* before the convention, there appeared the first seriously stated proposal in print of the abandonment of the party and the establishment of a political-action association. The *Discussion Bulletins* were a residual piece of party ritual. Before earlier conventions, these *Bulletins* had been published for a few weeks, designed to offer members an opportunity for a little democracy before centralism became paramount again. In 1956-57, these special publications were superfluous since sharp discussion had been conducted for months in regular publications. Bernard Burton, of Los Angeles, once of the *Daily Worker* staff, argued that a political-action association would better enable Communists to work within trade unions and would avoid the "certain air of duplicity [that] is fostered when . . . workers learn that a fellow-worker is not only active in an organization of one of the major parties, but is also a member of another party, the C.P." Doxey Wilkerson endorsed the idea in the same *Bulletin,* but John Williamson, writing from England a defense of orthodoxy that was almost devoid of the ideas that had rocked communism internationally, assailed all such proposals as "liquidationist" and "revisionist," two choice party epithets.[25] John Gates, in a clear

summary of his whole position, came out for a political-action association but was willing to postpone the change. He doubted that
the question could receive enough serious and unemotional consideration before the party convention. His main contention on party
organization was that democratic centralism had to be modified.
"Our experience has been the tendency for this to become trans-
formed into maximum centralization and minimum democracy.
. . . Democratic centralism apparently results in a semi-military
type of organization which is clearly not valid for our country in
this period." [26] Foster retaliated. He called such proposals "a mess
of Social-Democratic political and organizational pottage," and
argued that "Our Party must be based upon democratic centralism." [27] He later wrote that "to defeat the project for a political
action association is the life-and-death necessity now before the
Party." [28]

Early in December, the state committee of the New York party
debated a motion to put the organization on record favoring adoption of the political-association form. The committee members
could not agree among themselves. A majority wrote a statement
favoring such a change, and a minority prepared a dissenting statement.[29] The national committee, at its meeting in New York, December 17-19, amended the draft resolution and compromised the
issue. The compromise was to the effect that the party convention
would not "undertake to change the name and form of our Party,"
but that this action was not to "foreclose further consideration of
these proposals." The new national committee should "explore"
the idea further.[30] The majority in the New York State organization, the main center of sentiment for such a change, then agreed
to the compromise.[31]

The compromise on a change in the party's name and form
was the result of a larger spirit of compromise which permeated
the party. Everyone was very much afraid of a split. During the
national convention itself, speakers time and again unwittingly revealed that, although the factions had not been able to reconcile
their differences, they had an implicit agreement not to push their

view to the point that the other side would have no choice but to bolt.[32] Foster and his supporters were clearly a minority, although a sizable minority, so the compromise represented a greater yielding by the Gates wing than by the orthodox. Another piece of evidence to indicate the willingness of the Gates forces to compromise for the sake of unity was the conciliatory measures the New York organization took at its state convention, January 25-27, 1957, one of the series of local and state conventions that both preceded and followed the national convention.[33] This fear of a split gave Foster and his followers a great advantage. It enabled him to hang on until the tide eventually flowed strongly in his favor.

That the Foster wing of the party was not above a little skulduggery became apparent in the counting of the ballots cast in the New York State convention's election of delegates at large to the national convention. The state convention elected by secret ballot fourteen national convention delegates from a list of forty-six nominees. Tellers counted the ballots at the convention and disclosed that three of the fourteen elected were of the Foster faction and the other eleven were Gatesites, including Gates himself and state party chairman George Blake Charney. The *Daily Worker* four days later announced that the state convention had elected Foster, Dennis, Gates, and Charney, but did not list the others. The head teller, a supporter of Foster, took the ballots home with him and a few days later called the other tellers for a recount. The recount showed a change of party ballots, which if permitted to stand, would have made a majority of Foster supporters in the state delegation. The Gates wing learned of the change, accused the head teller of duplicity, and threatened to tell the whole story at the national convention if the original count were not certified. At an emergency meeting the weekend before the convention, the national committee decided to uphold the original count, destroy all the ballots, and keep the whole affair secret. The Gates faction agreed to keep still and not exploit the matter. But news of the affair leaked out, and although the party condemned "false press reports" as a "slander," the convention's credentials committee unwittingly confirmed the reports.[34]

No one doubted that the Russians supported Foster in the American party fight, and the Russians confirmed their backing of Foster just before the convention. Less than a week before the convention opened, American newspapers carried accounts of a story that had appeared in the Moscow newspaper *Sovetskaya Rossiya*. The Russian editors attacked "right wing elements" in the American party and singled out Joseph Clark for particular censure. Clark, the Russians charged, was as one with John Foster Dulles in support of "national communism" in an effort to "divide and conquer" the communist world.[35] The American battle, however, was beyond being stopped by the Russians. The "right wing elements" had rebuffed Moscow over Hungary and Russian anti-Semitism and were ready to do so again. Clark replied in his column of February 6. American Communists, he said, simply could not follow the Russian model: "Nothing can be more alien to Marxism than the view that all countries will come to socialism along the same path." [36] But Stalinists abroad—if they could still be called that after Khrushchev's speech—continued to try to shape the American party in their own image.

The sixteenth national convention of the Communist Party assembled on Saturday morning, February 9, 1957, in a ramshackle caterer's establishment called Chateau Gardens at Houston Street and Second Avenue in Manhattan's lower East Side. The building had once been a Russian Orthodox church, a fact that some observers found fraught with symbolism. The party had tried to rent better accommodations, but the proprietors of more than sixty New York hotels and halls had turned them down. Outside the door of Chateau Gardens stood a man with a camera who took photographs of all who entered. According to the report of an anti-Communist observer at the convention, "Uniformed and un-uniformed cops swarmed all over the place." He was reminded of the *New Yorker* cartoon in which a Communist began his address, "Comrades and members of the F.B.I." [37]

The report of the convention's credentials committee was interesting for the evidence it contained about the party's national composition. There were 298 delegates, of whom seventy-eight were women. Fifty-four of them were Negro, two were Mexican, and one was Puerto Rican. Slightly more than half the delegates were over forty-five years old, and most of them had been in the party for a long time. For a party supposed to be rooted in the masses, a breakdown of the delegates' "mass organization" activities was discouraging. Only three were farmers, only eighty were trade-union members, and only thirty-four of the fifty-four Negroes were "in Negro work." [38]

At the convention's first afternoon session, the delegates listened to messages of greeting from foreign Communist parties and leaders. The most important of these was a message from Jacques Duclos, which Foster had received on January 21. Duclos tried to influence the Americans as he had in 1945. He warned them not to deviate from orthodoxy. The French party's central committee cabled reaffirmation of the Duclos communication the night before the convention opened.[39] After the reading of these messages from France, Eugene Dennis delivered the convention's keynote address. His speech—a rather routine one, typical of Dennis in that he qualified everything controversial—tried to make a show of independence. The "main line of our convention resolution is Marxist-Leninist in content and fully in accord with the interests and democratic traditions of our country, with proletarian solidarity and with the new and ever developing generalized experience of the international working class. In any case, our decisions will be our own, made by the collective judgment of this convention, and will be based on *our* Marxist understanding of American reality and the needs of our people and nation." [40] Just precisely what this statement meant was anyone's guess, but Dennis hoped the convention would understand the sentences as a declaration of independence. The *Daily Worker* so interpreted them.[41] A declaration of independence that failed to mention the Soviet Union was, at best, ambiguous.

Foster addressed the convention immediately after Dennis. Benjamin Davis read Foster's speech for him, although Foster was seated on the platform. His speech was certainly not even intended to be interpreted as a declaration of independence. Duclos, in fact, "is correct in warning us of revisionist tendencies in our Party." Foster's speech revealed his convention tactics. The Gates wing had committed itself to avoid a split and not to press too hard for its position. Foster took advantage of their concern for "unity" to attack with all the vigor he could muster, to claw away for all he could salvage. Those opposed to Foster had the votes to defeat him, but they were less concerned with defeating him than with preserving unity. Under the circumstances, Foster could not lose any more than he had lost already; he could only gain. The harder he fought, the better his chance to gain, because Gates would not fight back. And Foster understood the situation. In his speech, he identified Gates with the "Right danger," which "is now threatening the life of the Party." Gates and the *Daily Worker,* he declared, had in their editorials on the Polish and Hungarian crises been guilty of "impermissible yielding before aggressive American imperialism." [42]

Neither Gates nor his followers ever defended their position on Hungary and Poland at the convention. Indeed, they regarded the subject as a forbidden topic. The convention ignored Hungary. If it had not been for Foster's reference—and the futile shouts of rank and filers who wanted to speak on the subject but could not get the floor [43]—one would not have known that Hungary was any more pertinent to the convention than, say, real-estate taxes in Saskatchewan.

The morning after Foster's speech, the convention considered the report of a subcommittee that had to do with the party's name and form. This report could have been the convention's hottest subject if Gates had wanted to make it so. The subcommittee report itself was a compromise to which the national committee had agreed in December: the convention would "oppose" the change to a political-action committee but "it should not close the door to all constructive exploration and discussion of the subject as may be organized by the incoming National Committee." All the speakers on the question at the convention were for the compromising subcommittee report. Many delegates wanted to state their differing views on the question of a political-action association, but all the speakers, including Gates, supported the report. One hard group tried to amend the report to change the word "oppose" to "reject," but after its motion was defeated, only three opposed and seventeen abstained on the vote to accept the compromise report.[44]

The hottest debate at the convention had to do with the party's attitude toward Marxism-Leninism, and the debate became one that a medieval theologian would have appreciated. The draft resolution had stated that the party based itself on "Marxist-Leninist principles as interpreted by the Communist Party of our country." [45] Twelve of the twenty-six members of the convention subcommittee charged with presentation of that part of the main political resolution, a group led by Esther Cantor, of New York, wanted to strike the word "interpret" and have the party "creatively apply" Marxism-Leninism. The majority of the subcommittee refused the amendment, and the minority presented a dissenting report. The editors of the *Proceedings* cut their document extensively at this point, but it is clear that the convention got four and one-half hours behind schedule in its debate on which report to accept, in effect whether to "interpret" Marxism-Leninism or "creatively apply" it. By a narrow margin, the word "interpret" remained in the final document.[46] That a national convention of a political body as badly divided as the Communist Party would debate at length and with heat the difference between "interpret" and "creatively apply" reflects much about the irrelevance of Communist thinking and the unviability of the Communist movement. Nevertheless, the defeat of the "creatively apply" group constituted a victory for the Gates wing, if that wing can be said to have won any victories at all.

One curious decision of the convention was proposed by Sam

Kushner, secretary of the convention committee on miscellaneous resolutions. Kushner proposed that the convention move its national headquarters to his home city, Chicago, within one year. The party had been founded in Chicago in 1919, and Kushner argued that it was time to move back. The stated reasons were that the central location would be more convenient for the national membership, and that it would place the national leadership nearer the farmers, workers in basic industry, and Negro unionists. Except for the matter of central location, the arguments were dubious. It is probable that the main reason was not expressed: a move from New York would get the national office away from the center of party unorthodoxy. The delegates did not expect Kushner's proposal, but they passed it unanimously because those who were against it knew the move would not be made.[47] Despite the furor in the party about bureaucracy, party headquarters did not move to Chicago within a year. According to the party constitution, a national convention is the party's highest authority and a convention's decisions may be rescinded only by another convention. Party headquarters did move, but not to Chicago. A month after the convention, the party moved from 101 West Sixteenth Street, at the corner of Sixth Avenue, in New York City, just a few blocks away to 23 West Twenty-sixth Street. The Twenty-sixth Street house, a lovely three-story Georgian structure, has an interesting history. Vincent Astor used it for his office until 1942, when he sold it to Frederick Vanderbilt Field. Field sold it in early 1957 —he has lived in Mexico for several years—to a corporation which leased the place to Charles Dirba, the old 1921 "Left opposition" leader. Dirba subleased the house to the party.[48] The reader may ponder the symbolism. The house of a conservative American capitalist became the property of a communistic capitalist, then was leased to a ghost from the party's past and subleased to the party for national headquarters in violation of the national convention's unanimous vote.

The convention's election of twenty members of the new national committee represented a compromise, as did almost everything the convention did. The new national committee was to be composed of sixty persons, twenty elected by the convention and the remaining forty by the subsequent state and district conventions. The twenty elected, in the order of their vote, were as follows: Charlene Alexander, Claude Lightfoot, James Jackson, Dorothy Healey, Benjamin Davis, Eugene Dennis, William Z. Foster, Earl Durham, Doxey Wilkerson, Carl Winter, John Hellman, Fred Fine, Anna Correa, Carl Ross, Al Richmond, John Gates, Sidney Stein, David Davis, Charles Loman, and George Blake Charney.[49] The group represented the entire party spectrum from Stalinist orthodoxy (Foster, Davis, and Loman) to as unorthodox as one could be and yet remain in the party (Gates, Richmond, and Wilkerson). Miss Alexander, of Los Angeles, who received the most votes, was relatively unknown in the party outside California. But for a Communist convention, she had tremendous advantages: besides being young and personally attractive, she was a woman and a Negro. Four of the five candidates receiving the most votes were Negroes.

The convention had instructed the twenty elected national committee members to elect seven of their number to be a temporary secretariat until the state conventions finished electing the full national committee. The elected members made another compromise. The twenty suggested unanimously that all the New York residents among them be the temporary secretariat, and the convention accepted their recommendation. The New York residents —Charney, Davis, Dennis, Durham, Fine, Foster, Gates, Jackson, Loman, Stein, and Wilkerson—were of all varieties of Communist.[50]

The convention ended on a note of self-conscious unity. Gates told the convention, "Some of us have lost out on . . . [our] points of view, but no matter who lost, the Party has won." Foster became downright chummy in his reply. "The work of this convention, it seems to me we have got to understand it, as Johnny said, as a victory for the Party, and not a victory for any particular group or faction in the Party." [51]

Who did win the convention? Surely it was not the party as a whole, as Gates and Foster claimed. The party faded after the convention even faster than it had in 1956. Nor had unity really been achieved. As one disgruntled neighborhood party leader put it in his letter of resignation from the party, "When Foster, Dennis, Davis, and Gates were proclaiming the Party's great winning of unity, the fighting went on as murderously and vindictively as during the prior nine months . . . while Davis was proclaiming the end to factionalism, both factions were organizing their second state, pre-state convention factional caucuses." [52]

The Gates forces, or at least the opponents of Foster's orthodoxy, won some things. The "Main Political Resolution" adopted by the convention,[53] a slight modification of the draft resolution written the previous September, would have been completely beyond the pale in 1952. Foster had voted against the draft resolution, but now he voted for it in its slightly revised form. The Main Political Resolution was the end product of an evolution of the party line that had been under way since the nineteenth, not the twentieth, congress of the Soviet party, the last congress in which Stalin participated. The twentieth congress, however, certainly hastened the evolution. Gone now were all references to the Negro nation in the Black Belt and "national self-determination." The document exuded a sweet reasonableness toward social democrats and non-Communist labor and Negro leaders. And the document did contain some guarded statements on the independence of the American party. But it was by no means a Gatesian document. It said nothing about Hungary or Soviet anti-Semitism.

The convention seemed, on the face of it, to be a compromise and a standoff between the Foster and Gates factions. Actually, it was a victory for Foster. Foster had gained time from the convention. He had saved himself and his point of view from elimination by exploiting the general fear of a party split. The unorthodox had not been united, and they had failed to strike when their opportunity was best.

Apparently the Russian party exerted no more than a general influence on the convention. The Russians' endorsement of Foster certainly strengthened his position with some of the delegates and confirmed their approval of him, but it did not deter other delegates from their determination to shape the party in a fashion Moscow would not approve. Why the Soviets did not do more than they did to get the party to endorse their position is a matter for speculation. Perhaps they thought they had done all they could successfully to affect thinking in the American party. Perhaps they thought the game was not worth the candle. Perhaps they operated from the assumption that their position could not lose in the end because they could always grant "recognition," award the "franchise," to Foster and his supporters in the event that there was a split at the convention and the hards lost the fight. In any case, as matters in the American party actually developed in due time, it was not necessary for the Russians to exert great pressure. The Russians did not have to bend the American party to their will; the American party bent of its own volition.

The failure to bring together into one camp all those who were in disagreement with Foster's hard position was partly the result of considered judgment and conviction and partly the result of poor tactics. The California party, unorthodox enough to publish a biting satire on party orthodoxy in its state discussion bulletin,[54] refused as a matter of conviction to unite with Gates to drive out the hards and try to create a party truly independent of Moscow. Dorothy Healy, leader of the party in southern California, a month before the convention said privately that although she had no use whatsoever for Foster's kind of Communism, she thought Gates was as dogmatic in his position as Foster was in his. She wanted a party representing many kinds of opinions and hoped that both Gates and Foster would be elected to the new national committee. She also predicted that neither Foster nor Gates would win at the national convention.[55] Months after the convention, Gates thought his side had made a tactical blunder. He recognized that he had been unable to get any unity from the anti-Foster forces, but he thought that what strength he had should have been directed at Foster. His associates had persuaded him to level most of his criticism at Dennis, rather than Foster, and Gates thought the attack on Dennis had only driven Dennis and Foster closer together when Dennis might have been used by the unorthodox.[56]

To Gates's analysis of his failure at the convention must be added some other factors. First of all, Gates was never able to develop with clarity and exactitude just what he was for; he knew only what he was against. Without a clear positive program, he was at a disadvantage in rallying support. Second, old party habits of thought led Gates to overemphasize the consequences of a party split, compromise too much for his own tactical advantage, and, in effect, walk into Foster's trap.

The old fox had planned it well. To compromise in a party resolution, he well knew, meant nothing at all. But many of Gates's followers were disgusted with their leader's compromises, and, from the convention on, Foster won major victory after victory.

FOSTER GAINS THE UPPER HAND

A disgruntled Gates supporter made a prediction at the convention that turned out to be remarkably accurate. While the convention chairman was declaring him out of order and trying unsuccessfully to get him to sit down, William Mandel, of New York, told the delegates that the convention, "having patched up unity between two irreconcilable viewpoints, has failed in what appears to be its very success." The convention "has only advanced far enough toward independence to make the Party useful to the Voice of America as a stick with which to beat Communist Parties abroad. It has not advanced far enough to be acceptable to the American working class or to the American people at large." Then came his prediction: "The fully independent element will be the distinct minority in the full National Committee of the Party. This is because the most convinced adherents of the Gates viewpoint will not reappear at the reconvened State Conventions to vote for New York's eleven members of the National Committee, and the same thing will happen elsewhere." [57]

Many members had quit in the fall of 1956; others had set up conditions which the convention would have to meet. Now many of these members quietly left the organization. One member on his way out was quite explicit: "I have no desire to 'help' the Gates forces fight the Foster forces. I consider that too many leaders of the Gates forces gave up their fight in compromise after compromise, until they compromised themselves into Foster's outdated position; and these leaders will continue to do so, leaving rank and filers to break their backs, alone." [58] Precisely how many left just after the convention is an unanswerable question. A letter to the *Daily Worker* much later in the year said that "thousands" had left.[59] Many who did not officially resign just ceased their activity, much to the dismay of their section leaders.[60] As one local leader who quit the party told a writer for the *Nation*, "In my [New York] party section we have 160 on the books. Seventy pay dues, maybe a couple of dozen come to meetings; we sit around and argue about Hungary and Leninism. What the hell else is there to do?" [61] With such floundering about within the party and with Communist passion directed against other Communists rather than against the "outside" world, some members left on the grounds that the party was no longer an effective organization. They quit the party not so much because their political and moral ideals were outraged as because they belatedly recognized that the party was no longer an effective instrument of social change. The party had become a futile sect, and continued association with it was equally futile.

Even before state conventions had met to elect the rest of the members to the new national committee, Foster began to press his advantage against Gates. He was not altogether successful in this first attempt to purge his opposition. The eleven New York residents who together composed the temporary party secretariat met on March 14. The Fosterites rebuked Gates and *Masses & Mainstream* for not dealing roughly enough with Howard Fast, whose departure from the party had only recently become public and who had, at last, criticized the Communists. Foster also tried to push through a motion demanding Gates's resignation as editor of the *Daily Worker,* but those in the middle ground refused to go along with Foster and defeated the motion. Someone at the meeting "leaked" the news to the general press. A week later, the temporary secretariat met, confirmed the news, and blasted news "leaks." "Any unauthorized individual issuance of such information to the press is contrary to working class principles, a violation of Communist ethics and conduct and is to be categorically condemned." [62] Someone who called herself "Paula" wrote a letter to the *Daily Worker* which accurately described the situation in the party. "Many people I know have gotten so emotionally carried away by factionalism that they have forgotten the main purpose of the party. To them it seems the most important thing is to get rid of this or that leader 'who is throwing out Marxism.' " She warned pointedly, "There's more ways of 'liquidating the Party' than by holding a meeting and voting 'now it's liquidated.' Another way . . . would be to make it an organization no one wants to belong to." [63] Apparently, it was already an organization that many no longer wanted to belong to.

Enough Gates supporters had left the party in New York so that by the time the state convention met, March 30-31, 1957, the Foster forces were able to gain more from compromise than they had at the national convention. In the election of state committee members at large, the Gates forces held their own—most of the state committee members were yet to be elected by county and regional conventions. The resolution of the state convention "On the Jewish Question in the USSR," however, was a clear setback for the unorthodox. The national convention had ducked that issue as one too hot to handle when the theme song was "Unite for Unity." The convention, over the objections of several delegates, had only passed the problem on to the new national committee.[64] The New York convention's resolution on the matter was a puzzling bundle of internal contradictions. One paragraph noted that the Soviet Union had not yet "carried to fruition" any of its announced projects for the stimulation of Jewish culture, and the next declared, "We reject the slander of anti-Soviet elements accusing the Soviet Union of anti-Semitism. There is no official state policy of anti-Semitism." Any sentence in the resolution that could be interpreted as critical of the Soviets was followed by one that absolved them of any evil.[65]

Fortunately for Gates, the ground rules provided that the state conventions rather than the subsequent county conventions would elect members for the unfilled places on the national committee, for between the two local conventions even more Gatesites left the party. The newly elected national committee, composed of sixty-six members rather than the sixty prescribed by the convention, contained only a small scattering of members who supported Gates completely. Twelve members were fully as orthodox as Foster. The rest of them were in between the two positions. The middle group shifted from time to time in its position because, although it held some mildly unorthodox ideas on some points, it put unity and compromise above all else.[66]

The first time the new national committee met, the first week of May 1957, the center group almost slipped out of its compromise position. The full committee decided to elect by secret ballot a seventeen-member executive committee. When the ballots were counted, they discovered that Foster had not placed among the first seventeen. Gates was among the first seventeen. The committee then enlarged the size of the executive committee to twenty, thereby including Foster. Further to make amends, the committee granted Foster the position of chairman emeritus. The position entailed no special power or responsibilities. The national committee then rejected another motion asking for Gates's resignation as editor of the paper—this time the motion also wanted Joseph Clark's resignation—but it did adopt a report that criticized "certain inadequacies and shortcomings" in the Communist press. There was a need, the report said, "of improving the reportage of life and events in the Socialist lands, especially for providing a more thorough-going Marxist analysis of the foreign policy of these countries." [67]

At the county party conventions in New York City, where Gates had had his greatest strength, the Foster forces triumphed. At the Queens County convention, the hards were obviously going to be in control, and the Gates crowd did not even attend. In Manhattan, there had been so many Gatesite resignations that the only battle, over the post of county organizer, was between a Foster supporter and a Puerto Rican "ultra-leftist" who considered Foster too soft. In Kings County (Brooklyn), the Foster group accused the Gatesites of "white chauvinism" when they opposed the election of Charles Loman as county organizer. At the national convention, Loman had been harder than Foster on most matters. In the uproar over the "white chauvinism" charges, about thirty Gatesites walked out.[68]

Among those walking out of the Brooklyn convention was Joseph Clark. As he and five friends got in a car to start for home, they were completely angry about the turn of events in the party and ready to quit. As they drove down the Belt Parkway toward Coney Island, their comments on the party were bitter. Then the driver noticed a car with two men passengers that seemed to be following them. He turned off the highway. So did the following car. He drove down side streets, and the following car stayed with them. Now they forgot their anger at the party and began to swear at the F.B.I., the presumed affiliation of their followers. The driver let his five passengers out at various subway stations, and the pursuers gave up. Most of the six disgruntled Communists eventually quit the party, but they would have left it sooner had not the two F.B.I. men, if that is who they were, picked an inopportune time to trail them.[69]

One of the functions of the county or regional conventions was to elect the rest of the members of the new state committee, some of which had already been elected at the state convention. Since Fosterites dominated most of the local conventions, they elected enough of their kind to dominate the state committee. The first meeting of the New York State committee, on May 25, elected Benjamin Davis the new state chairman, deposing George Blake Charney. Davis had been a consistent Foster supporter from the beginning. Charney remained in the New York organization as secretary, and party press releases asserted that "Davis and Charney will share equal responsibility." When one looked over the other state officers—Will Weinstone, who yielded to no one in his Marxist-Leninist purity, was education director—it was obvious that the Fosterites were in control.[70] Between the national convention and the county conventions, a matter of about ten weeks, enough Gatesites in New York, the seat of their greatest strength, had voted with their feet to create a Fosterite majority in the state organization.

Gates now had only a tenuous position in the party bureaucracy. Any time between June and the wild first weekend of November 1956, when the Russians moved back into Hungary and the French and English invaded Egypt, Gates would have emerged very strong from any kind of party elections. Had there been a party referendum—a fanciful supposition—any time during that period, it is altogether likely that Foster would have lost out completely. Foster was able to hang on because there were no elections then. Now the situation was reversed. As Gates himself put it, "My membership base is now on the outside." [71] And, ironically, what strength Gates had left in the party was due to the party's undemocratic structure, which prevented the rank and file from quickly and precisely expressing itself through the hierarchy. By the summer of 1957, Gates's greatest strength was at the top and his greatest weakness at the bottom. He had greater strength in the twenty-man executive committee of the national committee than in the full sixty-six-member body, and he had greater strength in the national committee than he had in the state and local organizations.

Before the national convention, it had been Gates's hope to transform the party within two or three years. If not much could be accomplished at the national convention, then much could be done, he thought, in the months and years to follow.[72] Gates's optimistic dream proved to be no more than a vision. His efforts after the spring of 1957 were necessarily defensive rather than designed to transform the party.

THE BICKERING FLICKERS ON

Much of the life disappeared from the *Daily Worker* after the national convention. Normally the dullest of newspapers, the *Daily Worker* acquired some sparkle after the twentieth congress. Although only a masochist could truly enjoy reading its files, the paper in 1956 and early 1957 did contain a great deal of conflict that lent it some interest. But in March 1957, the paper calmed down again and became almost, but not quite, its usual dreary self. Occasionally there was still something in its columns to indicate that Communists could break out of their intellectual dull gray mold.

For one thing, there was a dispute in the *Daily,* which must have been embarrassing for the staff, over what had actually happened at the recent national convention. Foreign Communist publications printed accounts of the convention that interpreted it as a victory for orthodox Marxism-Leninism. These accounts infuriated the *Daily* staff. Alan Max, the managing editor, tried to set the foreign comrades straight. When John Williamson wrote a story for *World News,* a British Communist weekly, that failed to mention that Foster and Dennis were no longer party chairman and secretary, respectively, Max took sharp issue with him. Williamson, as well as *Pravda* and *L'Humanité,* had written "accounts which completely missed the mark." [73] When Max discovered that a Soviet journal, *International Affairs,* had carried an article by T. Timofeyev which praised the convention for acknowledging "the vital force of proletarian internationalism," he could not restrain himself. It hurt that Timofeyev had written that the convention had "vigorously [opposed] revisionist and liquidationist tendencies," such as the idea of converting the party into a political-action association and organizing "a 'mass party of socialism,' into which the Communist party would dissolve itself." It hurt especially because Timofeyev had exaggerated only a little. Max replied with an open letter to *International Affairs.* The published *Proceedings,* he wrote, "read like an entirely different convention from the one discussed by your correspondent. . . . Such an account, especially if it remained uncorrected, could only tend to shake the confidence of your readers in the ability of your journal to give sound political estimates." [74]

Foster, naturally, could not let these words go unrebuked. Timofeyev was right, said Foster, Max was wrong. "The 16th Convention, while not without flaws [meaning he had not won entirely], was generally a constructive one [meaning he had won most issues]." The foreign journals were "correct," because the convention had rejected "revisionism" and "incorrect theoretical formulations" and made a "strong declaration for proletarian internationalism." "Thus the convention saved and reinforced the very spirit and structure of Communism in the United States." [75] It looked as if Foster intended to win by interpretation what little he had not been able to win in actuality.

The *Daily Worker* continued to criticize the Soviets occasionally, although usually in relatively mild language. In the spring of 1957, there was the complicated affair of Khrushchev and the Soviet bonds. The *Daily Worker* carried a paraphrased translation of Russian newspapers on the subject. For some years, Soviet citizens had been obligated to buy government bonds, which did not bear interest and were not negotiable, equivalent to from two weeks' to two months' earnings, depending upon the citizen's income. The Soviet Government ran a lottery for bondholders, and the lucky could hit a jackpot, but most bondholders received only their principal back in twenty years. Now Khrushchev proposed that the issuance of these bonds be stopped; the government, however, would not redeem any of the outstanding bonds at all until another twenty or twenty-five years. One sentence in the *Daily Worker*'s summary of the situation was entirely accurate: "Capitalists will never believe . . . that Soviet workers are accepting this voluntarily." [76]

Apparently not all Communists believed it either. George Morris, the *Daily*'s heavy-handed labor editor and a Fosterite, felt obligated to defend the Khrushchev action against criticism. The same thing happened in the United States, said Morris, except that the American Government accomplished its purpose by raising taxes. Furthermore, said Morris, all the Soviet people supported Khrushchev's action and not all Americans were for high taxes.[77] Joseph Clark could not agree with Morris, although the ghost of Robert A. Taft might have felt a certain sympathy for Morris's argument. To Clark, the whole affair of the bonds was undemocratic and indicated that the Soviet Union still had some distance to go in implementing the decisions of the twentieth congress.[78]

There was a far greater stir in the party and the *Daily Worker* when, in July 1957, Khrushchev ousted Molotov, Malenkov, Shepilov, and Kaganovich from power and banished them to obscure posts in the hinterland. Supposedly, the four had been removed from power because they resisted the growth of democracy in Russia. This was the emphasis Gates gave to his first editorial on the "recent historic Soviet events." The ousters were "a culmination of a series of sharp policy debates over questions of internal Soviet policy and foreign affairs." The four, under Molotov's leadership, had resisted the twentieth congress decisions for peaceful coexistence and "internal democratization." "We view with satisfaction . . . the rebuffing of a faction which opposed the steps to a new Geneva, to improved relations with all nations, to heighten the living standards and democratic rights of the Soviet peoples." Gates had one reservation: the debate on the issues within the Soviet party's central committee should have been public. In boldface type he declared, "The process of democratization requires such public debate." But Gates's editorial reservation was minor, "distinctly subordinate to the historic events themselves— events which will shape a peaceful world." [79]

Clark's column the next day was much more critical. He agreed with Gates that since the death of Stalin the Soviets had moved in the direction of relaxing international tension and of democracy, decentralization, and higher living standards internally. He had his doubts though about "the special demonology which says Malenkov was a foe of peaceful coexistence." "There was unquestionably an issue of policy behind every conflict in the Soviet party leadership. But this doesn't mean there wasn't also jockeying for leadership and power." Clark was more critical than Gates of the lack of public debate before the decision, although he conceded that "the fact that the Central Committee debated the issue is a far cry from the days when Stalin alone made decisions." If Malenkov was guilty, Clark wrote, "the Soviet people were entitled to evidence and a statement from both sides. They were never given the benefit of the public debate. . . . If anything, the methods used in the struggle against Stalinism show that it will take considerable time before democratic controls and procedures and direct working class control in all phases of Soviet life are established." He did not defend the four ousted Soviet officials. Quite the contrary. "It is fatuous to think that those ousted were not responsible for some of the achievements during the Stalin era as well as for the crimes. It would be just as fatuous to think that Khrushchev, Mikoyan, Bulganin and Voroshilov, [the] remaining collaborators of Stalin, were also not responsible for the Leningrad frameup and the repressions of the 30's, for which they now blame Molotov, Malenkov and Kaganovich." [80]

Clark was nothing but a "liberal bourgeois," raved one letter writer, who called himself "Red Gum." "Missouri Marxist" charged that Clark was "unscientific." [81] A considerable number of Foster-ite national leaders demanded that Clark be fired from the paper. Gates resisted the efforts to fire Clark, although he did not fully agree with him. When Gates threatened to resign if the national committee fired Clark, the Fosterites backed down. Unity was still the watchword for the party's public relations in the summer of 1957, and if Gates resigned, his action would be popularly in-terpreted—and rightly so—as the end of the party's "new look." [82] Then Gates wrote a long article which both differed with Clark on some aspects of his interpretation and agreed with him on other aspects, but which strongly defended Clark's right to interpret however he would for the *Daily Worker*.[83]

Interpretation of the Hungarian revolution continued to divide Communists and lend some life to the *Daily Worker*. In May 1957, Herbert Aptheker published a book entitled *The Truth about Hun-gary,* which he obviously considered a lasting contribution on the the subject if not the final word itself. Aptheker had some quali-fications for writing the book. A Ph.D. from Columbia University, he had specialized in American Negro history and clearly under-stood, even if he did not always practice, the canons of historical scholarship. *The Truth about Hungary* threatened to revive the whole controversy when Robert Friedman wrote a critical review of it for the *Daily Worker*. Uncritically favorable *Daily Worker* reviews for books by Communists who hewed to the party line had long been standard practice, but after the twentieth congress, the paper occasionally published intelligently critical essays. Fried-man's review was such an essay. He granted that Aptheker had performed a service in bringing together a great deal of scattered information. Aptheker had not interpreted his participants "either as all patriotic saints or all fascist sinners." Yet Friedman did not "believe that The Truth about Hungary is the full truth about Hungary." Its chief weakness, Friedman wrote, was that its con-clusions were not justified either by the events in Hungary or by Aptheker's description of them. Aptheker declared that Western imperialism was the underlying cause of the rebellion and saw in the Kadar postrevolution government hope for the future. Friedman could not accept either interpretation and said so, firmly but without malice.[84]

Again the Fosterites arose to swat down the heretics. "Faithful Reader" deplored Friedman's "obvious inadequacy in historical scholarship made all the more appalling by his dismissal of the book and his crude attack upon the Soviet Union which appears to have been his chief aim in the intellectually poverty-stricken review." [85] Then someone wrote an open letter to "Faithful Reader" which agreed that Friedman's review was poor but defended his right to publish such a review in the *Daily Worker*.[86] The discussion began to get a little silly when "Xaver" argued that Friedman's main difficulty was his failure to realize that the reason the Rakosi government had misruled was that there were so many imperialist warmongers elsewhere in the world; "if you expect people to behave normal under such conditions, you are asking too much." [87] Foster could not remain quiet in a squabble such as this one. He wrote another review of Aptheker's book, in which he praised the author's research and "well-organized and penetrating analysis." The book was a "very effective answer to this tissue of anti-Soviet vilification and warmongering." [88] Louis Weinstock, just out of prison, felt he had special qualifications for still another review. He and his wife had been born in Hungary, stayed there until after the overthrow of the Communist government in 1919, and then moved to the United States. He had visited Hungary during the Rakosi regime—and, he might have added, tried to get John Lautner to do likewise. Take it from one who was there, everything was fine in Communist Hungary. Everything was fine about Aptheker's book, too; it "is an outstanding Marxist contribution and deserves to be translated into many languages and circulated the world over." [89] After the Weinstock contribution, a reader begged Gates to call off the "symposium." "It is time to pause now, comrades, and ask—'Is the end in sight?' " [90]

THE END OF AN ERA

To many comrades, it seemed the end was indeed in sight. The party's new line was not breaking it out of its isolation any better than had its old one. The party, for example, had made a great deal of the Prayer Pilgrimage for Freedom, a big demonstration by non-Communist Negroes in Washington on the third anniversary of the Supreme Court's decision on school segregation. The *Daily Worker* gave the Pilgrimage consistent and favorable publicity, and some Negro Communists attended the Washington rally, but the Negro movement's leaders did not change their attitude toward Communists one bit. No matter that the party had changed its line, Communists were still anathema. A. Philip Randolph, co-chairman of the Pilgrimage, president of the Brotherhood of Sleeping Car Porters, and once a Norman Thomas Socialist, warned the Pilgrimage against accepting Communist help. The Communists, he said, "have no genuine interest in the solution of problems of racial discrimination, but seek only to use this issue to strengthen the foreign policy of the Soviet Union." [91] Nor did Communists make any advances in the labor movement. The national officers of the A.F. of L.-C.I.O. had too much experience with the Communists to submit themselves to any more. George Meany had his troubles with them back in the days when he was the A.F. of L.'s lobbyist at Albany, and Walter Reuther had not forgotten the attacks Communists had made upon him.

Some Communists, all of them unorthodox, were in the new and loosely organized American Forum for Socialist Education. This organization, founded in May 1957, was a curious collection of diverse political beliefs, Communist and non-Communist, from Stalinoid *National Guardian* followers at the most rigid left, through Gatesite Communists, Trotskyists of the various confessions, Dorothy Day *Catholic Worker* people, Musteite "reconcilers," philosophical anarchists, pacifists, and a sprinkling of Marxist professors. Fosterite Communists would have nothing to do with the American Forum, whose members were often as critical of the Soviet Union as they were of American policies.[92] Not many of the most optimistic radicals expected much from the American Forum, yet Gatesites were pathetically enthusiastic about the freedom of discussion and intellectual give-and-take of the Forum. If enthusiasm were a solution to the intellectual problems of radicalism and Marxism, the problems would have been solved long ago.

Several prominent Gatesites decided that trying to change the party was hopeless. Joseph Clark resigned from the party and from the *Daily Worker* in early September 1957.[93] Junius Scales, whose Smith Act "membership clause" conviction the Supreme Court had set aside in October, announced in December that he had quit.[94] Doxey Wilkerson, a national committee member, resigned November 26.[95]

Clark's resignation created quite a stir. In his letter of resignation he said that after twenty-eight years in the party—he had joined when he was only an adolescent—he found that "it is no longer possible to serve the cause of American socialism" within the organization. "Why didn't I resign at the time of the Khrushchev revelations on Stalin, or during the Hungarian uprising? The reason is that I had hopes for the cause of those opposing Stalinism within the party. . . . But . . . the hope I had for the party died." [96] According to Gates, Clark's hope had actually died sometime before he resigned, but Gates had been able to persuade him to stay on because his resignation would appear to be a major victory for Foster.[97] Gates replied to Clark's letter. He thought there still was hope for the party, but wrote that Clark and the *Daily Worker* staff "parted in sorrow and not in anger, as friends, not enemies." [98] A majority of the party's national administrative committee, a smaller unit of the national executive committee composed of Dennis, Benjamin Davis, Jackson, and Lumer for the "hards" and Gates, Fine, and Stein for the dissenters, issued a statement that was not so kind. Clark, the state-

ment said, had "lost all conception of a sound working-class attitude toward the Soviet Union" and had abused the freedom of
expression which the party had granted him.[99]

Many were to follow Clark's trail within a few months because
Foster and his wing of the party, obviously with the support of the
Russians, were attacking with all the force they could muster, in
effect demanding that the Gatesites surrender or get out. Foster's
energy in the attack was amazing, especially for a seventy-six-
year-old man with a heart condition. His frantic attack ended on
October 16 with a serious cerebral hemorrhage, which for weeks
paralyzed his right side and impaired his speech.[100] His writing
production was prodigious in the last weeks before the stroke. He
wrote a blast of the Gatesites and a personal statement of dedication to Moscow for the Russian magazine *Kommunist*. (*Kommunist* later came to his aid and condemned Gates for "bourgeois
nationalism." [101]) He engaged in a bitter exchange of letters with
one "M.G." in the *Daily Worker* in which he pulled all the stops;
"M.G." was "outlandish," guilty of "bourgeois national chauvinism," and a "crackpot," besides.[102] When another old man, Alexander Bittelman, wrote a long, tedious, and confused series of
articles for the *Daily Worker* entitled "I Take a Fresh Look"—a
grossly exaggerated title—that did not measure up on Foster's
orthodox yardstick, he wrote a blistering reply for *Political Affairs* so long that the editors had to divide it into two installments.[103] And he took time out from the party wars to glory in
the Russians' success with Sputnik I. "Triumphing over all the
capitalist enemies and the croakers and knockers in the labor
movement, the USSR . . . is now travelling ever faster along the
road to the eventual realization of the greatest social system of well-
being, democracy and mass happiness that the world has ever seen
or that man has ever dreamed of. The earth satellite is the har-
binger of still greater things to come; achievements which . . . had
to await the coming of Socialism upon the world scene." [104]

The battle between the Gatesites and the Fosterites came to a
head in December, and when the crisis was over, the Communist

Party had turned the corner from one era into another. Immediately following the giant celebrations in Moscow for the fortieth anniversary of the Bolshevik revolution, twelve Communist parties, each of them in power in its country, met and issued a declaration. The twelve parties were from Russia, China, Albania, Hungary, northern Vietnam, East Germany, Bulgaria, North Korea, Mongolia, Poland, Romania, and Czechoslovakia. The Yugoslavian party refused to participate. The meeting seemed to be 1948 all over again. The declaration hailed the Soviet Union as "the first and mightiest Socialist power" and contended that "the vital interests of the working people of all countries call for their support of the Soviet Union." The twelve parties did not revive the Cominform, defunct since Khrushchev and Tito kissed and made up temporarily, but they did discuss launching a new periodical to take the place of the Cominform's old *For a Lasting Peace, For a People's Democracy!* [105]

The *Daily Worker* ran a brief news story about the twelve-party declaration, shorter than those in the general press,[106] and said nothing editorially. Not until a month after the declaration did it print anything more about the Moscow meeting, and then it published only the text of the declaration.[107] There was a struggle going on behind the scenes in the party. On December 2, the national administrative committee of seven convened. The four Fosterites on the committee (Davis, Dennis, Jackson, and Lumer) had prepared a statement hailing the declaration. The three Gatesites (Stein, Fine, and Gates himself) tried to dissuade them, but they were outvoted. On such a major matter, they argued, any statement would have to come from a party echelon closer to the membership than the administrative committee, which was only part of the executive committee, which in turn was only part of the full national committee. The four Fosterites mailed their statement to the full national committee; the statement was not published.

The larger executive committee met for three days, beginning December 20, to consider the twelve-party declaration and the future of the *Daily Worker.* The Fosterites did not have a majority with Foster himself incapacitated. Robert Thompson, who had a few months before been released from prison, read a report on the twelve-party declaration. The return of Thompson, who had gained infighting experience as the chief hatchet man against Browder, was of great value to the Foster wing. But now the executive committee prepared a statement on the declaration that was at odds with Thompson's views. The statement declared, "We American Communists should not repeat the mistake we often made in the past, of accepting the views of brother parties regarding their own problems as necessarily applying in the same way to the problems our Party faces, or of accepting a generalized estimate of the world situation without our own critical appraisal as to whether it is fully correct, or applicable to our own country." To do anything else, the statement continued, would be contrary to the decisions made at the sixteenth national convention of the party. The statement also noted that the twelve-party declaration had said that Right opportunism was the "main danger at present," but that the American party had gone on record at the last convention to the effect that "left sectarianism" was the main danger. The executive committee approved the statement by a vote of eleven to seven, with two abstaining and two absent. Those voting for the statement were Charney, David Davis, Fine, Gates, Dorothy Healy, Lightfoot, Lima, Ross, Russo, Stein, and Martha Stone. Those voting against were Benjamin Davis, Dennis, Durham, Elizabeth Gurley Flynn, Jackson, Lumer, and Thompson. Carl Winter and Jack Stachel abstained, and Foster and George Myers were absent.[108] This vote was the last victory for the unorthodox.

At the same meeting, the executive committee began the complicated decision to cease publication of the *Daily Worker,* which was disastrous for the Gates faction. With only Gates voting no, the executive committee voted to recommend "to the owners and publishers of the Daily Worker that they consider suspending the Daily and make an all-out effort to preserve the Worker." Actually, the recommendation to the party's official publishers, a small group of relatively wealthy and aged party nonentities, was only a technicality. But the executive committee "also decided to poll the 60 members of the National Committee on this proposition, with the understanding that the NEC [national executive committee] proposal would not be final or operative until the full National Committee had made a collective decision." [109] Thus, on December 22, when the executive committee adjourned, the decision to cease publication of the *Daily* was not final, although it probably would be before long.

Those who voted for this recommendation to "consider" closing the *Daily* had two quite different motives. Those who agreed with Gates or were nearer agreement with him than they were with Foster wanted the *Daily* to continue but did not see how continued publication was financially possible. The Fosterites wanted the *Daily* to close shop to silence Gates.

The *Daily Worker* had been in a desperate financial condition for a long time. It had lost money for years—if it ever broke even —but special fund drives by the party and direct subsidies from the party treasury kept it going. In 1956 and 1957, the paper was in worse financial condition than ever because many in the Foster faction would not donate money and often would not renew their subscriptions. There is an abundance of evidence to indicate that Fosterites deliberately sabotaged the *Daily*. Back at the time of the sharp conflict in the party over Hungary, Foster, Dennis, and Davis had joined Gates in a desperate appeal for funds "regardless of . . . differences" within the party. "Any withholding of support to it would be disastrous to our entire movement." [110] There must have been cause for their concern about party "differences" affecting support for the paper. At the national convention, a Fosterite delegate had declared, "The *Daily Worker* has lost readers, and the support of many good old-timers. . . . They have stopped buying the *Daily Worker,* reading the *Daily Worker,* or supporting the *Daily Worker*. If we want to do work for the upkeep of our paper, of the saving of our paper, I think the first thing would be that the *Daily Worker* should change" its position on Hungary. The speech evoked applause.[111] When Clark resigned from the party, one O. H. Leeds, of Brooklyn, wrote, "Well, it's one gone and one to go. . . . A group of us in Brooklyn have pledged a week's pay for the paper, payable on the day Johnny Gates . . . is either dumped or quits." [112] The departure of many members from the party in 1956 and 1957 also seriously hurt the paper's finances. Some Gates supporters believed the rumor, which may have been true, that the party had $250,000 cached away, originally intended for the underground, which the Fosterites refused to use to keep the *Daily* going.

In October 1957, the paper cut down its size. It had been eight pages and five days a week, Monday through Friday. The *Worker* on Sunday ran sixteen pages. Beginning October 22, the *Daily* reduced itself to four pages and dropped the Friday edition altogether. The *Worker* dropped to twelve pages. The cutback reduced the number of pages a week by exactly one-half. The retrenchment did not save enough to make the paper solvent. Steve Nelson in early December announced there was a deficit of $175,000, which the staff hoped to pare down to $150,000 by further economies. National party officials, he said, had often discussed suspending the *Daily* to save the Sunday edition but had calculated that it cost only $50,000 a year more to publish both.

After the executive committee meeting adjourned on December 22, but before the poll of the full national committee had been completed, the Fosterite majority of four on the administrative committee double-crossed their parent body and released a statement to the press to the effect that the executive committee had voted to discontinue the *Daily*. Harry Schwartz, of the New York *Times,* telephoned Gates on Christmas Day to confirm the press release. Gates refused to comment, and Schwartz said the *Times* would print the story anyway. Gates then told Schwartz that the decision to cease publication was not yet final, that he wanted to see the paper continued, and that if there were any announcement to be made, the *Daily Worker* itself, not any party committee, would make it. Schwartz included Gates's statement in his story.[113]

The four Fosterites on the administrative committee then accused Gates of "leaking" to the press, in "violation of the most elementary organizational principles common to all working-class organizations." This accusation was too much for seven *Daily* staff members, who wrote a letter to the four saying their statement about Gates was "groundless, uncalled for, and too reminiscent of previous harmful practices which the Communist movement has criticized itself for and which it is trying to shed." The signers of the letter were Abner Berry (Negro affairs), Jesus Colon (Puerto Rican affairs), Max Gordon (politics), Ben Levine (television column), Alan Max (managing editor), David Platt (movies and plays), and Lester Rodney (sports).[114] A. B. Magil, Simon Gerson, George Morris, and Virginia Gardner did not sign the letter.

Gates and the *Daily Worker* were almost, but not quite finished. The national committee completed its poll on the question of whether or not to suspend publication of the *Daily* between Christmas, 1957, and New Year's, and the national committee voted to suspend. At a New Year's Eve party, Gates told Elizabeth Gurley Flynn and Jack Stachel that he probably was going to resign from the party soon. He had earlier told many people that if the *Daily* had to cease publication because of the pressure of the Foster group he would leave the party. On Monday, January 6, Dennis called a meeting of the administrative committee. All but Fine were present. Dennis began the meeting by saying that he understood "on good authority" that Gates was going to leave the party. Was that right? Gates replied that he probably would leave. Dennis wanted to know when he was going to quit. Gates replied he did not know yet, but that he would tell the administrative committee when he had made up his mind. Then Dennis introduced a resolution, already prepared, that would have removed Gates from all party offices because he was going to resign, and asked Gates what he thought of that. Gates replied that Dennis's motion was not in accordance with the procedures for suspension from office as provided in the party constitution adopted at the last convention.

Gates's constitutional objection jarred Dennis, who recessed the meeting and caucused with Davis, Thompson, and Lumer. They did not ask Stein and Gates to stay. When Dennis called for the meeting to resume, Stein refused to attend. Gates returned. Dennis read a modified resolution which had the same effect, and the committee passed it. Gates said they had held the party's constitution and convention in contempt but that their contempt was not as great as that which he held for them. Gates left the room and never saw Dennis again. Stein telephoned other members of the national executive committee, of which the administrative committee was a part, and the larger body reversed the administrative committee's resolution.[115]

On Thursday, January 9, the *Daily* announced that its last issue would appear the following Monday. On Friday, January 10, John Gates called a press conference in the little Albert Hotel on East Tenth Street, named for Albert Pinkham Ryder and built by the painter's brother. While press cameras flashed and television cameras whirred, Gates announced that after twenty-seven years in the party, he was resigning "to rejoin the American people and find out what Americans are thinking about." The party, he said, had "ceased to be an effective force for democracy, peace and socialism in the United States." Although the ideals that attracted him to the party still motivated him, he did "not believe it is possible any longer to serve those ideals within the Communist party." [116]

The *Daily Worker*'s last issue, thirty-four years to the day after its first issue in Chicago in 1924, was a curious document. The fight between the Gatesites and the Fosterites continued to the very end. Alan Max wrote, "Our tragedy was that we were unable to change ourselves. We could not keep up with the vast changes in the country. . . . Each attempt to change ourselves succeeded only briefly—then it foundered on the rocks of dogmatism." The administrative committee ran a statement on Gates's resignation that in effect said "good riddance." "For some time Gates has been politically disoriented and has been challenging many of the basic principles of scientific socialism, Marxism." And Will Weinstone, typical of the old-timers who now would dominate the party, had one final letter, which could just as well have been written ten or twelve years earlier: "In my opinion . . . the main attack must today be made against revisionism and liquidationism which undermine the very foundations of the party and its principles . . . and hinder the mobilization of the party and brass for their tasks in relation to the mass struggles of labor and the people." [117]

The same old words, the same old incantations, but an era in Communist history had passed.

CONCLUSION: AN IMPOTENT PARTY

The *Daily Worker* was dead. John Gates, the chief spokesman for the unorthodox Communists, had resigned, and those of his party supporters who had not already quit the party were in the process of leaving. The party settled down to its unexciting, orthodox, pre-Khrushchev style. The Sunday *Worker,* now officially edited by William L. Patterson but actually directed by Benjamin Davis, became a dull gray caricature of a newspaper. No more did it print angry letters to the editor on matters that made any difference. One letter denounced boxing as "the cruelest form of capitalist exploitation." The only controversy in the letters column was over the question of whether or not opera singer Maria Callas could "carry a tune." [1] The question of whether or not the staff members who had departed with the demise of the *Daily* would get the full severance pay required by the American Newspaper Guild contract received not one word of comment in the paper. The party itself was becoming the ideological home for aged and isolated Reds that some members really wanted.

The Fosterites demonstrated that they exercised effective control of the party at the national committee meeting of February 14-16, 1958, the first after Gates's resignation. Jack Stachel came armed with a resolution condemning Gates's ideas as "but the most extreme expression of a revisionist ideology . . . a product of the pressure of bourgeois ideology within the working-class and its organizations, including the Party, and an expression of accommodation to this ideology." Stachel called for members to demonstrate their "devotion and love for the Party" with a campaign to rout Gatesism from the organization. "There is no place in the Party for a Gates or his ideology. The departure of such individuals will not injure but strengthen the Party. The answer to his resignation must be a determination to reveal and defeat all alien ideology in our ranks." Sidney Stein, a middle-of-the-road party leader, offered the national committee a milder resolution. By a vote of 36 to 12 with seven abstaining, the national committee adopted Stachel's resolution.[2]

Another matter of business was a general resolution on the party's role, organization, and ideology. Carl Winter and Claude Lightfoot, who were not as rigid as Foster but were die-hards nevertheless, presented a compromise resolution with which they hoped all could agree. Their resolution was an amended version of one originally drafted by the northern California party. Stein gave the resolution qualified support. Dennis saw that there was no need for compromise since he and the other Fosterite hards had the votes. Dennis offered a resolution of his own, an affirmation of Communist orthodoxy. The party must be, he insisted, "a working class vanguard party guided by the science of Marxism-Leninism. It must not be confused with other types of political parties of a united front character, or with an idea of a so-called united socialist party in which adherents of Marxism-Leninism would be only one among a number of other ideological currents." After a sideswipe at Gates's "anti-Marxist views and actions," Dennis went on to the November 1957 declaration of the twelve Communist parties in Moscow, about which there had been "controversy in the national leadership." The declaration was "a document of far-reaching, historic importance. . . . It reinforces the unity both of the socialist countries and of the international working-class and Marxist movements. It is a major Marxist-Leninist contribution to the fight for world peace, democracy, national freedom and socialism." American Communists "should study it and learn from it." Dennis rejected "the erroneous and harmful views of those who regard the Declaration as a 'reversal' or a 'retreat' from the position of the 20th Congress of the CPSU." He urged the national executive committee to prepare a "definitive statement on the Declaration, to issue outlines and otherwise do everything possible to stimulate its widest study." Finally, Dennis, too, called for a party purge: "To defend and reinforce unity, it is necessary at all costs to eradicate all factional activities and groupings in our ranks." After considerable discussion, the national committee accepted Dennis's resolution by a vote of 32 to 20, with three abstaining.[3] A new national executive committee subsequently declared its full approval of the twelve-party declaration, thus reversing the statement on the declaration that the old executive committee had adopted December 22, 1957.[4]

Twenty dissenting votes on such a resolution were too many for the hards' comfort. These dissenting national committee members had been elected by the national and state conventions, and thus were not to be removed easily or constitutionally. The hards circumvented the problem by calling for a new national executive committee, one which they could pack with officers who had demonstrated "devotion and love for the Party" to their satisfaction. Outvoted on the proposal in the full national committee, the dissenters refused to accept nomination to the new executive body. One of the dissenters, Albert J. ("Mickie") Lima, of California, accepted nomination because he wanted to maintain a connection between the top leadership and the *People's World*. The hards' resolution called for fifteen members on the new executive committee (five less than the old one), and the national committee chose nine at the February meeting. The other six were to be elected later. The nine were Lima, Dennis, Benjamin Davis, Elizabeth Gurley Flynn, James Jackson, Hyman Lumer, George Myers, Jack Stachel, and Robert Thompson.[5] Foster, still incapacitated from his stroke, was unable to serve on the executive committee, but he later rallied enough to write for *Political Affairs* again.

Still elated by the sputniks—and gratified that the United States space satellite was smaller—Foster demonstrated that his stroke had not changed his views: despite "the mistakes of the 'cult of the individual' period under Stalin . . . Socialist democracy in the Soviet Union has achieved the greatest level of freedom for the working classes in the history of mankind." [6]

The Fosterites, now in complete control of the party organization, did not have to stage a full-scale purge. Most Gatesites simply quit. Alan Max, Lester Rodney, Abner Berry, and Max Gordon, all of the old *Daily Worker* staff and all bitter about their lack of severance pay, departed in February. George Blake Charney and two less important New York officials resigned their party positions but not their membership in March. So did Carl Ross, secretary of the Minnesota organization. On April 1, twenty-six state and local leaders of the California organization resigned from the party and declared their intention to organize a new group free of Moscow domination. Hundreds of rank and filers departed as quietly as possible, knowing that to resign noisily was only to identify oneself as having once been a member and thereby to jeopardize one's economic welfare and risk unpleasant social pressures. Thompson, back from prison and again the unofficial defender of the faith, lashed out at those who had resigned, charging that they were "an anti-party conspiracy." To Thompson, the answer to those who were disaffected by the drive for purity was to drive for even more purity. He seemed as disturbed by those who remained in the party and shrugged off the resignations as by those who quit altogether. "Unquestioned loyalty to the party and a readiness to fight for it against its attackers must be established as fundamental criteria for Communists. . . . The party cannot tolerate its continued belittling at the hands of people holding party membership; nor can it tolerate failure to defend it against slanders and attacks." [7]

Thompson's campaign for party purity succeeded in bringing about the departure of two more unorthodox leaders. Later in the spring of 1958, George Blake Charney resigned from the party altogether, as did Sidney Stein, who had helped Thompson hide out in the Sierras when Thompson was a fugitive from justice. The Fosterites now had almost the kind of party they wanted. The only significant center of opposition was in California, where Dorothy Healy refused either to resign or to capitulate. By June, the party was again quickly responsive to the desires of international Communism. Early in that month, the Soviets announced the execution of Imre Nagy and two of his associates in the Hungarian revolt. Almost at once, the *Worker* approved editorially of the execution. At a national committee meeting later in the month, a resolution criticizing the editorial failed of passage by a 3-to-1 vote.[8] Although Thompson continued to rail against factionalism, the party was almost as close to monolithic unity as is possible without the use of legalized terror. The party demonstrated again in the summer of 1958 that it was entirely serious about purity and unity when it expelled a curious little group of "ultra-leftist" sectarians.

After there has been a purge of the "right" in the Communist Party, it is usual for a small group of disgruntled "ultra-leftists" to charge that the purgers are as guilty of "revisionism" as the recently purged. The Left sectarians made such charges in 1946 and 1947. In the summer of 1958, this happened again. A small group from the New York waterfront and Harlem, with a few followers in Pennsylvania and Ohio, led by Harry Haywood, a hard champion of Negro nationalism, asserted that Dennis and Thompson were as contaminated with wrongheaded theories as Gates had ever been. Thompson promptly had them expelled. Eighty-three of the expelled "ultras" held a conference in New York in mid-August and organized themselves into the Provisional Organizing Committee for a Marxist-Leninist Communist Party. They had sufficient strength, most of it among Negroes and Puerto Ricans, to publish a four-page printed monthly newspaper, the *Marxist-Leninist Vanguard,* very much like the fugitive publications of earlier groups but slicker in its form than the usual mimeographed Left-sectarian publications.[9] The new group's chances of survival are remote. Even Haywood gave them up as hopeless before the year was over.

The party's crisis was over by the summer of 1958. The Fosterites had won everything: control of the party machinery, control of its press, control of its policies. Yet their victory was hollow. They had won little more than the "franchise" over a nearly dead party.

The weekly *Worker,* besides being lifeless and sterile, was in dangerous financial condition. After weeks of a drive to gain 9,000 subscriptions, it had sold only one-fourth that many.[10] At the end of May 1958, the staff did not see how it could afford to get out the June 1 issue, due to go in the mails on May 30. The staff raised some money from sympathizers in a desperate struggle for survival, got a priority on party funds, and persuaded the printer to postpone his bill twenty-four hours. Still the *Worker* could afford only four, rather than the usual sixteen, pages.[11] The situation was similar on the West Coast, where the *People's World* was down to one edition a week.

The party's schools, which had enrolled thousands of students, were all closed. The Jefferson School of New York, once the biggest, had had trouble finding enough students to make the operation pay since about 1953. The 1956 crisis finished off the already moribund institution. In November 1956, its board of trustees announced that the school would close at the end of the term.[12] In San Francisco, the California Labor School, which once had an "extension division" with classes throughout the Bay area as well as southern California, closed its doors a few months later.[13] In a desperate effort to eke out a Marxist living, a group of New York party intellectuals in the fall of 1957 tried renting a hall and selling courses themselves—$6.00 for seven lectures or $3.50 for four.[14] The tuition was cheap enough, but few took advantage of the bargain offer.

As an electoral group, the Communists showed how feeble was their power in the 1957 New York City elections, conducted while the *Daily Worker* was still publishing and before all the Gatesites departed. Elizabeth Gurley Flynn, as good a candidate as the party had, ran for the city council from the Twenty-fourth District, a lower East Side area. Under the label of the People's Rights Party, where she had polled 1,437 Bronx votes for the city council in 1954, she could in 1957 gather only 710 votes from a total of 70,168. The contrast to the elections twelve years earlier, when the Communists elected two city councilmen, was striking. The dismal showing was not due to lack of effort. Her campaign manager, Arnold Johnson, a faithful Fosterite, a graduate of Union Theological Seminary, revealed that the party had distributed 100,000 leaflets, conducted thirty outdoor meetings, and made three radio broadcasts.[15]

At no time during the party's crisis did even the top party leaders have better than a rough estimate of how many members had quit and how many remained. Just before the twentieth congress convened in Moscow, the party had conducted a membership registration, which showed there were over 20,000 members, 8,800 of them in New York City. In the summer of 1957, months after the party's convention, the national committee estimated the total membership at about 10,000, 3,500 of them in New York.[16] New York losses were proportionately greater because it was a center of party discontent. When Gates resigned from the party in January 1958, he estimated the national membership at less than 7,000.[17] Late in the winter of 1957-58, the party registered its members again, the first accurate count in slightly over two years, and the registration indicated that the estimates had been too high. More members had quit than national headquarters knew. The registration showed that there were slightly under 3,000 members of the Communist Party. In a little over two years, there had been a membership drop of over 85 per cent, the greatest decline in percentages (though not in total numbers) in the party's history. Robert Thompson, the party's new executive secretary, subsequently announced that his administration was "increasing and stabilizing" the membership, but it is not likely that the membership total today is much over 3,000.[18]

More members might have quit if the economic prospects of the former Communist had been better. The more prominent in the party a man had been, the more difficult it was for him to find steady employment. One former member was hired and fired from fourteen mediocre jobs in a six-month period in 1957. Every time his new employer discovered his Communist background, he was on the street again.[19] For a former Communist organizer or journalist to find a job suited to his training and experience is especially difficult; he is sure to be known as a former Communist, and employers are sensitive to the possibility of adverse public reaction. By the spring of 1958, few of the prominent former Communists had found the jobs they wanted; some were unemployed. John Gates had just written a book, published late in the year. Max Gordon was a part-time graduate student in history at Columbia University. Doxey Wilkerson had enrolled as a graduate student in the School of Education at New York University. Many of them were salesmen. Former Communists also face at least a brief period of difficult social and psychological adjustment. The former Communist needs something to fill the void the party had once occupied, something else to which to dedicate himself.

One sometimes hears stories of "professional ex-Communists" who reap large incomes as anti-Communist experts. Some of these people have done rather well financially; others have not. Most former Communists reject that kind of career, preferring, to use John Steuben's phrase when he quit the party, to live out their lives "in agony and silence." Actually, there are former Communists of both kinds at almost all income levels. The most curious former Communists, perhaps, are the few who have done well financially in Wall Street. A few are former members; more are former fellow travelers. To some observers, their Wall Street careers indicate that they never were good Communists; other observers argue that their success in capitalist speculation indicates the value of a Marxist economic education. To generalize even about the economic status of former Communists is impossible because there are so many of them—perhaps a quarter-million in the United States.

There are more former Communists in America than ever before because the party has never been smaller. The two Communist groups that split from the Debs Socialists in 1919 claimed a total of 70,000 members. Two years later, when they merged to form the present Communist Party, they claimed 10,000 to 12,000, and even this was three to four times their size in 1958. No longer does the Communist Party tower over the other Left Wing American parties. In January 1957, the Socialist Party of Norman Thomas merged with the Social Democratic Federation, which had split from the Socialists in the mid-1930's. The new combined organization is as large as the Communist Party, and, furthermore, it is growing slowly.[20]

The number of dues-paying Communists, of course, is not a fully satisfactory measure of the party's strength, for it continues to have sympathizers who support the movement financially and otherwise, and there may be a number of hidden members. In the summer of 1958, Thompson boasted that the party had recently raised $20,000 for the *Worker* in three weeks.[21] Thompson's boast revealed more than he realized. In 1947, the San Francisco Communists had collected one-third that amount at one mass meeting, and the national organization had raised $250,000 in twenty days.[22] As the membership has declined, so has the number of fellow travelers. The increasing futility of party action and the events of 1956 in East Europe disillusioned the fellow travelers as well as party members. The Communist Party today is almost dead as a political force. The American Communists' threat, or potential threat, to national security is another matter—a police and military matter—but as a political movement the Communists are impotent.

Those who are left in the party can be described as a "hard core," a phrase with chilling connotations. Certainly most of the Communists left are hard, and together they constitute only a core of what the party once was. But even some of the champions of hardness do not seem to have as much steel in their conviction as they once had. Foster, the old man himself, was not able fully to rally his old-fashioned vocabulary of contempt when he blasted Theodore Draper's coldly objective history of the party's origins and earliest years.[23] And Elizabeth Gurley Flynn was milder in her denunciation of Gates when he quit the party than she had been in her comments on Anna Louise Strong when Stalin exiled her from Russia in 1949.[24] Among the top leaders, only Robert Thompson, the soldier, seemed as ruthless in 1957-58 as he had been in exterminating Browderism in 1945-46.

It does not seem likely today that the Communist Party will revive, but such a prediction cannot be made with assurance. Communist parties elsewhere in the world have grown from nearly nothing into a formidable political force within a brief period when the conditions for their growth were right and when they developed a line with popular appeal. The conditions necessary for the growth of the American party certainly are not present today, and the party has not had a line attractive to Americans since the end of the war in Europe. Even if there were the necessary conditions —an end of American-Russian tensions, a major economic depression on the scale of the 1930's, widespread social discontent, and a consequent pervasive demand for far-reaching political and economic change—it could well be that the Communist Party's record of tailoring its policies to the zigzagging exigencies of Soviet foreign policy and its history of vituperative attacks on respected working-class leaders and of internal repression of freedom would badly inhibit really important growth of the party. This speculation, however, assumes that the American general public knows the history of the Communist Party; and the general public, even the usually informed public, knows relatively little of Communist history despite the flood of anti-Communist literature America has produced.

It is not likely that the Communist Party will die out completely. If it were going to dissolve, it would probably have done so during the Hungarian crisis. Such groups seldom sign their own death certificates. Even the Industrial Workers of the World still maintain an office, and the Greenback Party occasionally runs a candidate. It is not probable that the Communists will decline to the levels of the I.W.W. and the Greenback Party, relics of the pre-Communist era, because they will continue, we may assume, to stay abreast of current world problems, and the Communists have the U.S.S.R. to look to and to serve. Yet the party has done very little recruiting for some years now, and its average member is already middle-aged. The time may have already come when more Communists die annually than are recruited.

At this moment, the Communist Party seems destined to join a collection of other sects as an exhibit in the museum of American Left Wing politics. It is a nice irony that it was Leon Trotsky, the antichrist of Communism, who years ago and in another context coined the phrase that today fits the American Communist Party: "swept into the dust bin of history."

SUICIDE AND INFANTICIDE

How does one explain this decline of the Communist movement in the United States?

The Communist Party, in the first place, was never strong. The explanation of this failure involves the totality of American political, cultural, and economic history, especially the relative lack of class consciousness in the United States. Here, however, we are primarily concerned with why the Communists declined from their 1947 peak.

William Z. Foster and his hard followers—to the extent that they were concerned with the party's viability at all—held that the answer to the question lay in an analysis of conditions and forces outside the party, in what they called the "objective condition" or the "objective situation." They also used the term "life itself," an interesting choice of words. John Gates and his sympathizers held that the answer to the question lay in an exploration of the party's "errors," the mistakes of judgment it had made during the years it was in decline. Both Foster and Gates were right; but neither was completely right.

One important external condition that hurt the Communist Party was American postwar prosperity, the longest and most vigorous prosperity the United States has ever enjoyed. Postwar America has had economic recessions—in 1949, in 1953-54, and again in 1957-58—which brought hardship to large numbers of people, but these recessions were nothing comparable to the calamity of the Great Depression of the 1930's. During periods of prosperity, social discontent does not disappear entirely, but it is not as intense as it is during serious depressions. The average American worker who has been steadily employed since the war, who has bought a home, a car, and a television set, is not likely to be stirred by Communist denunciations of capitalism and imperialism even if he is behind on his installment payments. The era of the picture window and the tail-finned automobile has produced its own dissatisfactions and frustrations but not the kind that leads one to seek salvation in Left Wing politics. Postwar prosperity has tended to make American labor even more middle class than it was under the leadership of Gompers and Green and consequently less inclined than ever to pursue revolutionary purposes. Prosperity has affected youth as well as labor. Good times have sluiced off the natural revolt of young people into nonpolitical activities—beards and Zen Buddhism, for example—and the Communists' efforts to build a youth movement have failed conspicuously. All in all, prosperity's effects have been pervasive—the Communists would say "insidious."

A more important external condition hampering the Communists was the cold war and its many ramifications within American society. The American public, quite properly, identifies the Communist Party with the Soviet Union, which has never been more unpopular in the United States. Opposition to domestic Communism is nearly universal and more intense than ever before in America's long tradition of hostility toward that particular "foreign ideology." During the war, the fact that Russia and the United States were allies against the Nazis had brought a rather spectacular reversal of American opposition to Communism. At the end of the war, public-opinion polls indicated that Americans had less resentment against Communists than they had had before Pearl Harbor. But the public's tolerance of Communists, or at least its indifference toward them, quickly disappeared as tensions between America and Russia became severe. By the early 1950's, the American Communists had become community outcasts—and nearly outlaws.

This popular anti-Communism expressed itself partly in anti-Communist legislation and prosecutions. From 1949 on, the American Communists were forced to spend a large part of their time, energy, and money trying to stay out of prison and trying to maintain the legality of their organization. The party necessarily went on the defensive, and imprisonment deprived it of some of its abler leaders.

But another, and probably more important, aspect of postwar anti-Communism was the development of labor and non-Communist left-of-center groups into strong centers of anti-Communism. Before 1945, patriotic and business organizations had the field of anti-Communism almost to themselves, and although they certainly helped to condition the American population against Communist ideas, they had little influence in labor circles and among non-Communist critics of the *status quo*. The most important addition to the ranks of anti-Communism came in the early postwar years when the C.I.O. declared war on the Communists, and non-Communist liberals organized Americans for Democratic Action. The Communists had to "reach" the worker in basic industry and the political rebel, but the development of labor and liberal anti-Communism not only deprived the Communists of an audience, but developed hostility toward the Communists precisely where the Communists most wanted power. The decline of the American Communist Party can be told largely in terms of the conversion of the non-Communist Left into the anti-Communist Left.

The party would have had a difficult time confronting these external conditions even if it had adopted the wisest of policies. The Communists, however, were not wise, even in their choice of tactics. With postwar international relations and the conditions of American society in the late 1940's what they were, the Communists could hardly have selected a less propitious time to adopt a hard line.

At a time when most of organized labor was tying its political fortunes to the Democratic Party, the Communists embarked upon third-party adventures. The Communists so flagrantly dominated the Progressive Party that they thoroughly alienated many non-Communist critics of the *status quo,* and for years to come, many American political rebels who cannot feel altogether comfortable within the major political parties will resent the way that the Communists discredited the tradition of third-party revolt. At a time when American Negroes were beginning to make progress in their program for first-class citizenship and integration into the fabric of American life, the Communists returned to their old "self-determination for the Negro people in the Black Belt" position, which smacked too much of segregation, of "Red Crow," to attract Negro militants. When American writers were increasingly moving away from the social themes which permeated their product in the 1930's, the Communists insisted that literature be a "weapon" in the class struggle. When Americans were "returning to religion," the Communists went back to their old line that religion was an opium, a kind of superstition foisted upon a gullible public by self-serving economic interests. At a time when relations between the Soviet Union and the United States were dangerously strained, American Communists insisted that the Soviet position was entirely right and the American position entirely wrong. The Communists' "errors" made the "objective situation" worse.

The party's obeisance to Moscow was the source of its "errors" and the root cause of its unhappy "objective situation." If Foster ever perceived this fundamental fact about his party, he never expressed himself. And Gates, at least while he was still in the party, perceived it only dimly and without seeing all its ramifications, even though he favored loosening the Communists' tie to the Soviets.

The Communists made all their important "errors" either in direct response to obvious Soviet desires or in response to their habit of aping the Soviets and other foreign Communist parties. The Communist Party's 1948 electoral policy was a direct result of Zhdanov's speech in Poland and the organization of the Cominform in September 1947. Until news of the speech and the establishment of the new Communist international organization reached the United States, American Communists were still talking about a third party as a lever within the Democratic coalition rather than as an independent, competitive ticket. The Communists' other disastrous mistakes had their root cause in Russian policy. Their line on the American Negro derived directly from Stalin's theory—but not his actual policy—about the several nationality groups within the Soviet empire. The American party's wild estimate of the danger of total war and domestic fascism was the same as that of Communist parties everywhere. In their underground of 1949 and after, the Communists copied the tactics of European Communists with dire results. Indeed, their whole shift in policy from an accommodating line to a hard line in 1945 was dictated by their conformity to the zigzagging direction of Russian foreign policy.

The "objective situation" itself was not a result of the American party's connection to foreign Communism, but the party's reaction to the "objective situation" was. No one compelled the Communists to follow the Soviets' foreign policy against United States policy when relations between the two nations deteriorated. It would have been possible for the Communists to have criticized both American and Russian policy. A few genuine rebels did. Of course, the Communists would have no longer been Communists if they had done so, because compliance with Russian foreign policy has been the one constant, unvarying characteristic of Communist parties the world over. Nevertheless, the Communists could have decided to be American radicals rather than Russian weather vanes. They could have decided to be Left rather than East. And surely the attitude of the American public toward the Communists would have been different if the Communists had applied the same standards of criticism toward Russia as they did toward the United States.

Nothing but their own habits of mind compelled American Communists to defend themselves against anti-Communist attacks with a repression within their party at least as hysterical as that with which they were confronted; they reacted to McCarthyism with Stalinism. The closeness of the American Communists to the Soviet Union and other foreign Communist organizations—a tie unique in American politics—was their basic weakness.

And yet, paradoxically, their identification with the Soviets was, if one considers their whole history, a source of strength as well as a root of weakness. Their birth during and immediately after World War I was a result of the Bolshevik revolution. They survived the 1920's because the Bolsheviks survived the decade, and at that time the Russians subsidized them directly with "Moscow gold." In the 1930's, the American Communists profited from the fact that American capitalism was depressed and the Russian economy was expanding. Many Americans, thinking mistakenly that the Russian economy was truly socialist because the Russians despised capitalism, admired the Soviets for their material advancement—although even during the American depression, the American living standard was far higher than the Russian— and ignored the Russian totalitarian denial of individual liberty and dignity. The American Communists reaped advantage from their Russian connection in those days, as they did again during World War II, when the Soviet Union was an American military ally and its armies were slaughtering—and being slaughtered by— the Nazi *Wehrmacht*. Even today, the party finds some advantage in its Eastern bonds. The American Communists are relieved of the burden of having to think for themselves. That chore is performed by their abler European and Asian comrades; the American Communists have only to translate to the American scene. In addition, the party, to a slight degree even today, basks in the reflection of Soviet achievements, as it did to a greater extent from 1930 to 1945. The Soviet Union is a going concern, whether one approves of where it is going or not. Lincoln Steffens, after a trip to Russia when the Communist regime there was young, said he had been "over into the future, and it works." He was partly right. Whether or not it is the future still remains to be seen, but it does "work" if one applies the materialist value standard of industrial expansion, of tons of steel produced, kilowatt hours of electric power generated, or sputniks put into orbit, and does not apply the Western values of democracy, of diversity, and of individual liberty and due process of law. Whether the Russian economy "works" better than the American economy in the long run also remains to be seen. To the degree that Americans do admire the Soviet Union, the American Communist Party derives some reflected advantage from their Russian identification.

It is probable that the American Communist Party will continue to exist in some feeble form or other until the Soviet party finds it no longer useful. At the moment, at least, the Russians find the American party too useful to let it disappear entirely, though they think more highly of the French and Italian parties, which are of greater value to them. The Russians do not have any apparent hope for the success of their American comrades. Nor have the Russians pursued policies calculated to strengthen the American branch. The coup in Czechoslovakia and the Berlin blockade during the 1948 election campaign are cases in point. The Soviets find the American Communists useful primarily for propaganda purposes elsewhere in the world. Russia can maintain that the American Communists are the "vanguard" of the American working class and that the American people do not really support their "imperialist warmonger" rulers. Foreign Communists, especially the French, capitalized on the Rosenberg case to heighten anti-American sentiment and used *We Charge Genocide,* the American party's outrageous book on the treatment of the American Negro, for the same purpose. Some of the material on the United States in the Cominform's shrill newspaper, *For a Lasting Peace, For a People's Democracy!*, was only a paraphrased version of *Daily Worker* stories.

But such is the irony of history and life that, despite the degree of utility the American branch has for the Soviet party, the Soviet administered to the American Communists their last crushing blow. The disadvantages under which the American party labored had been becoming less severe before the twentieth congress and continued to ameliorate thereafter. McCarthyism clearly was in decline after the fall of 1954. The Supreme Court, in a series of important decisions—the Jencks case, the Yates case, and the Scales-Lightfoot case—removed some of the legal blocks that put the party at serious disadvantage. Before the twentieth congress of the Communist Party of the Soviet Union and Khrushchev's secret speech, the American party was ineffective; after the twentieth congress, it was impotent. The party's final crisis was not the result of either "error" or the "objective situation." It was precipitated entirely by the Russian denunciation of Stalin and the crushing of the Hungarian revolution.

To add to the irony, it was John Gates who, among the top leaders of the party, was most forcefully affected by these foreign events, and it was Gates who most wanted to loosen or sever the connection with the Soviet Union and to build an independent Communist Party which would look toward America rather than Moscow.

Of all the generalizations about the Communist Party of the United States and its history that might be made from the evidence, the most important and most nearly universally valid one is this: the American Communist Party was and is the willing instrument of the Soviet Union. The revolution does indeed devour the children it has borne and nursed and never weaned.

BIBLIOGRAPHICAL ESSAY / NOTES / INDEX

BIBLIOGRAPHICAL ESSAY

There are not available today the kind of manuscript sources on the Communist Party's history since 1945 that the historian likes to have. If the party itself has correspondence, unpublished reports, and membership records, it does not make them available. There is undoubtedly a rich store of materials on the party in the files of the Federal Bureau of Investigation, but their records are also unavailable. I have, therefore, been forced to rely primarily upon the party press, upon personal interviews, and upon what information I could glean from nonparty sources.

The party press is a much richer storehouse of information than one would expect. The press was the party's primary means of communication to the membership, and it necessarily revealed a great deal. Its press did not print its innermost secrets, but a great many matters that one would not expect to be printed did appear. Especially after the party crisis broke in 1956 did long-hidden incidents, plans, and conditions come to light.

I have been through the files of the *Daily Worker* and its Sunday edition, the *Worker,* throughout the period, as well as the *Daily People's World* of the West Coast. The Cominform newspaper, *For a Lasting Peace, For a People's Democracy!,* which I trust had a somewhat more abbreviated title in at least some of the several languages in which it was published from 1947 to 1956, was useful for the international Communist line. The best single source for the American party's line was *Political Affairs,* the monthly published by the party, until 1944 called the *Communist.* Communist pamphlets, most of them published by New Century, were also useful. One cannot ignore the "inner-party" press, the magazines intended only for party eyes. The publications of this type that I was able to unearth were *Contact,* published by national party headquarters in 1947, *Party Voice,* a monthly published by the New York organization from 1953, and the preconvention *Discussion Bulletins* published in 1945 and again in late 1956 and early 1957.

One has to learn to read Communist publications. First of all, one has to learn party jargon, or Communese, which differs from English in several important respects. In Communese, for example, the word "correct" means in harmony with the international line of the moment rather than "true." In fact, many things that were "correct" were demonstrably untrue. But even after mastering Communese, there is the problem of learning what is significant in party publications. Frequently, what a Communist left unsaid was as important as what he did say. Sometimes the mere fact that some subject or other received a considerable amount of attention in the press—for example, denunciations of Keynesianism in 1948—was more revealing than what was actually said. The reader of this book will be able to see the problems of interpretation involved in some of the quoted Communist writings. And in using the Communist press, one must exercise more than the usual scholarly caution about veracity.

Communist publications, especially pamphlets and inner-party publications, are not easy to find. I was fortunate in having available the small but invaluable collection of party materials that William Goldsmith gathered for the "Communism in American Life" project. This excellent collection should someday be made available to all scholars. Among the better public libraries on this subject are the New York Public Library and the Wisconsin Historical Society, at Madison, but I found two private libraries of great utility: the library of the now defunct Jefferson School of Social Science in New York and the personal library of Philip Jaffe, an assiduous collector of such materials, in Stamford, Connecticut. The librarian of the Jefferson School was most co-operative. He sometimes sold me duplicate copies of pamphlets and magazines. What has happened to the Jefferson School collections since the place closed late in 1956, I do not know, but those materials should be preserved. Finally, anyone working in this field of historical research must haunt party bookstores, which are never identified as such and have innocuous names. They are easily identified by the publications they sell. For some reason, most of these bookstores are presided over by rather vague old ladies who seldom have the right change.

Among the nonparty sources that were useful were the mimeo-

graphed minutes of the national committee of the Progressive Party
and the many press releases of that organization in Philip Jaffe's collection. I also found extremely revealing the testimony, cited in Chapter IV, that was taken by a C.I.O. committee in its hearings on
charges against the International Longshoremen's and Warehousemen's
Union. And then there is the testimony to be found in the published
hearings and reports of various Congressional committees investigating
Communism. On the whole, Congressional sources are a disappoint-
ment, although I sometimes found them useful. Both committee members and counsel were interested in names to be investigated further.
They frequently cut off a witness who seemed about on the point
of revealing something significant about the party's operations with
an exasperating request for more names. The most useful reports of
these committees were the result of traditional library research methods rather than of interrogation of witnesses.

I was able to get more interviews than a historian customarily can.
Earl Browder was helpful on the backgrounds of certain party leaders
and party problems. He also lent me some of the Left-deviationist
publications he had collected, as did Philip Jaffe. After the party
became engaged in a sharp internal struggle in 1956, I was able to
get information through interviews with party leaders and journalists,
primarily John Gates. Much that I learned in these interviews only
confirmed what I had already surmised, some of the information led
me to pursue new avenues of conventional research, and some of the
information I could have learned only through such interviews. Perhaps this book should be dedicated to Nikita Khrushchev, whose secret
speech on Stalin's crimes in February 1956 created conditions in the
American party which considerably facilitated my research.

Secondary sources useful in the writing of this book were dis-
tressingly few. Irving Howe and Lewis Coser in *The American Communist Party: A Critical History (1919-1957)* (Boston: Beacon,
1957) devote only sixty-three pages to the period after 1945, and
their volume is easily the most comprehensive history of the party
in this period heretofore published. John Gates, *The Story of an
American Communist* (New York: Nelson, 1958) is a useful autobiography. Its tenth chapter, pp. 157-191, is an account of the party's
crisis after the 1956 Khrushchev speech. The book appeared after I
had completed this volume, but it does not conflict with my account.
Through the party press and interviews with Gates and others in 1956
and 1957, I had been able to gather more details than Gates could
include in one chapter of an autobiography. J. Edgar Hoover's *Masters*

of Deceit: The Story of Communism in America and How to Fight It (New York: Doubleday, 1958) is rather superficial as a history of the party, although it is occasionally useful for the party's organization and methods. Actually, the F.B.I. director's book is a better primary source about anti-Communist activities. Quite useful to me were Max M. Kampelman, *The Communist Party vs. the C.I.O.: A Study in Power Politics* (New York: Praeger, 1957), Philip Selznick, *The Organizational Weapon* (New York: McGraw-Hill, 1952), Wilson Record, *The Negro and the Communist Party* (Chapel Hill: University of North Carolina Press, 1951), and the unpublished University of Chicago dissertation on the Progressive Party by John Cotton Brown, which I used extensively in Chapter V. William Z. Foster's *History of the Communist Party of the United States* (New York: International, 1952) is, for the postwar period, primarily a defense of the party's line and a denunciation of Browderism. Whatever value it has is as a primary source for the party line in the late Stalin period, and it is not as useful in this sense as the files of *Political Affairs*.

In 1955, the Fund for the Republic, Inc., published a large volume entitled *Bibliography of the Communist Problem in the United States*. Professor Joel Seidman, of the University of Chicago, is now engaged in enlarging and bringing that bibliography up to date. In view of these works, each of them far more comprehensive than anything I could append to this volume, it seems unwise to present the usual list of sources. For the materials I have used, the reader is referred to the notes.

NOTES

Abbreviations: *PA* for *Political Affairs*
 DW for *Daily Worker*
 Wkr for *The Worker*

CHAPTER ONE: NEW LEADER AND NEW LINE

1. Interview with Earl Browder, March 6, 1956.
2. Earl Browder, "Teheran—History's Greatest Turning Point," *The Communist*, XXIII (Jan. 1944), p. 8.
3. Wilson Record, *The Negro and the Communist Party* (Chapel Hill: University of North Carolina Press, 1951), pp. 203-5, 213-14.
4. Roy Hudson, "Labor's Victory Wage Policies," *PA*, XXIV (April 1945), p. 311; Irving Howe and B. J. Widick, *The UAW and Walter Reuther* (New York: Random House, 1949), pp. 114 ff.; Sidney Lens, *Left, Right and Center: Conflicting Forces in American Labor* (Hinsdale, Ill.: Regnery, 1949), pp. 343-5.
5. "Browder Answers Some Questions," *New Masses*, Jan. 2, 1945, p. 17; A. B. Magil, "Letter to a Liberal," *ibid.*, Jan. 9, 1945, pp. 7-8; "The Irresponsibles," *ibid.*, Jan. 2, 1945, p. 8; Magil, "Where Do the Liberals Go from Here?," *ibid.*, Jan. 23, 1945, pp. 9-12; Virginia Gardner, "Copperhead Field Day," *ibid.*, Jan. 2, 1945, pp. 13-14; Earl Browder, "Browder on National Service," *PA*, XXIV (Feb. 1945), pp. 115-16.
6. Earl Browder, "After V-E Day—What Next?," *PA*, XXIV (June 1945), p. 485.
7. Carl Ross, "Universal Military Training," *ibid.*, XXIV (Jan. 1945), pp. 60, 64; Roy Hudson, *op. cit.*, pp. 311-12; John Williamson, "The CPA—Our Most Indispensable Weapon," *PA*, XXIV (Jan. 1945), p. 46.
8. Earl Browder, "A Political Program of American Fascism," *ibid.*, XXIV (Feb. 1945), p. 107; Browder, "The Study of Lenin's Teachings," *ibid.*, XXIV (Jan. 1945), p. 4.
9. The January 1944 letter was published in *ibid.*, XXIV (July 1945), pp. 640-55; Foster quotation from "The Danger of American Imperialism in the Postwar Period," *ibid.*, XXIV (June 1945), pp. 494-5.

10. Eugene Dennis, *The People Against the Trusts* (New York: New Century, Dec. 1946), p. 4; interview with Earl Browder, May 14, 1956.
11. *Wkr*, March 4, 11, 1956; *DW*, June 22, 1956; interview with Earl Browder, March 6, 1956.
12. Eugene Dennis, "Yalta and America's National Unity," *PA*, XXIV (April 1945), pp. 302-10; Dennis, "Postwar Labor-Capital Cooperation," *ibid.*, XXIV (May 1945), pp. 415-22; *DW*, June 16, 1945.
13. "The Present Situation and the Next Tasks" as it was adopted by the national board, June 2, 1945, appears in *DW*, June 4, 1945, and *Wkr*, June 10, 1945; the text as it was approved by the national committee and then further edited is in *DW*, July 2, 1945, and *PA*, XXIV (July 1945), pp. 579-90; the resolution as finally adopted by the convention is in *Wkr*, Aug. 12, 1945.
14. Earl Browder, "On the Question of Revisionism," *DW*, July 24, 1945; W. Z. Foster, "Browder on Revisionism," *ibid.*, July 25, 1945.
15. *Ibid.*, July 3, 1945.
16. *Ibid.*, Jan. 28, 29, Feb. 14, 1946; "On the Expulsion of Earl Browder," *PA*, XXV (March 1946), pp. 215-17.
17. Interview with Earl Browder, May 14, 1956; *Distributors Guide*, Jan. 4–April 27, 1946. The newsletter had sixteen issues. William Browder formally announced the publication's demise in a mimeographed letter to the subscribers, July 8, 1946, over two months after the last issue appeared.
18. Interviews with Earl Browder, March 6, May 14, 1956.
19. *DW*, April 27, 30, 1946; *Wkr*, April 28, 1946.
20. Interviews with Earl Browder, March 6, May 14, 1956.
21. *DW*, April 14, May 24, 1946; "Statement of Comrade Heller to the Executive Committee of his Club," March 25, 1946, mimeographed document in the possession of Philip Jaffe, Stamford, Conn. Heller remained loyal to the party and the U.S.S.R. despite his expulsion. See his letters to the editors of the *DW*, June 25, 1956, and the *National Guardian*, June 4, 1956.
22. See, for example, W. Z. Foster, "On the Expulsion of Browder," *PA*, XXV (April 1946), pp. 339-48; Foster, "One Year of Struggle against Browderism," *ibid.*, XXV (Sept. 1946), pp. 771-7; Alexander Bittelman, "Problems of Peace, Democracy, and National Independence. On Earl Browder's book, 'War or Peace with Russia,'" *ibid.*, XXVI (June 1947), pp. 508-19; Howard Jennings, "Revisionism and American History," *ibid.*, XXV (Aug. 1946), pp. 742-62; Gilbert Green, "The Browderite Conception of History," *ibid.*, XXVIII (Oct. 1949), pp. 65-84; Robert Thompson, *The Path of a Renegade. Why Earl Browder Was Expelled from the Communist Party* (New York: New Century, April 1946).
23. "American Labor Faces May Day," *PA*, XXVII (May 1948), p. 394.
24. "The Convention Unanimously Rejects Browder's Appeal," *ibid.*, XXVII (Sept. 1948), pp. 935-6.
25. *DW*, Sept. 12, 1946; "The Minton-McKenney Flight," *New Masses*, Sept. 24, 1946, pp. 5-8.
26. "Statement of the National Board of the Communist Party on the Recent Expulsions of Vern Smith, Ruth McKenney, Bruce Minton and

William F. Dunne," *PA*, XXV (Nov. 1946), pp. 1011-15, and *DW*, Sept. 30, 1946. See also Jim Allan and George Morris in *DW*, July 7-9, 1947; Oleta O'Conner Yates, "The Struggle against Deviations and Factionalism in San Francisco," *PA*, XXV (Dec. 1946), pp. 1092-1103; and William Weinstone, "The Tactics of the Party in the New York State Elections," *ibid*. (Oct. 1946), pp. 911-13.

27. Interview with Earl Browder, May 14, 1956; *DW*, March 24, 1948; *Towards Socialism*, May 1, 1948, Oct. 10, 1949; *Turning Point*, Nov. 1949, p. 11.

28. Harrison George, *The Crisis in the C.P.U.S.A.* (Los Angeles: privately printed, 1947), p. 14.

29. *Towards Socialism*, May 1, 1949; interview with Earl Browder, May 14, 1956.

30. William Z. Foster, *The Twilight of World Capitalism* (New York: International, 1949), pp. 31-2; see also Foster, "American Imperialism, Leader of World Reaction," *PA*, XXV (Aug. 1946), pp. 686-95; and Foster, "American Imperialism and the War Danger," *ibid*., XXVI (Aug. 1947), pp. 675-87.

31. Eugene Dennis, *Peace or War: The People against the Warmakers!* (New York: New Century, May 1946), p. 7, a speech delivered at a May Day rally in Cleveland, 1946; *DW*, Aug. 8, 1946; W. Z. Foster, "American Imperialism and the War Danger," *loc. cit.*, pp. 675-6; James S. Allen, "The Policy of Anti-Soviet Encirclement," *PA*, XXV (Oct. 1946), pp. 879-92; Alexander Bittelman, "The Anglo-American Bloc," *ibid*., XXV (July 1946), pp. 588-96.

32. William Z. Foster, *The New Europe* (New York: International, 1947), p. 89; see also John Stuart, "The Aim of Soviet Policy," *New Masses*, April 16, 1946, pp. 10-13; Joseph Starobin in *DW*, Feb. 16, 1946; Max Weiss, "Oust the Trotskyites from the Labor and Progressive Movement," *PA*, XXV (Feb. 1946), p. 132; and Weiss, "The Struggle on the Ideological Front," *ibid*., XXV (Sept. 1946), p. 842.

33. William Z. Foster, *The New Europe*, p. 89; see also Joseph Clark in *DW*, Feb. 23, 1947.

34. *DW*, Aug. 7, 1947; also in *PA*, XXVI (May 1947), pp. 391-4.

35. The quotation is from Adam Lapin in *DW*, Nov. 24, 1945.

36. *Ibid.*, Feb. 13, 1946.

37. *Wkr*, Dec. 18, 1949; "Greetings to Joseph Vissarionovich Stalin on His Seventieth Birthday (December 21, 1949)," *PA*, XXIX (Jan. 1950), pp. 1-3; Alexander Bittelman, "Stalin: On His Seventieth Birthday," *ibid*., XXVIII (Dec. 1949), p. 1.

38. Eugene Dennis, "The London Conference," *ibid*., XXIV (Nov. 1945), pp. 965-6.

39. *DW*, March 30, 1946; see also Allen, "The Policy of Anti-Soviet Encirclement," *loc. cit.*, p. 879.

40. "Washington-London Axis," *New Masses*, March 19, 1946, p. 4.

41. *DW*, Oct. 14, 1946.

42. *Ibid.*, Feb. 5, 6, 8, 1947.

43. Joseph Starobin in *ibid.*, July 20, 1946.

44. Joseph Starobin, "The Truman Doctrine," *PA*, XXVI (May 1947), p. 403.

45. William Z. Foster, "Organized Labor and the Marshall Plan," *ibid.,* XXVII (Feb. 1948), p. 99.

46. Milton Howard, "The Ruhr—Can Liberals Support Revival of Reich Trusts?," *DW,* July 18, 1947, reprinted in *Fighting Words: Selections from Twenty-five Years of the Daily Worker* (New York: International Publishers, 1949), pp. 59-61; see also Joseph Clark, "American Labor and the German Working Class," *PA,* XXVII (April 1948), pp. 337-43.

47. James S. Allen, *Marshall Plan—Recovery or War?* (New York: New Century, 1948), p. 51.

48. *Ibid.,* pp. 48-9, 55, 62.

49. Arnold Johnson, "The North Atlantic Pact for Aggression," *PA,* XXVIII (May 1949), p. 16.

50. W. Z. Foster, *Twilight,* pp. 34-5.

51. Rob Fowler Hall, "Stop American Intervention in China!," *PA,* XXIV (Dec. 1945), p. 1065; James S. Allen, "The Policy of Anti-Soviet Encirclement," *loc. cit.,* p. 883; Frederick Vanderbilt Field, "Get Out of China," *New Masses,* Aug. 13, 1946, p. 11; Field, "Doublecross in China," *ibid.,* Sept. 10, 1946, pp. 8-11.

52. *DW,* Nov. 3, 1947.

53. Statement by the party secretariat, "Trieste and the Right of Self-Determination," *ibid.,* May 28, 1946; W. Z. Foster, *The New Europe,* pp. 18, 25-7, 77, 87.

54. *For a Lasting Peace, For a People's Democracy!* (Bucharest), July 15, 1948. This official Cominform newspaper, published in several languages, had appeared from Belgrade until the Tito schism.

CHAPTER TWO: THE PARTY LINE FOR AMERICA

1. Max Weiss, "The Struggle on the Ideological Front," *PA,* XXV (Sept. 1946), pp. 838, 847.

2. Jack Stachel, "Highlights of the Recent Labor Developments," *ibid.,* XXV (July 1946), p. 579.

3. Statement by the party's national board, "The People's Fight for Wages, Jobs, and Security," *ibid.,* XXIV (Nov. 1945), p. 1001; see also Eugene Dennis, "The Progressives Can and Must Unite," *ibid.,* XXVI (March 1947), pp. 195-203, and Hal Simon, "Some Lessons of the Recent Strike Struggle," *ibid.,* XXV (June 1946), pp. 499-500.

4. The editors, "Hit and Run," *New Masses,* Oct. 16, 1945, p. 8; Lewis Merrill, "Memo to Professionals," *ibid.,* Jan. 8, 1946, p. 15; J. B. S. Haldane, "The Party for Professionals," *ibid.,* March 12, 1946, p. 12.

5. Lillian Gates, "The People Fight Back for Rent and Housing," *PA,* XXVI (April 1947), pp. 316-27; Henry Schubart, "The Housing Crisis," *ibid.,* XXV (March 1946), pp. 240-53; Virginia Gardner, "Why You Can't Get a House," *New Masses,* Jan. 15, 1946, pp. 3-5; George Bernstein, "The People's Fight for Progressive Taxation," *PA,* XXIV (Dec. 1945), p. 1108.

6. Jacob Mindel, "Benjamin Franklin," *PA,* XXVI (May 1947), pp. 471-

80; see also Abner Berry, "The Fourth of July, 1947," *ibid.,* XXVI (July 1947), pp. 571-5.

7. Interview with Earl Browder, July 31, 1956.

8. Peter Seeger, "People's Songs and Singers," *New Masses,* July 16, 1947, pp. 7-8.

9. William Z. Foster, "Leninism and Some Practical Problems of the Postwar Period," *PA,* XXV (Feb. 1946), p. 106; Eugene Dennis, *What America Faces* (New York: New Century, 1946), pp. 58-9; Gilbert Green in "Speeches in Discussion on the Draft Resolution of the National Board at the Plenary Meeting of National Committee, C.P.A., June 18-20, 1945," *PA,* XXIV (July 1945), p. 596.

10. Foster, *op. cit.,* p. 106; Henry Winston, "Not Against but with the Stream," *PA,* XXVI (Aug. 1947), p. 737.

11. Eugene Dennis, "Postwar Labor-Capital Cooperation," *PA,* XXIV (May 1945), p. 415.

12. *DW,* Sept. 4, 1946.

13. *Wkr,* April 21, June 2, 1946.

14. *DW,* June 11, 1946.

15. James S. Allen, *Who Owns America?* (New York: New Century, June 1946), pp. 29, 6; Alexander Bittelman, "The Beginning of the Economic Crisis in the United States," *PA,* XXVIII (July 1949), pp. 22-32; Gil Green, "A Few Thoughts on Our Perspectives," *ibid.,* XXVIII (Aug. 1949), pp. 731-8.

16. Arnold Berman, "On Method in Political Economy," *PA,* XXXV (June 1956), pp. 44-57.

17. *Izmenenija vekonomike kapitalizma v itoge vtoroj mirovoj vojny* (Moscow, 1946).

18. *Commercial and Financial Chronicle* (New York), March 2, 1944. The biographical material here is from the introduction to this article.

19. Eugene Varga, "Toward a New Crash?," *New Masses,* Jan. 29, 1946, pp. 3-5, 15.

20. The present writer has based his account of Varga's book upon a manuscript translation by the Russian-born Irene Browder (Mrs. Earl Browder), in the library of Philip Jaffe, Stamford, Conn., and the excellent article by Frederick C. Barghoorn, "The Varga Discussion and Its Significance," *The American Slavic and East European Review,* VII (Oct. 1948), pp. 214-36.

21. Barghoorn, *op. cit.,* pp. 227-31; Leo Gruliow, translator, *Soviet Views on the Post-war World Economy* (Washington: Public Affairs Press, 1948); Joseph P. Lash, "Iron Curtain for the Mind," *The New Republic,* Dec. 27, 1948, pp. 13-15; New York *Times,* Sept. 8, Nov. 28, 30, 1946.

22. A translation of this article appears in *Communist* (Bombay), II (June-July 1949), pp. 108-22, along with another attack on Varga by his chief critic, K. V. Ostrovitjanov.

23. I. Kuzminov, "The Crisis Character of the Economic Development of the U.S. in the Postwar Period," *PA,* XXVIII (May 1949), pp. 54-70, translated from *Bolshevik* (Moscow), Dec. 15, 1948; Eugene Varga, "Against Reformist Tendencies in Works on Imperialism," *PA,* XXVIII (Dec. 1949), pp. 74-86.

24. James S. Allen and Doxey Wilkerson, eds., with an introductory essay by William Z. Foster, *The Economic Crisis and the Cold War* (New York: New Century, 1949). Foster's communication appears on pp. 1-10.

25. Bernard Karsh and Phillips L. Garman, "The Impact of the Political Left," in Milton Derber and Edwin Young, eds., *Labor and the New Deal* (Madison: University of Wisconsin Press, 1947), pp. 103-8.

26. William Z. Foster, "The Wage and Strike Movement," *PA*, XXV (Feb. 1946), pp. 121-9; Alexander Bittelman, "Wages and Prices under Monopoly Capitalism," *ibid.*, XXV (May 1946), pp. 434-6.

27. John Williamson, "For a Mass Party of the Working Class," *ibid.*, XXV (March 1946), p. 227.

28. *Final Proceedings* of the Eighth Constitutional Convention of the Congress of Industrial Organizations, 1946, pp. 111-14.

29. *Time*, Nov. 25, 1946; New York *Times*, Nov. 17, 24, 1946.

30. *DW*, Nov. 19, 29, 1946.

31. William Weinstone, *The Case against David Dubinsky* (New York: New Century, 1946), p. 5; *DW*, April 16, 19, 1946.

32. Carl Winter, "The Face of a Social-Democrat—Walter P. Reuther," *PA*, XXV (May 1946), p. 410.

33. See Max Weiss, "Oust the Trotskyites from the Labor and Progressive Movement," *ibid.*, XXV (Feb. 1946), pp. 130-148.

34. V. J. Jerome, "The Vatican's War on Peace," *ibid.*, XXV (April 1946), p. 325.

35. *Ibid.*, p. 311.

36. (New York: International, 1949), p. 94.

37. Jerome, *op. cit.*, p. 325.

38. W. Z. Foster, *The Twilight of World Capitalism* (New York: International, 1949), pp. 98, 92, 99.

39. William H. Melish, "The Church and Fascism," *New Masses*, March 12, 1946, p. 14.

40. Granville Hicks, *Where We Came Out* (New York: Viking, 1954), pp. 51-8.

41. New York *Times*, Feb. 28, 1943; *The New Yorker*, Feb. 27, 1943; interview with Earl Browder, March 6, 1956.

42. William Z. Foster, "Elements of a People's Cultural Policy," *New Masses*, April 23, 1946, p. 9; see also Foster, *Twilight*, pp. 145-6.

43. Albert Maltz, "What Shall We Ask of Writers?," *New Masses*, Feb. 12, 1946, pp. 19-22.

44. Eugene Dennis, *What America Faces*, p. 61.

45. Howard Fast, "Art and Politics," *New Masses*, Feb. 26, 1946, pp. 6-8; Joseph North, "No Retreat for the Writer," *ibid.*, Feb. 26, 1946, pp. 8-10; Alvah Bessie, "What Is Freedom for Writers," *ibid.*, March 12, 1946, pp. 8-10; John Howard Lawson, "Art Is a Weapon," *ibid.*, March 19, 1946, pp. 18-20.

46. *Wkr*, April 7, 1946; *DW*, April 8, 1946.

47. *DW*, Sept. 11, 1946.

48. Herb Tank, "A Christmas Story," *Fighting Words: Selections from Twenty-five Years of the Daily Worker* (New York: International Publishers, 1949), pp. 225-6.

49. Earl Browder, "On the Negroes and the Right of Self-Determination," *The Communist*, XXIII (Jan. 1944), pp. 83-4.
50. James W. Ford in *DW*, June 25, 1945; Benjamin J. Davis, Jr., in *Wkr*, July 22, 1945; see also letter from Edna Lewis, *DW*, June 29, 1945, and article by William Harrison, *Wkr*, July 15, 1945.
51. *Wkr*, Aug. 12, 1945.
52. Claudia Jones, "On the Right to Self-Determination for the Negro People in the Black Belt," *PA*, XXV (Jan. 1946), pp. 67-77.
53. Max Weiss, *ibid.*, XXV (May 1946), pp. 457-78.
54. Francis Franklin, "The Status of the Negro People in the Black Belt and How to Fight for the Right of Self-Determination," *ibid.*, XXV (May 1946), pp. 438-56.
55. Testimony of Wilkerson in Hearings before the Subcommittee To Investigate the Administration of the Internal Security Act . . . of the Committee on the Judiciary, United States Senate, 83d Cong., 1st sess., March 1953, pp. 637-43. This committee was popularly known at the time as the Jenner Committee.
56. Doxey Wilkerson, "The Negro and the American Nation," *PA*, XXV (July 1946), pp. 652-68.
57. James S. Allen, "The Negro Question," *ibid.*, XXV (Nov. 1946), pp. 1046-56; Allen, "The Negro People As a Nation," *ibid.*, XXV (Dec. 1946), pp. 1132-50; William Z. Foster, "On Self-Determination for the Negro People," *ibid.*, XXV (June 1946), pp. 549-54.
58. "Resolution on the Question of Negro Rights and Self-Determination Adopted by the National Committee, CPUSA, at Its December 3-5, 1946, Meeting," *ibid.*, XXVI (Feb. 1947), pp. 155-8. The resolution appears also in William Z. Foster and others, *The Communist Position on the Negro Question* (New York: New Century, Feb. 1947), pp. 9-13. For another account of the party line on the Negro immediately after the war, see Wilson Record, *The Negro and the Communist Party* (Chapel Hill: University of North Carolina Press, 1951), pp. 235-43.
59. Foster and others, *op. cit.*, p. 14.
60. William Z. Foster, "On the Question of Negro Self-Determination," *PA*, XXVI (Jan. 1947), p. 56.
61. *DW*, Feb. 23, Oct. 22, 1946, May 31, 1948, Oct. 2, 1950; *Wkr*, Feb. 10, 1946.
62. Henry Winston, "Party Tasks among the Negro People," *PA*, XXV (April 1946), pp. 358-9.
63. *Wkr*, July 22, 1945.
64. *Ibid.*, Aug. 12, 1945; Eugene Dennis, *What America Faces*, p. 55; Foster and others, *op. cit.*, p. 13.
65. Henry Winston, "Not Against the Stream," *op. cit.*, p. 734.

CHAPTER THREE: PARTY ORGANIZATION, PARTY STRENGTH, AND PARTY LIFE

1. *DW*, Aug. 24, Sept. 6, 1956.
2. The party constitution appeared in *Wkr*, Aug. 12, 1945.

3. Testimony of Barbara Hartle in Hearings before the Committee on Un-American Activities, House of Representatives, 83d Cong., 2d sess., June 15, 1954, p. 6111; Herbert A. Philbrick, *I Led 3 Lives, Citizen, "Communist," Counterspy* (New York: McGraw-Hill, 1952), p. 227.

4. *Theory and Practice of the Communist Party. First Course. Marxist Study Series #1* (New York: Communist Party, National Education Department, March 1948), pp. 44-5. The first printing of this pamphlet was June 1947.

5. *Ibid.*, pp. 44-5.

6. John Williamson, "New Organizational Problems of the Communist Party," *PA*, XXIV (Dec. 1945), p. 1119; Williamson, "For a Mass Marxist Party of the Working Class!," *ibid.*, XXV (March 1946), p. 224.

7. *DW*, May 22, 1947.

8. "National Committee Names Officers," *PA*, XXV (Sept. 1946), p. 770.

9. *Theory and Practice of the Communist Party*, p. 45.

10. A Bronx Negro Woman Comrade, "Social Relations among Communists," *Party Voice*, IV (June 1956), p. 22.

11. For further discussion of the military aspects of the party's organization see Philip Selznick, *The Organizational Weapon: A Study of Bolshevik Strategy and Tactics* (New York: McGraw-Hill, 1952).

12. New York *Times*, May 16, 1956; interview with Max Gordon, Aug. 29, 1958.

13. See House Committee on Un-American Activities, *The Communist Party of the United States as an Agent of a Foreign Power*, House Report No. 209, 80th Cong., 1st sess., 1947, pp. 32-4, for a list of Comintern representatives in the 1920's and 1930's.

14. *Ibid.*, pp. 33, 55-6.

15. For example, *New Times*, published in English by *Trud* in Moscow and available on some newsstands in the United States, the Cominform newspaper, *For a Lasting Peace, For a People's Democracy!*, the press of the European Communist parties, and reports by foreign correspondents in the general American press.

16. For the Coplon case, see David Dallin, *Soviet Espionage* (New Haven: Yale University Press, 1955), pp. 478-92; for the other cases, see New York *Times*, April 11, 27, Aug. 8, 10, Nov. 16, 1957.

17. Dallin, *op. cit.*, pp. 477-8.

18. J. Edgar Hoover, *Masters of Deceit: The Story of Communism in America and How to Fight It* (New York: Holt, 1958), pp. 293-5.

19. Claire Neikind, "U.S. Communism: Its Underground Plans and Its Secret Business Empire," *The Reporter*, IV (Jan. 23, 1951), p. 5; Bella Dodd, *School of Darkness* (New York: Kenedy, 1954), pp. 209-11. Weiner died in 1954. See Lem Harris, "William Weiner: An American Communist," *PA*, XXXIII (Nov. 1954), pp. 50-5.

20. Interview with Earl Browder, March 6, 1956; New York *Times*, Jan. 9, 1959.

21. *Proceedings*, Seventh General Convention, International Workers Order, June 16-18, 1947 (New York City), pp. 99-100; *Wkr*, June 29, 1947.

22. See speech by Sam Milgrom, I.W.O. general director, in *Proceedings, op. cit.*, pp. 12-51, and the speech by Benjamin Davis, *ibid.*, pp. 52-4.

23. James B. Haley, "Report on Examination of the International Workers Order, Inc., New York, N. Y., by the Insurance Department of the State of New York," mimeographed document in the files of the New York State Insurance Department, New York City, dated Jan. 15, 1950, p. 31.
24. *DW,* April 19, 1946, Jan. 8, 1948.
25. Carl Dorfman, "Training Good Leaders in Harlem," *Contact,* I (Feb. 1947), p. 10. *Contact* was an inner-party monthly magazine published by the party's National Organization and Education Commission in 1947.
26. John Williamson, "Improve and Build Our Communist Press—The Next Step in Party Building," *PA,* XXV (Sept. 1946), p. 826.
27. *DW,* Oct. 1, 1945, Oct. 4, 1949; *Wkr,* Oct. 6, 1946, Oct. 5, 1947, Oct. 10, 1948.
28. Morris Childs, "The Daily Worker—Problems and Prospects," *PA,* XXV (Sept. 1946), p. 834.
29. Interview with Joseph Starobin, Oct. 1, 1956. The emphasis in this account differs from that of Bella Dodd, *op. cit.,* p. 201, but it does not differ as to facts. Miss Dodd was a member of the national committee and abstained, but did not vote against the Gates appointment. Stachel's role in the direction of the paper is indirectly confirmed in Louis Budenz, *This Is My Story* (New York: Whittlesey House, 1947), pp. 216-17, 342.
30. Paul Morrow of the John Brown Club, Harlem, "Rest Day, Press Day," *Contact,* I (Aug. 1947), p. 12; see also *ibid.,* I (June 1947), p. 10.
31. John Williamson, "Improve and Build Our Communist Press," *loc. cit.,* p. 821; "The Plan That Gets the Subs," *Contact,* I (March 1947), p. 4. The *World's* circulation was as follows: 1946, 14,573; 1947, 15,411; 1948, 13,747—*Daily People's World,* Oct. 1, 1946, Oct. 2, 1947, Oct. 4, 1948.
32. *Wkr,* Oct. 13, 1946; Byron Edwards, "Detroit Shop Clubs Come Back to Life," *Contact,* I (Feb. 1947), p. 8.
33. *Wkr,* Feb. 10, 1946.
34. "Give It to 'Em—But Good!," *Contact,* I (July 1947), p. 1.
35. Interview with Earl Browder, March 6, 1956; John Williamson in *Wkr,* July 1, 1945.
36. *Wkr,* July 1, 1945.
37. John Williamson, "The C.P.A.—Our Most Indispensable Weapon," *PA,* XXIV (Jan. 1945), pp. 49, 54.
38. Interview with Earl Browder, March 6, 1956; John Williamson, "New Organizational Problems of the Communist Party," *PA,* XXIV (Dec. 1945), p. 1122.
39. Henry Winston, "Toward a Party of 100,000," *PA,* XXVI (Jan. 1947), p. 67; Winston, "For a Fighting Party Rooted among the Industrial Workers!," *ibid.,* XXVII (Sept. 1948), p. 838.
40. *Wkr,* Jan. 12, 1947; "Give It to 'Em —But Good!," *loc. cit.,* p. 11.
41. *DW,* March 24, 1947; *Wkr,* April 6, 1947.
42. Dorothy Jones, "Money Is Everybody's Job in San Francisco," *Contact,* I (June 1947), p. 14.
43. *DW,* April 18, 20, 1946.

44. John Lavin, "Harlem's Fighting Tenants' Group Gets Results," *Contact*, I (June 1947), p. 1; *DW*, June 2, July 1, 1947; Henry Davis, "God Must Have Sent You," *Contact*, I (April 1947), p. 4.

45. Joe Weiss, "Ulcers for Jim Crow," *Contact*, I (Nov. 1947), p. 3; John Williamson, "What Every Communist Should Do Now," *Wkr*, Jan. 20, 1946, and his article in *ibid.*, Jan. 27, 1946; *DW*, Jan. 31, 1946.

46. *New York County Control Bulletin*, June 1947, as cited in *Digest of the Public Record of Communism in the United States* (New York: Fund for the Republic, 1955), p. 553.

47. *Wkr*, June 23, 1946.

48. John Williamson in *ibid.*, March 24, June 23, 1946.

49. *DW*, Feb. 15, July 16, 1946.

50. An organizational study by the New York State party, dated Nov. 1952, cited in *Handbook on Puerto Rican Work* (New York: Communist Party of New York, 1954), pp. 64, 70.

51. Henry Winston, "Not Against but with the Stream!," *PA*, XXVI (Aug. 1947), p. 735; Winston, "Some Aspects of Party Work," *ibid.*, XXVII (March 1948), p. 247.

52. Jack Kling, at that time the party treasurer, "Dues, Dollars, Drives," *Contact*, I (Sept. 1947), p. 11.

53. Henry Winston, "For a Fighting Party Rooted among the Industrial Workers!," *PA*, XXVII (Sept. 1948), p. 838.

54. *DW*, Nov. 6, 1947; *Daily People's World*, April 17, 1947; *Labor Fact Book 10* (New York: Labor Research Association, 1951), p. 137.

55. New York *Times*, Nov. 18, 1945, Nov. 7, 1947, Nov. 22, 1949; New York *Herald Tribune*, Nov. 14, 1941, Nov. 9, 1943, Nov. 9, 1947; *DW*, Oct. 8, Nov. 5, 7, Dec. 2, 1947, May 19, 1948; *Wkr*, Sept. 7, 1947.

56. All returns are from *DW*, Nov. 7, 1946; *Wkr*, Dec. 15, 1946.

57. Commonwealth of Massachusetts, *Election Statistics, 1946* (Boston, 1947), p. 311; *Wkr*, Nov. 9, 1947.

58. State of California, *Statement of Vote, General Election, November 5, 1946* (Sacramento, 1946), p. 4.

59. State of New Jersey, *Result of the General Election Held November 5th, 1946* (Trenton, 1946); Robert M. Montgomery, Michigan Director of Elections, to the present writer, Lansing, March 23, 1956; *Annual Election Report of the Secretary of State of the State of Indiana, 1946* (Indianapolis, 1946), pp. 1032-5, 1040-1; State of Colorado, *Abstract of Votes Cast, 1946* (Denver, 1946), pp. 11, 16; Arthur Bary, "The Denver Elections," *PA*, XXVI (Jan. 1947), p. 52. Bary grossly exaggerated the Communist vote in this article. Then the Colorado State chairman and later the party's Rocky Mountain district organizer, Bary was expelled from the party in 1956 on a nonideological charge—*DW*, April 20, 1956.

60. Max Kampelman, *The Communist Party vs. the C.I.O.: A Study in Power Politics* (New York: Praeger, 1957); *Communist Domination of Certain Unions*, Report of the Subcommittee on Labor and Labor-Management Relations of the Committee on Labor and Public Welfare, U.S. Senate, 82d Cong., 1st sess., Senate Doc. No. 89, 1951. This important document is a reprint of the reports of the various C.I.O. committees that sat in judgment on the Left unions in 1950.

61. See, for example, *DW* editorials, Nov. 26, 1946, July 22, 29, 1947.
62. Letter from C. R. of Torrance, *Daily People's World,* May 23, 1956.
63. See testimony of Mike Quill in "Congress of Industrial Organizations, Hearings before the Committee to Investigate Charges against International Longshoremen's and Warehousemen's Union," May 17, 1950, pp. 37, 64, 66. This typescript document is a verbatim transcription of the hearings, available at A.F. of L.-C.I.O. headquarters, Washington, D. C.
64. John Williamson, "Trade Union Problems and the Third-Party Movement," *PA,* XXVII (March 1948), p. 236; see also his "New Organizational Problems of the Communist Party," *ibid.,* XXIV (Dec. 1945), pp. 1125-6; and his "Only Militant, United Action Can Defeat the Drive against the Unions!," *ibid.,* XXVII (Sept. 1948), pp. 866-7.
65. *On the Struggle against Revisionism* (New York: National Veterans Committee of the Communist Party, Jan. 1946); *DW,* Jan. 15, 17, March 25, April 18, 1946, May 2, 9, 1947; Carl Reinstein, "New D-Day in Washington," *Contact,* I (July 1947), p. 11; John Williamson, "New Organizational Problems of the Communist Party," *PA,* XXIV (Dec. 1945), pp. 1119-21; Robert Thompson, "Party Policy in the Veterans' Field," *ibid.,* XXV (Jan. 1946), pp. 42-9.
66. *DW,* June 24, 1947.
67. *Ibid.,* June 11, 1947.
68. See letter from "Young Marxist" headlined "GETTING ON WITH NORMAL PEOPLE," *ibid.,* Aug. 14, 1956.
69. Letter from L. D. headlined "IN DEFENSE OF COLUMN ON COMMUNIST CHILDREN," *ibid.,* Sept. 20, 1946.

CHAPTER FOUR: CREATING GIDEON'S ARMY—THE PROGRESSIVE PARTY

1. Adam Lapin, "Truman and the Republicans," *PA,* XXIV (Oct. 1945), pp. 876-81.
2. Eugene Dennis, *America at the Crossroads: Postwar Problems and Communist Policy* (New York: New Century, Dec. 1945), pp. 7-33. Foster's opening remarks appear on pp. 3-6.
3. V. J. Jerome, "Lenin's Method—Guide to the Grasp of Reality," *PA,* XXV (Jan. 1946), p. 16.
4. *DW,* Jan. 16, 1946.
5. Eugene Dennis, *What America Faces: The New War Danger and the Struggle for Peace, Democracy and Economic Security* (New York: New Century, March 1946), pp. 36-8; see also *Wkr,* Feb. 24, 1946.
6. George Blake Charney, "Lessons of the Congressional By-Election in N. Y.," *PA,* XXV (April 1946), p. 363. This account of the election is based on the Charney article and *DW,* Jan. 29, 30, Feb. 1, 3, 5, 7, 16, 19, 20, 1946, and *Wkr,* Feb. 3, 24, 1946.
7. *Proceedings,* Seventh General Convention, International Workers Order, June 16-18, 1947, New York City, pp. 113-15.
8. Dwight Macdonald, *Henry Wallace: The Man and the Myth* (New York: Vanguard, 1948), p. 101.

9. See, for example, Henry A. Wallace, "How To Guarantee the Peace," *New Masses,* June 19, 1945, pp. 6-7; Wallace, *Soviet Asia Mission* (New York: Reynal and Hitchcock, 1946).

10. Interview with Earl Browder, May 14, 1956.

11. Jacques Duclos, "On the Dissolution of the Communist Party of the United States," *PA,* XXIV (July 1945), pp. 670-1, 672.

12. Alexander Bittelman, "How Shall We Fight for Full Employment?," *ibid.,* XXV (Jan. 1946), p. 66; *DW,* May 27, June 12, 13, 1946.

13. New York *Times,* Oct. 28, 1955.

14. Account of the speech is based upon Russell Lord, *The Wallaces of Iowa* (Boston: Houghton Mifflin, 1947), pp. 577-8; Macdonald, *op. cit.,* pp. 107-9; New York *Times,* Sept. 13, 1946.

15. *DW,* Sept. 13, 14, 1946.

16. New York *Times,* Sept. 15, 19, 21, 1946, Oct. 28, 1955; Macdonald, *op. cit.,* p. 111.

17. Eugene Dennis, "Concluding Remarks on the Plenum Discussion," *PA,* XXVI (Jan. 1947), p. 15.

18. *DW,* July 25, 26, 1946.

19. Eugene Dennis, "Defeat the Imperialist Drive toward Fascism and War," *PA,* XXV (Sept. 1946), p. 802; *Wkr,* July 28, 1946.

20. William Z. Foster, "On Building a People's Party," *PA,* XXVI (Feb 1947), pp. 119-20.

21. Eugene Dennis, "Concluding Remarks on the Plenum Discussion," *PA,* XXVI (Aug. 1947), p. 696. Dennis had two speeches published under this title in *PA* in 1947, one in January and one in August.

22. Eugene Dennis, *The People Against the Trusts* (New York: New Century, Dec. 1946), p. 43.

23. For further criticism of "shotgun" anti-Communism see J. Edgar Hoover, "How To Fight Communism," *Newsweek,* June 9, 1947, pp. 30-2; Herbert A. Philbrick, *I Led 3 Lives: Citizen, "Communist," Counterspy* (New York: McGraw-Hill, 1952), pp. 249, 299-301.

24. Interview with Earl Browder, May 14, 1956.

25. *Time,* Sept. 9, 1946, pp. 22-3. Louis F. Budenz has asserted that the idea for I.C.C.A.S.P. was worked out in his office while he was on the *Daily Worker* and that the party assigned Alexander Trachtenberg and Lionel Berman to get the organization formed. Budenz, *Men Without Faces: The Communist Conspiracy in the U.S.A.* (New York: Harper, 1950), pp. 220-1; Budenz, *The Techniques of Communism* (Chicago: Regnery, 1954), pp. 33-4.

26. *DW,* March 11, Nov. 12, 1946; James A. Wechsler, *The Age of Suspicion* (New York: Random House, 1953), pp. 208-9.

27. Quotations from A. B. Magil, "Reveille for Progressives," *New Masses,* Jan. 14, 1947, pp. 3-6, and the preamble text reprinted on p. 6; *DW,* Dec. 30, 1946; New York *Times,* Dec. 30, 1946; New York *Herald Tribune,* Dec. 30, 1946; Harvey V. Brandt, "The Ideological Function of the Progressive Party of 1948," master's thesis in the library of Columbia University, dated 1949; Karl Marx Schmidt, Jr., "The Wallace Progressive Party," doctoral dissertation in Johns Hopkins University Library, dated 1951; Matthew Josephson, *Sidney Hillman:*

Statesman of American Labor (New York: Doubleday, 1952), p. 662n.

28. *DW,* Dec. 9, 1946, Jan. 6, 1947.
29. Wechsler, *op. cit.,* pp. 211-17; New York *Times,* Jan. 5, 1947; Arthur M. Schlesinger, Jr., "The Third Force in America," *ADA World,* Feb. 19, 1948; Robert Bendiner, "Revolt of the Middle," *The Nation,* Jan. 18, 1947; Wechsler, "Liberals without Reds," *The Progressive* (Madison, Wis.), Jan. 13, 1947. The U.D.A. turned over its treasury of $2,200 to A.D.A. See financial report attached to "Minutes of Joint Meeting of Executive and National Political Committees, ADA, July 16, 1947," a mimeographed document lent to me by Professor William E. Leuchtenburg of Columbia University.
30. A. B. Magil, "Progressive Unity or Division," *New Masses,* Jan. 28, 1947, pp. 6-9; see also editorials and columns by Max Gordon in *DW,* Jan. 7, 25, March 3, April 2, 1947.
31. William Z. Foster, "On Building a People's Party," *PA,* XXVI (Feb. 1947), p. 120.
32. *DW,* Aug. 14, 1947.
33. Simon W. Gerson, "Electoral Coalition Problems in New York," *PA,* XXVI (Oct. 1947), pp. 897-8.
34. Merrill Raymond Moremen, "The Independent Progressive Party of California, 1948," master's essay in the library of Stanford University, dated 1950; *Daily People's World,* July 26, 28, Aug. 25, 1947.
35. William Z. Foster, "Concluding Remarks at the Convention," *PA,* XXVII (Sept. 1948), p. 827; see *Daily People's World,* July 26, 29, 30, 1947; *DW,* Aug. 25, 26, 27, Sept. 7, 25, 26, 1947.
36. See Peter Cacchione in *DW,* Aug. 26, 1947, and the account of Marcantonio's speech to the Mine, Mill convention at St. Paul, *ibid.,* Sept. 7, 1947.
37. *Wkr,* Sept. 28, 1947.
38. Eugene Dennis, *The Communists Take a New Look* (New York: New Century, May 1956), pp. 20-1, 31.
39. This account is based upon New York *Times,* Oct. 6, 23, 1947; the resolutions appeared in *ibid.,* Oct. 6, 1947, *DW,* Oct. 7, 1947, and *PA,* XXVI (Nov. 1947), pp. 1051-1056. Two English translations of the Zhdanov speech are in *PA,* XXVI (Dec. 1947), pp. 1090-1111, and in the first issue of *For a Lasting Peace, For a People's Democracy!,* Nov. 10, 1947. I use the *PA* translation, which is much the more literate.
40. *L'Humanité,* Oct. 6-23, 1947.
41. The Communists determined on the third ticket a few days before the Zhdanov speech was published on Oct. 22, but after the publication of the resolutions on Oct. 5. The resolutions were a sufficient basis for action, but it is possible that the American party leadership knew of the Zhdanov speech before its publication.
42. *DW,* Oct. 7, 1947.
43. *Final Proceedings,* Ninth Constitutional Convention of the Congress of Industrial Organizations, Boston, Mass., Oct. 13-17, 1947, pp. 274-93. For the story of how the foreign-policy resolution was written, see Philip Murray's speech, pp. 290-1.

44. "Congress of Industrial Organizations, Hearings before the Committee to Investigate Charges against International Longshoremen's and Ware-housemen's Union," May 17, 1950, pp. 66-7, 98-101, 141-6, a type-script verbatim transcription of the hearings, A.F. of L.-C.I.O. head-quarters, Washington, D. C.

45. *DW*, Oct. 20, 1947.

46. *Ibid.*, Oct. 21, 1947.

47. Interview with Henry Wallace, Nov. 10, 1956.

48. Interview with Michael Straight, Nov. 14, 1956.

49. *DW*, March 27, May 26, 1947.

50. Interview with Michael Straight, Nov. 14, 1956. Straight was with Wallace on much of this trip.

51. *DW*, Sept. 21, 1947.

52. Michael Straight to the present writer, Washington, D. C., Oct. 10, 1956; interview with Straight, Nov. 14, 1956.

53. Interview with Henry Wallace, Nov. 10, 1956.

54. James A. Wechsler, "My Ten Months with Wallace," *The Progressive,* Nov. 1948, p. 5. *The Progressive,* founded by Robert M. La Follette, Sr., before World War I, is not to be confused with the Progressive Party. The magazine opposed Wallace in 1948.

55. Interview with Michael Straight, Nov. 14, 1956.

56. *DW*, May 26, Sept. 23, 1947; *Wkr,* Dec. 14, 1947.

57. New York *Times,* April 18, 1947; *Proceedings,* I.W.O. convention, *op. cit.,* pp. 23, 52-4, 113-5.

58. William H. Miller to Michael Straight, Chicago, June 9, 1947, in files of *The New Republic* correspondence, Washington, D. C. Miller was a New York lawyer and a twice-defeated A.L.P. state assembly candidate whom P.C.A. sent to Chicago to be state executive director.

59. "Minutes of the Joint Meeting of Executive and National Political Committees," A.D.A., July 16, 1947.

60. *DW*, Jan. 14, April 19, 1946; interview with Norman Thomas, Aug. 2, 1956.

61. *DW*, June 7, 1947.

62. *The Progressive,* April 1948, pp. 36-7.

63. *DW*, Sept. 3, Oct. 16, 1947.

64. *Ibid.*, Nov. 3, Dec. 11, 1947; *Wkr,* Dec. 14, 1947.

65. Michael Straight to the present writer, Washington, D. C., Oct. 10, 1956; interview with a former *The New Republic* editor who prefers to remain anonymous, June 1957. Wallace confirmed the stories of the delegations in an interview, Nov. 10, 1956, but it had not occurred to him before that the visits came at opportune times, such as after a Murray denunciation of a new party.

66. *Wkr,* Dec. 21, 1947; interview with Henry Wallace, Nov. 10, 1956.

67. *Wkr,* Oct. 5, 1947; *DW,* Nov. 6, 1947; Gil Green, "The Chicago Elec-tions," *PA,* XXVI (Dec. 1947), pp. 1112-19.

68. Albert E. Kahn to Louis Adamic, Croton-on-Hudson, N.Y., Dec. 12, 1947, carbon copy in files of the N. Y. Insurance Commission, New York City. Kahn used his home address in the letter but it was typed by an I.W.O. stenographer and bore the legend "uopwa #16," the union "bug" of the United Office and Professional Workers of America, Local

16. This "bug" appeared also on mimeographed material from the Communist and Progressive parties. The U.O.P.W.A. was expelled from the C.I.O. in 1950.
69. *DW,* Dec. 19, 29, 1947; *Wkr,* Dec. 28, 1947.
70. P.C.A. press release, dated Dec. 29, 1947, in library of Philip Jaffe, Stamford, Conn.

CHAPTER FIVE: PROFESSIONAL SOLDIERS IN A CAMPAIGN THAT FAILED

1. Editorial and Max Gordon column, *DW,* Dec. 30, 31, 1947.
2. *Wkr,* Jan. 4, 1948.
3. William Z. Foster, "The Political Significance of Keynesism," *PA,* XXVII (Jan. 1948), p. 43; Jacob Mindel, "The Economic Theories of John Maynard Keynes," *ibid.,* XXVII (Feb. 1948), pp. 156-66; Joseph Roland, "The Question of the National Debt," *ibid.,* XXVII (March 1948), pp. 266-78; Albert Prago, "Notes on Keynes' Concepts of Saving and Investment," *ibid.,* XXVII (April 1948), pp. 367-75; Max Weiss, "Wallace's 'Toward World Peace,'" *ibid.,* XXVII (May 1948), pp. 400-11; James S. Allen, "A Comment on State Capitalism and Socialism," *ibid.,* XXVII (May 1948), pp. 426-39; Celeste Strack, "The Keynesian Palace Revolution," *ibid.,* XXVII (May 1948), pp. 448-59; I. G. Bliumin, "The Economic Teachings of Keynes," *ibid.,* XXVII (July 1948), pp. 638-61, translated from a Russian journal; Milton Howard in *DW,* April 7, 1948.
4. (New York: Reynal and Hitchcock.)
5. Weiss, *op. cit.,* pp. 407, 410.
6. New York *Times,* Jan. 2, 1948.
7. "Congress of Industrial Organizations, Hearings before the Committee to Investigate Charges against International Longshoremen's and Warehousemen's Union," May 17, 1950, pp. 72-3, 104-11, A.F. of L.-C.I.O. headquarters, Washington, D. C.
8. *Ibid.,* pp. 71-2.
9. William Z. Foster, "Organized Labor and the Marshall Plan," *PA,* XXVII (Feb. 1948), p. 106; John Williamson, "Trade Union Problems and the Third-Party Movement," *ibid.,* XXVII (March 1948), p. 233. John Gates, then editor of *DW,* told me in an interview, Dec. 6, 1956, that although he never heard Foster express himself in the words Quill quoted, he had heard Foster express himself to the same effect, and Gates did not doubt the truth of Quill's testimony.
10. Eugene Dennis, "The Role of the Communist Party in the Present Situation," *PA,* XXVII (March 1948), p. 213; also see his published pamphlet, *The Third Party and the 1948 Elections* (New York: New Century, March 1948), p. 46.
11. C.I.O., Hearings . . . to Investigate I.L.W.U., *loc. cit.,* p. 72.
12. *DW,* Feb. 18, 1948.
13. Samuel Lubell, *The Future of American Politics* (New York: Anchor, rev. ed., 1956), pp. 91-3.
14. *DW,* April 28, 1947.

15. Alexander Bittelman, "New Tasks and Realignments in the Struggle for the Jewish State in Palestine," *PA*, XXVII (Feb. 1948), pp. 146-55.
16. Michael Straight, "What Happened in the Bronx," *The New Republic*, March 1, 1948, pp. 7-8.
17. Lubell, *op. cit.*, p. 93.
18. *DW*, Feb. 18, 1948; Straight, *op. cit.*, pp. 7-8.
19. *DW*, Feb. 16, 1948.
20. New York *Times*, Feb. 19, 1948.
21. *National Guardian*, Nov. 12, 1956, described Miss Petran as one of the Wallace movement's "chief advisers in foreign affairs." For her ideology, see her article in *ibid.*, June 25, 1956.
22. Frederick Vanderbilt Field, "American Imperialist Policy in the Far East," *PA*, XXV (Nov. 1946), pp. 988-1000.
23. New York *Herald Tribune*, March 22, 1948; for further information about the group, I am indebted to a person who was briefly one of the "researchers" and who prefers to remain anonymous. This informant is not the person who gave the Alsops their story.
24. Hearings before the Committee on Foreign Affairs, House of Representatives, 80th Cong., 2d sess., pp. 1581-1625, quotations from pp. 1582, 1593, 1613-14; Victor Perlo and David Ramsey, "Europe and American Aid," *The New Republic*, Jan. 12, 1948, pp. 15-20; Michael Straight repudiated Perlo and Ramsey in "ERP: Aid to Peace or Road to War?," *ibid.*, March 15, 1948, pp. 11-12; Jennie Lee in London *Tribune*, reprinted in *ADA World*, Aug. 7, 1948.
25. Henry A. Wallace, "Where I Was Wrong," *This Week*, Sept. 7, 1952, p. 7.
26. *Henry A. Wallace: The First Three Months* (Washington: A.D.A. Publicity Department, 1948).
27. Milton Howard in *DW*, March 7, 1948.
28. *Wallace: The First Three Months*.
29. New York *Times*, March 18, 1948; "The People's Victory in Czechoslovakia: An Editorial," *PA*, XXVII (April 1948), p. 296.
30. Interview with Henry Wallace, Nov. 10, 1956.
31. Quoted in Matthew Spinka, *Church in Communist Society: A Study of J. L. Hromádka's Theological Politics (Hartford Seminary Foundation Bulletin, No. 17)* (Hartford, Conn.: Hartford Seminary Foundation, 1954), pp. 28, 30.
32. Spinka, *op. cit.*, p. 21; Joseph L. Hromádka, *Doom and Resurrection* (Richmond, Va.: Madrus House, 1945); New York *Times*, May 30, 1958.
33. Dorothy Thompson, "How I Was Duped by a Communist," *The Saturday Evening Post*, April 16, 1949, pp. 19, 75-85; Hermann Budzislawski, *"Ich war Amerikas berühmteste Frau," Die Weltbühne* (East Berlin), III (Dec. 7, 1948), pp. 1531-4; interview with Mrs. Ida Landau, widow of Overseas News Agency Manager Jacob Landau, Dec. 10, 1956.
34. Interview with Henry Wallace, Nov. 10, 1956; Henry Wallace to the present writer, South Salem, N. Y., Nov. 20, 1956.
35. *Wkr*, May 30, 1948; also in *PA*, XXVII (June 1948), p. 506.

36. William Z. Foster, "The 1948 Elections and the Struggle for Peace," *PA*, XXVII (Sept. 1948), p. 775. This entire issue was devoted to speeches and documents of the 1948 Communist convention. There was no October 1948 issue of *PA*.

37. William E. Leuchtenburg, "Wallace in the Rockies," *The New Leader*, Sept. 25, 1948, p. 5; Merrill Raymond Moremen, "The Independent Progressive Party of California, 1948," master's essay in the library of Stanford University, dated 1950, pp. 110-12.

38. *DW*, July 23, 1948.

39. *ADA World*, Aug. 7, 1948.

40. John Cotton Brown, "The 1948 Progressive Campaign: A Scientific Approach," unpublished doctoral dissertation in the library of the University of Chicago, dated 1949, pp. 122-4, 140-2, 145. This dissertation is important. It is the best account available, since the press was excluded, of the platform committee's deliberations. Brown was one of Tugwell's graduate students. Tugwell arranged for Brown to sit in on the platform committee meetings, technically as his assistant, but actually to take notes for his dissertation. Interview with Rexford Tugwell, April 17, 1956.

41. Brown, *op. cit.*, pp. 156-7; interview with Rexford Tugwell, April 17, 1956.

42. Brown, *op. cit.*, pp. 161-5.

43. *Ibid.*, pp. 168-79.

44. *DW*, March 15, 1948.

45. Interview with Rexford Tugwell, April 17, 1956; Brown, *op. cit.*, pp. 180-7; *Labor Action*, Aug. 2, 1948. *Labor Action*, a Shachtmanite weekly, is a useful source. It is special in its slant, but the Shachtmanites were well informed on Communist tactics.

46. Brown, *op. cit.*, pp. 187-90.

47. Hearings before the Committee on Un-American Activities, House of Representatives, 83d Cong., 2d sess., Jan. 13 and 18, 1954, pp. 3869-70.

48. James A. Wechsler, "The Philadelphia Pay-Off," *The Progressive*, Sept. 1948, p. 9; *Labor Action*, Aug. 2, 1948.

49. Wechsler, *op. cit.*, pp. 9-10; *Labor Action*, Aug. 2, 1948; James A. Wechsler, *The Age of Suspicion* (New York: Random House, 1953), p. 231.

50. Brown, *op. cit.*, pp. 194-5; *Labor Action*, Aug. 2, 1948; Wechsler, *Age of Suspicion*, p. 232; *Daily People's World*, July 26, 1948; interview with C. B. Baldwin, Nov. 15, 1955.

51. Brown, *op. cit.*, pp. 239-40; *Labor Action*, Aug. 2, 1948; "Report by Steve Muller of Students for Democratic Action on the Founding Convention of the Young Progressives of America," appendix I of *Henry A. Wallace: The Last Seven Months of his Presidential Campaign* (Washington: ADA Publicity Department, 1948). Quotations from this appendix.

52. Interview with Rexford Tugwell, April 17, 1956; *Wallace: The Last Seven Months;* Henry A. Wallace to Herbert A. Philbrick, South Salem, N. Y., Feb. 1, 1952, printed in New York *Herald Tribune*, Feb. 4, 1952.

53. Leuchtenburg, *op. cit.;* Moremen, *op. cit.*, pp. 133-4; Baltimore *Sun*

story as quoted in New York *Herald Tribune* editorial, Aug. 23, 1948; interview with Rexford Tugwell, April 17, 1956.

54. John Williamson, "Only Militant, United Action Can Defeat the Drive against the Unions!," *PA*, XXVII (Sept. 1948), p. 864; William Z. Foster, "Concluding Remarks at the Convention," *ibid.*, XXVII (Sept. 1948), pp. 824-5.

55. *DW*, Oct. 20, 1948; I. F. Stone, "Confessions of a Dupe: Why I Was for Wallace," *The Truman Era* (New York: Monthly Review Press, 1953), pp. 67-8. The column originally appeared Aug. 25, 1948.

56. Interview with Henry Wallace, Nov. 10, 1956; Henry Wallace to the present writer, South Salem, N. Y., Nov. 20, 1956.

57. Joseph and Stewart Alsop in New York *Herald Tribune*, March 22, 1948; A.D.A., *Bat Boy for Reaction*, a small pamphlet, 1948; Moremen, *op. cit.*, pp. 187, 216-17, 242.

58. Rexford G. Tugwell, "Progressives and the Presidency," *The Progressive*, April 1949, pp. 5-6; New York *Times*, Sept. 7, 1948.

59. *Statistical Abstract of the United States* (Washington: Government Printing Office, 74th ed., 1953), p. 321. The *World Almanac* for 1953 gave Wallace 1,137,992 votes. State figures cited here are from the *World Almanac* unless otherwise indicated.

60. Mimeographed text of Wallace's address at a dinner of the National Wallace for President Committee, New York City, April 19, 1948, in library of Philip Jaffe, Stamford, Conn.

61. State of California, *Statement of Vote, General Election, Nov. 2, 1948* (Sacramento, 1948), p. 5.

62. Lubell, *op. cit.*, p. 219. Lubell estimated (p. 220) that three-fourths of the Wallace voters were Negro or Jewish.

63. Max Gordon in *DW*, Nov. 10, 1948; George Blake [Charney] and Al Terestman, "The People Win with Marcantonio," *PA*, XXVIII (Jan. 1949), pp. 85-94; James W. Ford, "The 1948 Elections in Bedford-Stuyvesant," *ibid.*, XXVIII (Feb. 1949), pp. 70-81.

64. See, for example, M. Marinen, "Election Struggle and Onslaught of Reaction in U.S.," *For a Lasting Peace, For a People's Democracy!*, Sept. 1, 1948; and Jan Marek, "Political Notes," *ibid.*, Nov. 15, 1948.

65. *DW*, April 14, 1948.

66. New York State Committee, "The Election Results in New York," *PA*, XXVII (Dec. 1948), p. 1082.

67. William Z. Foster, *The Twilight of World Capitalism* (New York: International, 1949), pp. 124-6.

CHAPTER SIX: THE PARTY AND ANTI-COMMUNISM

1. Eric F. Goldman, *The Crucial Decade: America, 1945-1955* (New York: Knopf, 1956), pp. 116-17.

2. For further details see Hadley Cantril, ed., *Public Opinion, 1935-1946* (Princeton: Princeton University Press, 1951), pp. 130-1; Samuel A. Stouffer, *Communism, Conformity and Civil Liberties: A Cross-Section of the Nation Speaks Its Mind* (Garden City: Doubleday, 1955), pp. 43-4.

3. William Z. Foster, "Keynote Message of Greetings to the Plenum," *PA*, XXIX (May 1950), p. 11; Michael Bianca, "How To Fight McCarthyism," *ibid.*, XXX (Oct. 1951), p. 23.

4. William Weinstone, "The Fight to Repeal the Legislative Blueprint for Fascism," *ibid.*, XXIX (Oct. 1950), pp. 35, 43; see also Alexander Bittelman, "Who Are the Conspirators?," *ibid.*, XXX (July 1951), p. 21; Gus Hall, "The Present Situation and the Next Tasks," *ibid.*, XXIX (Oct. 1950), p. 7; William Z. Foster, in "Is the United States in the Early Stages of Fascism?," *ibid.*, XXXIII (Nov. 1954), pp. 4-21, concluded that at that time, while the Senate was in the process of censuring McCarthy, fascism was a growing danger.

5. Foster in *Wkr*, Jan. 15, 1950; Weinstone, *op. cit.*, p. 38.

6. Abner Berry in *DW*, Oct. 2, 1950; James W. Ford, "The Communist Party: Champion Fighter for Negro Rights," *PA*, XXVIII (June 1949), p. 48.

7. Weinstone, *op. cit.*, p. 40.

8. James Rorty and Moshe Decter, *McCarthy and the Communists* (Boston: Beacon, 1954), p. 150; *DW*, Aug. 15, 1946, and Rob F. Hall, "The People Won't Mourn La Follette," *ibid.*, Aug. 19, 1946.

9. "America's Hour of Peril—Unite! Save Democracy and Peace!," *PA*, XXX (July 1951), pp. 1-8.

10. Editorial, "The Trap against Unity," *DW*, July 14, 1949.

11. *DW*, Jan. 12, 1946.

12. *Ibid.*, Feb. 1, 1946.

13. *Ibid.*, Aug. 5, 1946.

14. *Digest of the Public Record of Communism in the United States* (New York: Fund for the Republic, 1955), pp. 194-6.

15. New York *Times*, Jan. 18, 19, 1949.

16. C. Herman Pritchett, *Civil Liberties and the Vinson Court* (Chicago: University of Chicago Press, 1954), p. 233.

17. *Ibid.*, pp. 233-6, 280 note 7

18. *DW*, Feb. 25, 1949.

19. *Wkr*, Jan. 30, 1949; *DW*, March 22, 1949.

20. *Wkr*, Sept. 19, 1948; Elizabeth Gurley Flynn in *ibid.*, April 3, 1949.

21. See his introduction to George Marion, *The Communist Trial: An American Crossroads* (New York: Fairplay Publishers, 2d ed., 1950).

22. For a critical discussion of the constitutional issues involved in the decision see Pritchett, *op. cit.*, pp. 71-7.

23. *DW*, March 7, 1952.

24. Subcommittee . . . of the Committee on the Judiciary, United States Senate, 84th Cong., 1st sess., Committee Print, *The Communist Party of the United States of America . . . A Handbook for Americans* (Washington, D. C., 1955), p. 34.

25. Foster, "Keynote Message of Greetings to the Plenum," *PA*, XXIX (May 1950), pp. 10-11; see also *DW*, March 21, 1950.

26. Committee on Un-American Activities, House of Representatives, 81st Cong., 2d sess., House Report No. 1954, *Review of the Scientific and Cultural Conference for World Peace Arranged by the National Council of the Arts, Sciences, and Professions and Held in New York City, March 25, 26, and 27, 1949.* This report has utility, but it is a typical

report of this committee in that its emphasis was on lists of names rather than analysis.

27. *DW*, Oct. 3, Dec. 5, 6, 1949.

28. *Ibid.*, Nov. 21, 1950, Nov. 14, 15, 1951; *Wkr*, Sept. 11, 1949; *For a Lasting Peace, For a People's Democracy!*, March 31, Nov. 24, 1950.

29. *DW*, May 18, 21, 23, June 14, 1950; *Wkr*, June 11, Oct. 1, 1950; *Labor Fact Book 10* (New York: Labor Research Association, 1951), p. 26.

30. *Wkr*, May 18, 1947, March 28, 1948; *DW*, Sept. 29, Oct. 11, 14, 19, 30, 1947.

31. Dyson Carter, "New Ways of Killing," *New Masses*, Sept. 3, 1946; *DW*, March 19, 20, April 9, 1952

32. Frederick Vanderbilt Field, "Wall Street's Aggression in Korea and the Struggle for Peace," *PA*, XXIX (Sept. 1950), p. 15; for secretariat statement, "Halt Wall Street Aggression in Asia!," *ibid.*, XXIX (Aug. 1950), p. 2; *For a Lasting Peace, For a People's Democracy!*, Sept. 22, 1950.

33. *DW*, June 26, 1950.

34. Betty Gannett, "Wall Street's War against the Korean People," *PA*, XXIX (Aug. 1950), p. 7; Field, *op. cit.*, p. 26.

35. Interview with Joseph Starobin, Oct. 1, 1956; Joseph Starobin, "A Communication," *PA*, XXXVI (Jan. 1957), pp. 60-2.

36. Eugene Dennis, "The MacArthur Ouster: A Letter to the Members of the Communist Party, U.S.A.," *PA*, XXX (May 1951), pp. 3, 6. Italics in original.

37. *Wkr*, July 13, 1952.

38. *DW*, July 28, 30, 1953.

39. John Swift, "Some Problems of Work in Right-Led Unions, II," *PA*, XXXI (May 1952), p. 32. Not to be confused with the "John Swift" articles of 1953. "John Swift" was clearly a pen name.

40. *DW*, June 29, 1950.

41. Joseph Rockman, "Tasks in Broadening the Fight for Peace," *PA*, XXXI (June 1952), pp. 15-29. "Rockman"—another obvious pen name —pointed out that sectarianism hurt the party cause in the peace movement. In his sharpest sentence he wrote that "We place an impossible task for ourselves if we . . . insist that the Negro people fight for peace under the leadership of the Left or not at all" (p. 29).

42. Gus Hall, "Through United Front Struggle to Peace," *ibid.*, XXIX (May 1950), p. 37; Hall, "The Present Situation and Next Tasks," *ibid.*, XXIX (Oct. 1950), p. 21. Each of these articles was a report to the national committee.

43. Wallace speech at second national convention of Progressive Party, Ashland Auditorium, Chicago, Feb. 24, 1950, Progressive Party press release in library of Philip Jaffe, Stamford, Conn.

44. *DW*, March 30, 1950; see also William Z. Foster in *ibid.*, March 3, 1950.

45. *Ibid.*, July 30, 1957, for denunciation of Walter Wallace.

46. "Minutes of the Meetings of the Executive Committee of the Progressive Party on the Situation in Korea and China, July 6, 8, 9, 10, 11, 1950," mimeographed documents in library of Philip Jaffe, Stamford, Conn.

47. New York *Times,* April 26, Aug. 18, 19, 21, 1957, Jan. 3, March 16, 1958.
48. "Minutes," July 10, 11, 1950. See note 46.
49. "Minutes of Special Meeting of National Committee, Progressive Party, 13 Astor Place, New York City, July 15, 1950"; Wallace's press release of same date. Both in library of Philip Jaffe, Stamford, Conn. See also Wallace's brief account of his leaving the Progressives in "Henry Wallace Tells of His Political Odyssey," *Life,* May 14, 1956, pp. 183-4.
50. *Daily People's World,* Oct. 10, 1950.
51. In January 1952, for example, she appeared on a program with *DW* staff writers Joseph North and John Pittman to increase the paper's circulation—*DW,* Jan. 18, 1952.
52. Richard M. Scammon, comp. and ed., *America Votes: A Handbook of Contemporary Election Statistics* (New York: Macmillan, 1956), pp. 33, 259, 421-2.
53. Max M. Kampelman, *The Communist Party vs. the C.I.O.: A Study in Power Politics* (New York: Praeger, 1957), pp. 157-8.
54. *Wkr,* Dec. 19, 1948.
55. John Williamson, "Two Conventions of Labor: The Situation in the Trade Union Movement," *PA,* XXVIII (Jan. 1949), p. 35.
56. *Proceedings,* Tenth Constitutional Convention, Congress of Industrial Organizations, 1948, pp. 281-2.
57. *Wkr,* Jan. 9, 1949.
58. *Proceedings,* Eleventh Constitutional Convention, Congress of Industrial Organizations, 1949, pp. 272-3. For background on the Quill union and its peculiar combination of Irish Catholic membership and Left leadership', see James J. McGinley, S.J., *Labor Relations in the New York Rapid Transit Systems, 1904-1944* (New York: King's Crown, 1949), pp. 316-25.
59. *DW,* May 20, 1949. For background on W.F.T.U., see Kampelman, *op. cit.,* pp. 233-45.
60. *Proceedings,* Fourteenth Convention, United Electrical, Radio, and Machine Workers of America (U.E.), Cleveland, 1949, pp. 205-25.
61. *Proceedings,* Eleventh Constitutional Convention, C.I.O., 1949, pp. 240, 281, 288, 302, 305.
62. Kampelman, *op. cit.,* pp. 167-222.
63. Even the *DW*'s labor columnist, George Morris, saw U.E.'s situation as hopeless. See *DW,* Sept. 28, 1956.
64. Vernon Jensen, *Nonferrous Metal Industry Unionism, 1932-1954* (Ithaca: Cornell University Press, 1954), p. 305.
65. *Testimony of the Director on February 3 and February 7, 1950 . . . on the 1951 Appropriation Estimates for the Federal Bureau of Investigation,* Department of Justice, 1950; *Digest of the Public Record,* p. 550.
66. *DW,* Oct. 4, 1950, Oct. 2, 1953; *Wkr,* Oct. 8, 1950, Oct. 11, 1953.
67. *DW,* May 25, 1950.
68. *Ibid.,* April 6, 9, 1951.
69. *National Guardian,* Aug. 15, 1951.
70. Committee on Un-American Activities, House of Representatives,

Trial by Treason: The National Committee to Secure Justice for the Rosenbergs and Morton Sobell (Washington: Government Printing Office, 1956), pp. 13, 15-24.

71. For Communist denials of anti-Semitism, see Klement Gottwald, "The Prague Treason Trials," *PA*, XXXII (Feb. 1953), pp. 46-50; and Samuel Rosen, "Zionism and Bourgeois Nationalism," *ibid.*, XXXII (June 1953), pp. 38-48, and (July 1953), pp. 57-65; Jacques Duclos quotation from Robert B. Glynn, *"L'Affaire Rosenberg* in France," *Political Science Quarterly*, LXX (Sept. 1955), p. 509.

72. Glynn, *op. cit.*, pp. 514-15.

73. Irwin Edelman, "An Open Letter to the Rosenberg and Sobell Friends," undated one-page mimeographed flier. Internal evidence indicates the "letter" was written between June 19 and July 16, 1953. For this document I am indebted to Mr. Edelman.

74. Edelman, "The Rosenberg Case: Some Observations," *Contemporary Issues* (London), V (Oct.-Nov. 1954), p. 319. This article indicates that Edelman had some highly unusual ideas, to say the least. In the article, he argued that Bloch, the Communists, and the F.B.I. conspired to execute the Rosenbergs. Nevertheless, he did suggest a legal argument which a Supreme Court justice thought warranted consideration.

75. S. Andhil Fineberg, *The Rosenberg Case: Fact and Fiction* (New York: Oceana, 1953), pp. 110-13; Edelman, "The Rosenberg Case," *loc. cit.*, p. 319.

76. Communist Party national committee, "The Rosenbergs: Heroes of Democracy," *PA*, XXXII (July 1953), pp. 2-3.

77. *DW*, Feb. 16, 25, June 22, 1953; Edith Segal, *Give Us Your Hand! Poems and Songs for Ethel and Julius Rosenberg in the Death House at Sing Sing* (New York: National Committee to Secure Justice in the Rosenberg Case, 1953).

CHAPTER SEVEN: THE PARTY'S INTERNAL SECURITY

1. Edmund Wilson, *The American Earthquake: A Documentary of the Twenties and Thirties* (New York: Doubleday, 1958), p. 212.

2. *Testimony of the Director on February 3 and February 7, 1950 . . . on the 1951 Appropriation Estimates for the Federal Bureau of Investigation*, Department of Justice, 1950, pp. 142, 145. How many F.B.I. agents were in the party and how highly they were placed is a matter known only to the F.B.I. Earl Browder said in an interview, May 14, 1956, that he had always operated on the assumption there was at least one agent in the national office, but that he never suspected any of the leaders who were prominent after the war. John Gates in an interview, Dec. 6, 1956, said he did not suspect any of the top leaders of the party.

3. Interview with John Gates, Dec. 6, 1956; for verification of the small club organization, see Lee Amistad, "For a Marxist-Leninist Policy on Party Organization," *Party Voice*, I (March 1953), supplement, pp. 8, 12.

4. Amistad, *op. cit.*, p. 8.
5. Testimony of John Lautner in *United States* v. *Kuzma,* #11,655 (3d Circuit, 1954), Record on Appeal, transcript, pp. 1689-1701.
6. "The Status of Our Party," *Party Voice,* IV (July 1956), p. 4.
7. *DW,* Aug. 31, 1950; interview with Joseph Starobin, Oct. 1, 1956; interview with John Gates, Dec. 6, 1956.
8. See J. Edgar Hoover, *Masters of Deceit: The Story of Communism in America and How To Fight It* (New York: Holt, 1958), pp. 273-89. This account emphasizes underground methods and the difficulty of "shadowing" people using such methods.
9. Alex Parker, *Organizing the Party for Victory over Reaction. Report Delivered at the National Conference of the Communist Party* (New York: New Century, Dec. 1953), pp. 11-12.
10. *Ibid.,* pp. 15-17; interview with Max Gordon, Aug. 29, 1958.
11. Peggy Dennis, "Comradely Yours," *Wkr,* June 11, 1950.
12. See "The Status of Our Party," *loc. cit.,* p. 4.
13. A letter to the editor of *DW,* June 11, 1956, asserted that "thousands" were expelled, including whole clubs in some cases.
14. B. S., "Party Democracy and Dissent," *Party Voice,* IV (June 1956), p. 3.
15. *D.W.,* Feb. 23, 24, March 30, April 8, 1949.
16. *Ibid.,* June 8, 1956.
17. *U.S.* v. *Kuzma,* transcript, pp. 1398-1408.
18. Zoltan Deak, "The Tito-Rajk Conspiracy against the Camp of Peace and Democracy," *PA,* XXVIII (Dec. 1949), pp. 87-94.
19. This account is based upon Lautner's testimony in *Brownell* v. *Communist Party of the United States,* Subversive Activities Control Board Hearings, 1952, pp. 9259-61, 9294-9309; *DW,* Jan. 17, 1950; and *U.S.* v. *Kuzma,* transcript, p. 1749. Professor Herbert Packer of Stanford University Law School, who is making a study of government witnesses and counsel in Communist cases, reports that Lautner was one of the most consistent of government witnesses in his testimony.
20. B. S., *op. cit.,* p. 3.
21. William Z. Foster, "Keynote Message of Greetings to the Plenum," *PA,* XXIX (May 1950), p. 13.
22. *DW,* April 3, 1950.
23. Eugene Dennis, "Let Us March Forward with Supreme Confidence," *PA,* XXIX (July 1950), p. 14.
24. Interview with Max Gordon, Aug. 29, 1958.
25. Henry Winston, "Building the Party—Key to Building the United Front of Struggle," *ibid.,* XXIX (May 1950), p. 80; *Wkr,* June 11, 1950.
26. George Siskind and Harry Martel, "Psychoanalysis: Ideological Instrument of Imperialism," *PA,* XXIX (Dec. 1950), pp. 61-74, quotations from 61-2, 73-4.
27. *Scientific Session on the Physiological Teachings of Academician I. P. Pavlov* (Moscow, 1951).
28. Alvin S. Herwitz, "Pavlov's Teachings in Psychology and Physiology," *PA,* XXXI (Sept. 1952), pp. 57-64; see also Joseph C. Clayton, "Some Problems in the Struggle Against Psychoanalysis," *ibid.,* XXXIII (April 1954), pp. 40-52.

29. Howard Fast, *The Naked God: The Writer and the Communist Party* (New York: Praeger, 1957), pp. 148-53.
30. See *We Charge Genocide: The Historic Petition to the United Nations for Relief from a Crime of the United States Government against the Negro People* (New York: Civil Rights Congress, 1951).
31. Richard O. Boyer, *Pettis Perry: The Story of a Working Class Leader* (New York: Self Defense Committee of the 17 Smith Act Victims, April 1952).
32. *Brownell* v. *Communist Party,* S.A.C.B. Hearings, p. 9314.
33. Robert Thompson, "Strengthen the Struggle against White Chauvinism," *PA,* XXVIII (June 1949), p. 18
34. *DW,* May 25, 1949, April 24, 1950; I. C., "Left Errors in Trade Union and Negro Work," *Party Voice,* IV (June 1956), p. 6.
35. *DW,* July 7, 1949; I. C., *op. cit.,* p. 6.
36. Pettis Perry, "Press Forward the Struggle against White Chauvinism," *PA,* XXIX (May 1950), p. 144; "A Statement on Florida Vacations," *DW,* April 19, 1951; interview with John Gates, Dec. 6, 1956.
37. *DW,* Aug. 27, 1951. Party headquarters subsequently moved to the Jefferson School building at Sixth Avenue and Sixteenth Street.
38. *Wkr,* June 18, 1950.
39. Fast, *op. cit.,* pp. 144-5; William Z. Foster, "Left Sectarianism in the Fight for Negro Rights and Against White Chauvinism," *PA,* XXXII (July 1953), p. 28.
40. Foster, "Left Sectarianism," *loc. cit.,* pp. 17-32, quotation from p. 24.
41. Amistad, *op. cit.,* p. 2.
42. "The Status of Our Party," *loc. cit.,* p. 4.
43. Amistad, *op. cit.,* pp. 2-3; see also Parker, *op. cit.,* pp. 31-42.

CHAPTER EIGHT: SLOW THAW IN THE COLD WAR

1. The draft resolution, under the stated authorship of the party's national committee but obviously the work of a smaller body, appeared in *PA,* XXXI (Dec. 1952), pp. 4-13; John Swift, "The Struggle for a Mass Policy," *ibid.,* XXXII (Feb. 1953), p. 17; "Readers Guide to *Economic Problems of Socialism in the U.S.S.R.* by Joseph Stalin," *ibid.,* XXXII (June 1953), pp. 66-96.
2. Draft resolution, *loc. cit.,* pp. 10-11; National Committee, C.P.U.S.A., "Resolution on the Situation Growing out of the Presidential Elections (Final Text)," *PA,* XXXII (July 1953), p. 12.
3. William Z. Foster, "Left Sectarianism in the Fight for Negro Rights and Against White Chauvinism," *ibid.,* XXXII (July 1953), pp. 17-32; Foster, "The 34th Anniversary of the Communist Party," *ibid.,* XXXII (Sept. 1953), p. 8.
4. As an article in *ibid.,* XXXIII (April 1954), pp. 4-19; as a pamphlet, with the same title, published by New Century the same month. The party hoped the pamphlet would have a circulation of a million, but it achieved only 650,000.
5. *Draft Program of the Communist Party, loc. cit.,* pp. 17-18.

6. Committee on Program Drafting, "A Letter on the Draft Program," *ibid.,* XXXIII (April 1954), pp. 20-7.
7. Betty Gannett, "The Communist Program—A Vital Document," *ibid.,* XXXIII (Sept. 1954), p. 48; for the final version see *ibid.,* XXXIII (Oct. 1954), pp. 1-20, and *DW,* Aug. 9, 1954.
8. Draft resolution, *loc. cit.,* p. 11.
9. See, for example, "A Letter on the Draft Program," *op. cit.,* p. 21; Pettis Perry, "The November Elections and the Struggle for Jobs, Peace, Equal Rights, and Democracy," *PA,* XXXIII (Sept. 1954), p. 15; Andrew Stevens, "Perspectives for Political Action," *ibid.,* XXXII Oct. 1953), p. 5; William Z. Foster, "Perspectives for a Labor-Farmer Party in the U.S.," *ibid.,* XXXIV (Feb. 1955), p. 15.
10. *DW,* April 22, 1955.
11. A.L.P. news release, Nov. 4, 1953, in library of Philip Jaffe, Stamford, Conn.
12. *National Guardian,* Nov. 7, 1955.
13. Alex H. Kendrick and Jerome Golden, "Lessons of the Struggle Against Opportunism in District 65," *PA,* XXXII (June 1953), pp. 26-37.
14. *Ibid.,* XXXII (July 1953), p. 4.
15. John Swift, "The Left and the Struggle for Labor Unity, I," *ibid.,* XXXII (July 1953), pp. 33-42, quotations from pp. 36, 41, 42. Italics in original.
16. John Swift, "The Left-Led Unions and Labor Unity, II," *ibid.,* XXXII (Nov. 1953), p. 64.
17. V. I. Lenin, "Preface to 'Letters to Sorge,'" *ibid.,* XXXII (Nov. 1953), p. 64.
18. V. J. Jerome, "May Day—1954; What Faces Us?," *ibid.,* XXXIII (May 1954), p. 7. Italics in original.
19. See George Morris, "The AFL-CIO Merger," *ibid.,* XXXIV (March 1955), pp. 30-40, and his columns in *DW,* Jan. 19, 21, 1955; see also editorial in *DW,* Dec. 29, 1954, and William Z. Foster in *ibid.,* Dec. 31, 1954, Dec. 1, 1955.
20. William Z. Foster, "Notes on the Struggle for Negro Rights," *PA,* XXXIV (May 1955), p. 31.
21. Hugh Bradley, "The N.A.A.C.P. Convention," *ibid.,* XXXII (Nov. 1953), pp. 57-9; Pettis Perry, "The Third Annual Convention of the National Negro Labor Council," *ibid.,* XXXIII (Feb. 1954), pp. 1-8.
22. Pettis Perry, "The Negro People in the Struggle Against McCarthyism (Draft-Program Discussion)," *ibid.,* XXXIII (May 1954), pp. 40-2.
23. Gannett, *op. cit.,* p. 59.
24. Frederick C. Hastings and Charles P. Mann, "For a Mass Policy in Negro Freedom's Cause," *PA,* XXXIV (March 1955), pp. 11-12; William Z. Foster, "Notes on the Struggle for Negro Rights," *loc. cit.,* pp. 40-41.
25. Doxey Wilkerson, "The 46th Annual Convention of the NAACP," *ibid.,* XXXIV (Aug. 1955), pp. 7-10.
26. Benjamin J. Davis, *The Negro People on the March* (New York: New Century, Aug. 1956), p. 30.
27. Betty Gannett, *The Communist Program and the Struggle for Jobs,*

Peace, Equal Rights, and Democracy (New York: New Century, 1954), pp. 29-30. Italics in original.
28. "The American Way to Jobs, Peace, Equal Rights and Democracy: Program of the Communist Party," *PA,* XXXIII (Oct. 1954), p. 20.
29. William Z. Foster, "Reply to a Priest's Letter," *ibid.,* XXXIII (Oct. 1954), pp. 45-8.
30. All from the May 1955 issue.
31. "The American Way," *loc. cit.,* p. 19.
32. Andrew Montgomery, "Our National Pride," *Party Voice,* II (July-Aug. 1954), pp. 8-9.
33. V. J. Jerome and Betty Gannett, "Patriotism and National Pride," *ibid.,* II (Sept.-Oct. 1954), pp. 21-7; published also in *PA,* XXXIII (Oct. 1954), pp. 28-35. Italics in original.
34. James S. Allen, "Democratic Revival and the Marxists," *Masses & Mainstream,* Oct. 1955, pp. 1-11, quotations from pp. 9, 11; see also Herbert Aptheker, "Patriotism and the Nation," *PA,* XXXIV (July 1955), pp. 22-33.
35. *DW,* Sept. 20, Dec. 1, 7, 8, 1955.
36. *Ibid.,* June 29, 1953.
37. *Ibid.,* July 13, 1953.
38. Nemmy Sparks, "The Yugoslav-Soviet Rapprochement," *PA,* XXXIV (Dec. 1955), pp. 27-34.
39. *Daily People's World,* Nov. 4, 16, 1955.

CHAPTER NINE: TARNISHED HEROES: STALIN AND FOSTER

1. New York *Times,* Feb. 15, 1956; *For a Lasting Peace, For a People's Democracy!,* Feb. 17, 1956; N. S. Khrushchev, "Report to the XXth Congress, CPSU," *PA,* XXXV (March 1956), pp. 51-64.
2. *DW,* Feb. 16, 17, 1956; *Wkr,* Feb. 19, 1956.
3. *DW,* Feb. 20, 1956.
4. *Wkr,* March 4, 1956.
5. *DW,* March 13, 1956.
6. *Wkr,* March 18, 1956.
7. *DW,* March 16, 1956.
8. New York *Times,* March 16, 1956; New York *Post,* March 16, 1956.
9. *New Times* (Moscow), March 1, 1956, special supplement, pp. 10-11.
10. As quoted in New York *Times,* March 28, 1956.
11. *Ibid.,* March 30, April 7, 1956.
12. *Ibid.,* March 24, 1956; see also account in *DW,* March 26, 1956.
13. *DW,* March 27, 1956.
14. *Ibid.,* March 26, 1956.
15. Important Communists admitted there were these divisions in the party. See Charney speech cited in note 12.
16. *Ibid.,* April 2, 1956.
17. See editorial in *ibid.,* March 19, 1956, and story under headline "WHAT WILL THE WORKER SAY?," *Wkr,* March 25, 1956.
18. *DW,* March 28, 1956; New York *Times,* March 28, 1956.
19. New York *Post,* March 28, 1956; *Time,* April 9, 1956, p. 35.

20. Howard Fast, *The Naked God: The Writer and the Communist Party* (New York: Praeger, 1957), pp. 50-1; interview with John Gates, Dec. 6, 1956.

21. New York *Times*, March 30, April 3, 1956.

22. *DW*, May 25, 1956.

23. *Time*, April 9, 1956, pp. 98, 100.

24. New York *Post*, March 28, 1956; New York *Times*, March 31, 1956.

25. John Gates, *Evolution of an American Communist* (New York: privately printed, 1958); interviews with Gates, Dec. 6, 1956, July 30, 1957. *Evolution* is a pamphlet version of the articles Gates wrote for the New York *Post*, Jan. 20-26, 1958. See also Gates, *The Story of an American Communist* (New York: Nelson, 1958).

26. *DW*, April 11, 1956.

27. *Ibid.*, April 5, 6, 1956; see also the cautious statement on civil liberties in a communist state in Editors of *PA*, "Socialism—USA and USSR," *Monthly Review*, VII (April 1956), pp. 497-500. The cover of this issue mistakenly says April 1955.

28. From notes made by the present writer at the meeting, April 4, 1956.

29. The March issue explained that "circumstances beyond our control" prevented publication of the February issue.

30. From personal observations of the meeting, April 30, 1956. A letter in the *DW*, May 4, 1956, complained about the meeting.

31. *DW*, April 11, 12, 1956; "What Happened to Soviet Jewish Culture? The First Authentic Statement and Our Comments," *Jewish Life: A Progressive Monthly*, X (May 1956), pp. 3-7, 27, 40. The present account is based on the *Jewish Life* translation.

32. *DW*, April 13, 1956.

33. *National Guardian*, June 25, 1956.

34. Letter from "A. F.," *DW*, April 24, 1956; letter from A. Unger, *ibid.*, April 25, 1956; see also Dora Teitelboim, *"We* Will Mourn Our Dead," *Masses & Mainstream*, IX (June 1956), pp. 1-7.

35. *DW*, June 25, 1956.

36. *Draft Resolution for the 16th National Convention of the Communist Party, U.S.A. Adopted Sept. 13, 1956* (New York: New Century, Sept. 1956), p. 58.

37. *DW*, Oct. 29, 1956.

38. *Ibid.*, May 3, 1956.

39. *Wkr*, April 8, 1956.

40. *DW*, April 16, 1956.

41. Eugene Dennis, *The Communists Take a New Look: Report to the National Committee of the Communist Party, U.S.A.* (New York: New Century, May 1956).

42. *DW*, May 3, 1956.

43. New York *Post*, July 22, 1956; *DW*, July 25, 1956. Subsequently, letters in the *DW* complained that party members had to rely on the "capitalist press" for full information about national committee affairs. See issue of Aug. 2, 1956, for example.

44. *Party Voice Discussion Supplement*. This four-page report by Norman Schrank was undated, but it appeared some time in May 1956. It discussed the national committee meeting that ended May 1, and the pres-

ent writer obtained a copy of it on May 31. Hereafter cited as Schrank report. For the votes on the report, John Gates to the present writer, Brooklyn, July 8, 1958.

45. Schrank report.
46. A Bronx Negro Woman Comrade, "Social Relations among Communists," *Party Voice,* IV (June 1956), p. 22; Food Worker, "A Rank and Filer Speaks his Piece," *ibid.* (July 1956), p. 9; D. V., "A Letter," *ibid.,* p. 23.
47. *DW,* July 25, 1956; for background of Dirba see Theodore Draper, *The Roots of American Communism* (New York: Viking, 1957), pp. 335, 339-40.
48. Interview with Earl Browder, July 31, 1956; *Party Voice,* IV (Sept. 1956), pp. 27-32; (Oct. 1956), pp. 21-5.
49. Don Lester, "One Essential in the Fight Against Left Sectarianism (From the discussion at the State Committee Meeting)," *ibid.,* IV (July 1956), p. 14.
50. These quotations are from the text as published in New York *Times,* June 5, 1956. A more convenient and better-edited version is in Russian Institute, Columbia University, ed., *The Anti-Stalin Campaign and International Communism* (New York: Columbia University Press, 1956), pp. 2-89, hereafter cited as *Anti-Stalin Campaign.* Another edition of the text of the speech, with annotations by Boris I. Nicolaevsky, was published by the *New Leader* under the title *The Crimes of the Stalin Era* (New York, 1956). Bertram D. Wolfe in *Khrushchev and Stalin's Ghost* (New York: Praeger, 1957), pp. 88-253, reproduces the speech and provides a thoughtful commentary on it.
51. Fast, *op. cit.,* p. 51.
52. *National Guardian,* May 14, 1956.
53. *DW,* June 6, 7, 1956.
54. *Ibid.,* June 12, 1956.
55. Fast, *op. cit.,* p. 27.
56. *DW,* Aug. 23, 1956.
57. Reprinted in *Anti-Stalin Campaign,* pp. 148-65.
58. *DW,* June 25, 1956; also in *Anti-Stalin Campaign,* pp. 269-73, and *PA,* XXXV (July 1956), pp. 34-6.
59. *Anti-Stalin Campaign,* p. 148.
60. New York *Times,* June 29, 30, July 1, 1956.
61. *DW,* July 2, 1956.
62. *Anti-Stalin Campaign,* p. 148.
63. Text of the resolution is in *ibid.,* pp. 276-306; *DW,* July 3, 1956; and *PA,* XXXV (Aug. 1956), pp. 32-47.
64. *DW,* July 5, 1956.
65. *Ibid.,* July 4, 1956; also in *Anti-Stalin Campaign,* pp. 326-7.
66. *DW,* July 3, 1956, incorrectly dated June 3 on front page but correctly dated on other pages; editorial also is in *Anti-Stalin Campaign,* pp. 323-4.
67. *DW,* July 5, 6, 1956.
68. *Ibid.,* July 9, 1956; see also July 10, 23, 1956.
69. *Ibid.,* July 26, 1956; also in *PA,* XXXV (Aug. 1956), pp. 48-9; John Gates, Brooklyn, to the present writer, July 8, 1958.

70. New York *Times,* July 26, 1956; *DW,* July 27, 1956.
71. "On the National Committee Statement," *Party Voice,* IV (Sept. 1956), pp. 8-10.
72. For Davis, *Wkr,* Sept. 2, 1956; for Foster, *ibid.,* Aug. 26, 1956.
73. *Ibid.,* Aug. 12, 1956.
74. Quotations from Bill Norman in *ibid.,* Aug. 19, 1956, but see also, all in *ibid.,* "B. S.," July 8, 1956; Albert Blumberg, July 15, 22, 1956; Fred Blair, July 29, 1956; Lillian Gates (Mrs. John Gates), Carl Hirsch, and "C. E. W.," Aug. 5, 1956; William Albertson, Aug. 12, 1956; Frank Carlson, Aug. 19, 1956; and "A Party Member," Sept. 3, 1956.
75. *Draft Resolution . . . 1956;* published also in *Wkr,* Sept. 23, 1956; New York *Post,* Sept. 22, 1956.
76. *Wkr,* Sept. 23, 1956; New York *Times,* Sept. 23, 1956; New York *Post,* Sept. 22, 1956.
77. New York *Times,* Sept. 24, 1956.
78. *DW,* Sept. 27, 1956.
79. *DW,* Oct. 3, 1956.
80. *Draft Resolution . . . 1956,* p. 56. Italics added.
81. William Z. Foster, "On the Party Situation," *PA,* XXXV (Oct. 1956), pp. 15-45, quotations from pp. 15, 20, 34.
82. From notes of the present writer at the meeting, Oct. 5, 1956; *Wkr,* Oct. 21, 1956.
83. Decca Truehaft, *Lifeitselfmanship, Or How To Become a Precisely-Because Man: An Investigation into Current L (or Left-Wing) Usage* (Oakland, Calif.: privately published, 1956), p. 11. Also published in *Mainstream,* IX (Oct. 1956), pp. 36-45.

CHAPTER TEN: HUNGARY AND FURTHER DISILLUSION

1. *DW,* Oct. 22, 1956. This editorial evoked criticism. See letters in *ibid.,* Oct. 25, 26, 1956.
2. *Ibid.,* Oct. 24, 1956.
3. *Ibid.,* Oct. 25, 1956.
4. *Ibid.,* Oct. 29, 30, Nov. 1, 1956.
5. *Ibid.,* Nov. 5, 1956. For Soviet statement of Oct. 30, see *ibid.,* Nov. 1, 1956, and Paul E. Zinner, ed., *National Communism and Popular Revolt in Eastern Europe: A Selection of Documents on Events in Poland and Hungary, February-November, 1956* (New York: Columbia University Press, 1956), pp. 485-9. The two translations differ slightly.
6. *DW,* Nov. 6, 1956.
7. *Ibid.,* Nov. 5, 1956.
8. *Ibid.,* Nov. 7, 1956.
9. Quoted in *ibid.,* Nov. 8, 1956.
10. *Ibid.,* Nov. 13, 21, 1956. See also letters from Helen Turner and "Constant Reader," Nov. 19, 1956.
11. *Ibid.,* Nov. 12, 1956.
12. *Ibid.,* Nov. 15, 1956.

13. See letter of Jack Goldring, in *ibid.,* Nov. 15, 1956. Goldring disassociated himself from the Connecticut party statement.
14. Appears in *ibid.,* Nov. 20, 1956, under title "An Open Letter to the Membership," and in *PA, XXXV* (Dec. 1956), pp. 1-5, under title, "On the Events in Hungary."
15. *DW,* Nov. 20, 1956.
16. *Ibid.,* Nov. 21, 1956.
17. *Ibid.,* Nov. 29, 30, 1956.
18. *Ibid.,* Nov. 26, 1956.
19. New York *Times,* Feb. 1, 1957. Fast told the present writer in an interview, in Dec. 1956, that he had left the party some weeks before.
20. New York *Times,* Jan. 19, 1957.
21. *Ibid.,* Dec. 18, 1956.
22. New York *Herald Tribune,* Nov. 24, 1956.
23. New York *Times,* Dec. 16, 1956.
24. Interview with John Gates, Dec. 6, 1956.
25. *16th National Convention Discussion Bulletin, No. 1,* Nov. 1, 1956. There were five of these *Bulletins,* all published by party headquarters in New York. Their dates were No. 2, Nov. 27, 1956; No. 3, Dec. 10, 1956; No. 4, Jan. 1, 1957; and No. 5, Jan. 15, 1957.
26. John Gates, "Time for a Change," *PA, XXXV* (Nov. 1956), pp. 53-5.
27. Foster, "Marxism-Leninism in a Changing World (Part II)," *ibid., XXXV* (Dec. 1956), p. 62.
28. Foster, "Origins of the Crisis in the CPUSA," *Party Voice,* V (Jan. 1957), p. 25.
29. *DW,* Jan. 2, 1957.
30. *Discussion Bulletin, No. 5,* Jan. 15, 1957.
31. George Blake Charney and Bill Norman, "A Letter to the Readers," *Party Voice,* V (Jan. 1957), p. 2.
32. *Proceedings* (abridged) of the sixteenth national convention of the Communist Party, U.S.A. (New York: Communist Party, 1957), pp. 17, 46, 72. Hereafter cited as *Proceedings.*
33. New York *Herald Tribune,* Jan. 31, 1957; New York *Times,* Jan. 31, 1957.
34. New York *World-Telegram and Sun,* Feb. 7, 1957; *Proceedings,* p. 174; *DW,* Feb. 8, 1956.
35. New York *Times,* Feb. 4, 1957.
36. *DW,* Feb. 6, 1957.
37. Notes by Bernard Rosenberg on the Communist Party convention, typescript report prepared by Mr. Rosenberg, a lecturer at the New School for Social Research, for the Fund for the Republic, Inc. A briefer version of Rosenberg's report is in *Dissent* (New York), IV (Spring 1957), pp. 152-6. Subsequent citations to Rosenberg are to the unpublished report. The convention admitted thirteen non-Communist observers to its meetings.
38. *Proceedings,* pp. 173-4.
39. *Ibid.,* pp. 42-5.
40. *Ibid.,* pp. 45-7, quotation from pp. 51-2.
41. *DW,* Feb. 11, 1957.
42. *Proceedings,* pp. 37-67, quotations from pp. 63-6.

43. Rosenberg, *op. cit.*
44. *Proceedings,* pp. 70-85.
45. *Draft Resolution for the 16th National Convention of the Communist Party, U.S.A., Adopted Sept. 13, 1956* (New York: New Century, Sept. 1956), p. 56.
46. *Proceedings,* pp. 164-73, 318; Rosenberg, *op. cit.*
47. *Proceedings,* p. 175; Rosenberg, *op. cit.*
48. New York *Times,* May 3, 1957.
49. *Proceedings,* p. 195.
50. *Ibid.,* pp. 232-3, 239.
51. *Ibid.,* pp. 235-6.
52. Letter of James McCluskey to the Inwood Section, C.P.U.S.A., February 1957, copy in the author's possession.
53. The document appears in *Proceedings,* pp. 253-328.
54. C. L. of Los Angeles, "The 'Main Task'—or Candide Revisited," *The Party Forum* (San Francisco), Nov. 1, 1956.
55. Interview with Dorothy Healy, Jan. 16, 1957.
56. Interview with John Gates, July 30, 1957.
57. *Proceedings,* p. 237.
58. Letter of McCluskey to Inwood Section.
59. *DW,* Oct. 11, 1957.
60. Interview with Merle Brodsky, a leader in the California East Bay area, March 28, 1957.
61. Robert Claiborne, "Twilight on the Left," *The Nation,* May 11, 1957, p. 414.
62. New York *Times,* March 18, 23, 1957; *DW,* March 22, 1957.
63. *DW,* April 3, 1957.
64. *Proceedings,* p. 247.
65. *DW,* April 3, 4, 1957.
66. Interview with John Gates, July 30, 1957.
67. New York *Times,* May 6, 11, 1957; *Wkr,* May 12, 1957. Gates said in an interview, July 30, 1957, that he had a higher percentage of supporters in the executive committee of twenty than in the full national committee. The executive committee members were: George Blake Charney, Benjamin Davis, Eugene Dennis, Earl Durham, Fred Fine, Elizabeth Gurley Flynn, William Z. Foster, John Gates, James Jackson, and Sidney Stein, of New York; David Davis, Philadelphia; Claude Lightfoot, Chicago; Hy Lumer, Cleveland; George Myers, Baltimore; Carl Ross, Minneapolis; Michael Russo, Boston; Martha Stone, Newark; Carl Winter, Detroit; Dorothy Healy, Los Angeles; and Albert J. ("Mickie") Lima, San Francisco.
68. New York *Times,* May 11, 1957.
69. Interview with Joseph Clark, Dec. 30, 1957.
70. New York *Times,* June 7, 1957; *DW,* June 7, 1957.
71. Interview with John Gates, July 30, 1956.
72. Interview with John Gates, Dec. 6, 1956.
73. *DW,* April 4, 1957.
74. *Ibid.,* June 4, 1957.
75. *Ibid.,* June 12, 1957.
76. *Ibid.,* April 19, 1957.

77. *Wkr,* May 5, 1957.
78. *Ibid.,* May 19, 1957.
79. *DW,* July 9, 1957.
80. *Ibid.,* July 10, 1957.
81. *Ibid.,* July 17, 18, 1957.
82. Interview with John Gates, July 30, 1957.
83. *DW,* July 24, 1957.
84. *Ibid.,* June 19, 1957.
85. *Ibid.,* June 26, 1957.
86. *Ibid.,* July 2, 1957.
87. *Ibid.,* July 19, 1957.
88. *Ibid.,* July 9, 1957.
89. *Ibid.,* July 23, 1957.
90. *Ibid.,* July 26, 1957.
91. New York *Times,* May 18, 1957.
92. See letters from Harold Collins, *DW,* Dec. 17, 26, 1957.
93. *Ibid.,* Sept. 9, 1957.
94. *Ibid.,* Dec. 19, 1957.
95. *Wkr,* Dec. 15, 1957.
96. *DW,* Sept. 9, 1957.
97. Interview with John Gates, July 30, 1957.
98. *DW,* Sept. 10, 1957.
99. Ibid., Sept. 12, 1957.
100. *Ibid.,* Oct. 21, Nov. 20, 1957.
101. New York *Times,* Dec. 9, 1957, Jan. 12, 1958.
102. *DW,* Oct. 2, 8, 11, 1957.
103. The Bittelman series was in *ibid.,* Oct. 1 to 16, 1957; William Z. Foster, "The Party Crisis and the Way Out," *PA,* XXXVI (Dec. 1957), pp. 47-61, and *ibid.,* XXXVII (Jan. 1958), pp. 49-65. Foster obviously had a copy of the Bittelman articles before they were published entirely. The last appeared on the day of Foster's stroke.
104. *DW,* Oct. 9, 1957.
105. New York *Times,* Nov. 22, Dec. 3, 1957.
106. *DW,* Nov. 25, 1957.
107. *Wkr,* Dec. 15, 22, 1957.
108. *DW,* Dec. 31, 1957; the executive committee's statement appears in *PA,* XXXVII (Jan. 1958), pp. 1-4; Robert Thompson's report appears in *ibid.,* XXXVII (Feb. 1958), pp. 26-35. An editorial footnote on p. 30 of the Thompson report repeats the gist of the *DW's* Dec. 31 account of the administrative committee's actions.
109. *DW,* Dec. 31, 1957; New York *Times,* Dec. 26, 1957.
110. *DW,* Nov. 13, 1956.
111. *Proceedings,* pp. 242-3.
112. *DW,* Sept. 13, 1957.
113. New York *Times,* Dec. 26, 1957; see also *DW,* Dec. 30, 31, 1957.
114. *DW,* Dec. 30, 1957.
115. Interview with John Gates, Feb. 23, 1958.
116. New York *Times,* Jan. 11, 1958.
117. *DW,* Jan. 13, 1958.

CONCLUSION: AN IMPOTENT PARTY

1. *Wkr,* March 16, Jan. 26, Feb. 16, 1958.
2. *Ibid.,* March 9, 1958; "On the Resignation of John Gates," *PA,* XXVII (March 1958), pp. 7-9; interview with John Gates, Feb. 23, 1958.
3. *Wkr,* March 9, 1958; "On Uniting and Strengthening the Party and Its Mass Base," *PA,* XXVII (March 1958), pp. 1-6; New York *Times,* Feb. 22, 1958.
4. "On the Peace Manifesto and the 12-Party Declaration," *PA,* XXXVII (June 1958), pp. 22-6; the older statement appeared in *ibid.,* XXXVII (Jan. 1958), pp. 1-4.
5. *Wkr,* March 9, 1958; New York *Times,* Feb. 22, 1958; interview with John Gates, Feb. 23, 1958. At a national committee meeting in June 1958, four more members—Andrew Krchmarek, Claude Lightfoot, Burt Nelson, and Carl Winter—were elected to the executive committee—New York *Times,* July 12, 1958.
6. William Z. Foster, "The Superiority of World Socialism Over World Capitalism," *PA,* XXXVII (May 1958), pp. 19-28, quotation from p. 26.
7. New York *Times,* March 8, 28, May 3, 1958; New York *Post,* April 16, 1958; *Wkr,* May 4, 1958.
8. New York *Times,* July 12, 1958.
9. *The Marxist-Leninist Vanguard* (New York), Sept.-Nov. 1958. The first issue appeared in Sept. 1958.
10. New York *Times,* May 3, 1958.
11. *Ibid.,* May 31, 1958; *Wkr,* June 1, 1958.
12. New York *Times,* Nov. 28, 1956; *DW,* Nov. 28, 1956.
13. San Francisco *Chronicle,* May 3, 1957.
14. Original announcement in *DW,* Oct. 11, 1957.
15. New York *Times,* Nov. 7, 1957.
16. Interview with John Gates, July 30, 1957.
17. New York *Times,* Jan. 11, 1958.
18. New York *Post,* April 16, 1958; New York *Times,* May 3, July 12, 1958.
19. Interview with Joseph Clark, Dec. 30, 1957.
20. Theodore Draper, *The Roots of American Communism* (New York: Viking, 1957), p. 272; Irwin Suall, national secretary of the combined socialist organization, to the present writer, New York, March 6, 1958.
21. Bob Thompson, "On the Work and Consolidation of the Party," *PA,* XXXVII (Aug. 1958), p. 46.
22. Dorothy Jones, "Money Is Everybody's Job in San Francisco," *Contact,* I (June 1957), p. 1; *DW,* March 24, 1947; *Wkr,* April 6, 1947.
23. William Z. Foster, "Draper's 'Roots of American Communism,'" *PA,* XXXVI (May 1957), pp. 34-40.
24. Elizabeth Gurley Flynn in *DW,* April 8, 1949, and in *Wkr,* Jan. 26, 1958.

INDEX

Abel, Rudolf Ivanovich, 78, 79
Abraham Lincoln Brigade, 12, 281
Abraham Lincoln School, 86
Abt, John, 103, 128, 149, 171, 212
Acheson, Dean, 32, 188
Adamic, Louis, 148, 166, 172, 177
Adams (Samuel) School, 86
Addes, George, 103
Albam, Jacob, 79
Albertson, Vaughn, 212
Alexander, Charlene, 329
Allan, William, 195
Allen, James S., 15, 64, 120, 269, 273-74, 315
Alman, David, 221
Alman, Emily, 221
Alsop, Joseph, 160
Alsop, Stewart, 130, 160
Amalgamated Clothing Workers, 103, 125, 128, 131, 154
Amalgamated Meatcutters Union, 262
American Civil Liberties Union, 83, 280
American Committee for Cultural Freedom, 280
American Committee for the Settlement of Jews in Birobidjan, Inc., 83
American Communications Association (A.C.A.), 102
American Federation of Labor (A.F. of L.), 9-10, 36, 45, 46, 103, 139, 145, 149, 156, 193, 259, 261-62, 344
American Forum for Socialist Education, 344-45
American Labor Party, 3, 98, 99, 114-17, 121, 124, 131-33, 140, 149, 154, 157, 158, 210, 211, 213, 218, 220, 256-59, 266
American Legion, 123
American Newspaper Guild, 49, 75, 354
American Peace Crusade, 221
American Slav, 91
American Slav Congress, 83, 91, 147, 149, 205
American Veterans Committee (A.V.C.), 47, 83, 143-44
Americans for Democratic Action (A.D.A.), 124, 129-30, 145, 166, 366
Anti-Semitism, 30, 222, 260, 284-86, 294, 296, 297, 320, 324, 330, 335
Aptheker, Herbert, 221, 342-43
Arizona, 95
Astor, Vincent, 328
Auriol, Vincent, 222

Bachrach, Marion, 159
Bacteriological warfare, charges of U.S. use of, 206

Baldanzi, George, 130
Baldwin, C. B., 125-27, 142, 143, 169-71, 173, 177, 211, 212
Balokovich, Zladko, 149
Bary, Arthur, 165
Bary, Mrs. Arthur, 165
Bass, Charlotta, 165, 213, 256
Basztovanski, S., 134
Bedacht, Max, 22
Begun, Isadore, 71, 201, 245
Bell, Donald. *See* Budzislawski, Hermann
Bendiner, Robert, 130
Benson, Elmer, 125, 150
Beria, Lavrenti P., 252, 270, 284, 288
Berlin, 178, 370
Berry, Abner W., 101, 351, 357
Bessie, Alvah, 57
Bevan, Mrs. Aneurin, 160
Bilbo, Theodore, 65
Bittelman, Alexander, 26, 117, 346
Black, Hugo L., 198, 200
Blair, Fred, 246
Bloch, Emmanuel H., 220, 223
Bogart, Humphrey, 126
Boston, 100
Brainin, Joseph, 221
Brandt, Joseph, 237-38
Bridges, Harry, 7, 102, 104, 132, 137-39, 149, 154, 155, 217, 262
Brotherhood of Railroad Trainmen, 128
Brotherhood of Sleeping Car Porters, 344
Browder, Earl, 5, 7-13, 15-20, 37, 52, 55, 61-65, 81, 88, 91-92, 96, 106, 113, 114, 117, 125, 135, 265-66, 274, 291-92, 302, 307, 348
Brown, Archie, 100
Brownell, Herbert, 224, 279
Bryson, Hugh, 102, 132-33, 149, 150, 171
Buchanan, Frank, 178
Buchanan, Scott, 171
Budenz, Louis, 76, 89
Budzislawski, Hermann, 163
Bulganin, Nikolai A., 286, 294, 341
Bunche, Ralph J., 65-66, 193
Bureau of Internal Revenue, 278, 280

Burkhart, Carolyn, 20
Burnham, Louis, 212
Burton, Bernard, 321
Byrnes, James F., 120

Cacchione, Peter V., 99, 133
California, 6, 12, 20, 48, 71, 95, 98, 100, 103, 131-34, 176, 178, 189, 319, 331, 357
California Labor School, 86, 359
Callas, Maria, 354
Calomiris, Angela, 236
Cameron, Angus, 128-29
Cantor, Esther, 327
Carey, Homer F., 148
Carey, James B., 128, 130
Carver (George Washington) School, 86
Catholic Worker, The, 344
Chambers, Whittaker, 80, 179, 186-87
Charesyez (Hungarian "Titoist"), 236
Charney, George Blake, 201, 276, 323, 329, 337, 348, 357
Chervenkov, Vulko, 134
Chiang Kai-shek, 185
Chicago, 10, 92, 94, 148, 210, 328; University of, 166
Childs, Marquis, 130
Childs, Morris, 89
China policy, 32
Churchill, Winston, 27, 46
Civil Rights Congress, 83, 199, 220, 221, 234-35, 244
Clark, Joseph, 277, 300, 307, 314, 315, 324, 336, 340-42, 345-46, 350
Clark, Tom C., 198, 200
Cold War, 26-32, 36, 251-52
Coleman, Sam, 295
College of the City of New York, 281
Colon, Jesus, 351
Colorado, 101, 164-65, 176
Columbia University, 342, 361
Cominform. *See* Communist Information Bureau
Comintern. *See* Communist International

Committee for the Defense of the Pittsburgh Six, 83
Committee on Foreign Affairs, House of Representatives, 160, 161
Committee on Un-American Activities, House of Representatives, 27, 57, 103, 187
Communist, The, 6, 159
Communist Information Bureau (Cominform), 18, 134-37, 146, 178-79, 205, 347, 368, 371
Communist International (Comintern), 17, 73, 76, 135, 302
Communist Labor Party, 22
Communist Party, Belgium, 297
Communist Party, Canada, 299
Communist Party, Denmark, 297
Communist Party, Finland, 297
Communist Party, France, 5, 136, 325, 370
Communist Party, Great Britain, 136, 338
Communist Party, Italy, 136, 147, 240, 297
Communist Party, Norway, 297
Communist Party, U.S.A.: characteristics of leadership, 73-75; conventions, 5, 11, 13, 19, 72, 164, 176, 255, 323-37, 349; membership, 91-97; organization and strength, 3-4, 9, 13, 34-67, 202, 214-18, 227-48, 295, 318, 333, 359-71; position, 5-7, 13-15, 23-33, 68-110, 113-22, 131-34, 137-40, 152-57, 191-95, 198-99, 203-10, 218-26, 239-48, 252-71, 286, 296-97, 300-1, 303-4, 312, 316, 330, 347-48, 358, 367
Communist Party, U.S.S.R. *See* Russia
Communist Political Association (C.P.A.), 5, 7, 8, 13, 92, 93
"Concentration policy," 70-71
Congress of Industrial Organizations (C.I.O.), 3, 4, 29, 36, 44-51, 101-6, 113, 116, 125, 127-29, 131-32, 137-39, 145, 147, 149, 154-56, 177, 193, 214-18, 259, 261-62, 366; Political Action Committee (C.I.O.-P.A.C.), 125, 128, 156

Connecticut, 315
Connolly, Eugene P., 99
Coplon, Judith, 78-79, 80, 186
Cornell University, 147
Correa, Anna, 329
Counts, George S., 130
Crockett, George W., 197
Crum, Bartley C., 149
Curran, Joe, 102, 127
Czechoslovakia, Communist coup, 161, 178, 370

Daily People's World, 22, 90, 116, 223, 271, 314, 356, 359
Daily Worker (London), 273
Daily Worker (New York), 9, 16, 22, 25-27, 37, 40, 50, 54, 57, 58, 65, 68, 75, 76, 84-110 *passim,* 117-21, 133, 137, 152, 154, 162, 166, 177, 181, 194, 198, 201, 206, 207, 211, 218-20, 234, 236, 238, 242, 245-46, 270-321 *passim,* 325, 326, 334-59 *passim,* 362, 371
Darcy, Sam, 20
Daughters of the American Revolution (D.A.R.), 122-23
Davidson, Jo, 126, 127
Davies, A. Powell, 130
Davis, Benjamin J., Jr., 62, 66, 89, 99, 196, 265, 289, 300, 304, 312, 318, 326, 329, 330, 337, 345, 347, 348, 349, 352, 354, 356
Davis, David, 329, 348
Davis, Elmer, 130
Day, Dorothy, 344
Debs, Eugene V., 4, 9, 69, 73, 262
De Caux, Leonard Howard, 103
"Democratic centralism," 73, 322
Democratic Party, 7, 46, 69, 113, 115, 121, 122, 123, 124, 127, 128, 131, 132, 133, 140, 143, 151, 156, 157, 158, 178, 181, 193, 253, 256, 257, 263, 266, 367
Denikin, Anton, 194
Dennis, Eugene, 12-13, 19, 25, 38, 40, 56, 73, 89, 99, 113-15, 120-22, 131-39 *passim,* 156, 194, 196, 200, 208, 234, 240, 279, 287-91, 297-304 *passim,* 312-32 *passim,* 338, 345, 347, 348, 351-52, 355-56, 358

Dennis, Peggy (Mrs. Eugene), 233, 241
Department of Justice, Internal Security Division, 79-80
Depression, 31, 39-44, 365
Detroit, 92
de Valera, Eamon, 213
"Devil-conspiracy" theory of history, 26, 34-35, 41, 51, 206, 243
Dewey, Thomas E., 114, 121, 152, 177, 179, 180, 214
D'Fonseca, Lydia, 212
Dickstein, Samuel, 115
Dilling, Elizabeth, 123-24
Dilworth, Richardson, 130
Dimock, Edward J., 201
Dirba, Charles, 291, 328
Discussion Bulletin, 321
Distributors Guide, 16, 18
District 65, United Retail, Wholesale, and Department Store Workers Union, 103, 149, 246, 260
"Dixiecrat" movement, 179-80
Djilas, Milovan, 134
Dmitrov, Georgi, 44
Dodd, William E., 212
Dolan, Graham, 165
Dorner, Hannah, 126, 128, 170
Douglas, Helen Gahagan, 178, 213
Douglas, Paul, 178
Douglas, William O., 198, 200, 223
Douglass, Frederick, 69
Dowling, Lyle, 20
Doyle, Bernadette, 98
Draper, Theodore, 363
Dubinsky, David, 45, 124, 130
Du Bois, W. E. B., 221
Duclos, Jacques, 5, 9, 11, 16n, 39, 40, 62, 117, 134, 222, 287, 302, 325, 326
Dulles, John Foster, 206, 273, 313, 324
Dunne, William F., 20, 22
Durham, Earl, 329, 348
Durkin, James, 139, 211

Edelman, Irwin, 222-23
Eisenhower, Dwight David, 189, 193, 208, 210, 224, 252, 258, 263, 272-73, 274, 275, 278, 279, 310, 313-14

Eisler, Gerhart, 76, 138, 163, 186
Emerson, Thomas, 212
Emspak, Julius, 139, 215, 216
Engels, Friedrich, 261
Ernst, Morris, 130
Espionage, 27, 77, 78-81

Fadiman, Clifton, 55
Fair Employment Practices Commission, 6
Fajon, Etienne, 134
Farkasz, M., 134
Farm Equipment Workers (F.E.), 102, 214
Farmer, Fyke, 223
Farrell, James T., 56
Fast, Howard, 57, 149, 242, 246, 293, 295, 317, 320, 334
F & D Publishing Company, 279
Federal Bureau of Investigation (F.B.I.), 77, 78, 79-80, 199, 202, 218, 219, 220, 227-30, 233, 236, 238, 270, 324, 336-37
Feinglass, Abe, 139
Fellowship for Reconciliation, 209
Feltin, Cardinal, 222
Field, Frederick Vanderbilt, 159-60, 328
Field, Noel and Herman, 237
Fine, Fred, 270, 304, 329, 345, 347, 348, 351
Fischer, Louis, 130
Fitzgerald, Albert J., 169-70, 171, 172, 214, 215
Flaxer, Abram, 49, 154
Flint, Michigan, 70
Flynn, Elizabeth Gurley, 181, 198, 201, 235, 247, 348, 351, 356, 360, 363
Folk music, 37-38
Folks-Shtimme, 284, 298
Food, Tobacco, Agricultural, and Allied Workers of America (F.T.A.), 102, 214
For a Lasting Peace, For a People's Democracy! (journal), 240, 347, 371
Ford, James W., 62
Foreman, Clark, 128, 212
Forrestal, James, 146

Foster, William Z., 9-13, 16*n*, 18, 19, 22, 26, 30, 38, 41, 44, 51, 53, 55, 64, 65, 67, 73, 75, 113, 121, 122, 131-34, 140, 153, 155-56, 164, 168, 176-77, 182, 193, 196-98, 202-4, 208, 229, 239-40, 247, 253-54, 263-67, 270, 274-79, 289, 291, 293, 298-308, 312, 316, 318-39 *passim*, 343, 346, 348, 349, 355, 356, 363-65, 367

Four Continents Book Company, 276

Frank, Lewis, 143-44, 159, 160, 163, 169

Frankfeld, Philip, 201

Frankfurter, Felix, 198, 200

Franklin, Benjamin, 37

Franklin, Francis, 21, 63

Fraternal Life, 91

Freiheit. See *Morning Freiheit*

Freudianism, Communist position on, 240-43

Friedman, Robert, 342, 343

Fuchs, Klaus, 78, 186, 188, 219, 221

Furtseva, Ekaterina, 285

Galbraith, John Kenneth, 130

Gannett, Betty, 265, 268

Gardner, Virginia, 282, 351

Gary, Indiana, 70

Gastonia strike (1929), 37-38

Gates, John, 89, 196, 277-79, 281-83, 285, 289, 290, 295-365 *passim*, 367, 371

Gaulden, Rose, 96

Gellert, Hugo, 107

General Motors strike (1946), 46

George, Harrison, 20, 22

George Washington Carver School, 86

Georgia, 246

Gero, Erno, 310, 311

Gerson, Simon, 99, 131-32, 201, 351

Gheorgiu-Dej, George, 134

Gitt, Josiah, 177

Gladstein, Richard, 197

Gold, Ben, 49, 104, 105, 139, 154

Gold, Harry, 219-20, 221

Gold, Mike, 56-57

Golden, Jerome, 260, 261

Gompers, Samuel, 365

Gomulka, Wladyslaw, 134, 276, 289, 309-10, 311

Gordon, Max, 351, 357, 361

Gorglione, Michael, 93

Gorman, Patrick, 262

Graham, Charles, 165

Green, Gilbert, 38-39, 196, 211, 232-33, 270, 304

Green, William, 365

Greenback Party, 364

Greenglass, David, 219-20, 221

Gubichev, Valentin, 78, 79, 186

Haldane, J. B. S., 37

Hall, Gus, 196, 197, 232-33

Hallinan, Vincent, 213, 256, 257-58

Hammett, Dashiell, 199

Hand, Augustus, 197

Hand, Leonard, 200

Harap, Louis, 221

Harlem Leadership Training School, 87

Harlem Women's Committee on Peace, 205

Harrison, William, 100

Hartle, Barbara, 203

Hathaway, Clarence, 89

Havenner, Frank R., 178

Hayford, James, 173

Haywood, Harry, 358, 359

Haywood, William D., 217, 262

Healy, Dorothy, 201, 329, 331, 348, 358

Heller, A. A., 18, 91

Hellman, John, 329

Hellman, Lillian, 211

Henderson, Donald, 154

Henderson, Leon, 130

Herriot, Edouard, 222

Hicks, Granville, 55

Hillman, Sidney, 45, 125, 143

Hiss, Alger, 78, 186-88, 189

Holifield, Chet, 178

Hollywood, 56, 57

Hoover, J. Edgar, 80-81, 218, 224, 228

Horthy de Nagybanya, Nicholas, 311

Hotel and Restaurant Employees' International Alliance, 104

Howard, Charles P., 170, 205
Howard, Milton, 241
Howell, Charles, 178
Hromádka, Joseph L., 162-63
Huberman, Leo, 167
Hull, Cordell, 7
Humphrey, Hubert, 130
Hungarian Revolution, 309-16, 324, 326, 330, 337, 342-43, 345, 363, 371

Ickes, Harold, 126-27
Illinois, 95, 178, 180
Imbrie, James, 147
Imperialism, Communist interpretations of, 23-24, 32, 60, 113, 119-20, 135-36, 191
Independent Citizens Committee of the Arts, Sciences, and Professions (I.C.C.A.S.P.), 116, 118, 126-27, 128
Independent Progressive Party, California (I.P.P.), 133
Industrial Workers of the World (I.W.W.), 9
Inprecorr (Comintern journal), 42
International Affairs, 339
International Association of Machinists (I.A.M.), 217
International Brotherhood of Electrical Workers, 217
International Brotherhood of Teamsters, 262
International Fishermen and Allied Workers of America, 102
International Fur and Leather Workers Union (Furriers), 49, 102, 104, 105, 149, 214, 246, 262
International Ladies Garment Workers Union (I.L.G.W.U.), 45, 124
International Longshoremen's Association (I.L.A.), 104, 214, 262
International Longshoremen's and Warehousemen's Union (I.L.W.U.), 102, 262. *See also* Bridges, Harry
International Publishers, 18, 91
International Typographical Union, 104
International Union of Electrical, Radio, and Machine Workers (I.U.E.), 217

International Union of Mine, Mill, and Smelter Workers (Mine, Mill), 102, 147, 217
International Workers Order (I.W.O.), 22, 83-85, 91, 116, 138, 140, 145, 148, 320
Iran crisis (1946), 26
"Iron Curtain," 27
Isaacson, Leo, 155, 157-58, 173
Isserman, Abraham J., 197

Jackson, James, 270, 304, 312, 329, 345, 347, 348, 356
Jackson, Joe, 94
Jackson, Robert H., 200
Jefferson, Thomas, 69
Jefferson School of Social Science, 86-87, 95, 240, 281, 282, 307, 359
Jerome, V. J., 115, 268
Jewish Daily Forward, 50
Jewish Life, 91, 284, 285
Jewish Peoples Fraternal Order, 84, 148, 149
Johnson, Arnold, 360
Johnson, Joseph E., 168
Johnston, Eric, 14
Joliot-Curie, Frederic, 204
Jones, Alvin, 173
Jones, Claudia, 62, 65
Joseph Weydemeyer School of Social Science, 86

Kadar, Janos, 313, 314, 317, 353
Kaganovich, Lazar M., 341
Kahn, Albert E., 148, 204
Kahn, Elinor, 133, 165
Kaiser, Henry, 11
Kansas City, Missouri, 70, 73
Kardelj, Edward, 134
Kasenkina, Oksaka Stepanova, 179
Kaufman, Irving R., 219, 220, 223
Kefauver, Estes, 307
Keith, Charles, 20
Kendrick, Alex H., 260, 261
Kennedy, Stetson, 318
Kenny, Robert W., 149
Kenya, 263
Keynesian theories, Communist attitude toward, 38, 39, 40, 141, 153
Khrushchev, Nikita, 239, 248, 250-52, 270, 271, 286, 292-94, 297,

299, 309, 315, 317, 324, 340, 341, 345, 347, 371
Kingdon, Frank, 127, 149
Klein, Arthur G., 115, 116
Kling, Jack, 237-38
Kommunist, 316-17, 346
Korean War, 202, 205-8, 209-10, 211, 212-13, 220, 227, 252
Krchmarek, A. R., 98
Krug, Julius, 11
Kushner, Sam, 328

Labor. *See under names of labor organizations*
Labor-Management Charter, 14
Labour Party of Great Britain, 29, 160
La Follette, Robert M., Sr., 131, 175
La Follette, Robert M., Jr., 194
La Guardia, Fiorello, 113, 116
Lamont, Corliss, 257, 258
Lampell, Millard, 170
Lardner, Ring, Jr., 274-75
Lash, Joseph, 289
Lautner, John, 235-38, 343
Lawrence, William H., 175
Lawson, John Howard, 57
Lee, Jennie, 160
Leeds, O. H., 350
Left, non-Communist, 35, 106, 122-30, 158-59, 366
"Left-deviationists," 20, 69, 358
Lenin, V. I., 23, 25, 38, 115, 254, 261, 284, 294
Lenin School (Moscow), 12
Leonard, Richard, 103
Levine, Ben, 351
Lewis, John L., 44, 45, 48
Liberal Party, 128, 157
Lie, Trygve, 219
Lightfoot, Claude, 287, 304, 329, 348, 355
Lima, Albert J. ("Mickie"), 348, 356
Lincoln, Abraham, 69
Lincoln (Abraham) Brigade, 12, 281
Lincoln (Abraham) School, 86
Linfield, Seymour, 174
Literature, Communist attitude toward, 54-58
Little, Brown, and Company, 129

Livingston, David, 260
Loeb, James, Jr., 130, 145, 166
Loman, Charles, 329, 336
Longo, Luigi, 134
Longshoremen's strike (1945), 71
Los Angeles, 100, 103, 132, 165, 180, 213, 244-45
Louisiana, 95, 246
Lovestone, Jay, 15, 302
Lubell, Samuel, 157-58
Lumer, Hyman, 345, 347, 348, 352, 356

MacArthur, Douglas, 207, 208
McCabe, Louis F., 197
McCarran Internal Security Act, 189, 194, 227
McCarthy, Joseph R., 188, 189, 194, 224, 252
"McCarthyism," 188-89, 252, 369, 371
MacDougall, Curtis, 178
Macedonian issue (1948), 171-72
Maceo Snipes School, 87
McGee, Willie, 244
McGranery, James P., 219
McGrath, J. Howard, 158
McKeesport, Pennsylvania, 70
McKenney, Ruth, 20, 55
McManus, John, 211, 258, 307
Magil, A. B., 351
Mainstream, 58
Malenkov, Georgi M., 134, 340, 341
Maltz, Albert, 56-57
Mandel, William, 332
Manuilsky, Dmitri Z., 76
Mao Tse-tung, 32, 185
Marcantonio, Vito, 133, 149, 158, 169, 170-71, 180, 211, 213, 256-58
March of Labor, 215, 317
Mardo, Bill, 57
Maritime Committee for a Communist Party, 20
Marsh, Herbert, 139
Marshall, Daniel G., 223
Marshall, George C., 28, 32, 135, 137, 146, 160
Marshall Plan, 27, 28-31, 32, 106, 132, 135, 136, 137, 140, 143, 145, 155, 159, 160, 161, 214

Martin, James S., 171
Marx, Karl, 261
Marxism-Leninism, 33, 38, 62, 65, 68, 305-6, 325, 327, 337, 338, 355
Marxism-Leninism-Stalinism, 199
Marxist-Leninist Vanguard, 358
Maryland, 180
Masaryk, Jan, 161, 162
Mason, Chick, 291-92
Massachusetts, 72, 180
Masses, The, 57
Masses and Mainstream, 58, 91, 241, 283, 334
Matles, James, 139, 154, 215, 216
Matusow, Harvey, 201
Mau Maus, 263
Max, Alan, 274, 311, 314, 338-39, 351, 352, 357
Mead, James M., 121
Meany, George, 344
Medina, Harold R., 197, 199-200
Melish, William Howard, 54
Merrill, Lewis, 37, 104
Michelson, Clarina, 93-94
Michigan, 95, 101, 180, 315
Michigan Herald, 90
Michigan School of Social Science, 86
Mikoyan, Anastas, 273, 341
Militant, The, 283
Minc, H., 134
Minton, Bruce, 20
Mitford, Nancy, 307
Molotov, Vyacheslav, 17-18, 30, 215, 340
Montana, 95
Montgomery, Andrew, 267-69
Mooney-Billings case, 225
Morgan, J. P., Jr., 5
Morgenthau, Henry, Jr., 128
Morning Freiheit, The, 85, 90, 95, 279, 284, 320
Morris, George, 50, 340, 351
Morris, Newbold, 113
Morros, Boris, 212
Moysey, Donald R., 279, 280
Multer, Abraham J., 178
Murray, Milton, 49
Murray, Philip, 14, 31, 48-50, 106, 128, 129, 137, 147, 154, 155, 156, 177, 193, 214

Muste, A. J., 344
Myers, George, 348, 356
Myrdal, Gunnar, 63

Nagy, Imre, 290, 310, 311, 313, 316, 358
Nation, The, 333
National Association for the Advancement of Colored People (N.A.A.C.P.), 14, 66, 83, 128, 209, 263-65
National Citizens Political Action Committee (N.C.-P.A.C.), 116, 118, 125, 127, 128
National Committee to Secure Justice in the Rosenberg Case, 221
National Conference of Progressives, 128-29
National Council of the Arts, Sciences, and Professions, 204
National Farmers Union, 128
National Guardian, 159, 211, 220, 223, 257, 258, 285, 294, 307, 344
National Labor Conference for Peace, 204
National Lawyers Guild, 166
National Maritime Union (N.M.U.), 102, 127
National Negro Labor Council, 263-64
"National self-determination," for Negroes, 60-61, 62-65, 264, 330
National Union of Marine Cooks and Stewards (M.C.S.), 102, 132, 149, 214
NCP Report, 20
Negro, and Communist Party, 6, 14, 23, 35, 54, 58-67, 87, 96, 97, 209, 242-47, 262-65, 330, 367, 370. *See also* National Association for the Advancement of Colored People
Nelson, Donald M., 11
Nelson, Steve, 350
Nevada, 165
New Century Publishers, 91
New Challenge: The Magazine for Young Americans, 267
New Committee for Publications, 20
New England, 72
New Jersey, 100, 178, 180

New Leader, The, 51, 123
New Masses, 20, 56, 57-58, 91, 104, 107, 206
New Mexico, 95, 176
New Republic, 142, 147, 161
New Times, 276
New York City, 3, 4, 48, 71-72, 92, 93-95, 99-100, 103, 110, 115-16, 137, 178, 180, 210, 213, 360
New York *Post,* 144, 289
New York State, 12, 71, 89, 91, 95, 131-34, 180, 229, 289, 290, 301, 315, 319, 322-23
New York *Times,* 50, 55, 77, 175, 276, 292, 301, 305, 350
New York University, 361
New Yorker, The, 324
Nichols, Louis, 80*n*
Niebuhr, Reinhold, 129, 130
Nixon, Richard M., 187, 188, 210
Norman, William, 270
North, Joseph, 57
North American Committee to Aid Spanish Democracy, 83
North Atlantic Treaty Organization (N.A.T.O.), 31
North Dakota, 95
Northwestern University, 146, 148, 178

Oakes, Grant, 178
O'Casey, Sean, 271
Ohio, 95, 98, 180
Ohio School of Social Science, 86
Orwell, George, 281
Osman, Arthur, 103, 139, 260
Overseas News Agency, 160
Overthrow of government, 69

Pacific Northwest Labor School, 86
Padover, Saul, 130
Paine, Thomas, 69
Paine (Tom) School of Social Science (Philadelphia), 86
Paine (Tom) School of Westchester, 86
Parker, Alex, 231
Party Voice, 267-68, 283, 290-91, 292, 301, 307
Patterson, William L., 354
Patton, James, 128

Pauker, Anna, 134
Pauley, Edwin W., 126
Pavlov, Ivan, 242
Pennsylvania, 72, 95, 178, 180
People's Songs, Inc., 165
Pepper, Claude, 119, 121
Percy, William Alexander, 194
Perlman, Leo, 95
Perlo, Victor, 159, 160-61
Perlow, Max, 104
Perry, Pettis, 244-45, 247
Petran, Tabitha, 159, 166, 167, 168, 285
Philadelphia, 9, 72, 165
Pittsburgh, Pennsylvania, 72
Platt, David, 351
PM, 7, 159
Point Four, 31, 209
Polish Revolution, 297-98, 308-12, 326
Political Affairs, 6, 7, 19, 26, 43, 52, 91, 113, 115, 131, 153, 159, 236, 242, 245, 247, 253, 260, 274, 305, 346
Popper, Martin, 166, 167, 168, 170
Poptomov, V., 134
Porter, Paul A., 130
Potash, Irving, 104, 105, 139, 154, 196
Potofsky, Jacob, 128
Pravda, 134, 135, 276, 297-98, 301, 305, 310-11
Prayer Pilgrimage for Freedom, 344
Pressman, Lee, 103, 129, 155, 166, 170, 172, 173, 178
Price, Earl, 20
Progressive, The, 146
Progressive Citizens of America (P.C.A.), 127, 129, 145, 149, 150, 151, 204
Progressive Party, 164-82, 209, 210-13, 214, 215, 218, 256-58, 367
Proletarian novels, 54-55
Provisional Organizing Committee for a Marxist-Leninist Communist Party, 358
Puerto Ricans, Communist efforts among, 96, 168-69
Publisher's New Press, Inc., 280

Quad City Committee for Peace, 83
Quill, Michael, 49, 99, 102, 105, 137-39, 154, 155-56, 158, 215, 318

Rajk, Laszlo, 236, 276, 277-78
Rakosi, Matyas, 276, 311, 343
Ramsey, David, 159, 160-61, 166, 167
Randolph, A. Philip, 6, 65, 344
Reale, Eugenio, 134
Red International of Labor Unions (Profintern), 10
Religion, Communist attitude toward, 52-54
Republican Party, 47, 69, 113, 116, 119, 121, 122, 127, 128, 140, 145, 146, 157, 158, 193
Reuther, Walter, 14, 47, 49, 51, 103, 127, 130, 195, 344
Revai, Joseph, 134
"Review commissions," 77-78, 228
Rhee, Syngman, 206
Richmond, Al, 314, 329
Riesel, Victor, 51
Rieve, Emil, 49, 130
Robeson, Paul, 158, 169, 174, 211
Robeson, Mrs. Paul, 166, 167, 169
Rodney, Lester, 316, 351, 357
Rodos (of Soviet police), 293
Rogge, O. John, 204-5
Rohrer, Charles, 167
Roman Catholic Church, 48, 51, 52-54, 266-67
Roosevelt, Eleanor, 130
Roosevelt, Franklin D. (Sr.), 6, 7, 123, 125, 126, 128, 137, 141, 146, 188
Roosevelt, Franklin D., Jr., 130
Roosevelt, Theodore, 142, 158
Rosenberg, Ethel and Julius, 78, 80, 186, 218-26, 370
Ross, Carl, 329, 348, 357
Rubin, Morris H., 146
Russell, Sam, 273
Russia (U.S.S.R.), 4-5, 10, 23-37 *passim*, 42, 60, 81, 117-19, 127, 133-37, 154, 157, 159-61, 173, 178-79, 209, 213, 215, 219, 234, 242, 251-52, 267, 270, 272-74, 276, 285, 289-301 *passim*, 309-12,

315, 320, 324, 330-31, 334-35, 339-42, 346-47, 357, 363-71
Russo, Michael, 348
Ruthenberg, Charles, 69
Ryan, Joseph P., 71
Ryder, Albert Pinkham, 352

Sabath, Adolph, 121
Sacco-Vanzetti case, 225
Sacher, Harry, 197
Samuel Adams School, 86
San Francisco, 6, 93, 132, 180, 213
Santo, John, 154, 316
Santo, Mrs. John, 318
Scales, Junius, 345
Scarlett, Bishop William, 130
Scheer, Maximillian. *See* Schlieper, Walter
Schlesinger, Arthur M., Jr., 130
Schlieper, Walter, 159-60, 163
Schneiderman, William, 196, 201, 304
School of Jewish Studies, 86, 240
Schrank, Norman, 290-91
Schuman, Frederick L., 166, 168, 169-70
Schutzer, Arthur, 211
Schuyler, George, 193
Schwartz, Harry, 305, 350
Schwellenbach, Lewis B., 93
Seeger, Pete, 38, 107, 165
Selly, Joseph, 139, 154
Shea, William S., 116
Shepilov, Dimitri T., 340
Sherbell, Kenneth, 149
Sillen, Samuel, 283
Simon, Hal, 104, 139
Slansky, Rudolf, 134, 222
Sloane, Allan E., 170
Smith, Howard, 195
Smith, Lillian, 56
Smith, Verne, 20, 22
Smith Act, 99, 159, 168, 189, 194, 195-203, 218, 230, 234, 270, 281, 282, 345, 366
Snipes (Maceo) School, 87
Sobell, Morton, 219-20
Soble, Jack and Myra, 78, 79
Sobolev, A. A., 311
Social Democratic Federation, 51, 362

Social Security Administration, 75
Socialist Call, 123
Socialist Party, 4, 9, 22, 53, 65, 73, 123, 124, 129, 145, 262, 344, 362
South Dakota, 95, 165
Southern Conference for Human Welfare, 83, 128, 212
Sovetskaya Rossiya, 324
Spark: A Marxist Monthly, 20
Spodick (New Haven delegate), 172
Springmeyer, George, 165
Sputnick I, 346
Stachel, Jacob ("Jack"), 89, 196, 304, 348, 351, 354-55, 356
Stalin, Joseph, 23, 26-27, 41, 60, 62, 65, 68, 134, 233, 235, 248, 250-51, 253, 254, 266, 272-77, 284, 288, 292-94, 296, 297, 298, 309, 310, 330, 341, 345, 357, 363, 368, 371
Stanley, Emma, 98
Starobin, Joseph, 207, 307
Stassen, Harold, 126
State, County, and Municipal Workers of America, 49
Steel, Johannes, 115-16, 141-42, 204
Steel strike (1946), 71
Steffens, Lincoln, 370
Stein, Leonard, 171
Stein, Sidney, 233, 304, 307, 329, 345, 347, 348, 352, 355, 358
Stern, Alfred K., 211, 212
Stern, Martha Dodd (Mrs. Alfred K.), 212
Stettinius, Edward, 7
Steuben, John, 317, 361
Stevenson, Adlai, 256, 307, 314
Stockholm Peace Petition, 204, 205
Stone, I. F., 177
Stone, Martha, 304, 348
Straight, Michael, 142, 143, 144
Strong, Anna Louise, 234-35, 238, 363
Strong, Ed, 289, 304
Suez crisis (1956), 313-14, 337
Sutta, Bert, 20
Sweezy, Paul, 167, 168
Sylvis, William H., 69
Syndicalist League of North America, 10

Taft, Robert A., 152, 340
Taft-Hartley Act, 97, 132, 143, 146, 179
Tampa, Florida, 180
Tank, Herb, 58
Taunton, Massachusetts, 9
Taylor, Glen, 158, 165, 167, 174
Texas, 95, 246
Thomas, Cedric, 167-68
Thomas, J. Parnell, 57, 143, 187
Thomas, Norman, 51, 110, 344, 362
Thomas, R. J., 47, 103, 104
Thompson, Dorothy, 163
Thompson, Robert, 12, 19, 73, 89, 99, 107, 131, 137, 139, 196, 200, 232, 236, 239, 245, 348, 352, 356-58, 360, 362
Thurmond, Strom, 180
Time, 50, 126, 159, 187, 279
Timofeyev, T., 339
Tito, Marshal, 19, 33, 135, 172, 179, 236, 270, 289, 347
Togliatti, Palmiro, 297, 298, 300
Togliatti, Mrs. Palmiro, 147
Toledo, Ohio, 70
Tom Paine School of Social Science (Philadelphia), 86
Tom Paine School of Westchester, 86
Townsend, Francis E., 133
Trachtenberg, Alexander, 19, 201, 238
Trade Union Educational League (T.U.E.L.), 10
Trade unions, 35. *See also* Congress of Industrial Organizations, American Federation of Labor, *and under names of unions*
Transport Workers Union (T.W.U.), 49, 102, 215, 318
Trieste dispute, 33
Trotsky, Leon, 364
Trotskyists, 15, 51, 56, 194, 196, 282, 283, 298, 344
Trud, 276
Truehaft, Decca, 307, 308
Trujillo, Robert, 164-65
Truman, Harry S., 28, 29, 31, 32, 113, 114, 117-21 *passim,* 128, 129, 133, 135, 141-58 *passim,* 177, 179,

180, 185, 187, 189, 194, 207, 208, 212, 214, 215
Truman Doctrine, 27-28, 29, 132, 143, 145, 162
Tugwell, Rexford G., 166, 167, 168-69, 175, 176, 179
Turning Point, 21
Twilight of World Capitalism, The (Foster), 53, 240

"Underground," 77-82, 193, 230-33, 270, 368
Union for Democratic Action (U.D.A.), 129-30
United Auto Workers of America (U.A.W.), 6, 46, 47, 103, 104, 127, 150, 194, 195, 214
United Electrical, Radio, and Machine Workers of America (U.E.), 102, 104, 144, 147, 170, 174, 177, 214, 215-16, 217
United Furniture Workers, 102, 104, 214
United Gas, Coke, and Chemical Workers of America, 103
United Harlem Tenants and Consumers Organization, 94
United Mineworkers of America, 48
United Nations, 160, 212, 244, 313
United Office and Professional Workers of America (U.O.P.W.A.), 37, 102, 104, 173, 211, 214
United Packinghouse Workers, 103, 147
United Public Workers of America, 102, 214
United Retail, Wholesale, and Department Store Workers Union (District 65), 103, 149, 246, 260
United Shoe Workers of America, 102
U.S. Youth Sponsoring Committee for the World Peace Appeal, 205
United Steelworkers of America, 217
United Textile Workers, 49
University of Chicago, 166
Urban League, 264
Utah, 95

Vandenberg, Arthur H., 114, 152
Varga, Eugene S., 41-44

"Vermont Resolution," 173, 210
Veterans of the Abraham Lincoln Brigade, 83
Veterans for Peace, 205
Vishinsky, Andrei, 215
Voice of America, 332
Voorhis, Jerry, 187, 213
Voorhis Act, 76
Voroshilov, Kliment Y., 341

Wagner, Robert F., Jr., 258
Waldorf Peace Conference, 204
Walker, Christine, 173, 174
Wallace, Henry A., 7, 106, 114, 116-21, 125-39 *passim,* 140-54, 155-81 *passim,* 210-14, 253
Wallace, Walter, 211
Wallach family, 108
Walt Whitman School of Social Science, 86
Warren, Earl, 100
Washington, 180
Watt, Richard, 167
Wechsler, James A., 130, 144, 172
Weiner, Robert William, 81-82, 91
Weinstock, Louis, 236, 343
Weinstone, Will, 192, 193, 337, 353
Weiss, Max, 34-35, 63, 153-54, 270, 282, 287
Wellman, Saul, 237
Western Federation of Miners, 217
Weydemeyer (Joseph) School of Social Science, 86
Wherry, Kenneth, 185
White, Eliot, 54
White, Walter, 14, 128, 263
"White chauvinism," 66, 240, 242-47, 260, 262-63
Whitman (Walt) School of Social Science, 86
Whitney, A. F., 128
Wichita, Kansas, 10
Wiggins, Ella May, 38
Wilkerson, Doxey, 63-64, 264, 321, 329, 345, 361
Williamson, John, 8, 48, 70, 73, 92, 95, 105-6, 137, 138, 139, 154-55, 156, 176, 196, 304, 321, 338
Wilson, Edmund, 227
Wilson, Woodrow, 142
Winant, John, 162

Winston, Henry, 66, 67, 73, 96-97, 140, 196, 197, 230, 232-33, 241, 270
Winter, Carl, 196, 289, 304, 329, 348, 355
Wisconsin, 12, 95, 246
Woodward, C. Vann, 282
Worker, The. See *Daily Worker*
Workers Freedom League, 20
Workmen's Circle, 83
World Federation of Trade Unions, 215
World News, 338
Wright, Richard, 56
Wyatt, Wilson, 130
Wyoming, 95

Yakovlev, Anatoli A., 219, 220
Yale University, 212
Yates, Oleta O'Conner, 201
Yonkers, New York, 15
Young, Howard, 117
Young Communist League (Y.C.L.), 34, 107, 281
Young Progressives of America (Y.P.A.), 173-74
Yugoslavia, 32, 46, 311. *See also* Tito

Zhdanov, Andrei A., 134, 135-36, 290, 368
Zinoviev, Grigori, 73
Zorin, Valerian A., 161